A Southern Renaissance

A Southern Renaissance

The Cultural Awakening
of the American South,
1930–1955

Richard H. King

New York   Oxford
OXFORD UNIVERSITY PRESS
1980

Library of Congress Cataloging in Publication Data

King, Richard H
  A Southern Renaissance.

  Bibliography: p.
    1. American literature—Southern States—
History and criticism. 2. American liter-
ature—20th century—History and criticism.
3. Southern States—Civilization. 4. Southern
States—Intellectual life. I. Title.
PS261.K45   810'.9'975   79-9470
ISBN 0-19-502664-0

Grateful acknowledgment is given to publishers and copyright holders for permission to reprint selected passages from the following:

The Collected Poems of James Agee, edited by Robert Fitzgerald. Copyright © 1962, 1968 by The James Agee Trust. Reprinted by permission of Houghton Mifflin Company.

Let Us Now Praise Famous Men by James Agee. Copyright © renewed 1969 by Mia Fritsch Agee. Reprinted by permission of Houghton Mifflin Company.

Letters of James Agee to Father Flye, by James Agee. Reprinted by permission of James Harold Flye.

Selected Letters of William Faulkner, by William Faulkner, edited by Joseph Blotner. Copyright © 1977 by Jill Faulkner Summers. Reprinted by permission of Random House, Inc.

Brother to Dragons, by Robert Penn Warren. Copyright 1953 by Robert Penn Warren. Reprinted by permission of Random House, Inc.

The Collected Poems of William Alexander Percy, by William Alexander Percy. Copyright 1943 by Leroy Pratt Percy. Reprinted by permission of Alfred A. Knopf, Inc.

The Letters of Thomas Wolfe, edited by Elizabeth Nowell. Reprinted by permission of Charles Scribner's Sons.

Allen Tate, *Collected Poems 1919–1976*. Copyright © 1952, 1953, 1970, 1977 by Allen Tate. Copyright 1931, 1932, 1937, 1948 by Charles Scribner's Sons. Copyright renewed © 1959, 1960, 1965 by Allen Tate. Reprinted with the permission of Farrar, Straus & Giroux, Inc.

The Literary Correspondence of Donald Davidson and Allen Tate by John T. Fain and Daniel Young, by permission of the University of Georgia Press. Copyright © 1974 by the University of Georgia Press.

"Sequel of Appomattox," by Donald Davidson. Reprinted by permission of Mary Davidson Bell.

To My Parents,
Dorothy and Dawson King

Preface

The origins of this book lie in the early 1960s when I was an undergraduate at the University of North Carolina. During those years the activist phase of the Civil Rights movement began in nearby Greensboro and soon spread throughout the South. No one who was a Southerner or who lived south of the Mason-Dixon line at that time could help but be aware that enormous changes were in the offing. At roughly the same time, I first read Faulkner and was immediately and permanently hooked. Indicative of Faulkner's impact was my response to a question posed in an interview for a graduate fellowship. One of my interrogators asked whom I considered the leading Southern historian. Though I had read W. J. Cash and C. Vann Woodward, my immediate reply was, "William Faulkner." Needless to say, this was not the right answer, or at least the answer he was looking for. I did not win the fellowship. But, caught up as I was in Faulkner's world, still registering that shock of recognition which his work touched off in me, I could have hardly answered otherwise.

Chapel Hill was an ideal place in many ways to be in the early 1960s. Liberalism was a tradition there, not an aberrant impulse. The names of Howard Odum, Rupert Vance, and Thomas Wolfe, the university's most famous alumnus, were heard often. Cash's *The Mind of the South* was assigned in history classes and C. Vann Woodward's *The Burden of Southern History* had just appeared in paperback. I heard Robert Penn Warren lecture in Chapel Hill. James Agee's *Let Us Now Praise Famous Men* was re-issued around that time, and several of us were put onto it by our teachers. In my senior year at Chapel Hill I wrote an honors thesis on "Faulkner and Southern History." That thesis contained the seeds of much of what is in this longer study.

While working on this project I often encountered friendly skepticism when I described what I was doing as an intellectual history of the South between 1930 and the mid-1950s. Typically, the response would be, "Is there one?" It was as though I had proposed a study of Spiro Agnew's political ethics or of Norman Mailer's poetry. But, yes, there *is* one. As I indicate, the Southern Renaissance was much more than simply a story of William Faulkner's achievement, much more than a strictly literary movement. I have also sketched in the historical context within which the Southern Renaissance flourished. Intellectual historians, literary scholars, and sociologists of culture urgently need to take up a comparative investigation of cultural creativity. How can we explain those amazing outbursts of intellectual production which, as often as not, seem to appear in the most unlikely places, far from the centers of political, economic, and social power?

Some readers may find this study excessively theoretical. My general approach has been shaped by psychoanalytic theory and its recent applications in the work of literary critics such as Harold Bloom and the French Freudians. Like Bloom and unlike the French I have not been shy in evaluating as well as analyzing texts. I have been less interested in doing psychohistory (an unfairly maligned subspecialty in the historical profession) than I have been concerned with using Freud's theory as a way of talking about cultural change as expressed in written, "high" cultural works. This study is a form of cultural anthropology in the broadest sense of the term. It investigates a regional culture's symbol and image systems—its conscious articulations and hidden underpinnings—as they responded to historical change.

My own proclivities aside, I have made heavy use of theory for two reasons. First, the writing of American history has suffered from a paucity of theory; this seems particularly true of intellectual history. (It is less true of much recent work in the history of slavery, and that historiography is much the richer for its theoretical content.) Why this is true is a matter which is not my purpose to investigate here. Suffice it to say that graduate students in history are seldom asked to study Marx or Freud, Weber or Durkheim, Nietzsche or Hegel, or even the speculative philosophers of history in any thorough way. The result is a certain theoretical "tone deafness" among historians trained in this country.

Second, much of the writing about the South, particularly by Southerners, has been intensely autobiographical, even confessional. It seemed time to draw back and try to make sense of the cultural context within which Southern writers and intellectuals—and articulate Southerners in general—have tried to formulate their ambivalent feelings about the region. In fact, this Southern tradition of self- and regional scrutiny was brought to fruition by the writers of the Renaissance. From them many of my generation learned something about what we had "experienced" as we grew up in the region. We had been speaking "Southern" without even knowing it. That shock of recognition from reading Faulkner brought with it the realization that one could live in the region and still care for it, that the final definition of "being Southern" had not been established, and that the region's recent experience and its tradition, particularly in the twentieth century, encompassed far more than the Klan and the segregationists, the cynical politics of race and class domination, and a collection of timid academic and religious institutions. Thus I had to step outside the immediate world of the South and the Southern Renaissance in order better to apprehend it. A theoretical approach allowed this simultaneous "distance" and "closure."

By now it is probably not hard to figure out that my general political sympathies are of the liberal and populist variety. (Of course these two traditions are by no means synonymous.) Moreover, coming as I do from Tennessee, East Tennessee at that, I did not grow up with the glories of the Old South reverberating in my ears. When I told one Southern writer that I came from Tennessee, he replied, "Hell, that's not even in the South." To be sure, there are figures such as Allen Tate or William Alexander Percy on "the other side" from whom one can learn. But finally, I have little use for Southern conservatism of the Agrarian or aristocratic or any other sort. Yet, as I suggest at the end of the book, the Southern liberalism voiced by intellectuals by the mid-1950s was more an attitude than a program, less activist and politically cogent than one might have hoped. It was a world-view rather than a fighting creed. In a sense, my study falls in this tradition of Southern intellectual liberalism; still, I hope that the quarter century since the mid-1950s has added something to that tradition.

One does not complete a study such as this without incurring numerous debts of gratitude along the way. Nor did this work come to fruition without certain costs. My debt to those who helped me through rather trying times is incalculable.

Much gratitude goes to Dr. Frank Ryan of the History Department at Chapel Hill who supervised my honors thesis. His quiet intensity and passion for ideas provided me with a much needed intellectual model in those early years. Jerry Kindred and I began talking about history and historical consciousness in the late 1960s. Our conversations on these and related matters helped sharpen my thinking considerably. One can often learn as much from the "lay" reader of, say, Faulkner as from the professional. Jon Connolly, Louise Strawbridge, Jenny Cashdollar, and Tim Bird have provided me with many hours of stimulating conversation—and insights—about the South and its writers. My trip through the South a few years back with Jim Wagner was a delightful way to re-acquaint myself with the region. Students at both the University of the District of Columbia and the University of Nottingham helped me see things in the texts we were studying together that I would not have come to on my own.

I am also grateful to Paul Gaston for his general encouragement of this project and to Bertram Wyatt-Brown who helped me find a publisher after he had read parts of the manuscript. Erik Wensberg has been very supportive of my work over the years and provided valuable information on James Agee and a close reading of the pages that deal with Agee. My year as a Fulbright lecturer in England brought me into contact with Brian Lee and Dave Murray. Their intellectual acumen, knowledge of American literature and culture, and friendship were invaluable. Gib Ruark, Jim Herbert, Larry Friedman, and Steve Whitfield have been exacting but valuable companions. The readings which Friedman and Whitfield gave of my first draft helped bring the manuscript into coherent shape. Sheldon Meyer at Oxford Press forced me to rethink parts of the manuscript and his advice resulted, I think, in a better and more accessible book. Also, Kim Lewis at Oxford has gone over the manuscript closely and pointed out the most glaring stylistic infelicities and obvious errors.

At the most personal level I want to thank Nancy King for her encouragement through most of this project. Without her it would never have been begun. Charlotte Fallenius has been much more than a help; she's been an "älskade vän." To my parents, Dorothy and Dawson King, I can only—and inadequately—say, thanks.

Washington, D.C.   R.H.K.
October 1979

Contents

A Southern Renaissance

1

A Southern Renaissance

In 1975 the leading historian of the South in the post-World War II era, C. Vann Woodward, sought to define the Southern Renaissance and to specify the conditions of its emergence.[1] "Why the Southern Renaissance?" was characteristically Woodwardian in its lack of dogmatism, its lucid summations and deft criticisms, and its tendency toward equivocation. Locating the origins of the Renaissance in 1929, the year that saw the publication of Thomas Wolfe's *Look Homeward, Angel* and William Faulkner's *The Sound and the Fury*, Woodward characterized it as a flowering of the "literary arts—poetry, fiction and drama."[2] Although Woodward suggested no point at which the literary well ran dry, one might conveniently locate the end of the main phase of the Renaissance somewhere around 1955. After that year the South was preoccupied with "other voices, other rooms."

This is not to say that Southerners stopped writing or that nothing of worth appeared after the mid-1950s. Far from it. But by this point the figures dealt with in my study were either dead or past their creative peaks. Though he won a Nobel Prize in 1949, Faulkner's powers as a novelist had waned considerably. Allen Tate and John Crowe Ransom had all but ceased writing poetry, while their critical and cultural essays appeared with decreasing frequency. W. J. Cash, William Alexander Percy, and Thomas Wolfe were dead; and James Agee was to succumb to a heart attack in 1955. After the middle of the decade, Lillian Smith published little and turned her attentions to the civil rights struggle, as well as to her own battle with cancer. Neither Howard Odum nor Rupert Vance sounded any fresh notes on the theme of Regionalism after World War II, while V. O. Key shifted his energies from the political culture of the South to other aspects of political science. To be sure, C. Vann Woodward was to emerge as one of the most prominent American historians in the 1960s, but his pioneering work in Southern history lay behind him. And though Robert Penn Warren's reputation as a poet waxed tremendously in the 1960s and 1970s, his fiction never regained the heights of *All the King's Men*. The apogee had been reached; the Renaissance had become a tradition.

Woodward went on to survey the various explanations that had been advanced for the Renaissance. He rejected as absurd the "sociological" explanations that saw the cultural flowering as the issue of Southern prosperity or industrialization, a newly discovered liberal spirit, or the infusion of new blood from the outside. He then proceeded to dismiss the "defensive" theory, which he attributed to W. J. Cash. In this account the Renaissance was the attempt of Southern writers to justify themselves and their society in the face of a hostile American society. Finally, however, Woodward gave a qualified nod of approval to Allen Tate's "backward glance" thesis: the Renaissance was the product of the creative tension between the Southern past and the pressures of the modern world.

But the Tate thesis did not entirely satisfy Woodward either. First, it failed to explain why the Renaissance happened precisely when it did; and, second, it failed to account for the literary productivity of Southern writers after World War II. Thus the backward glance notion provided the "necessary conditions" but not any sort of final explanation. To add specificity to Tate's thesis, Woodward drew upon Cleanth Brooks, a critic who had been closely associated with the Agrarians at Vanderbilt University in the 1920s and their hostile view of modern culture. According to Brooks, the Southern experience had been marked by a feeling for the concrete and specific, a familiarity with conflict, a sense of community and religious wholeness, a belief that the mystery of human nature defied rational explanation or manipulation, and a sense of the tragic. This was the fertile ground in which the South's artistic and intellectual promptings took root and flourished.

Woodward was properly skeptical that any determinate relationship between historical causes and cultural results could be drawn; but he was also perhaps overly defensive. Indeed it is difficult to imagine what a scientific (in the sense of "natural" scientific) explanation of the Southern Renaissance would look like. Besides this knotty theoretical issue, however, Woodward's essay suggested other matters that called for further analysis.

First, the Southern Renaissance was more than "just" a literary movement. It was certainly that; but it also represented an outpouring of history, sociology, political analysis, autobiography, and innovative forms of journalism. W. J. Cash, James Agee, Lillian Smith, Howard Odum, and William Alexander Percy were as central to the Southern Renaissance as William Faulkner, Robert Penn Warren, Allen Tate, and John Crowe Ransom. To be specific, Woodward's biography of the Georgia Populist leader Tom Watson, which appeared in 1938, deserved the kind of attention which Warren's novel about a Huey Long-like figure, *All the King's Men* (1946) attracted. This is not to say that *Tom Watson* and *All the King's Men* are the same kind of book. They are, however, embedded in the same historical context and informed by a "structure of feeling and experience" (to use Raymond Williams's phrase) common to the writers and intellectuals of the Renaissance.[3] In that sense they can and should be considered together.

Woodward's essay presents other problems. He never identifies the source of the sociological explanation of the Renaissance, and it seems to me a straw man. Though he attributes the "defensive" thesis to W. J. Cash, nowhere in *The Mind of the South* does Cash claim that the Southern Renaissance was the product of

Southerners under siege, except in the case of the Agrarians, where there is a lot to be said for Cash's claim. Cash paid high tribute to the realistic romanticism of Thomas Wolfe, Faulkner, and Erskine Caldwell. They were examples of the newly emerging critical spirit at work in the "mind" of the South after World War I. But though he mentions Faulkner and Caldwell together, Cash never equates them, as Woodward claims he does.

Finally, though there is no gainsaying some of the regional characteristics that Woodward draws from Brooks, it should be noted that they are generally conservative traits or tend to be most eagerly embraced by the party of the past. But the Renaissance was by no means the exclusive property of the conservative spirit and those who protested the appearance of the modern world. Second, some of these alleged characteristics of the Southern experience are questionable. It is difficult to see, for instance, how one can speak of the Southern fear of abstraction when the section has been addled over the years by all sorts of chimerical causes and collective delusions. Nor does the Southern claim on the tragic sense appear very strong if one assumes that the tragic sense requires insight into the circumstances which have led to grief. The South has rarely shown much of that insight. More generally, Woodward might have placed greater emphasis upon what is implied in the Tate thesis: the *dissolution* of the social and cultural context that nurtured these characteristics made way for the literary and intellectual resurgence in the South circa 1930.

If Woodward's essay represents the conventional account of the origins of the Southern Renaissance, there are other accounts which bid for attention. Writing in what might be called the neo-Catholic tradition of the Tate wing of the Vanderbilt Agrarians, Lewis Simpson claims that the Renaissance was most centrally about "memory and history." Though the restoration of an agrarian order was ostensibly its goal, the Renaissance sought "to assert the redemptive meaning of the classical-Christian past in its bearing on the present."[4] Thus, according to Simpson, the Renaissance was less literary than religious; it was, "a search for images of existence which will express the truth that man's essential nature lies in his possession of the moral community of memory and history."[5] What the Renaissance resisted was the corrosive pessimism of modernity and the utopian faith that knowledge can change "the very constitution of being" and that history can be abolished.[6]

Simpson's interpretive account of the Renaissance is both more interesting and less pertinent than Woodward's. Surely history and memory, loss and absence, were central preoccupations in much Southern writing in the years after 1930 (as they were in much writing before those years). But Simpson's claim that Faulkner and his contemporaries were essentially religious writers is debatable, to put it mildly. Nor does Simpson give any examples of powerful utopian impulses at work in the South in these years. Whatever else may be said about Southern liberals and reformers, they were hardly wild-eyed radicals or soft-headed dreamers. Finally, Simpson's account fails to ground the Renaissance in its specific (Southern) historical setting. Instead, he sees it as a counterattack against the spirit of modernity and the gnostic strain in Western political thought articulated first by Joachim of Floris in the twelfth century. His was intellectual history with a vengeance.

What then was the Southern Renaissance? Put briefly: the writers and intellectuals of the South after the late 1920s were engaged in an attempt to come to terms not only with the inherited values of the Southern tradition but also with a certain way of perceiving and dealing with the past, what Nietzsche called "monumental" historical consciousness. It was vitally important for them to decide whether the past was of any use at all in the present; and, if so, in what ways? Put another way, the relationship between present and past which the Renaissance writers explored was fraught with ambivalence and ambiguity. The "object" of their historical consciousness was a tradition whose essential figures were the father and the grandfather and whose essential structure was the literal and symbolic family. In sum, the Renaissance writers sought to come to terms with what I call the "Southern family romance."

This study is not intended as a complete intellectual (or literary) history of the Southern Renaissance. Rather, I will trace the attempts of various (white) Southern writers and intellectuals to come to grips with the tradition of the Southern family romance, white Southern racism, and the received truths about Southern political culture. Related to, though distinct from, this concern with the family romance is my concern with the varieties of historical consciousness at work in Southern culture in the 1930s and 1940s. Put succinctly, I see in this period an emerging self-consciousness in Southern culture, a quasi-Hegelian process as it were. Increasingly, in those years, the Southern tradition was not only raised to awareness, it was also progressively demystified and rejected.

By historical consciousness, I do not mean "philosophy of history." William Faulkner, for instance, was neither an interesting thinker nor a profound philosopher. But I am interested in the ways he and his contemporaries articulated the tortuous process of dealing with the past of the region. Thus, by historical consciousness, I do not mean a philosophically rigorous discussion of the ultimate constituents of historical reality, the driving force(s) of the historical process, or the *telos* of that process. If Freud and Nietzsche are anywhere near correct, our systematic and "cognitively responsibile" views of the past are rooted in personal and cultural experience; and if Hayden White is correct, our accounts of historical reality are filtered through literary "figures," written according to certain standard plots and shaped by various ideologies or world-views.[7] Thus historical consciousness refers to the way we understand and articulate our perception of the past.

Beyond this I will generally focus on works which take the South and its tradition as problematic. For this reason I do not deal with black writers such as Richard Wright or Ralph Ellison or with women writers such as Eudora Welty, Carson McCullers, Flannery O'Connor, and Katherine Anne Porter. All of these writers would demand extensive treatment in a complete history of the Renaissance. Black writers are not taken up because for them the Southern family romance was hardly problematic. It could be and was rejected out of hand. Their great theme was the attempt (literally) to escape the white South which had historically oppressed their people. The case with the women writers is more difficult, but my reading of them indicates that whatever the merits of their work—and they are considerable—they were not concerned primarily with the larger cultural, racial, and political themes that I take as my focus. For whatever reasons—and the one woman I do treat, Lillian Smith, urged women to address themselves to these larger themes—they did not place the region at the center of their imaginative visions.[8]

Not surprisingly, Faulkner dominates my study. One is often tempted to pass off the Renaissance as the exclusive product of its one undeniably "great" writer, Faulkner. It is with some reluctance that one dares say anything additional about Faulkner, since so much has already been said. But John Irwin's *Doubling and Incest/Repetition and Revenge* (1976) both anticipated some of the things I had to say about Faulkner and compelled me to extend the extraordinarily insightful thesis he developed.[9] At any rate, no study of Southern historical consciousness and the family romance can avoid confronting Faulkner's profound exploration of these themes.

Further, my study is most centrally informed by Freud's theory of memory, culture, and therapy. "Informed," however, is a weasel word, and there is no need to be coy. I would suggest that what Freud did in and for European culture, Faulkner (and to a lesser extent Cash and Lillian Smith) did in and for the modern Southern cultural tradition. My reading of the "literature of memory" is mediated by my understanding of Freud; in turn my grasp of Freud has been enriched, I think, by my immersion in the texts of Faulkner and his Southern contemporaries. Their modes of expression and their truth-claims differ, but Freud, as well as the Southern writers of the Renaissance, explored the engagement of memory with and in a tradition which was frighteningly powerful even in its death throes.

This is not to suggest that I am interested in direct or conscious influences between Freud and Faulkner or anyone else. Faulkner's biographer records that Faulkner may have read Freud in the 1920s. But when asked later about possible influence, Faulkner replied in typical fashion that all the psychology he knew came from his characters and his poker-playing.[10] Of course

Faulkner was notoriously perverse in his response to such questions. But whether he was a reader, much less a close student of Freud, is of little interest to me. Most well-read Southerners would have read or heard something of Freud by the 1920s. There *were* a few oases in the "Sahara of the Bozart," as H. L. Mencken called the South of the time; Lillian Smith and Cash had read their Freud and taken him seriously.

But I also have more than interesting cultural analogies in mind when I say that Freud's influence is strong in this study. For the way Freud went about his explorations of the psyche—his own and others'—exemplifies the difficult role of the historian and the vicissitudes of historical consciousness in general. As in Freud and his patients, so in the writers of the Renaissance: repetition and recollection, the allure of the family romance, the difficult attempt to tell one's story and be freed of the burden of the past, and the desire to hold onto the fantasies of the past, were all powerfully at work. "Only" the language and the ostensible intent were different.

Finally by "informed" I mean that Freud's theory of therapy —the movement of memory in repetition, recollection, and working through—seems to me a normative model against which we can gauge the power of a work which takes the past as thematic. It is the mark of seminal historical works, and of fiction such as Faulkner's, that they take us back, then through, and out the other side—which turns out to be the way we came in, only at a different level.

Southern Intellectuals: Tradition and Self-Consciousness

Ante-bellum Southern intellectuals provided one of the few sources of dissent from the prevailing American cultural ethos and historical consciousness.[11] More generally, if American intellectuals have traditionally been marginal to actual political and economic power, post-Civil War Southern intellectuals were even more so. As provincials they suffered under the suspicion (from others and from themselves) that they were "rustic and boorish," out of touch with the main action in the centers of cultural ferment.[12] Though this subjective burden, mixed with envy and resentment, was shared with other American intellectuals, it was accentuated by the South's trauma of defeat and occupation during Reconstruction and the South's historical association with racial bigotry, religious primitivism, and lack of cultural achievement. If this were not bad enough, the Southern intellectual has measured his status in the South and the nation against the dominant intellectual role played by the Virginians in the founding and formation of the nation. As Allen Tate wrote in "Aeneas at Washington": "The city my blood had built I knew no more."[13] Thus not only has the South been a cultural province, it has had to live with a decline from prior cultural and political pre-eminence.

Historically, the choices open to the white Southern writer or intellectual have been limited, though not as restricted as those imposed on black Southerners, or, say, upon the intelligentsia in Czarist Russia. He could leave the South, perhaps under pressure, assimilate to the national culture, and "forget" his origins. Or he could leave, but remain a "Southerner" in manner and sympathies, serving as an explainer of the region to the rest of the nation. As recently as the 1960s, under the editorship of Willie Morris, many émigré white Southerners found in *Harper's* an outlet for their writings, which offered a mixture of criticism and nostalgic good feelings toward the land they had left. There are several ironies in the title of Morris's autobiography *North Toward Home*.

Those intellectuals who remained in the South could either become spokesmen, however sophisticated, for the Southern tradition, or speak out for change. To take the latter position was to run the obvious risk of being accused of "fouling one's nest," of being a fifth column for alien, that is, "Yankee," notions. For spokesmen of the tradition, the problem was that as intellectuals they were alienated from those to whom and for whom they spoke. To be an intellectual in the South was to talk to oneself or at best a close group of sympathizers—or to be set upon as an arrant traitor for daring to suggest that intellect might be used for something other than the exigencies of regional self-defense. For instance, in the 1920s, sociologist Howard Odum came under heavy fire from ministerial and business groups in the Piedmont for allowing essays on modern science and religion and industrial working conditions to appear in the newly founded journal *Social Forces*. Either no one listened—or the wrong sort listened.

One of the chief problems was that the South had neither a strong "enlightenment" tradition nor mass tradition of intellectual or educational concern. The Jeffersonian ideal of intellectual curiosity about whatever bore on man's fate had long since faded. By the 1930s the Jeffersonian legacy was a rather tame affair, something honored more in the breach than observance. Virginius Dabney's attempt to show the pervasive influence of Jeffersonian liberalism served mainly to show how weak and amorphous it had been.[14] And of course no better example exists than the Scopes "Monkey" trial in Dayton, Tennessee, in 1925, about the teaching in public schools of Darwin's theory of evolution, and the controversy surrounding it to show that it was not simply a matter of hostile and fundamentalist masses against a beleaguered intelligentsia. Humanism and a defense of the Christian tradition in the South were considered compatible with religious fundamentalism. Nor did the Populist movement in the 1890s provide any lasting education of the masses, whatever its immediate political successes.[15]

On the institutional level, the university tradition in the South was notably weak, though by the 1920s several departments of history and sociology (along with Vanderbilt's English department) were beginning to make their mark. As Howard Odum would note in *Southern Regions* (1936), no Southern university belonged in the top rank of American universities. There was but a small and rather precarious space of freedom within which to consider, much less advocate, new ideas. There was certainly no tradition of academic radicalism in Southern institutions of higher education. Nor, needless to say, was there a vital and intellectually astute clergy in the largely Protestant and fundamentalist South. In general, the steadiest voices of moderate enlightenment came from newspapermen. Dabney, George Fort Milton, John Temple Graves, and—a bit later—Ralph McGill, Hodding Carter, and Mark Ethridge would stand for a certain civil dissent, but they were either unable or unwilling to break any lances against mass opposition.

In addition, Southern cities such as Atlanta or Birmingham, New Orleans or Charleston, lacked strong, dissident artistic communities or influential universities. While black scholars such as W. E. B. Du Bois, earlier at Atlanta, and Charles Johnson at Fisk did important sociological work, the black minority lacked the power or opportunity to be a major factor in Southern intellectual ferment.

All this is to say that, prior to the 1930s, there was little contact between the political and cultural elites, a point made in W. J. Cash's gloomy conclusion to *The Mind of the South*. Agrarian conservatives ruled as they always had—according to tradition and self-interest, which were often synonymous. Neo-populist leaders depended more upon the life of the mouth than of the mind, more on rhetoric than applied intelligence. Business progressives went to school at the Chamber of Commerce and businessmen's clubs. Put simply, by around 1930, Southern intellectuals inhabited another country.

And yet, as Cash might have said, something began happening in the 1920s. The "introspective revolution" of the 1930s and 1940s was prepared by a series of historical events which had profound symbolic reverberations among Southern writers and intellectuals.[16] These events served as historical precipitates, crystallizing cultural themes and solidifying individuals into groups, thus setting the stage for much of the *Kulturkampf* in the 1930s.

The first of these events was World War I itself, which marked the end of a century of European peace and the stable bourgeois order which marked that period. Though less so than among the intellectuals of the European nations, the war profoundly affected American writers.[17] The center did not hold. For sensitive Southerners, World War I represented the occasion for the South, as Allen Tate put it, to "rejoin the world."

Nor was the effect of that war lost on young Southern writers such as William Faulkner, who wrote of the disillusionment of the returning veteran in *Soldier's Pay* and *Sartoris*. William Alexander Percy, then a young poet, was later to write in *Lanterns on the*

Levee of the exhilaration of combat—and then the sense of being adrift after his return from the trenches. Many young Southerners must have seen World War I not only as a great adventure but also as a sort of historical second chance. Having grown up in a Southern tradition powerfully shaped by the Civil War and Reconstruction, young Southerners saw World War I as a chance to demonstrate the heroism which had been drummed into them as one of the transcendent virtues of the Southern tradition. In the long run the war's cultural reverberations gave a final blow to the genteel tradition in literature. In this sense the Southern Renaissance, at least in its literary manifestations, drew less from the Depression experience than from the cultural impact of the war.

In these years the most frontal (and notorious) assault on Southern cultural esteem came from H. L. Mencken.[18] His "Sahara of the Bozart" (1917) was read by many devoted Southerners, including liberals, as an unfair attack by an outsider. It is less well known that Mencken did not attack only to withdraw and gloat at the havoc he had wreaked. Rather, he helped keep alive fledgling literary magazines such as *The Double Dealer* in New Orleans and *The Reviewer* in Richmond, and later opened the pages of *The American Mercury* to young Southerners, such as W. J. Cash and Gerald Johnson, who were critical of the region's cultural aridity. For him, as for the poets associated with *The Fugitive* in Nashville, the enemy was the genteel tradition, New South boosterism, and the cultural wasteland of rural society. Indeed, when it suited his purposes, the sage of Baltimore fancied himself a Southerner of sorts. His reading of the region's history told him that a golden age had existed in the South sometime prior to 1800; and he even bemoaned the decline of aristocratic influence in the post-Civil War South. Thus, Mencken's attack on the contemporary South was grounded in a certain nostalgic fondness for the Virginia dynasty, and his later championing of Howard Odum and Cash was a strange one. Mencken was no modern liberal, and his affection for the aristocratic ethos should logically have placed him nearer the Agrarians. But Mencken, unlike most American conservatives, had even less use for the clergy and the spirit of religious fundamentalism than he had for social reform. What led to the enmity between Mencken and the Vanderbilt group was the publicist's savage dissection of the fundamentalist mentality at work in the Scopes trial. It was in response to Mencken's attack on the South in Dayton that poets and intellectuals in Nashville readied the counterattack which was to appear in 1930 as *I'll Take My Stand.*

By then even for defenders of the Southern tradition, not to mention its critics, the tradition had become an "entity" which could not be simply assumed; it had to be reappropriated.[19] Accompanying this reification of the tradition was an upsurge in historical self-consciousness, a sign itself of the distance between self and tradition. As Allen Tate was to write in 1930, "[T]radition must, in other words, be automatically operative before it can be called tradition."[20] The very act of trying to re-present the tradition pointed to its absence. In fiction and poetry the tradition was often symbolized in the portraits of the heroic generation, the presiding presences of the tradition, who had wrested the land from the Indians and defended it against the Yankees and the aggressions of Reconstruction. The portraits of these men—stern, untroubled, and resolute—hung in the entrance halls or the parlors of the homes; and from there they judged the actions of their successors. Their example was a standing rebuke to a decline in energy and will. The next generation was of necessity less heroic; charismatic origins were institutionalized, perpetuated by hard work, and marked by less glamor, for the generation between the heroic one and the one that experienced the tradition as absent had to live in the world rather than die heroically. They were too near their sons to be quite heroic. The meaning of the Civil War was, in Donald Davidson's words:

> Something for grandfathers to tell
> Boys who clamor and climb.
> And were you there, and did you ride
> With the men of that old time?[21]

> ("Sequel of Appomattox")

And yet, a crucial segment of the third (and in some cases fourth) generation, which was born around the turn of the century and lived through the cultural crisis of World War I, came to feel increasingly estranged from the tradition. That tradition loomed distressingly distant and overpoweringly strong, insupportable yet inescapable.²²

This in turn raises the question which has haunted the modern world and has remained central to the culture of modernism: what does it mean to live without a tradition? Insofar as Southern writers and intellectuals were concerned with this question, they expressed a central concern of the modernist movement. The answers to the question are various, some of which this century has seen embodied in ghastly forms. Here Hannah Arendt's work sheds light, for the loss of "the thread which safely guided us through the vast realms of the past" renders memory helpless. In the face of these difficulties "old verities which have lost all concrete relevance" may be "rehashed." Also in the absence of its traditional authorizations, present authority may degenerate into the application of violence which in turn provokes counterviolence. Or finally the world may grow "fantastic."²³

Certainly of the rehashing of old verities there was no end in the 1930s. One thinks here of the Agrarians or of William Alexander Percy. Calling upon the past to aid the present, they attempted to revitalize the tradition by turning it into a conservative, even reactionary ideology. Some, like Percy, realized that the tradition could not be revitalized in any binding, collective way and that it had become "merely" a personal code by which they could at least live.

Nor was violence far from the surface of much of the writings in the 1930s. One thinks here of Tate's call for violence to reclaim the lost Southern tradition or his evocation of the lost possibility of an expansionist slave empire in his biography of Jefferson Davis. And no matter how far removed they were from the ideological violence of contemporary European fascism, the fictional fantasies of Faulkner's Gail Hightower in *Light in August* or the lacerating self-destructiveness of Bayard Sartoris in *Flags in the Dust* and the sophisticated poetry of Tate or Donald Davidson in his "Lee in the Mountains," all testified to the barely submerged violence that threatened to surface in the Southern tradition at its time of dissolution.

Certainly Arendt's description of reality become "fantastic" could stand as a general characteristic for much of the literature of Renaissance, a sort of modernist gothic style. What else is Faulkner wrestling with in his work up through, say, *Absalom, Absalom!*? And surely W. J. Cash and Lillian Smith were preoccupied with the fantastic aspects of Southern culture, the ways in which historically shaped desires and their inverse, self-destructiveness, had woven a texture which stifled rather than gave comfort. Though the question of when a culture becomes fantastic is terribly complicated, not least because all cultures are based upon certain fantasies, a provisional answer might apply the pragmatic criterion: when it no longer "works." Themes and motifs split off and become isolated from the whole; they are spun out into whole visions. One might also say, following Freud, that in fantasy there is a refusal to acknowledge that we must die, that we have a body which imposes certain limits on us, and that we must live in a world with other people.[24] In cultures grown fantastic, the regressive or reactionary form of memory is dominant. Time is denied.

Paul Ricoeur extends Freud's discussion of the relationship of fantasy to reality by noting that in aberrant cultural situations the cultural principle in the individual, the super-ego, is more than normally driven by aggressive impulses, guilt (aggression against the self), and over-idealizations. Such a "culture of melancholy" becomes death-dealing: "the super-ego reveals itself as a pure culture of the death instincts, to the point of suicide."[25] Rather than enforcing the binding power of Eros, guilt unravels the collective and individual worlds. As we shall see in works such as Faulkner's *Flags in the Dust* and *Light in August* and Percy's *Lanterns on the Levee*, cultural melancholia embodied the lost tradition in figures of death, at once idealized and feared because of their powerful hold over the present and because of their absence. Thus a tradition grown fantastic denies death and the workings of time on one level only to be obsessed by death at a deeper level. The monumental or reactionary form of historical consciousness is not necessarily wrong in a moral or substantive sense, since there are traditions which one might wish revitalized. Rather it is "wrong" insofar as it desires the impossible—repetition—rather than the necessary recollection and working through of the past.

But in the Southern Renaissance a second movement of memory despaired of the repetition which marked the culture of melancholy and set about scrutinizing the tradition of the family romance itself. As seen in Faulkner's Quentin Compson of *Absalom, Absalom!* and in Tate's work, beginning with "Ode to the Confederate Dead" and culminating in *The Fathers,* this form of historical consciousness ends in a tragic confusion between past and present, fantasy and reality. Neither repetition nor recollection can triumph. What recollection reveals is the violence and horror at the heart of the tradition itself, or its weakness and contradictions. Time becomes an obsession, and the founding of the tradition and the costs thereby incurred are emphasized.

The third mode of historical consciousness moved toward a reconstitution of "reality" after having carried through on a demystification of the family romance. Building upon the agonized analysis of the second stage, it incorporated and transcended the Southern tradition as previously conceived. As seen in Faulkner's "The Bear" and the writings of W. J. Cash and Lillian Smith, memory emerges from the trap of fantasy which is organized around the judgments of the founding fathers. Recollection triumphs over repetition; not only the impossibility but the undesirability of resurrecting the tradition become clear.

These three stages of historical consciousness present analogies to the unfolding and transformation of memory in psychoanalysis. In both instances, the past is problematic: now overpowering, now completely absent from memory, it is debilitating. What had been assumed as "mine" now appears as "other" and strange. In the final stage this "otherness" is demystified and reassimilated after having been worked through. It is incorporated into a new synthesis. The movement is from incapacitating repetition to recollection and then to self-consciousness, from identity to estrangement and back to incorporation at a higher level. Beyond Nietzsche's monumental and critical forms of historical consciousness, a new form—the analytic or the ironic—emerges. One awakens from the nightmare of history.

Thus the modes of historical consciousness which emerged in the 1930s and 1940s were manifestations of the ambivalent spirit of cultural modernism. The prototypical historical consciousness of the modern period is obsessed with the past and the precarious possibilities of its survival. In addition, the preoccupation with the past among Southern writers and intellectuals in this period was typically Southern. Still, they were by no means united in their attitudes toward the past in general or toward the family romance in particular. The decades after 1930 were to see a reassessment of the Southern tradition, and it is to that effort which we will now turn.

2

The Southern
Family Romance
and Its Context

Historically, the South has been a "peripheral" or "underdeveloped" region within the European world-system and within the United States itself.[1] Before the Civil War the South's cotton went directly to England and the Continent or so ended after calling at New York. Lacking significant home industries and unable to raise enough foodstuffs to meet its own needs, the South had to import most of what it consumed. Besides its economic disadvantage in the larger world economic system, the South was starkly divided along class and racial lines. A planter elite dominated Southern life; and it was just accessible enough to ambitious—and lucky—strivers from the sizable Southern yeomanry to keep social tensions among whites from becoming unmanageable.

But if the plantation system was the key to understanding Southern economy and society, the presence of an enslaved black population (around one-third of the total population of the South) explained much else about the South. Slavery placed the South on the defensive in the modern world. From its early cosmopolitanism, the South after 1830 increasingly turned inward, developing a siege mentality to justify itself and its essential institutions. Under attack from the outside, the region came to see itself as different from the rest of the United States. Though the South was still a frontier society in many ways, its planter elite was attracted to what historian Eugene Genovese calls "pre-modern," i.e. pre-bourgeois, values.[2] In the planter ideology, leisure was valued over hard work; the cultivation of the social graces and hospitality was preferred to the pursuit of the main chance; a patriarchal hierarchical society came to seem preferable to an egalitarian one; the agrarian way of life was preferred to the urban, industrial sort. Cultured Southerners were struck by the resemblance between the South they thought they inhabited and the fictional world of Sir Walter Scott's novels. In the Southern conception of itself, master and slave, rich and poor, male and female, knew their place before men and before God.

In all these ways, and others, the South was not born traditional, but became so. Its insistence upon cultural superiority masked anachronistic cultural values. The relative prosperity of the planter class hid the fact that the South was itself enslaved by the demands of the larger world economy. Its defenses of slavery diverted attention from the fact that slavery rested upon the master-slave relationship, upon plain exploitation, not benevolence or concern for the less fortunate. And the white South's uneasy balancing of democratic aspirations with aristocratic ethos produced contradictions of its own.

The central "event" in the history of the South was the Civil War and Reconstruction. In defeat, in the memory of the common struggle against the Yankee and the Freedman, the white South became united as it rarely had been before the war. Many white Southerners professed relief that the "peculiar institution" of slavery was a thing of the past. But the destruction of slavery did not automatically lead to the economic "take-off" of the South.[3] Its cotton was still in demand in the outside world. The plantation system, it turned out, could run quite well with "free" labor. In place of chattel slavery for blacks and freehold farming for middle-level and poorer whites came tenancy and sharecropping. If the small farmer did manage to hold onto his land in the grim years after 1865, he often was little better off than the sharecropper. He was caught in the "crop lien" system by which he mortgaged his crop to a merchant in exchange for a loan to see him through the coming year. By 1880 cotton production had reached its highest prewar levels. In place of the dignified old planter or the fiery Cavalier, the merchant and banker as absentee landlords now played a prominent part in the plantation economy.

The 1870s saw something new in Southern history—the rise of an indigenous commercial class linked with the emerging railroad, coal, and iron interests but still tied by interest, family, and sentiment to the agricultural sector. Encouraged by the "Redeemer" governments which had rescued the Southern states from "radical" governments imposed by the North during Reconstruction, efforts were made to attract investment capital to the region from the Northeast and Europe. In the manner of most elites in underdeveloped areas, the ideology of this new class—the "New South" ideology—expressed both reactionary sentiments and progressive desires, particularist pride and national sentiments.[4] Ultimately, however, the rhetoric of sectional development masked the South's continuing dependence upon the outside investment that flowed into the South as the century came to a close. Though the illusion of rapid growth and regional prosperity was widespread, World War I saw the South still dominated by "low-wage, low-value-creating industries."[5] The case of textile manufacturing told much of the story: goods produced in the South were then sent North for final processing. Though economic diversity grew, the Southern economy remained a pawn of outside interests.

World War I saw the rapid growth of the lumber, shipbuilding, explosives, textile, coal, oil, and iron and steel industries. Cotton prices soared; the years 1917 through 1919 were the best ever. Yet after 1919 and the return to "normalcy," cotton prices plummeted: from a high of 35¢ in 1919 to around 20¢ in 1927 and then to 6½¢ in 1932. The invasion of the boll weevil, the exodus of blacks and poor whites, and the shift of cotton production toward the Southwest contributed to the growing awareness that cotton was no longer king. By 1930 some 55 per cent of farm operators were tenants. The region's economy stood somewhere between miserable failure and utter disaster. Though state and local governments continued to try to lure industries to the South with the promise of a docile labor force, weak unions, and generous tax breaks, the South was still the "nation's number one economic problem," or so the *Report on the Economic Conditions of the South* (1938) had it.[6]

Though industries grew and cities developed in the post-Reconstruction South, race relations in the South reached their nadir in the 1890s. That decade saw the peak period of lynchings in the South but more significantly it saw the formalization of social segregation in Dixie. The years between 1890 and World War I represented the culmination of trends in race relations at work since 1865. In a systematic and "legal" way, following largely upon the *Plessy v. Ferguson* decision of 1896, which declared that segregation by public authorities was constitutional if "separate but equal" facilities were maintained, barriers were erected to delimit the social contact between the races. Southern society from top to bottom was segregated. Upon assuming office in 1913 the country's first Southern-born President since the Civil War, Woodrow Wilson, ordered the segregation of Washington's government buildings, and in 1915 historian Wilson gave his approval, after a private screening, to D. W. Griffith's racist film epic *The Birth of a Nation*. This "Jim Crow" South not only survived the 1930s, it lasted on down into the 1960s.[7]

With the inexorable growth of tenancy and sharecropping, the poor of both races left the South in large numbers in the Great Migration north which began with the onset of World War I. Rural poverty was endemic; dietary and nutritional problems among the poor were legion; and the dual school system of the South exhausted the meager financial resources available for public education. The only thing approaching a mass social movement after the 1890s was the revival of the Ku Klux Klan between 1915 and 1925. Nativism, the expression of anti-Catholic and anti-Jewish sentiment, joined hands with the endemic white racism to create a movement of considerable political power.

By the 1930s the Southern social structure bore a family resemblance to Barrington Moore's description of pre-World War I German and pre-World War II Japanese society, like "Victorian houses with modern electrical kitchens but insufficient bathrooms and leaky pipes hidden decorously behind newly plastered walls." Several social prerequisites for a bourgeois, democratic order were missing in the South. The region historically lacked a "vigorous and independent class of town dwellers" (though Southern cities were growing); and the process of "getting rid of agriculture as a major social activity . . . taming the agrarian sector" had been only partially completed. The South seemed to be engaged in a halting economic development "without changing the social structure."[8]

In Southern politics, as in race relations, the 1890s was the crucial decade. The first six years of the decade saw a growing agrarian insurgency culminate in the emergence of a mass political movement, Populism. Strongest in Texas, Alabama, Georgia, and North Carolina, the Populists dared to break with the "party of the fathers," the Democratic party, and challenge the conservative elite formed by planter, merchant, lawyer, banker, and industrialist for political control of the region. Though scoring significant electoral victories at the local, state, and even national level, the Populists collapsed after William Jennings Bryan's candidacy as a free-silver Democrat in 1896 and the end of the severe depression of the early 1890s.[9]

The 1890s also witnessed the removal of blacks from Southern politics. Beginning in 1890 with Mississippi, Southern states passed a series of measures—the poll tax, the grandfather clause, literacy and understanding tests, property qualifications and the white primary—which "constitutionally" disfranchised blacks and a significant number of poor whites as well. These disfranchisement measures were generally spearheaded by the regular Democratic party and were aimed in part at the poorer white farmers who were potential supporters of the Populist party. After the turn of the century, white political participation and voter turnout dropped precipitously, though never of course to the levels forced on blacks. Thus by the early years of the century the South was a solidly one-party section, dominated by a white elite.[10] This was to remain largely the case down to the 1950s.

As the 1930s approached, Democratic politics was dominated by three distinct, though overlapping, groups. The most powerful was the conservative coalition of "Bourbons" and "Big Mules" (to borrow the nomenclature of Alabama politics), the alliance of large planters and industrialists. But prior to World War I the Progressive movement exerted a considerable influence on Southern politics, though, as C. Vann Woodward has emphasized, it was "for whites only." Southerners played a vital part in Woodrow Wilson's administration. Progressivism in the South concentrated on "efficiency" and "public service" measures (road building, education) and muted whatever earlier impulses there had been for expanded democracy, social justice, regulation of business, or pro-labor policies. This was what George Tindall has called the "business progressives," a sort of neo-New South movement.[11] The third force in Southern politics drew on the rhetoric and some of the substance of the agrarian insurgency surviving the demise of Populism. The period from 1900 to World War II was the heyday of the Southern demagogue, who gathered "redneck" support by rhetorical attacks on the "big shots" and the blacks. Once in office these demagogues either sold out to the conservatives or pushed through mildly progressive reforms. Besides the demagogues there were authentic agrarian leaders such as Hugo Black in Alabama and especially Huey Long in Louisiana who kept the Populist spirit alive.

As with the Wilson administration, Southern Democrats proved to be an important part of the New Deal coalition; and Southern politicians proved to be as "liberal" as any others on economic issues. Southern liberals played important roles in various New Deal agencies, especially those having to do with farm policy, but they were without political clout in the region itself. Still the New Deal failed to redesign the basic political landscape of the South; and the decade saw no repetition of the Populist insurgency of the 1890s.

An overview of the South circa 1930 would suggest a society in some ways resembling Franco's Spain or the Latin American republics. On the other hand, important cultural and institutional factors make this parallel misleading. The South was part of a national society whose political-legal structure was formally based on individual legal and political equality rather than ascriptive caste structures. The small white farmer still took his cultural bearings from the yeoman, republican ideal rather than harkening back nostalgically to an organic peasant order. "Plebeian anti-capitalism," so crucial in the appeal of authoritarian and proto-fascist ideologies elsewhere, found little popular resonance. In addition, economic distress, the residual effects of the Populist movement, and a general anti-aristocratic animus meant that the white classes and masses lived in an uneasy tension rather than forming a united front. The industrial development so assiduously pursued by the burgeoning urban and Piedmont middle classes and state government support of industrialization pointed to significant departures from the agrarian ethos which had dominated the region up to that time.

Finally, whether the term "colony" or "semi-periphery" or "underdeveloped" best describes the South's position circa 1930 is of no consequence. The important point is that the South was caught between two worlds—the old and the new—and two traditions—the regional and the national. Its ramshackle structure was founded on historical devotion to an increasingly unprofitable one-crop economy, an industrial infrastructure dominated by extractive industries and "primary production" and still significantly controlled by outside interests, a large surplus labor force lacking skills and training or the consumption power to support an industrial economy, and a cultural ethos which discouraged innovation and divided its allegiance between an outdated tradition and enthusiasm for a new order perpetually aborning.

Whatever benefits the South had once enjoyed during prosperity as a "favored colony,"[12] the national economy in the 1930s was trapped in a world-wide depression. The Great Depression of the 1930s did not "cause" the intellectual reassessment of and in the South, at least not its initial manifestations, but it did provide the context for its expression and its elaboration.

The Southern Family Romance

"Every culture lives inside its own dream," Lewis Mumford once observed;[13] and the Southern family romance was the South's dream. Though related to the "plantation legend" of ante-bellum popular fiction and similar expressions in post-Reconstruction popular fiction, the Southern family romance was never expressed in any consistent theoretical or literary way.[14] One must find it "between the lines," as it were, of Southern literature and life, for it was the collective fantasy which made up the "structure of feeling" of that culture. It constituted the values, attitudes, and beliefs that white Southerners expressed in their attitudes toward the region itself, the family, the relationship between the races and sexes, and between the elite and the masses.

But why "family romance"? The South was historically an agrarian society which lacked strong extra-familial institutions. The plantation itself was conceived of as structured like a family. It was relatively homogeneous and resolutely patriarchal in fact and in self-conception. It was not uncommon, as W. J. Cash noted in his *The Mind of the South,* for a rural Southern county to be dominated by a very few families and its populace, both black and white, to bear a small number of surnames and certain striking physical resemblances. Moreover, intermarriage among close kin was not at all uncommon and had a certain economic rationale among upper-class whites.[15] Beyond this there was a strong strain in Southern thought which saw society as the family writ large. For thinkers such as George Fitzhugh, the society-as-family was the ideal toward which Southern society should strive. Individual and regional identity, self-worth, and status were determined by family relationships. The actual family was destiny; and the region was conceived of as a vast metaphorical family, hierarchically organized and organically linked by (pseudo-) ties of blood.

Further, the term "family romance" has a specific meaning within psychoanalytic thought. In a brief introduction to Otto Rank's *The Myth of the Birth of the Hero,* Freud used "family romance" to describe the situation in which a child begins to view realistically the parents he had originally idealized and taken to be the sum of all human virtue. In reaction to his disappointment and what is often displacement from the center of attention, his "royal highness," the child, may imagine that he is adopted or a stepchild whose "real" (imaginary) parents are of noble lineage or powerful station. At the core of the young child's reaction Freud saw resentment at having been abandoned and a fantasized denial of abandonment.[16]

The notion of the family romance was elaborated further in Rank's essay. According to Rank, myths were the "dreams of the masses of people."[17] In the presence of an actual hero, a group will draw upon its own childhood fantasies, most centrally the family romance, which is a variation of the Oedipus story, to explain the hero's origins and his fate. By idealizing the cultural hero, the members of the group can justify their own revolt (in reality or fantasy) against their parents.

Rank went on to elaborate upon and explain the pattern which he had found in the stories of mythical figures. For instance, in the life of the hero the desire to be rid of the parents is reversed; it is the parents who wish to be rid of the young man. In the collective myth and in the family romance, the parents are generally split into "real" and "foster" and sometimes into "good" and "bad." Sometimes the foster parents are of lowly origin or are even animals. The myth of the hero culminates when the son returns to displace the father and, in the case of Oedipus, to marry the mother. Thereby he assumes the high or noble station which is rightly his.[18]

It was in the context of thoroughgoing social change after 1830 that an early version of the Southern family romance first surfaced—"the plantation legend." Writers in both sections of the country, particularly popular novelists, found much that troubled them in the restless, acquisitive society of those times. To these writers and their readers, the Revolutionary era seemed the age of heroes, one marked by public-spirited heroism and cultural achievement. By contrast, American society in the age of Jackson seemed hopelessly materialistic and a cultural wasteland. Decline had set in.

By way of cultural compensation, popular fiction pictured Southern society as essentially different from the rest of the country. It was more stable and settled than the chaotic West, less acquisitive and venal than the commercial Northeast. At the center of this popular image of the South was the plantation legend, which expressed a yearning for "intellectual distinction, genteel taste, private and public decorum."[19] But the legend was also shadowed by the fear of the family's dissolution. Its hero, the Southern Cavalier, had to "kneel down before the altar of femininity and familial benevolence."[20] It was felt that if somehow Yankee energy and Southern grace could be united, ultimately, America's future would be right.

Besides the idealization of the planter, the celebration of the feminine, and the lip service paid to the family, the plantation legend also existed to justify slavery or at least minimize its malevolence. The slave was pictured in "his dependence and helplessness" and "unquenchable happiness"; in more tense moments his "animality" was emphasized.[21] The process of sentimentalization was reflected in both the image of the woman and the slave. All were made part of the family. Not surprisingly, Southerners rejected the notion that they were peculiarly cruel or unjust. Rather, slave-holding became emblematic of a higher concern for a helpless and uncivilized race whom the Southern "fathers" and "mothers" gently but firmly disciplined.

If the prewar plantation legend emphasized the differences between the sections, the popular literature of the post-Reconstruction period served as a means of sectional reconciliation. Even more than the prewar plantation literature, this fiction was suffused with nostalgia for a way of life which had "gone with the wind." Once again the cultural distinctiveness of the Old South was emphasized. While the rest of the nation was becoming increasingly heterogeneous, the South prided itself on its aristocratic origins and bemoaned the destruction of the aristocratic way of life. Indeed, as late as the 1930s (and some will remember more recently), sociologist Hortense Powdermaker observed that middleclass white Southerners were obsessed with establishing their aristocratic credentials. Those who denied or disdained such connections were rare.[22] Another central theme in the fiction of writers such as Thomas Nelson Page and Thomas Dixon, author of *The Clansman*, from which the film *The Birth of a Nation* was made, was the way in which the good white folk of both sections united against those who insisted upon black equality, now that slavery had been destroyed. "The devoted slave" was contrasted with "the confused freedman."[23] Though few favored the restoration of the peculiar institution, the justification for racial segregation and black subordination stood at the center of this popular fiction.

This post-Reconstruction popular fiction was the imaginative expression of the "New South Creed," a vision advanced by Southern intellectuals and publicists. The New South Creed emphasized the need for industrial development, diversified agriculture, sectional reconciliation, and racial comity, with blacks placed in a subordinate position. Though the New South Creed was a "modernizing" ideology, it also paid homage to the Old South and the Lost Cause. In this sense it was the post-Reconstruction expression of the Southern attempt to square the cultural circle, to combine the best of the Old South with the spirit of modern industrial capitalism.

To pull off this bit of ideological legerdemain, the New South spokesmen took one of two positions regarding the ante-bellum South. For some the Old South had divided into two parts: the Jeffersonian legacy provided the justification for national. unity and cultural achievement, while the decades after 1820 were seen as an unfortunate interregnum. But for the most part, the arcadian fantasy of the Old South was embraced wholeheartedly. This move was reinforced by the North itself, which came increasingly to admire the Southern ethos as a cultural alternative to the industrial, polyglot society emerging above the Mason-Dixon line. "A national love feast for the Old South" was the result.[24] Sectional reconciliation could proceed apace. Assuring the North that it would do right by freedmen, the South encouraged Northern investment in nascent industries. In sum, then, the New South Creed plumped for modernization and development on the one hand and cultivated the cultural fantasies of the ante-bellum days on the other.

Of further interest is the way in which the New South Creed itself became a myth. Where they began by stressing the lack of sectional development, New South spokesmen eventually replaced reality with wish. The new day, they came to assert, had already dawned. Not only were the apparently incongruous fantasy of the Old South and the dream of the New South yoked together, the future was converted into an already existing reality. What the New South advocates attempted in reality contradicted their allegiance to the tradition of the family romance. The cultural superstructure to which educated and "enlightened" Southerners gave their allegiance and by which they understood themselves was out of phase with the reality of Southern life. Indeed the cultural superstructure was divided against itself. The monumental and critical views of the past, one hallowing the past and the other rejecting it, vied with one another for dominance.

Between approximately 1900 and World War I a new generation of Southern intellectuals came on the scene. These men might best be described as genteel progressives, the more sophisticated heirs of the New South movement of the previous decades. Publicists, academics, and clergymen, born generally between 1855 and 1875, they were intermediaries between the backward South and the developed North. Except on the matter of white supremacy, they "criticized the entire life of the South . . . searchingly, sometimes scathingly."[25]

Though coming from small-town and rural backgrounds, they supported Southern industrialization. From solidly middle-class families, they were advocates of the ethic of work and rationality to their more backward fellow Southerners. Not for them the idealization of each and every Confederate ancestor. Rather they paid homage to the time-honored favorites of Southern moderates who wished to remain loyal Southerners yet affirm a more seemly Southern tradition, one less strident and harsh. For them Jefferson and Robert E. Lee, not John C. Calhoun or Nathan Bedford Forrest, were the figures of the past who deserved emulation. Though the most prominent of these Southern progressives—Woodrow Wilson—was less emancipated from "the romantic myths of the virtuous South,"[26] others such as Edwin Mims had little sympathy for the Lost Cause.

But the decisiveness of their break with the Southern tradition is hard to credit. Leaving aside their unquestioning commitment to white supremacy (a matter to which we will return), they were hardly ideological or temperamental radicals. They pursued "no rebellion against their fathers."[27] Like every white Southerner, they believed wholeheartedly in the "myths of Reconstruction."[28] The Populist movement's bare-knuckles approach was "anathema"; and the closest they came to grass-roots appeal was in support of public education, hardly a fighting issue. Any discussion of politics or economics which focused on class interest or conflict was taboo. Finally, their cultural-literary tastes were thoroughly genteel.

In his study of a number of these figures, *The Savage Ideal*, Bruce Clayton's assessment of their racial attitudes shows the degree to which they were still mesmerized by the family romance. Not only did they not challenge their fathers, they had no "real understanding of racism's hold on the Southern mind,"[29] including their own. They were thoroughgoing paternalists and looked longingly back to the ante-bellum days when loving cooperation had allegedly marked the relationship of master and slave. Nor did these men believe in political equality among whites ("Herrenvolk" democracy). They feared the white masses as much as or more so than the black masses.[30]

Except for Edwin Mims, who became chairman of the English department at Vanderbilt University, the influence of these Southern progressive intellectuals waned after World War I. They, like their New South predecessors, remained fundamentally divided in their attitudes toward the past and future. With their blindness toward matters having to do with class or race, with their optimistic belief that modernization could take place without the South's abandoning its central cultural values, they remained sophisticated apologists for things as they were—and had been. They were willing to give a little to keep the rest.

The years between Reconstruction and World War I saw the emergence of a new racial fantasy, though it was one which had lurked around the edges of (white) Southern racial consciousness from the beginning.[31]

What white Southerners wanted after the Civil War was a docile black population; their fundamental fear was that the freedman would resist being consigned to a subordinate position. Three separate though related modes of race relations emerged. The first, articulated by Hinton Helper, called for ridding the South of its black people by colonization; for obvious economic reasons such a plan was never adopted. (Exclusionist tendencies lingered on well into the new century.) The second position, one proposed by Helper's ideological opposite, George Fitzhugh, called for a position of "integrated subservience." It assumed continuing black docility and subservience, while Helper's assumed black defiance and considered the close contact with blacks as "impure and revolting."[32] The third position came as a compromise between the two. As articulated by Tennessee politician Parson Brownlow and others, it sought to keep the docile, "good" blacks at hand and somehow to isolate or get rid of defiant, "uppity" ones. Behind these plans lay the "perennial racist dichotomy between the Negro as child and the Negro as beast."[33] The New South ideologues, as we have seen, set forth a quasi-paternalistic racial ideal, in which whites claimed responsibility for black moral guidance and education, while at the same time urging black self-help and self-reliance. They were caught somewhere between an aristocratic paternalism of the Fitzhugh sort and a bourgeois paternalism of moral and educational "uplift." Their ideological heirs were the Southern moderates of the Progressive period already alluded to, who also stressed the "benevolent" paternalism of the educated and enlightened middle-class Southerner. Horrified by lynching and egregious forms of racial domination, these moderates were still firmly committed to separate but equal development and to black inferiority.

But alongside this moderate paternalism, a new more brutal motif appeared in racial thought around the turn of the century —the Negro as "beast" or "the diseased Negro." Always lurking behind the earlier racial paternalism, this form of racism flourished in the 1890s and during the first decades of this century. The black man was seen less as the perennial child or docile old uncle who offered ease to the frantic strivings of whites and more as the barely tamed savage, the oversexed rapist, and/or the carrier of polluting disease which threatened the health, indeed the very survival, of the pure white race. The logic of this position was eventual black extinction by natural selection. In the meantime, blacks were kept in line by both legal and extra-legal means.

Thus what emerged in these years were two forms of white racism, which Pierre van den Berghe has labeled "paternalistic" and "competitive."[34] Taken strictly, the Southern family romance, modeled as it was upon the ante-bellum racial order, viewed blacks as permanent and harmless children in the larger Southern family. From a psychoanalytic perspective, paternalistic forms of racism are understandable in Oedipal terms: parent-child relationships are paradigmatic. Further, though racial equality is denied, intimacy and contact between the two races is not forbidden as long as the subordinate caste keeps its place. This paternalistic view, however, came steadily into conflict with the laissez-faire ideology of the Southern progressives and with the turbulent reality of the 1890s and early part of the new century.

Yet, the family romance had also pictured blacks as potential savages, in need of the firm hand of white mastery. At the heart of competitive racism lies not the paternalist relationship but the sexually menacing image of blacks. With the white South threatened in the decades on either side of 1900 by political and social rebellion, blacks became the displaced embodiment of those repressed individual and collective impulses which threatened to emerge as the old order came under attack. The solution was to segregate blacks socially and to exploit them economically, just as the unconscious pre-Oedipal drive fragments had to be repressed and driven from consciousness—affirmed, in short, by denial.

At this point, it would be well to draw back and flesh out more fully the notion of the family romance, Southern style, as it stood at the beginning of World War I. At the center of the family romance, in its patriarchal expression, was the father. Powerful though the Southern woman might be in fact, she was distinctly subordinate in the romance to the powerful and heroic father. As the romance emerged in the post-Civil War years less emphasis was placed upon the Cavalier per se. The "father" came to be the gracious, courteous, but tough planter of the pre-War years who had led the heroic and collective struggle against the Yankees. He was the "presiding presence" in the romance; and, as he faded from the scene, the grandsons in the early years of the century idealized the great hero of the romance even more. Measured against the heroic generation of the grandfathers, the fathers seemed rather unheroic and prosaic to their sons. The family romance thus pitted son against father and often joined grandson and grandfather. Further, though many Southerners embraced the gospel of progress in the post-Reconstruction years, this optimistic stance was shadowed by the strong suspicion that the age of heroes lay in the past. Decline was an integral part of the Southern family romance.[35]

If the Southern family romance placed the father-son relationship at its center, the white woman was expected to play the role of the mother. As mistress of the plantation she was the lady bountiful, caring for the wants and needs of her family, both white and black. A prime, though late, example of this characterization is Ellen O'Hara, Scarlett's mother in *Gone With the Wind*. The Southern woman was caught in a social double-bind: toward men she was to be submissive, meek and gentle; with the children and slaves and in the management of the household, she was supposed to display competence, initiative, and energy. But she remained a shadowy figure, always there and ever necessary, but rarely emerging in full force. She was "queen of the home."[36]

Another way of understanding the role of the mother in the Southern family romance is to observe that sexuality or erotic appeal was denied her. In extreme form she was stripped of any emotional, nurturing attributes at all. Eventually, she came to assume a quasi-Virgin Mary role as the asexual mother of the Southern male hero. It is of course difficult to know what the relationship between this cultural role and the reality of Southern life was. Lillian Smith was to observe that her mother's generation (that of the late nineteenth century) shied away from anything having to do with sexuality or the body. It became an object of disgust, a matter of shame. And though Anne Firor Scott has challenged Smith's indictment of Southern women's coldness and antisensuality, the accepted values of the culture, reinforced by Victorian morality, surely had a profound effect.[37]

One can only speculate that the cultural denial of sexuality or nurturing warmth to the white woman must have something to do with the lack of strongly sexed women in much of the literature of the Southern Renaissance. One thinks here of Tate's *The Fathers*, which opens with the funeral of Lacy Buchan's mother, of Faulkner's series of neurasthenic women, castrating bitches, spiky but asexual older aunts and grandmothers, and the absence of the mother in "The Bear" or her shadowy role in *Absalom, Absalom!*; of Will Percy's neglect of his mother in his autobiography; of Carson McCullers's *A Member of the Wedding*, and indeed all her stories in which a mother scarcely appears; and of Lillian Smith's *Strange Fruit* and *Killers of the Dream*. In the case of Faulkner, it was not, as we shall see, that his mother played a minor role—far from it. But Southern women remained neglected figures in the cultural articulations and literary renderings of the family romance.

If (in the family romance) the white father and mother assumed dominant positions, blacks occupied the role of permanently delegitimized and often literally illegitimate children. Yet there was a central contradiction at the core of the notion of the South as a "family." On the one hand racial ideology dictated that blacks could not be acknowledged as literal members of the family, a theme explored in *Light in August, Absalom, Absalom!*, and *Go Down Moses* most clearly. To recognize blacks would be to soil the purity of the racial-social lineage, the infrastructure of the tradition. One the other hand the family romance also claimed that blacks were "childlike" and thus permanent members of the metaphorical Southern family. To take the family romance literally would be to negate it; and this is what happened in the writings of Faulkner and Lillian Smith.

Emotional ambivalence and role reversals can readily be seen in the actual and fantasized roles of black men and women in the romance. The black male was ideally a loyal figure of childlike wisdom and Christian charity, a wise and forgiving grandfather or naïve, childlike retainer. Yet he might also be the "bad Nigger," the rapist and the insurrectionist, bent on exacting his blood lust from whites. D. W. Griffith's *The Birth of a Nation,* based on Thomas Dixon's *The Clansman,* and again *Gone with the Wind* present both of these aspects quite clearly.

Similar contradictions existed in the role of the black woman.

In his analysis, Rank observed that the foster "mothering agent" of the mythological hero was usually someone of low or peasant origin or even, as in the Romulus and Remus legend, an animal. With this in mind, the ambiguities inherent in the role of the black "mammy" became clearer. Because of her skin color, she was an illegitimate sibling, childlike though not without force of will. Yet the romance, and sometimes reality, contradicted this image by presenting her as the loving foster mother to whom the Southern hero owed all. In this role, as the legendary "kind animal," she was a cultural rebuke to the stereotypically cold and distant white mother. In Lillian Smith's work she becomes the "real" mother; that is, the one who nurtures and truly mothers. And yet the black woman was also regarded as sexually ardent and animal-like in passion. Thus she was a sultry temptress and nurturing mammy, inferior sibling and true parent, incestuous object and idealized mother. What linked these rather contradictory roles was the fact that to the black woman were attributed the emotional impulses denied to the white woman.

Thus, in the reality and cultural fantasy of the South, the roles of parent and child attributed to white and black respectively were affirmed, denied, and inverted. Emotional acknowledgment was often accompanied by social denial. The burdens of this psycho-cultural romance fell most heavily on the black male and the white female. The white woman was denied sexual and nurturing attributes, which were displaced onto the black woman. Analogously, the black man suffered the worst of both worlds: as symbolic phallus he was particularly open to violent retaliation, most horribly in the castration rituals that accompanied lynching, while as wise "uncle" he was denied authentic manhood. The actual black family was most vulnerable in its paternal role, for the black father lacked control over the actual or symbolic systems of survival, while the white family was weakest in its maternal position. To the former was denied power; to the latter, sexuality. Hence, as we shall see, the ultimate challenge to the family romance was the sexual relationship of black men and white women, a violation of the incest and the miscegenation taboos.

This then was the Southern family romance, the central fantasy structure of Southern culture, as the 1920s gave way to the Depression decade. As we have seen, the family romance was riven with contradictions, particularly in its vision of blacks and its ambiguous assessment of the claims of the past measured against the vision of the future. With social and economic stability disappearing, the tradition of the family romance came under intense scrutiny. This was the assignment and the burden of the generation of the 1930s.

3

Modernizers
and Monumentalists:
Social Thought in the 1930s

Southern intellectual life in the 1930s was centered at Chapel Hill, North Carolina, and at Nashville, Tennessee. Whereas the Regionalists (and their allies) at the University of North Carolina were trained in sociology, geography, economics, and history, the Vanderbilt Agrarians were poets, novelists, men of letters, and only incidentally social analysts. In moments of exasperation the Regionalists saw the Agrarians as romantic obfuscators, while the Vanderbilt group accused the Regionalists of being New South advocates in modern dress, Yankee wolves in sheep's clothing. The Agrarians looked to the past for guidance in forging a vision of what the South and ultimately modern society should be, while the Regionalists attempted to transcend the South's inherited culture and imagine a significantly new South for the future. In matters of detail and immediate programmatic suggestions not a great deal separated the two groups; still their opposing visions were different enough to allow them to define the boundaries of discourse about the South in the 1930s.

Howard W. Odum and Southern Regionalism

The dominating figure in the Chapel Hill group, Howard Odum, enjoyed a long and influential career as educator, scholar, and social planner.[1] Along with Rupert Vance, Guy and Guion Johnson, Harriett Herring, and others, he published a series of works, primarily in the 1930s, which charted a course for the revitalization and maturation of the South.

Odum was born in 1884 and grew up in Georgia. A shy and retiring child, he was close to his mother, from whom he acquired a love of nature and a passion for education. Odum's fundamentalist religious training developed in him a certain asceticism, a desire for justification, and a sense of continually being on trial. He was also shaped by his two grandfathers, with whom he spent long hours talking. His paternal grandfather was a man of modest means, and from him young Howard learned shame over the South's defeat, a shame rooted in John Wesley Odum's own sense of shame for having deserted the Southern cause after an emotional crisis. His maternal grandfather was from the planter class; and from him Odum learned open bitterness toward the North. Not shame but vindictiveness was his guiding emotion.

Through these two figures Odum came to identify with the South and its condition. During his life Odum was to exhibit both resentment over the South's defeat and a desire for the South to be vindicated in the eyes of the world. These emotions were united, however, in a vision of ultimate harmony and reconciliation within the South and between the South and the rest of the nation. The basic characteristics of his life and work were a "deep aversion to conflict, his great hope that reason could reduce it, his intense moralism, and, above all, his love for the South."[2]

Though trained in the classics at Emory University in Georgia, Odum shifted his interest to sociology after teaching in rural Mississippi and coming into contact with T. P. Bailey at the University of Mississippi. Odum's first sociological projects concerned Southern blacks; and in 1910 he published *The Social and Mental Traits of the Negro.* His central concern in this monograph was with Negro "progress," that is, how blacks could be accommodated in the post-slavery South. Odum dissected the black character and found it woefully lacking. The main obstacle, he wrote, "in the way of the Negro's industrial efficiency as well as in his mental and moral character is his lack of sustained application and constructive conduct."[3]

Odum's book was a prime example of the racist transformation of social "facts" into natural "givens." He had no doubt that the Negro was different "not only in development but also in kind";[4] and thus Odum foresaw no immediate or long-range equality. Only with white help could the black man prosper. Invoking the *sine qua non* of Southern racism, Odum saw intermarriage as the chief obstacle to black progress. Equality and regional progress were mutually exclusive.

Race would remain an important concern when he began teaching at the University of Georgia in the early teens. He increasingly stressed development over fixity of traits, the factors contributing to racial differences rather than their permanence.[5] He published a trilogy of "novels" based on black folklore and folktales in the late 1920s which, though more sympathetic than his earlier writings, still carried the conventional stereotypes of blacks. In his sociological works of the 1930s, Odum quietly questioned the impoverished South's insistence on maintaining dual school systems and even suggested that graduate education be interracial. For Odum, the key to progress in race relations lay with the leadership of both races. Always a gradualist, he was instrumental in the founding of the Southern Regional Council. And in 1944 he wrote privately to John Temple Graves that segregation violated scientific, democratic, and Christian precepts, if it was taken to be a permanent condition.[6]

At the University of Georgia, Odum took up what became the other focus of his scholarly writing—rural sociology. Odum's vision of regional reform and regeneration was informed by the New South spirit as well as the Progressive notion of social science in the service of the rationalization and organization of Southern rural life. Modernization of the South was to be achieved by cooperation not conflict. Behind this general goal lay his dream of restoring the rural South to a position of self-respect, a desire rooted in his own experience plus the rural apologetics of Virgil and Horace, whom he had read as a student, and the American agrarian ideology. More theoretically, Odum's sociology was organicist in nature. Change in one sector of social life was accompanied by change in all the other sectors. He vacillated between the conservative Darwinist view that progress would come gradually and naturally and the vision of progress through rational planning. This tension was to appear in all his later works, particularly *Southern Regions.*

In 1920 Odum moved to Chapel Hill, which, under President Harry Chase, had embraced the Wisconsin plan of the university as a service institution. Odum founded the journal *Social Forces* in 1922 and immediately began calling for the South to abandon its outmoded romanticism and stifling intolerance and to adopt an open, objective attitude toward its problems and potentialities. But over the next several years the various articles he (and others) published in *Social Forces* dealing with science and religion, the labor movement and race aroused considerable opposition from the North Carolina clergy and business community. Odum deeply regretted the publicity surrounding the Scopes trial and considered it an example of the failure of intellectuals to make contact with the "people" and educate them. There had been "more pathos than joke, more futility than fighting, more tragedy than comedy" in the Scopes trial and the hoopla surrounding it.[7] Thus he took a conciliatory position somewhere between H. L. Mencken and the Vanderbilt Agrarians.

Odum's collisions with entrenched economic and religious interests revealed several salient traits. With his belief in the persuasive power of facts and objective research, he tended to see all conflicts as misunderstandings. He "abhorred conflict and confrontation"[8] and was always surprised that he was considered a radical. His genuine but rather paternalistic faith that the "people" would respond to wise leadership gradually lessened; and by the late 1920s he had to admit that *Social Forces* would have to be a journal for specialists, not for a general audience. Still his faith that science could offer solutions to social problems and bring order and harmony to chaos and conflict remained fundamentally intact. His was a positivism with a human face.

Odum's concept of Regionalism began taking shape in the late 1920s under the influence of thinkers such as Lewis Mumford. *American Epoch* (1930) used Odum's family experience as a way of talking about the Southern past.[9] Odum praised the planter aristocracy but noted that the planters and the yeomen were descended from common stock. He did score the aristocracy's inadequate grasp of reality and blamed them for the weakness of the family among both races. The focus of the book fell on "Uncle John", a non-slave-owner who had fought with the South against the North. He stood as a representative of the "common folk" of the South, its backbone. Odum also criticized Northern self-righteousness in dealing with the South and particularly the imposition of black rule upon the defeated South in Reconstruction. Defeat and occupation led to a loss of Southern confidence. But in uncritically idealizing its leaders and its cause, the South had not been without blame for its own problems.

There were several more general themes in *American Epoch* which Odum developed more fully in *Southern Regions*. Though the South possessed abundant physical resources and cultural advantages, its great failure had been in political leadership.[10] Here Odum pointed to Tom Watson, the Georgia Populist who had succumbed to a rabid sort of racial demagoguery after the turn of the century. In focusing on Watson, Odum revealed a bit of the uneasiness the Regionalists harbored toward the Southern farmers' revolt of the 1890s. It had been too extreme, too irresponsible. Instead the South needed the steady vision of a quiet professional middle class, the "hand of science and statemanship."[11] Odum also noted that black Southerners had never been given an "opportunity for natural development."[12] As a result the Negro, despite advances in certain areas, lagged far behind the Southern white.

Finally, after calling for the South to be understood in the national context, Odum ended with a plea for a South which thought "less highly of the past than of the future."[13] With this critical perspective on the past, the South could and should shed the memories which had embittered it and the characteristics which had hindered the full development of its potential. Only then could it rejoin the nation.

In Rupert Vance's *Human Geography of the South* (1932), the Regionalist case was set forth with greater detail and precision.[14] Underlying Vance's work was a tension which the Regionalists exploited but with which they never quite came to terms. Vance was concerned as a geographer to analyze the ecological setting within which Southern society had developed. He observed that the South "has various physiographic regions" but went on to say that "History, not geography made the Solid South."[15] This contradiction had dogged the South historically and was the despair of those who envisaged a South which would exchange the blandishments of tradition for the necessity of regional planning. The Regionalists were to keep hammering at this dichotomy between geography and history, and, in Odum's *Southern Regions,* between social and economic indices and historical-cultural forces.[16] If only, they wanted to believe, the South could wipe the historical slate clean, then its abundant natural and human resources could be fully utilized.

Another theme in both Vance's book and Odum's *Southern Regions* followed from Odum's emphasis upon the middling, yeoman farmer—the importance of the frontier in Southern history. Even the plantation society, claimed Vance, "retained many of the frontier traits," and much of the South, according to Odum, still reflected "a sort of arrested frontier pattern of life."[17] The rationale behind this emphasis was, first, to provide the South with an alternative to the aristocratic tradition and to assert the need for the South to abandon its cotton monoculture for a more diversified economy. The Piedmont had avoided the plantation hegemony and was "entering the stage of industrialization. Here the South is making her first coherent break with the agrarian tradition."[18] Thus no longer should the black-belt South dominate the region or provide the leadership for the South. Finally by stressing the frontier experience as central to the South and minimizing the planter influence, the Regionalists could also claim that Southern culture, far from wilting, was waiting to flower. The South presented the "immaturity and vitality of regional folk capable either of superior achievement or of pathological developments."[19]

Vance and Odum both stressed the abundance of natural and human resources at the South's disposal. As of 1932 Vance was inclined to reject the notion of congenital black inferiority and certainly rejected the less widely held but nevertheless common notion that poor whites were of inferior stock.[20] But both he and Odum pointed to the fact that from the beginning the South had been saddled with a colonial economy—a cotton monoculture, debtor status, soil exhaustion, and cheap wages. In addition, technology and capital were in short supply. Moreover, Vance and Odum saw the need to keep the educated and professional classes from leaving the South; otherwise what little strength the South possessed would be sapped. And both pointed as well to the burden of what Odum would euphemistically call the "dual load of dichotomous education"[21] and the shortcomings of Southern higher education generally.

But if Vance and Odum presented substantially the same analysis of the South's plight, it was Odum's massive *Southern Regions* (1936) which proved to be the Bible for Regionalism. *Southern Regions* was the result of some four years' work funded by the General Education Board through the Social Science Research Council.[22] Rejecting the Vanderbilt Agrarians' sectional truculence, Odum emphasized that Regionalism was a theory and a praxis which aimed to reintegrate the region into the nation. Integration would not come at the expense of the Southern economy but would allow the South to escape its colonial position. Thus the South would regain its self-respect, but not at the expense of national unity.

Odum also contended that there no longer was a single "South" but rather two Southern regions—the Southeast and the Southwest. Here Odum was forcing the hand of history and tradition; his "indices of capacity" would establish this new truth against the mystic chords of Southern unity. In the Southeast the most pressing problem lay with the agricultural sector, with race running a close second. Agriculture must be developed and diversified and industrial development begun where appropriate.

In the area of race Odum waffled a bit but called for a special effort to improve race relations and for the abandonment of the notion of black inferiority. This did not mean, however, that segregation would be abolished, only that the "inequalities" would be taken out of the biracial system. This could be done "without destroying the integrity of the races."[23]

Here Odum was faced with the classic political dilemma of Southern moderates and the theoretical fuzziness in the sociological priority given to "folkways" over "stateways," customs over laws. Southern liberals assumed that any real (or suspected) advocacy of social equality would doom their proposals to defeat. Thus one assumes that Odum's equivocation was an Aesopian tactic, for if the races were biologically equal, the notion of racial integrity was emptied of significance.

But then there was the theoretical problem. Odum quoted Guy Johnson with approval: "The old question of social equality is not necessarily involved, for there is no equality except that which is bestowed willingly in the attitudes and behavior of individuals. The races can go the whole way of political and civic equality without endangering their integrity."[24] The confusions here were legion. It was not clear, for instance, why political and civic equality did not also involve folkways. This confusion was compounded by the assumption that social equality, as opposed to political and civic equality, was essentially a matter of individual preference. Ultimately the hidden assumption here was the taboo on intermarriage, which underlay all white Southern advocacy of racial "integrity" and opposition to social equality. It is difficult to say whether or not this legal-sociological double-talk was Aesopian as well. Odum was always the conciliator and may have thought that such tortured formulations offered something for everyone. Still the whole cultural-psychological problem was one which neither Odum nor the Regionalists were willing to tackle. Odum's specific solution to Southern racial problems was educational, institutional and inadequate. There should, he felt, be some "inter-institutional education of Negroes in three or four regional universities," which were yet to be built.[25]

And yet in areas having to do with regional development, Odum trusted in the power of facts to show the right direction and did not hesitate to have stateways override folkways. In fact the positive thrust of his program was for state and regional planning boards to be set up, on the model of the TVA, to provide facts and a framework for alternative policies.[26] These boards would, however, not have actual decision-making power. Thus in all areas but race, the "rational" should triumph over the historical; the folk was a potential force for change not stasis.

Though Odum was to publish *American Regionalism* in 1938 with Harry Moore, the rest of his work only elaborated what had come before. He continued to insist on the distinction between regionalism and sectionalism and to affirm the Regionalist commitment to national unity and the "new pluralism of the American nation."[27] He added a vague attack on "unrealistic all-inclusive 'isms' and plans so often offered as substitutes for fundamental processes and extensions of the American order."[28] This wooly yet abstract prose camouflaged Odum's distaste for socialism or an internal class analysis of the South. Indeed the striking thing about Odum and the Regionalists was their almost unbroken silence on Marx and socialism. A perusal of *Social Forces* in the 1920s and 1930s reveals only a handful, if that, of articles or reviews dealing with socialism, the Soviet Union, or the importance of class factors in social analysis. Instead of labeling the yeoman as a "middle class" farmer, Odum preferred to use the more all inclusive term "folk" and thus to divert attention from the possibility of analyzing the region in terms of class relationships.

Nor did Odum change his attitude toward the Populists after *American Epoch*. In *Southern Regions* he dismissed Tom Watson as a "rabble rouser" who "stands as a sign and symbol of the South's political dilemma."[29] And later, in 1947, he referred to the Georgia Populist as "maniacally bitter."[30] In his review of Woodward's biography of Watson, Rupert Vance was less harsh toward, though still skeptical of, the Populists' limited programs and accomplishments.[31] Though Regionalism was for the people, it was not by the people. *Southern Regions* ended with a call for "scholarship and statesmanship, reputed symbols of the Jeffersonian ideal." There was no talk of political or social conflict. Analogously, racial problems were best handled by the elites of both races.[32] Odum feared the "culture conflicts arising from the impatience and enthusiasm of the younger generations of Negroes."[33] Later, during the war, he wrote of his desire for "orderly change . . . realistic education rather than revolutionary action"[34] to ease the racial tensions which had arisen during the war as a result of the conflict of Southern folkways and the war effort.

In summary then, Odum was committed to the "folk" without

desiring their direct participation in the development of the South. General education and wise leadership would satisfy their needs. Yet, ironically, the larger implication of the Regionalist program resembled a sort of vulgar Marxism. Once economic problems had been solved, racial and class conflicts would disappear. It would be too much to call the Regionalists "technocrats," particularly in the context of the 1930s, when that term had a specific meaning; and their proposals were in broad harmony with the New Deal. But they did have an atypical Southern faith in the power of facts, analysis, and planning to change minds and to move the entrenched interests without unseemly political or social conflict.

Moreover, though Odum and Vance clearly identified the South's colonial status, they did not analyze the exploitative class relationships within the region. This is not to say that they neglected poverty; far from it. Rather they tended to talk of general income levels or to point to the rise of tenancy and sharecropping; and their solutions were either very general—the call for regional economic planning—or quite specific—the call for better vocational and higher education. They assumed that if the masses received better education, they would receive better jobs and improve their lives. The rising tide of future Southern prosperity would lift all boats. Education took the place of politics, planning the place of participation.

But to some students of the South during the 1930s the calls for sectional harmony and national integration were inadequate. When they looked more closely at the social and economic relationships within the South, they saw that certain segments of the population—small farmers and tenants, workers in the mills and factories, and blacks in general—were clearly being exploited as a "class." Most forthright and adamant were probably Broadus and George Mitchell. In their *The Industrial Revolution in the South* (1930), the Mitchells called for "a revolution in our social habit and procedure."[35] The Mitchells refused to shed any tears for the Old South and contended that what industry had killed should have long since perished. To bring about this industrial revolution they looked to the unions to "remove the inferiority complex" of the workers and the paternalism and "superiority complex of the employers."[36] The goal was some sort of "collective industrial control."

Arthur Raper and Ira Reid in *Sharecroppers All* (1941) pointed to the racial division between whites and blacks as the cause of depressed wages among both groups.[37] Raper and Reid were quite forthright in linking racial and class inequalities and relating both to the South's other ills: "From race and attendant class demarcations stem the South's economic feudalism, one party system, white primary and poll taxes. The result has been the disinheritance and disfranchisement of nearly all the Negroes, a majority of the whites and of the region itself in national affairs."[38] It was time that the South stopped blaming everyone else for its problems. The authors of *Sharecroppers All* were not unaware of the colonial economic position of the South vis-à-vis the rest of the nation, but for them racial and social disparities within the South matched or outweighed those between the South and the rest of the country.

As always, what was to be done was less clear. Raper and Reid called for cooperative production and distribution and looked with hope to the Southern Farmers Tenant Union and the Southern Conference on Human Welfare. Concerning race they wrote: "To rid the region of lynch law, programs must be launched which deal realistically and constructively with Jim Crow laws and residential segregation, the right to education, right to trial by jury, the right to be represented when taxed."[39] Though the ambiguity of the phrase "realistically and constructively" is obvious, they did not feel called upon to pay homage to the "integrity" of the races.[40]

Besides supporting unionization and cooperative enterprises, W. T. Couch called upon analysts of Southern agriculture, the Agrarians included, to recognize that the interests of large commercial farmers, small farmers, and tenants were not identical simply because they all worked the land. He urged the New Deal, which had primarily helped the first two categories of farmers, to set up "experimental farm villages" to help tenants. Property would remain private, but specialization, rationalization of task, and diversification of crops could be worked out on each unit. Such communities would remedy the isolation of rural life.[41]

But perhaps the most forthright analysis of race and class came from H. C. Nixon, an apostate Agrarian who had made the symbolic move from Nashville to Chapel Hill and beyond. His *Forty Acres and Steel Mules* (1938) was praised by C. Vann Woodward, whose biography of Tom Watson had just appeared, for focusing upon class divisions within the South.[42] According to Woodward, the South had been "an agent as well as victim of economic exploitation"; and he called for analysts to focus upon class divisions within the South rather than harping on its colonial position.[43] Nixon's book amply fulfilled this desire.

In *Forty Acres* Nixon called for group, cooperative solutions, not the "individualistic remedy of '40 acres and a mule.' "[44] Since the Civil War the South's colonial economy had been run by a "commercial gentry," along with the "merchant and the planter who had been tied to the financial East" and had become the "equivalent of a concessionaire in a backward country."[45] Nixon saw plans such as Mississippi's BAWI scheme to attract industry as merely ways of confirming the South more fully in its colonial dependency. Imaginative plans for land reform and rural coopera-tives such as existed in Scandinavia and Ireland were needed; rural villages and planned communities were also necessary to provide human and cultural contacts. They should also include Negroes. Nor was Nixon at all hesitant about drawing upon "extra-regional capital and a measure of extra-regional control" but on the condition that it came "from Washington, not Wall Street."[46]

Finally Nixon was anxious to transcend Southern chauvinism and Yankee-baiting, since for him class divisions were more im-portant than sectional rivalries.[47] The dice had been loaded against both the Negro and the South, but "with many Southern-ers participating in the winnings." "There can be no inter-regional justice," Nixon ended, "without inter-class justice."[48]

But for all their insights and efforts to address the complexly interwoven connections between race, class, and region, such radi-cal voices generally went unheeded. As has been the case gen-erally in America, class and race were to be addressed separately.

With President Roosevelt becoming Dr. Win-the-War instead of Dr. New Deal, Southern underdevelopment was to be "solved" in other ways. Still, the Regionalists' modernizing ideology provided a valuable first step toward imagining a South which had abandoned its traditional cultural, racial, and social attitudes and had set forth in a new direction. The reintegration of the South in the nation as an equal partner was their goal.

The Agrarians and Literary Catonism[49]

Along with their ideological precursors in the ante-bellum period, the Vanderbilt Agrarians offered the closest thing to an authentic conservative vision which America has seen. They were the party of the past, yearning for an organic, hierarchical order such as had allegedly existed in the ante-bellum South or the European Middle Ages. Like most defenders of aristocracy, they were literary intellectuals and displayed considerable hostility to the natural sciences, modern technology, and the philosophical position— broadly known as positivism—they associated with the modern world. There were differences among them regarding literary modernism. John Crowe Ransom and Donald Davidson preferred literary modes which mirrored the orderly and hierarchical world of the past, while Allen Tate displayed the complex, dislocated rhythms and imagery of the modern world in his poetry, and in his criticism defended T. S. Eliot and other modernist writers.

The cultural vision of the Agrarians falls under Barrington Moore's "Catonist" rubric. The Catonist response to modernization has surfaced in every European society, most fatefully in Germany; and, as Moore's rubric indicates, its legacy traces back to the Roman Republic of the Punic Wars. Catonism is the ideological response of a landed upper class (and its spokesmen) which is economically, socially, and politically on the defensive. The Catonist fears the encroachment of alien values and impersonal commercial forces which disrupt an aristocratic and organic order cemented by ties of family, status, tradition, and, sometimes, race or nationality. The Catonist also fears the "people" politically, though he may often celebrate the organic, cultural linkages that constitute hierarchical unity. As Moore sees it, the "sterner virtues, militarism, contempt for decadent foreigners and anti-intellectualism" make up the core of the Catonist response. The Catonist takes the collapse of his specific world for the end of virtue and order generally. In cultural-psychological terms the Catonist manifests "wholeness hunger," the yearning for an earlier time before the dissociation of sensibility. And the Catonist's historical consciousness is "monumentalist"; it seeks to resurrect the past and to revivify a former, more heroic ethos in the present.[50]

More familiar to Europe than to America, the Catonist critique of industrial capitalism sounds very much like its Marxist opposite. Underlying both positions is the assumption that modern capitalism has been the most revolutionary and disruptive force in the modern world. Where they differ, of course, is that the Catonist seeks to revoke the world created by the cash nexus, the marketplace and the industrial system, while the Marxist vision incorporates and transcends it. The South for the Agrarians was an economic, even cultural, colony of the capitalist North. While not explicitly anticapitalist, the Agrarian vision evoked an agrarian order based upon personal private property and held together by the cooperation of planter and yeoman. Their overriding concern was that economics should not dominate social or personal life. The Agrarian solution to the South's economic colonization by the North was not, as with the Regionalists, a desire for a more equitable share of the system, but a rejection of integration into the modern economy of industrial and financial capitalism altogether.

As the Southern tradition loomed problematic after World War I, a not uncommon reaction was to defend it all the stronger, shearing it of what little complexity it possessed. This was the upshot of the Agrarians' message in their famous manifesto *I'll Take My Stand* (1930), which appeared paradoxically both more cogent and less relevant as the Depression deepened. In an earlier incarnation as the "Fugitives," several of the Agrarians had distanced themselves from the sentimentality and stifling gentility of conventional Southern culture. Ironically, in the 1930s they came to advance only a more sophisticated version of the Southern family romance. Gentility was replaced by veneration of aristocracy; nostalgia was given added bite by combativeness.

I'll Take My Stand has been analyzed more than enough by students of American literature and culture. A reading of *I'll Take My Stand* now hardly engages the mind or the emotions; and one would have to agree with Louis Rubin that the most compelling and valuable works of the individual contributors lie elsewhere.[51] Whether one agrees with the Agrarians' vision of the past or their prescriptions for the future, the manifesto's tone is so polemical, so self-serving and self-exculpatory that all irony or distance, all complexity of thought about the South or its history are lost. Self-consciousness is so impressed into the service of a particular view of the Southern tradition that it fails to engage itself. The result, with only few exceptions, is a work which is at once flat and hysterical.

The occasion for *I'll Take My Stand* followed discussions among John Crowe Ransom, Allen Tate, Donald Davidson, and Robert Penn Warren on the heels of the Scopes trial and H. L. Mencken's savage attacks on the fundamentalist South. Before that, Tate, for instance, had been rather favorably disposed toward Mencken and had even defended him against Chancellor Edwin Mims's harsh response to the "Sahara of the Bozart" article. In 1923 Tate wrote to Donald Davidson that "the trouble is in the damnably barbaric Southern mind."[52] Four years later, however, Tate promised Davidson: "I've attacked the South for the last time, except in so far as it may be necessary to point out that the chief defect [it] had was that in it which produced . . . the New South." Davidson replied in the same vein by noting that he was catching the "anti-New South" spirit himself.[53]

In 1930 John Crowe Ransom, the literary mentor of the Fugitives, published his *God Without Thunder*.[54] There he attacked modern religious liberalism and spoke strongly for a god of wrath and thunder. For Ransom, religion and myth were the modes of comprehending the world which most satisfactorily located man in nature. Transmuting the spirit of Dayton into a rather dubious historico-theological generalization, Ransom claimed that "all first class religionists are Fundamentalists,"[55] an assertion that must have made Mencken jump with glee. The problem with *God Without Thunder* was that Ransom clearly was neither a fundamentalist nor a "religionist" in any conventional sense of the term.

His justification for religion, his defense of mythic thinking, and his startling contention that authentic religion was "almost inevitably agrarian rather than industrialist,"[56] all came down finally to a matter of aesthetics. As one early critic observed, Ransom's tract was neither philosophy nor religion, but mythopoeia, "as if" raised to a cultural imperative.[57] *God Without Thunder* was a self-conscious defense of naïveté, that strangest of modern secular intellectual productions: a non-religious defense of religion, a masterpiece of bad faith and bad religion.

Ransom's confused mixture of religion, aesthetics, and economics anticipated the larger confusions (not complexities) in the Agrarian polemic. At its heart *I'll Take My Stand* revealed an economic-social distinction (agriculture vs. industry, agrarian vs. capitalist) made into a regional one (South vs. North) and in turn conflated with the cultural distinction between tradition and modernity, religion and science, the political distinction between states' rights and centralization of power, and contrasting philosophies of history. The aesthetic problem with *I'll Take My Stand* was that few surprises lay in store; inevitably, the oppositions sorted themselves out the same way every time.

Nor are these confusions surprising, since the contributors to *I'll Take My Stand* were far from unified over the title or the essential meaning of what had been put between two covers. No wonder, then, that critics, then and now, have found the Agrarians more than a little slippery in the defenses of the manifesto. While Davidson and Frank Owsley were specifically concerned with a defense of the historic South and an agrarian way of life, Tate wrote Davidson that the mention of "agrarian principles" in the title "reduces our real aims to nonsense."[58] Tate and Ransom saw the South in much less literal and much more symbolic terms than Davidson or Owsley. Further, Tate, Andrew Lytle, and Robert Penn Warren saw *I'll Take My Stand* as a defense against Communism. And there were other divergences. Tate envisioned the ante-bellum South as essentially aristocratic and feudal, while Owsley and Lytle were more attuned to a vision of a yeoman society leavened by a relatively small number of planters. Some raged against industry per se, while others called for a better balanced economy. Donald Davidson, always a true believer, was profoundly disturbed by Warren's essay on the Negro which he felt went "off at a tangent" and was "not our main concern." It "smack[s]" too much of "latter-day sociology," so much so that Davidson wondered if his younger colleague had really written it.[59] Still the differences fade before the general sameness of tone, a litany of complaints and accusations against a world the Agrarians had never made.

Our main interest in *I'll Take My Stand* lies in its rendition of the Southern past. The Agrarians' great good time was the antebellum South, a felicitous, harmonious balance of yeoman and planter, culturally the bastion of non-materialistic values, and economically opposed to the expanding capitalism of the North. When slavery was mentioned, the message was usually something like Ransom's contention that, while slavery had been bad in theory, it had been rather benevolent in practice.[60] Sectional strife and then the War were seen as a betrayal by the North of the compact hammered out at Philadelphia in 1787; far from centering on slavery as a moral issue, the Agrarians tended to see the War as a conflict of economic systems and of ways of life. Once defeated, the South received, according to Frank Owsley, "a peace unique in history. There was no generosity."[61] If that were not bad enough, the ensuing years were marked by Northern efforts to brainwash Southerners through control of education and culture. Since Reconstruction a decline in the quality of Southern life had set in, marked by the emergence of Southern fifth columnists—the New South advocates—as well as the more obvious growth of cities and industry and encroachment of secular and scientific forms of thought. Extreme measures were called for. Conspiratorial language came easy to some of the Agrarians. The serpent of modernization and modernism had invaded the Southern garden.

One of the few essays in *I'll Take My Stand* marked by any degree of subtlety was Allen Tate's "Remarks on Southern Religion." There Tate acknowledged the paradox at work in his and Ransom's defense of religion—reason was enlisted in the defense of faith, self-consciousness was to preserve an inherited tradition.

Unlike most of his colleagues Tate looked critically at the Old South; it was "a feudal society without a feudal religion."[62] Because it never "created a fitting religion,"[63] it could not preserve its unique culture after defeat. Having "lived by images"[64] not ideas, the South not only failed to develop an appropriate religion, it failed to break with the political culture of the American nation. From this intellectual weakness flowed the South's vulnerability to modern ideas and capitalist gewgaws.

The wider significance of Tate's essay was that it turned the focus inward and pointed to a crucial intellectual blind spot in the ante-bellum South. Whatever the genuine merits of the tradition, its flaws would have to be remedied were it to be revitalized. Tradition would have to become self-conscious. But Tate saw that this also presented potential dangers. In European culture, reason had gradually moved from supporting faith to undermining it. Historical estrangement from the tradition led to psychic estrangement engendered by the very act of its theoretical defense. To realize that the tradition was a "tradition" was to be alienated from it.

With most of the Agrarians a defense of the Southern heritage took on a quality which they claimed was the central flaw in the secular, progressive intellect—abstraction. If God is in the details, *I'll Take My Stand* was a highly irreligious book. A latter-day Agrarian (in fact, not rhetoric), Wendell Berry, has also scored the sentimentality of the Agrarians: ". . . their withdrawal [later to the North] was facilitated by a tendency to love the land, not for its life, but for its historical associations—that is, their agrarianism was doomed to remain theoretical by a sentimental faith that history makes the grass green whether the land is well farmed or not."[65] Their historical account reinforced the Southern tradition and family romance in its essentials. Whatever the validity of their critique of the modern world, most of the Agrarians avoided hard questions about the South itself. Had they quarreled with themselves, the result might have been poetry; but in *I'll Take My Stand* the quarrel was directed against others and remained rhetoric.

Sectionalism vs. Regionalism:
Nashville and Chapel Hill

After the publication of *I'll Take My Stand* the Agrarian cause became the subject of considerable intellectual controversy; and on the Agrarian side the argument was extended and refined. Whatever else can be said about the reception of Agrarianism, it can hardly be claimed that the voices of the Vanderbilt writers were stifled. They published prolifically in several journals, especially *The American Review* (1933–37), *Southern Review* (1935–42), and to a degree in *The Virginia Quarterly Review*. John Crowe Ransom never jumped wholeheartedly into the fray; the essays he published on the Agrarian theme were of a very general nature, usually plumping for subsistence over commercial farming, for farming as a way of life over farming as a business. His interest turned instead to literary criticism and the forging of the New Criticism. Allen Tate, however, managed to write cultural and literary criticism as well as to engage in the small-scale debate and polemic with opponents about the nuts and bolts of Agrarianism. Warren devoted little attention to social, economic, or political themes, confining himself largely to literary criticism and poetry. The spear-carriers of the movement in the 1930s, the voices crying in and for wilderness, were Frank Owsley, Andrew Lytle, and especially Donald Davidson.

Before examining the Agrarian critique of the Regionalists, it may be well to examine in more detail the Agrarian account of the Southern past as it was developed after 1930. In 1931 Andrew Lytle published *Bedford Forrest and His Critter Company*.[66] Lytle saw Forrest as the quintessential ante-bellum Southerner: the combination of "planter and pioneer, the European and American . . . merged under the common influence of cotton."[67] Jefferson Davis had been a timid and overly defensive leader, who established "the foundations of the Confederacy on cotton and not on the plain people."[68] Always the daring general, Forrest had given his men the feeling that "the South was one big democracy, fighting that the small man, as well as the powerful, might live as he pleased."[69] Born as a common man, Forrest illustrated the promise of (white) Southern life, that the move from pioneer to planter was possible.

Lytle's portrayal of Forrest is less interesting for what it says about Forrest than for what it says about Lytle's vision of the past. He whitewashed Forrest's role as a slave trader and excused Forrest's lack of control over his troops, which led to the Fort Pillow massacre of black troops. Leaving nothing to the imagination, Lytle ended the biography with a panegyric to the Ku Klux Klan as "the last brilliant example in Western Culture of what Feudalism could do."[70] Seen in this light, its founder and leader's life "was a symbol of the Southern Feudalism. He emerged from the cabin, grew rich on cotton, established himself as a strong man of his Culture, and was cut down in his prime, with the virtues and vices of the Wilderness still part of his character."[71]

Besides selecting such dubious heroes as Forrest, Lytle also published essays on John Taylor of Caroline and John C. Calhoun. Frank Owsley wrote that Robert E. Lee was "the most convincing evidence in support of an agrarian aristocracy." Voicing the patriarchal theme which vied with the yeoman theme for ascendancy, Owsley wrote that "Marse Robert" was the "grand patriarch and father of his 'boys.' "[72] And of Mississippi Senator L. C. Q. Lamar, Owsley wrote that he was "one of the truly great men of American history,"[73] the type of man who should have been president of the Confederacy instead of the ever unpopular Jeff Davis.

Not only did the Agrarians fail to question the morality of the peculiar institution, they voiced no doubts as to the wisdom of white racial hegemony. In a laudatory review of black sociologist Charles Johnson's *The Shadow of the Plantation*, Ransom contended that the miserable plight of blacks portrayed in the book resulted from the destruction of the plantation, "a casualty of our money economy."[74] The wider implication was that blacks had been better off in slavery than freedom. Indeed, the Agrarians were fond of a bit of ideological legerdemain which combined a critique of capitalism with an attack on racial equality and suggested that somehow the two—capitalism and equality—went hand in hand. As Warren suggested, "the Radicals . . . were in reality the agents of capitalistic conservatism."[75] This was Charles and Mary Beard with deep South accents.

But it was left to Frank Owsley to extend the argument into the realm of absurdity. Writing on the Scottsboro trial of nine black youths for rape, which attracted national attention, historian Owsley claimed to see a new abolitionism at work. Once again Northern interests were putting forth moral arguments and standards of abstract justice as a smokescreen for economic domination of the South. The soul of the South was being vied for by capitalists and communists; and blacks were the pawns in the game. Owsley warned ominously but innocently that such a situation could only enflame the section, encourage the Klan, and lead to "violent retaliation."[76] Again capitalism and socialism were the common enemies. Northern entrepreneurs and Northern radicals had nothing to teach the Agrarians about dissimulation.

As Warren's essay in *I'll Take My Stand* made clear, the Agrarians were at best committed to a policy of separate-but-equal in racial matters. As the decade proceeded, it was left to Tate to discuss race in deceptively moderate terms, while Donald Davidson would take a harder line. In his review of W. T. Couch's *Culture in the South,* a Chapel Hill response to the Agrarians, Tate addressed the plight of black Southerners directly. Tate's effort demonstrated his usual intellectual acumen combined with considerable doses of casuistry and moral obtuseness. On the one hand, Tate urged that blacks be allowed to buy land, since only in that way could they really protect themselves and their rights. Otherwise liberal concern and black efforts would go for naught. If this happened, Tate foresaw a general improvement in the welfare of all Southerners. On the other hand, Tate offered a perverse syllogism to justify his own acquiescence in white supremacy. "The white race seems determined to rule the Negro race . . . ," he wrote, while obliquely distancing himself from responsibility. But he went on to say: "I belong to the white race; therefore I intend to support white rule."[77] This was intellectual and moral sophistry masquerading as realism.

Davidson, however, expressed the brutal underside of Agrarian racial views. Throughout the 1930s Davidson suggested that

Southern liberals, particularly the Regionalists, were a bit soft on race, as indeed they were. But in his essay, "Still Rebels, Still Yankees," an otherwise bucolic evocation of rural Georgia and Jeffersonian virtue, Davidson took time to ask: "What did a few lynchings count in the balance against the continued forbearance and solicitude that the Georgian felt he exercised toward these amiable children of cannibals?"[78] Further, Davidson's review of John Dollard's *Caste and Class in a Southern Town* was openly insulting to blacks. Not surprisingly, Davidson found Dollard's discussion of the "sexual gain" from the caste system "revolting and obscene"; the South had been "convicted on evidence procured from the sewers of Freudian psychology."[79] Davidson concluded in a manner which recalled Mencken's earlier observation that Davidson "passes for an advanced thinker" but when outside criticism comes "he simply throws up his hands and yields to moral indignation."[80] The South, wrote Davidson, "will not support a program of improvement which implies a change of [racial] status," for at issue are "self-preservation and pride of race and tradition."[81]

The Agrarians also responded directly to the Regionalists. For the Agrarians, the Chapel Hill sociologists and their allies were uncomfortably reminiscent of New South spokesmen such as Henry Grady and Walter Hines Page who had wanted to modernize the South, and thus acquiesce in Northern domination. Aside from these fellow travelers, Davidson held that "it can hardly be said that Southern liberals have any ancestors in the South."[82] Davidson feared that the regional focus of the sociologists (which he liked) would ultimately lead to federal government control, to the "Leviathan" state. Thus the bureaucrats and the plutocrats threatened Southern control of its destiny. The logic of the liberal position, claimed Davidson, led to a huge federal government, "socialistic caste," science, irreligion, and "equality for the Negro." But he added the Regionalists "may escape their dilemma by becoming more Southern," that is, like the Agrarians.[83]

The Agrarians also criticized Odum and Vance for their lack of political realism. According to Tate and Davidson, Odum was naïve to think that the South could take concerted action as a region without outside interference. For Davidson in particular, the Regionalist position meant ultimate conflict with the industrial Northeast and not the smooth cooperation for which Odum hoped. Odum in short softpedaled the issue of "colonial degradation."[84]

Still, Odum and Vance were preferable to the militant group represented by Arthur Raper, who was too sympathetic to blacks; H. C. Nixon; and C. Vann Woodward, who in his defense of Nixon betrayed, said Davidson, a suspicious "Marxian flavor." Though adamant in his opposition to Northern control of the South, Davidson firmly rejected the "class approach" on principle as only helping the enemy.[85] Rather, the struggle was a sectional one against outside financial and industrial interests. Home rule, not rule at home, was the issue.

But the Agrarian position was not exclusively negative. In his "Notes on Liberty and Property" Tate saw American history as a working out of the original conflict between Hamilton and Jefferson. Returning to the Jeffersonian fold, Tate saw that "small ownership had been worsted by big, dispersed ownership—the corporation." Using Berle and Means's study of corporate control, Tate asserted that "corporate structure strives toward the condition of Moscow."[86] Thus again we have the ultimate convergence of modern capitalism and socialism. To strengthen individual ownership of property, Richmond Beatty and George O'Donnell, two recruits to the Agrarian cause, called for the rescue of the yeoman farmer and the ambitious tenant, while giving up on the poor whites, who were "generally, beyond salvation."[87]

But Owsley was quite specific in his plans for Southern recovery. For him monopoly must be destroyed, "property restored and the proletariat abolished."[88] Specifically, Owsley called for the rehabilitation of the agricultural population, particularly the planter and the tenant. Sounding for all the world like W. T. Couch and other New Deal Southerners (and Thad Stevens), Owsley supported government programs to give 80-acre plots to tenants, along with a house, livestock, and living expenses for a year. Those who had fled rural poverty would be lured back from the cities. In the short run, subsistence farming would be strengthened, while, in the long run, a political economy of balanced agriculture, industry, finance, and commerce would be achieved. Davidson supported such a land reform program in essence, though how he could do so and still be against the "class approach" is hard to say.

One final set of changes which both Owsley and Davidson suggested was in the political-constitutional structure of the nation. They called for the establishment of regional autonomy, a "New Federalism" as Davidson called it, which would check "Leviathan" and allow internal tariffs, a modification of the Fourteenth Amendment so that corporations could no longer be considered as "persons," and grant the South power to tax and to control race relations. This was Calhoun's concurrent majority idea in modern dress.[89] And hardly an example of superior grasp of reality.

Still, the specific programmatic suggestions of the Agrarians were not all that different from those of the Regionalists. Agriculture was the sick man of the South, and something had to be done about it. Nor were the principal figures in either group committed to a "class" analysis of Southern society. The differences lay rather in tone and implication. Where the Regionalists supported economic integration and national cooperation with aid from the New Deal, the Agrarians were much more wary of help from the national government. In contrast they felt that the South's fate depended on control of its own affairs. Where the Regionalists advanced vague and rather safe suggestions about changes in the racial order, the Agrarians were adamantly against them, though within a biracial order Tate supported black ownership of land. Both groups agreed that the position of the small farmer should be strengthened; but while the Regionalists were generally resistant to the charms of the aristocracy, the Agrarians held to the ideal of a hierarchical society, led by an elite. But their worldviews probably diverged most. The Agrarians yearned for a restoration of a hierarchical Christian order, while the Regionalists were secularists, relatively deaf to the appeal of religion. Where the ideal of a pre-capitalist society and economy was the yardstick against which the Agrarians measured modern life, the modern world was the condition toward which the Regionalists worked.

Capitalism and socialism were not only economic systems; they implied a distinct cultural order for the Agrarians. For the Regionalists the capitalist economic order, though shaped by governmental planning, was the future which should be embraced. In sum, whereas the Agrarians wanted to draw rigid distinctions, the Regionalists hoped to have it both ways.

In a curious way World War II, the postwar prosperity, and the 1954 Supreme Court decision, outlawing segregation in schools, rendered both the Regionalist and the Agrarian visions nugatory. The South was gradually integrated economically into the nation, but under no comprehensive regional plan. Odum and Guy Johnson were influential in the early years of the Southern Regional Council, but Odum's congenital moderation on racial matters came increasingly to look like temporizing. Of Regionalism as an ideology little more was heard in the postwar years, having already become something of a curiosity in the Depression. The Agrarians had never attracted much specific support for their vision. And except for Warren, most of the original Agrarians were silent as the middle of the century approached. After the 1954 Supreme Court decision, Southern conservatism increasingly couched its arguments in the distasteful idiom of racism or the fussy rhetoric of constitutionalism. But of Agrarianism there was scarcely a word.

From Agrarianism
to the New Criticism

Though the social and cultural thought of the Agrarians was suffused with a nostalgic belligerence, the critical aesthetic forged by Ransom and Tate and applied by Warren and Cleanth Brooks was spare and classical in its avoidance of psychological or ideological concerns. Celebrators of an Agrarian ethos and defenders by default of a fundamentalist sensibility, they broke with the mindlessness which historically plagued Southern culture. Men of wide classical learning and traditionalists to the core, they led a revolution in literary criticism, whose consolidation would dominate American literary study for a couple of decades after World War II.

It will not do to see the "New Criticism" as an inevitable expression of the Catonist vision, but neither can it be totally severed from it. William Empson and F. O. Matthiessen, for instance, showed that a liberal or left-wing commitment was not incompatible with adherence to the techniques of close textual explication. As Richard Ohmann has noted, the New Criticism became the reigning academic orthodoxy in the 1950s, fitting quite nicely with the retreat from politics of that decade, and was thus quite compatible with the disengaged liberalism of most academics. Indeed, one of the ironies of the history of New Criticism lies in its rapid move from a fighting creed to established dogma.[90]

An even larger irony is that, though the New Critics had no use for positivism in philosophy and its self-designated role as a handmaiden for natural science, they quite analogously excluded serious consideration by literary critics of the larger cultural, political, and social implications of literature. If, as Shelley contended, the poets were the world's unacknowledged legislators, then the New Critics refused even to run for the seat.

And yet the Southern wing of the New Criticism was most decidedly political, despite its own protestations. To refuse to pronounce on ideological or ethical matters was itself a way of making such judgments. In particular, the early critical work of Ransom and Tate was informed by cultural and ideological assumptions which they considered intrinsically bound up with the proper study of literature. Later Ransom and Tate became less and less engaged with the social and cultural issues which they had spoken for in the 1930s, a disengagement roughly parallel to their waning Agrarian commitment and their move northward. By the time of Brooks's *Well Wrought Urn* (1947) the political and social assumptions had all but disappeared or had become ideological frosting on the critical cake.

At issue then is how the Southern intellectuals who had been so conscious of the past and the problematic status of tradition in *I'll Take My Stand* could have formulated what appears to be an ahistorical mode of criticism; and how these ardent, even fanatical opponents of the scientific spirit could have ended by apparently formulating a narrow technique, even science, of criticism.

John Crowe Ransom:
The New Critic as Theoretician

Ransom was an unlikely critical revolutionary. Born in 1888, the son of a Methodist minister in Pulaski, Tennessee, Ransom from early on seems to have been mature and serious, reserved and assiduous. After graduating from Vanderbilt he was a Rhodes Scholar at Oxford, where he read "Greats" (classical studies) and concentrated upon philosophy. He returned to teach at Vanderbilt on the eve of World War I, and remained there until 1937. At Vanderbilt Ransom quickly gathered a group of young poets and critics around him and was the guiding light in the emergence of the "Fugitives" in the early 1920s. While his poetic production was confined largely to a few years in the 1920s, most of his life was occupied with teaching, organizing, and raising money for the *Kenyon Review* and developing his critical theory.

If Ransom's personal life was relatively untroubled and his professional life marked by a remarkable steadiness, his fundamental vision was informed by a hostility to modernity, particularly an implacable opposition to the abstract vision of modern science and technology. Nor was Ransom a particular champion of literary modernism, at least in its formative years of the 1920s. Though in any conventional sense apolitical, he devoted nearly a decade of his life to social and economic criticism, only in the mid-1930s to return to his first love, literary criticism. Ransom's old-fashioned courtliness and reserve disguised a considerable talent for promotion of the literary causes he embraced. He was always at the center of some literary enterprise or other—the Fugitives, the Agrarians, *Kenyon Review* and the School of English at Kenyon College, and Institute of Letters at Indiana University—and managed to keep these enterprises afloat in difficult times.

By his own account Ransom was, he wrote, "In manners, aristocratic"; yet he was open and accessible as a teacher and refused at later Fugitive reunions to wear the mantle of leadership which had once been his. He was "in religion, ritualistic," yet Ransom, ironically, came to consider himself a Unitarian, that most spare and desiccated of modern ersatz-religions, a far cry from the god of thunder he invoked in 1930. And though he called himself a "traditionalist in art," he eventually came to recant his early harsh evaluation of Eliot and later judged Wallace Stevens to be one of the great modern poets.[91] Never wide ranging as a thinker or a poet, he led a critical revolution in this country.

For Ransom the modern age was marked by the triumph of science and positivism, a secular vision based on social engineering, the triumph of democracy, industry, and city. Through the abstractions of the scientific vision, the concrete had been lost. Though Ransom dealt rarely with modern poetry and hardly ever with the modern novel, he claimed that the poets of the modern age were "post-traditional: they are only heirs of a tradition."[92] Where formerly the poet had "proposed to make virtue delicious," in the modern world the good and the beautiful had been tragically dissociated.[93]

As a counter to modernist currents, Ransom held that the poem was "an order of existence" possessing ontological status; it was, "a desperate ontological or metaphysical manoeuvre."[94] Though poetry is "an event in time," it is "an inevitable and perhaps spectacular event which *interrupts* [my emphasis] the history of men officially committed under civilization to their effective actions and abstract studies. It is revulsive, or revolutionary, by intention."[95] Crucial in this description was Ransom's notion that the poem is an intervention running counter to history and thereby triumphant over time. The poem should not improve the world but "realize the world, to see it better."[96] It is thus a cognitive still-point, transcending rather than being subjected to the workings of time. It offers an aesthetic cognition of the world but one mediated by memory: "[The poems] which we cherish as perfect creations . . . are dramatizing the past," he wrote, "the tense of poetry is the past," recording and preserving the fugitive experience and insight in an impersonal way.[97]

Of particular importance in *The World's Body* was Ransom's incessant and insistent polemicizing against liberal and radical tendencies to read literature as a set of proposals for future social orderings or to reduce literature to sociological determinants. Whatever the validity of these attacks against (vulgar) Marxist, utilitarian liberal, and reductionist readings of all stripes—and I think they are convincing in a limited way—it should be recognized that the New Critical strictures advanced by Ransom represented a political position as well as an aesthetic stance.

In Ransom's case this negative polemic was supplemented by the positive critical injunction that the critic should concern himself with the *forms* at work in the poem, handed down by the tradition, which the "old society—the directed and hierarchical one" had used.[98] Poetic form provided the aesthetic counterpart of the essential structures, particularly religious and ritualistic ones, of traditional society. Form foreclosed all immediacy of emotion or impulse and blunted the desires of the ego or the dictates of utility. For Ransom, the critic sought to remind the reader of the absent tradition by his formal reading of the work of art. Criticism became, like the poem, a private skirmish against the modern world. The world revealed by the poem nostalgically mirrored the lost world.

There is thus in Ransom's aesthetic an historically mimetic action at work: the ideal order of society is properly recalled to mind in the ideal reading of the poem. The special ontology of the poem mirrors a lost order of being. By extension, then, Ransom's famous call for the professionalization of criticism in "Criticism, Inc." was a way of preserving the Western tradition. At its moment of creation the charismatic leader and founding father of the New Criticism pointed to the desirability of routinization rather than permanent revolution.

In *The New Criticism* (1941) Ransom took on several contemporary critics with whom he felt in some sympathy. There Ransom presented a more balanced description of the poem as composed of "structure" and "texture." By structure Ransom referred roughly to the central theme or main ideas, the rational content, the denotative aspect; in short, that which could be paraphrased. Though granting structure its place, Ransom located the essence of the poetic work in the texture—meter, diction, and particularly metaphor and conceit. Texture was that which was inherently unparaphrasable.

Ransom also questioned the attempts of T. S. Eliot and Tate to bring explicit historical-traditional concerns to bear in critical evaluation. For Ransom, the place of a poem in the tradition told nothing of its "worth."[99] While historical context might be interesting and important, there was a fundamental difference between presenting it and evaluating the poem itself. Thus Ransom's vision was no longer rooted in specific time or place. The tradition he sought to resurrect—or at least preserve—was rarified, a sort of meta-tradition, a timeless way of seeing things. Against Eliot, he doubted that there had been any time when sensibility had not been "dissociated"; rather the dissociation of thought and feeling, the concrete and the universal, the good and the beautiful marked the human condition. The focus upon structure and texture mirrored the perennial split; their interaction revealed the human approximation to the ideal.

Finally the critic who followed Ransom was left beyond history or any specific historical tradition. This move by Ransom was not absolute—he had kind words for Dante's vision and society—but it represented a tendency in his critical theory. It also reflected, I suspect, Ransom's waning interest in the Agrarian cause to which he finally bid adieu in his recantation of 1945. In "Art and the Human Economy" he granted that the only way of returning to the past was "formally"; that is, through art or in thought. Given the nature of the modern world, it was impossible to expect an actual restoration; nor, he added, was such a life compatible with those things he treasured, i.e. art, criticism, the academic life, his work as editor of the *Kenyon Review*.[100] Indeed the *Review* signaled the Agrarians' *apertura a la sinistra*. Decidedly apolitical and indifferent to Southern apologetics (or to World War II), *Kenyon Review* became the meeting ground for the Southern New Critics and the emerging New York Jewish intelligentsia. Lionel Trilling, Paul Goodman, and Delmore Schwartz appeared cheek by jowl with Ransom, Brooks, Warren, and others. Art and music criticism vied with literary criticism for a major place. Here indeed was a fruitful confusion of realms, but culture was severed from politics with a vengeance.

By the early 1950s Ransom had drifted even farther away from any sort of engaged conservatism. In a review of Russell Kirk's *The Conservative Mind,* Ransom observed that historical (or empirical) conservatism was bankrupt. It opposed first, but then had to defend all historical change, including the rise of big business, once the change had taken place. For Ransom, the only genuine conservatism was a "theologically" grounded one. That lacking, conservatism became merely a modern form of opportunism.[101]

Allen Tate:
The New Critic as Cultural Critic

If Ransom was the chief theoretician of the New Criticism, Allen Tate was its leading cultural critic and polemicist.[102] Unlike Ransom, who seldom addressed himself to modern poetry (or fiction), Tate felt that the critic should deal with contemporary literature, since, as he once said, all literature was contemporary anyway. Where Ransom's own poetry avoided the modernist style, Tate's dense and allusive verse epitomized high modernism. Finally, by way of comparison, if Ransom made a theoretical virtue of bracketing general cultural questions, Tate was always tensed between being the New Critic and being the cultural critic, the explicator of texts and the secular moralist, the academic and the man of letters who located the work of art and the life of the artist in relation to one another and to their times. It is indeed ironic that Tate's essays have defined the general conditions necessary for cultural creativity and specifically the origins of what we now call the Southern Renaissance.

One did not have to strain to see a political and polemical intent in Tate's writings. At the height of the Cold War, Tate asserted that, though poets should not pronounce directly on politics, they should be concerned with the "vitality of language" and take the side of "the eternal society of the communion of the human spirit" against the "dehumanized society of secularism."[103] Not beholden to any political creed, the poet is "responsible to his conscience—his special *areté* for the mastery of disciplined language."[104] Though more temperate and defensible than his animadversions against liberalism and radicalism in the late 1930s, which he felt betokened the coming of "slave society," (Tate was remarkably silent on the threats from fascism or Nazism), Tate's essential commitment was to criticism as a secular form of preaching.

Tate shared Ransom's distaste for "social poetry" and had just as little use for any aesthetic which considered poetry a projection of the poet's feelings onto the world or as the record of his response to an external stimulus. Good poetry defied formulation or use; and its central quality was imagination, not the will of romantic poetry or the practical-moral concerns of allegory. Indeed, Shakespeare provided the best "poetry of the imagination" which "finds its true usefulness in its perfect inutility."[105] Tate was less systematic than Ransom and less interested in close textual analysis than his onetime mentor. Not the truth so much as the coherence of a poet's informing ideas determined the worth of the verse.

In an essay on Emily Dickinson (1928) Tate regarded as unfortunate the contemporary lack of "a rational insight into the meaning of the present in terms of some imaginable past implicit in our own lives." The strength of Dickinson as a poet and her importance as a cultural symbol arose from the fact that she came at a time when the New England theocracy, one of "heroic proportion and a tragic mode," was breaking up and before the Emersonian reduction of it to a "genteel secularism"[106] had quite taken hold. He thus saw reflected in her poetry the "clash of powerful opposites."[107] Hers seemed the ideal moment of creativity; and Tate's explication of her cultural setting anticipated his later explanation for the flourishing of Southern letters in the 1930s.

It is important to note here Tate's variation on Ransom's mirror relationship between the poem and the historical moment. For Ransom the perfect work reflected the stable, yet complex rituals, forms, and hierarchies of traditional society. Tate offered a similar mirroring notion, but concentrated his attention on the way fractured and broken verse, replete with contradiction and ambiguity, reflected the disruptive forces at work in modern life. "The poet," wrote Tate, "finds himself balanced upon the moment when such a world is about to fall." He must be "cultured" not in the sense of possessing an arsenal of learning and highly formalized education; indeed, his vision can be "blunted by a too rigid system of ideas."[108] Rather, the poet must have his culture as a second nature, in order that his imaginative capacities can take shape.

As mentioned, Tate was less concerned with the truth of the poet's system than he was with its coherence. Whether it was Christian or a "minor mythology" made little difference;[109] instead, the poet must have some tradition, some metaphysical or formal convention, within which imagination could be articulated. In contrast with Dickinson and Yeats stood the great cautionary example of modern poetry, Hart Crane, one of Tate's good friends. Tate saw Crane as a "romantic," suffering from the disjunction of intellect and sensibility. His life and poetry had been marked by a "locked-in sensibility, the insulated egoism" which could never be translated into an imaginative whole. Lacking an "objective pattern of ideas,"[110] Crane had tried vainly to create his own mythos and, with it, to dominate his material. That failing, his only way out was suicide.

Thus in these essays Tate defined the essential problem of the modern poet—the loss of tradition. Yet, paradoxically, the conditions most conducive to artistic productivity came in such a transition period between the old and new traditions. Presumably the existence of a society of unified sensibility, a framework of theological and metaphysical systems, and an hierarchical social ordering did not provide the needed conditions. Tension in the work of art—its sign of vitality and authenticity—mirrored the tensions in the society and culture on the verge of dissolution. One could either, as Yeats had it, perfect the life or the art. When Tate wrote in 1935 that it was "a good age to write about but a hard age to live in,"[111] he was defining the two foci of his thought—secular modernism and the desire for religious consolation. Having long since abandoned the Agrarian cause and permanently residing in the North, Tate then embraced Roman Catholicism in the early 1950s. What more venerable refuge from the modern world and more ironically inimical to the fundamentalist South which some of his colleagues had apostrophied? But then for Tate the crucial flaw in the Southern tradition all along had been its lack of an appropriate religion to embody the traditional order. The order was gone, and all that remained was the religion.

Brooks and Warren:
The New Criticism Domesticated

In an early issue of *The Fugitive* (IV), Ransom claimed that irony was the "ultimate mode" of modern poetry because "it is the most inclusive."[112] In Cleanth Brooks's critical work the ironic mode was coupled with its characteristic trope—the metaphor. Irony and metaphor became critical touchstones for judging literary excellence. Though not one of the original Agrarians or Fugitives, Brooks had studied at Vanderbilt and then Oxford as a Rhodes Scholar. In 1935 he joined his fellow Kentuckian, Robert Penn Warren, as managing editor of the new *Southern Review*, which ceased publication in 1942. Their *Understanding Poetry* was the text by means of which a whole generation of teachers and students was instructed. With Brooks and Warren the New Criticism, now a bit more expansive and less polemical, established its dominance in postwar academic literary studies.

Both Brooks and Warren made more sophisticated the New Critical objection to propagandistic art. As Brooks emphasized in *Modern Poetry and the Tradition*, the worth of a poem was simply not proportionate to its truth; *how*, not *what*, was central. Science was concerned with unambiguous messages; poetry with the "organization of experience."[113] To be true to reality (and here Brooks and Warren followed Tate's mimetic notions), the structure of a poem "involves resistances, at various levels, and involves the reader." Statements, themes, messages—whatever one called them—had to be "earned by the entire poem . . . the statement is meaningful, not for what it says but for what has gone before."[114]

In *Modern Poetry and the Tradition*, Brooks demoted the Victorians (except for Hardy) and the Romantics (except for Blake and Keats) while elevating the metaphysical poets to prominence. Their hegemony in British literature had been ended, claimed Brooks, by the triumph of the new science, an enterprise with a tendency toward "order and simplification."[115] Tragedy and irony, however, demanded a more complex ordering of experience; and only within this century had there been a resurgence of metaphysical poetry. Modernist writing became a sort of updated metaphysical poetry. Thus there was a strange optimism in Brooks's radical revision. The growing self-doubt of science and the questioning of the belief in historical progress signaled a cultural situation more favorable to tragic complexities. The poetry of an age reflected the dominant cultural tendencies of that age.

Nor was it strange that Brooks's colleagues—Ransom, Tate, and Warren—along with Eliot and Yeats were singled out for special praise. Situated as they were between past and present, traditionalists in a modern age, it was natural, Brooks implied, that irony and "structures of synthesis" would dominate their verse. The complicated and dense metaphors—particularly those of Tate and Warren—attempted to include opposites and reconcile contradictions, an effort which mirrored the historical situation of the South and its absent tradition. Thus the essence of the Agrarians' poetry lay not so much in its structure, which was not necessarily or recognizably Southern, as in its texture—the convoluted diction, the centrality of metaphor which attempted to bridge the gap between the past tradition and the present age.[116]

A retrospective and complete evaluation of the New Criticism is not central to our purposes. Clearly, in *The Well Wrought Urn* (1947), Brooks domesticated the passions of Ransom and Tate and offered a subtle and rather tolerant approach to literature. This domestication was in the service of the religion of literature as it developed after World War II. Literature replaced philosophy or politics as a source of guidance or object of dominant interest. Aesthetic sensibility replaced political awareness as the prime virtue in the higher realms of culture, particularly English departments. With poetry and fiction granted co-equal ontological status with reality itself, it was easy for the latter to be neglected and for literature to step into its place.

Still, as Gerald Graff has recently noted, it is important to remember the academic and political contexts in which the New Criticism was forged. In the 1930s, when literature was supposed to fulfill various political or cultural functions, the New Critical emphasis upon the work itself was distinctly liberating. As an attitude rather than a theory, the New Criticism was shared in spirit by left-wing, anti-Stalinist critics such as Philip Rahv and William Phillips, who tried to separate artistic and imaginative achievement from political or ideological intent. The attitude toward Eliot was a litmus test on these matters. Indeed, the examination of texts apart from their explicit message proved more liberating for the "left" than the "right," since much modernist poetry and fiction was "reactionary" in content and elitist in intention. Quite simply it allowed a leftist critic to do justice to a work of the highest quality with whose conclusions he disagreed or to whose "message" he objected. Conversely, not only radicals but also liberal Southerners such as Cash, Lillian Smith, and Paula Snelling were blind to the literary merits of much of the Agrarians' writings because of their understandable distaste for the social and cultural vision expressed.

Moreover, Tate's commitment to the vitality of the language and its nuanced use was a lesson which George Orwell, certainly no man of the right or quondam aristocrat, taught with eloquence in his essay "Politics and the English Language." In an age of mass communications and brainwashings and Newspeak left and right and center, it was potentially of radical import to defend language's ability to clarify and illuminate rather than to obfuscate.

That being said, one searches in vain in the criticism of Ransom or Tate or Brooks or Warren for denunciations of "social poetry" or fiction advocating the virtues of a hierarchical society or fascism or anti-Semitism. Socially engaged art for the New Critics meant exclusively writings from the left of center. Tate, in particular, edged at times toward an inexcusable confusion of totalitarian with liberal ideologies, a move which clouded rather than clarified political and cultural discourse.

The later critics who claimed that the New Criticism fell prey to a sort of scientism seem to me wrong. Clearly, Ransom called for a disciplined and rigorous criticism as well as for the bracketing of personal emotions, but this was far from any sort of literary-critical positivism. But as Gerald Graff notes, the opposite fault was more troublesome—the tendency toward subjective, individual response. In stressing texture over structure, technique over message, there were no substantive judgments to be made. If the modernist ethos was traditionless, it was difficult to see from what privileged position the critic could speak. Put another way: to make normative judgments about literary works, ones which transcended private or coterie tastes, implied the inadequacy of the internal, formal criteria which the New Critics emphasized. There was, finally no necessary connection between the critical tools which the Southern critics developed and the cultural-moral values which they defended. And, clearly, technique triumphed over mystique in the postwar years. The historicism of Tate and Brooks left them with nothing other than private or historical judgment to fall back upon, unless, that is, there was a transcendent order to provide an ultimate standard of judgment; and with both men such was the case. But their Christian vision was one which few shared.

Moreover, the invocation of irony, ambiguity, complexity, and tragedy rapidly assumed the status of dogma, fitting quite well the postwar mood of political quiescence. Rather than "earning" (to use Warren's term) the ironic perspective on historical change, the New Critics too often simply assumed it. Attempts to change society were doomed from the start—as well as being undesirable in the first place—and thus irony came a bit cheap. Never did one read, for instance, of the ironic contrast between the aristocratic image of the old South and the brutal and oppressive realities which such a vision masked. Their version of Southern history and ultimately of modern Western culture came nearer to being a melodrama with clearly labeled "good" and "bad" guys. Though Tate did identify the intellectual soft spot in the mind of the South, he never really confronted the moral problem of slavery. And as late as 1952 Tate could write that at least the slaves in the ante-bellum South could talk back to their masters, in contrast with the situation in the Soviet Union. This was a distinction without much of a difference, a Cold War form of "you-too-ism."[117]

Finally, like most protests against the loss of a tradition, the

Agrarian-New Critical version of Southern and European culture was a strange one, which failed to do justice to the complexity of modern history. As Dudley Wynn pointed out quite early, the Agrarian notion of the "tradition" consisted largely of the pre-modern culture of Christian feudalism.[118] They dismissed Western history and culture after that as largely a disaster. And it must be said that the Agrarian-New Critical claim to moral superiority as defenders of a classical-Christian humanism showed how vulnerable that humanism was on the matters of slavery and racism and how inadequate it was for the modern world.[119] But to repeat something said earlier: whatever one's moral discomfort with the Agrarian vision, its fatal weakness lay in its desire to repeat the past rather than recollect and transcend it. The New Critics' distaste for modern society and their desire to isolate the world of literature from it mirrored and extended the Agrarian rejection of the modern South and its yearning for an earlier, imaginary version of the ante-bellum South. Their rejection of history was matched by history's rejection of their vision.

4

Repetition and Despairing Monumentalism: William Faulkner and Will Percy

In the decaying patriarchal tradition of the South in the 1930s, cultural criticism had to begin with the father and culminate in a critique of the tradition of the fathers as expressed in the family romance. The actual and symbolic, historical and literary aspects were too intimately connected to be avoided. Born into a family which had come down in the world, William Faulkner was uniquely situated to devote his life to a fictional exploration of the Southern family romance.

Faulkner's attitude toward his family tradition reflects the classical pattern of the family romance, but also departs significantly from it.[1] On the one hand Faulkner saw the past in heroic terms, with the "fathers" standing in judgment upon the modern world and the often neurasthenic, over-refined *artistes manqués* who populate Faulkner's early fiction. Like Will Percy's grandfather, Colonel William C. Falkner played an active role in defying scalawags and carpetbaggers and in intimidating blacks who had the temerity to exercise their newly granted political rights during Reconstruction. Accompanying such heroic figures came the vain hope that somehow the outcome of the Civil War could be undone, at least fleetingly in fantasy. As Faulkner was to write in

Intruder in the Dust: "For every Southern boy fourteen years old, not once but whenever he wants it, there is the instant when it's still not yet two o'clock on that July afternoon in 1863 . . . it hasn't happened yet, it hasn't ever begun yet, it not only hasn't begun yet but there is still time for it not to begin . . . *This time. Maybe this time* with all this much to lose and all this much to gain. . . ."[2]

The loss of the War paradoxically marked the founding of the tradition built upon death and defeat. The centrality of memory in Faulkner's art can be seen in the description he gave of his state of mind when he began work on *Flags in the Dust* (*Sartoris*). He had resolved, he wrote, to:

> try by main strength to recreate between the covers of a book the world I was already preparing to lose and regret, feeling, with the morbidity of the young, that I was not only on the verge of decrepitude, but that growing old was to be an experience peculiar to myself alone out of all the teeming world, and desiring, if not the capture of that world and the feeling of it as you'd preserve a kernel or a leaf to indicate the lost forest, at least to keep the evocative skeleton of the dessicated [*sic*] leaf.[3]

Of interest here is Faulkner's melancholy stance and the lack of a vision of vitality or plentitude. He desires less the re-creation of the lost world than its evocation and stresses the vanity of attempts to revive it. It is also important to note Faulkner's sense of standing uniquely alone and of being old before his time. Though younger in years, the latecomer is older in accumulated experience, weighed down by the awareness of past heroism and its absence in the present. Action is seemingly foreclosed. As he wrote in *The Unvanquished*: "Those who can, do, those who cannot and suffer enough because they can't, write about it."[4] Recollection remains caught in the past rather than transcending it.

Yet there was another side to Faulkner which saved him from the pure melancholy of the artist born too late and which meant that he never completely accepted the family romance in his own life or in his fiction. He always possessed a certain distance from the Southern tradition, a detached irony toward the grandiose posturings and suicidal adventures of Confederate daredevils. Whether it was the needless death of Carolina Bayard Sartoris in *Flags in the Dust* or the death of Gail Hightower's grandfather in the henhouse in *Light in August,* the Rebels seemed more given to *le beau geste* than *l'acte gratuité.* They were figures of comedy as well as grandeur. The Sartoris family was modeled rather closely on Faulkner's own family, but young Faulkner "emphasized the drama and color at the expense of substance and achievement." Instead of making them "hill country versions of Delta planters," he highlighted the "adventurous, the picturesque, even the raffish."[5] Behind this ambiguous and complex exploration of the family and the region's past was Faulkner's assumption, expressed most clearly in *Flags in the Dust* and then in *Absalom, Absalom!,* that reality was transformed by the action of memory into high tragedy—and farce. Faulkner's are less historical novels than novels about the workings of memory and the varieties of historical consciousness.

This ambivalent attitude toward the past was reflected in young Faulkner's protean efforts to define himself. In his formative years he vacillated between the romantic and the cynic, the figure who wanted more than anything to be a war hero and the belletristic trifler and brooder. Yet if he struck heroic but slightly ludicrous poses, he also came to underplay his own artistic ambitions and achievements, fancying himself a simple Mississippi dirt-farmer who happened to write stories.

This ambivalence about his vocation and its value paralleled his attitude toward his male ancestors. William seemed to identify strongly with his fabled great-grandfather, who was a novelist in addition to his other "heroic" accomplishments. Yet Faulkner later wrote to Malcolm Cowley about the change in his name that "Maybe when I began to write . . . I secretly was ambitious and did not want to ride on grandfather's coat-tails, and so accepted the 'u,' . . . The above was always my mother's and father's version of why I put back into it the 'u' which my greatgrandfather, himself always a little impatient of grammar and spelling both, was said to have removed."[6] Faulkner was never close to his father, and there was apparently no love lost between them. More important, by *Go Down Moses* Faulkner was to reject the equation of biological and spiritual kinship altogether. There Ike McCaslin declines his family inheritance and adopts Sam Fathers as his spiritual father. The family was not destiny. Chronological succession did not establish spiritual subordination. One could finally choose one's own fathers.

Though Faulkner's fiction was populated with strong fathers, his immediate family was dominated by Maud, not Murry, Falkner. Reflecting a pattern as much American as Southern, the mother "assumed the fundamental responsibility for disciplining the children . . . She was the steady force," but also "sometimes overdid it."[7] Artistically inclined herself, she imparted to William, her eldest son, and to his brothers a love for literature. Yet Faulkner later denied the great influence of his mother, who considered him a genius, "the light of my life."[8] "Being the eldest of four boys," he wrote, "I escaped my mother's influence pretty much, since my father thought it was fine for me to apprentice to the business."[9] This denial was at odds with apparent reality. Even after his marriage Faulkner made daily pilgrimages to his mother's house for morning coffee.

Faulkner's denial of his mother's influence was reflected in his fictional treatment of women. An attitude bordering on misogyny was undoubtedly strengthened by his resentment of his wife Estelle's having first married another man and by the difficulties the couple had in their years of marriage. If his actual great-grandfather became the model for heroic figures such as John Sartoris, his mother and aunt undoubtedly provided materials for several of Faulkner's feisty, yet asexual, older women. Aside from these figures Faulkner's women are mindless, mysterious, or often destructively sexual. Faulkner's great fiction of the 1930s offers no white mothers who are central to the action; and indeed the mother is often literally or psychologically absent. By way of contrast, the "foster" parents, that is, the black man and woman, appear as trustworthy and nurturing figures against whom the fragmenting white world can be measured.

Thus Faulkner's fiction represented a complex affirmation and

denial of his own family tradition and of the regional family romance. In place of his own family and the patriarchal ethos of the
South, he created another world, itself a vast metaphorical structure which simultaneously affirmed and denied "reality." At first
this world was much like the skeleton of the desiccated leaf, but
by "The Bear" it had become a rich and teeming forest.[10] Faulkner
was to call himself the sole proprietor of this plenitudinous world
and thus revenge himself on his status as latecomer. Unable to be
a hero, this decrepit young man became a demiurge.

In the literature of the Southern Renaissance Faulkner's Benjy
Compson in *The Sound and the Fury* serves as the point of departure for an investigation of historical consciousness. The disorder in the Compson family is embodied in both Benjy's and
his brother Quentin's difficulties with time, in the other brother
Jason's disordered sense of values, in their sister Caddy's promis-
cuity, and in the cynicism of their father and the neurotic self-
pity of their mother. Standing apart and providing a point of observation and implicit judgment is the black servant, Dilsey.

Benjy is less an idiot than animal consciousness in human
form. He neither remembers nor forgets in the conventional sense
of those terms, since past and present are scarcely distinguishable
in his awareness. Benjy does react to difference and to absence;
but they are scarcely temporalized. His "memory" is the repository
of accumulated stimuli, arranged in no sequential order but rather
by a "qualitative" logic of smells and sounds. When he smells
trees he associates this with Caddy, who also smells of trees. The
Compson property adjoins a golf course; and when Benjy hears
the word "Caddy," he thinks it refers to his sister.

Thus Benjy's is a "stimulus-response reality."[11] "Caddy" is a
context-free signal which elicts desire and the pain of loss in
Benjy. He is like the sightless, deaf Helen Keller before her realization that words denote concepts and not objects directly.[12] As
one critic has observed, "We can trust Benjy's perceptions because
they're never filtered through any conceptions."[13] In Freudian
terms, Benjy is almost pure primary process, desire unmediated
by self-consciousness. All this points to the fact that the distinc-

tions between self and other, present and past, accompany self-consciousness. Benjy is not aware of these distinctions and thus cannot articulate them. The world does not stand over and against him; rather he is part of it. He is "lived."

Finally, because he cannot conceive of time, Benjy's world is constituted by repetition. At the end of the novel when Luster, one of the family's servants, drives around the town square the wrong way with Benjy in the wagon, Benjy's howl denotes the violation of this fixed pattern. For him difference signifies disruption. His experience of the world foreshadows the development of historical consciousness in Faulkner's fiction. He is the truth of the desire to escape time and history, which brings not bliss but merely dumb existence.

With the Sartoris saga, we enter the historical world in which the Southern tradition has grown destructive. This world is presided over by the great-grandfather, John Sartoris, "that arrogant ghost which dominated the house and its occupants and the whole scene himself."[14] The fourth generation of Sartorises—John and Bayard—bear the same names as their ancestors in the Civil War, an emblem of the repetitious, death-dealing quality of the tradition. Indeed, in *Flags in the Dust* Faulkner suggests that the monumentalizing, mythopoeic power of memory itself is at fault. The narrator sardonically comments on Aunt Jenny's tale of the hijinks of the original John and "Carolina" Bayard Sartoris during the Civil War: "As she grew older the tale itself grew richer and richer . . . until what had been a hare-brained prank of two heedless and reckless boys wild with their own youth, was become a gallant and finally tragical focal-point to which the history of the race had been raised from out of the old miasmic swamp." Thus in remembrance the heroic vision is forged, acquiring its compelling power over the descendants who take it seriously.

But it is in the life of young Bayard Sartoris, recently returned from World War I, that we see the destructive compulsions of the tradition work themselves out. Even if he knows his problem, Bayard cannot clearly articulate it. Already his own life and that of his twin brother have repeated his great-grandfather's and his cousin's. Carolina Bayard dies from a capricious bit of derring-do in the 1860s; and we learn that young Bayard feels responsible for the useless death of his brother in World War I.[15] The guilt arising from this useless repetition leads young Bayard to mope about the house and then to hell about the country in his newly purchased automobile, eventually causing the death of his grandfather, Bayard. This compulsion to repeat, this death wish of Bayard's, is not only determined by the events of his own life, but also by the family romance with death. He is defined by his actions, yet they are not his own.

Young Bayard tries haltingly to express what it is that holds him prisoner. He senses that it has to do with the Civil War and says bitterly that it was a "two bit war." Yet his life denies his own better judgment and shows the way in which he is engulfed by the family legend. Lacking a future, his life becomes a series of self-destructive repetitions which aim at rectifying his brother's useless death. Yet the tradition of his family and the region demands death as the great rectification. Life transmuted into heroism by latecomers comes to wreak havoc on the descendants. Only Bayard's grandfather possess a modicum of detachment. When Will Falls asks—"what the devil were you folks fighting about anyway?"—he answers, "Damned if I ever did know."

Thus in *Flags in the Dust* we see the Southern tradition out of control and embodied in the Sartoris family whose very name is "a game outmoded and played with pawns shaped too late and to an old dead pattern and of which the Player himself is a little wearied." In the world of the novel there is no possibility of breaking the repetition. Recollection leads not to transcendence but to repetition. As such recollection becomes a romantic fantasy of death, the mirror image of the myth of romantic love, which also culminates in death. While the narrator presents us with the critical vantage point and allows us to see raw materials out of which the fantasy is constructed, this perspective is closed to the characters in the novel for whom it could make a difference. From this point on Faulkner's work will move toward the creation of an historical consciousness *within* the narrative which will be able to comprehend and tell his story and thereby transcend that disastrously repetitious pattern.

In Gail Hightower, the deposed minister in *Light in August,* we have one of Faulkner's great historical fantasists. To be sure, Hightower is not precisely the central character in the novel. But his obsession with the past counterpoints neatly the tortured efforts of the "mulatto," Joe Christmas, to escape his fate, that is, his color; and with the rather simpler existences of the pregnant Lena Grove and her eventual companion, Byron Bunch.

Though he re-enacts the past in fantasy rather than acting it out, his retreat into private fantasy is a step forward in awareness. Unlike Bayard Sartoris, Hightower vaguely realizes the nature of the fantasy which controls his life. Still his essential being lies outside the present. Bunch, and especially Lena and Christmas, come close to forcing him back to present "reality" where he must take action of his own.

Hightower's life is constituted by three repetitions. Like his father he becomes a minister and an amateur doctor. More crucially, however, his psychic life is dominated by the memory of his grandfather's "martyrdom"—"a swaggering and unchastened bravo killed with a shotgun in a peaceful henhouse." As in *Flags in the Dust,* Faulkner suggests that Hightower's memory has transformed his grandfather's absurd death in a useless Civil War episode into the very stuff of which epics are made. Hightower's own martyrdom comes when he allows himself to be removed from his pulpit in Jefferson after his wife has been involved in a sordid domestic scandal. Once he has suffered his professional and public martyrdom he spends the rest of his life reliving in fantasy at twilight the heroic scene of his grandfather and his comrades riding into Jefferson during the Civil War.

Hightower "grew to manhood among phantoms, and side by side with a ghost."[16] The phantoms were his father, mother, and a black servant; the ghost was his grandfather. Like so many Southern grandfathers, Hightower's grandfather was a plain, gruff, hard-drinking man who practiced "simple adherence to a simple code." Once young Hightower hears of his grandfather's exploits from the black servant, the rest of his life is aimed at "return[ing] to the place to die where my life had already ceased before it began." Thus his grandfather defines the source and goal of his life and exerts a hold which he cannot escape. With his grandfather's life-death at the center of his memory, Hightower must continually return to and identify with it: "And if I am my dead grandfather on the instant of his death . . ." At that point in the fantasy, his grandfather and his men ride into town.

But in *Light in August* as in *Flags in the Dust*, Faulkner makes us aware of the glaring disparity between the monumental aura surrounding Hightower's grandfather and the reality of his death. Having realized that his obsession cost his wife's life, Hightower recognizes the controlling power of his grandfather fantasy ("I could neither let my grandson live or die."). These words indicate, I think, an advance of Hightower over Bayard Sartoris. He can neither live in the present, nor can he repeat the fantasy and die a hero. For Hightower, the latecomer, the heroic generation had been the lucky one, allowed to live and die in the completion of a life guided by a simple creed. For him, however, such heroism becomes a private fantasy, and all the more powerful for that. But, finally, Hightower does not want to be free of the fantasy nor can he articulate it to others.

If we can talk of a progression in historical consciousness here, it would lie in Hightower's awareness, at one level, that his fantasy has ruined his life. He edges toward a critical awareness of the power of the Southern tradition. Once the tradition of the family romance is raised to consciousness, it becomes available for analysis. Only by going backwards and then inward is a return to and progress forward possible

Will Percy and
the Tradition of the Fathers

What the Vanderbilt Agrarians advanced as a relatively untroubled defense of the Southern tradition against the onslaughts of modernity and what Faulkner depicted in his early novels as the sense of entrapment in the repetitions of a death-dealing tradition was in William Alexander Percy's *Lanterns on the Levee* (1941), a melancholic reflection on a time out of joint.[17] His autobiography was an elegy for an ethos, mourning the loss of a father, Leroy

Percy, and the tradition of the fathers. Ultimately, the Agrarian vision was an academic one, a stance rather than a rooted position. By contrast, Percy was a serious man, whatever else he was, who attempted to live by a tradition that had been created by the Civil War and irrevocably destroyed by World War I; or, perhaps as accurately, destroyed by the Civil War and re-created by World War I. Therein lie the difference and the greater authenticity which Percy embodied.

As a "last gentleman" Percy became a figure to be conjured with by those who knew him. To his friends and admirers Percy was something of a saint, a man of "fastidiousness and delicacy of manner," to quote his fellow Greenvillian and intimate friend, David Cohn. Hodding Carter, whom Percy helped persuade to come to Greenville, Mississippi, and found the *Delta Democrat*, remembered Percy's "giving of self," his willingness to aid those in distress. All remember his capacity for suffering fools. An outsider to the South and to the Delta, anthropologist Hortense Powdermaker wrote of Percy's kindness in facilitating her access to Indianola, where she studied race relations in the 1930s. John Dollard consulted with Percy while researching his famous study of race and class; and while Percy took strong exception to Dollard's conclusions and would never comment on the substance of Powdermaker's study, he was unfailingly courteous to them when called upon for aid.[18]

Will Percy was not a happy man. Novelist Walker Percy remembers that his uncle's eyes were "shadowed by sadness" and wonders in his *The Message in the Bottle* (1975) "why he was sad from 1918 to 1941 even though he lived in as good an environment as man can devise . . . ?"[19] Cohn struck much the same note when he wrote that Will Percy "was the loneliest man I have ever known." If the message of *Lanterns on the Levee* is any clue, it is no wonder that Will Percy was possessed by melancholy: the prophet of decline can hardly be expected to exhibit rising spirits. Yet the most apocalyptic of voices may privately be joyful and the jests of the humorist underlain, as is well known, with private sadness. Still, in Percy's case the private man seemed to reflect the essential pessimism of the cultural critic. Where the Agrarians had hoped to reinstate a past cultural ethos, Percy had no confidence that the old order could be restored, nor did he suggest a way of doing so. He was the melancholic Roman to the end—rarely the joyous and tragic Greek—and found a provisional solace only in the Stoic maxims of Marcus Aurelius and the ethical precepts of the Gospels. And though he presided over his own small realm in the Delta, he felt no more sense of freedom in the world at large than that experienced by another great Stoic, the slave Epictetus.

Thus, *Lanterns on the Levee* seems to present the Will Percy whom his friends knew and cherished. According to Cohn, Percy had begun his autobiographical reflections in the late 1930s, but put the manuscript aside when several friends had discouraged him from completing it. Cohn found the fragments scattered throughout the Percy living room and upon reading them urged his friend to continue. *Lanterns on the Levee* is anything but depressing: it is often charming, ironical, and informed by a winning self-deprecation. Despite his own angle of vision, W. J. Cash thoroughly enjoyed the book and forgave Percy his biases, while James Agee was fond of reading aloud to his friends those portions of *Lanterns on the Levee* which had to do with Sewanee.[20] As Percy suggested, if the South's fate boded forth a "sideshow Götterdämmerung," it was a twilight of the gods Will Percy contemplated with the equanimity of a man who knew that he and his vision would surely die. But never is *Lanterns on the Levee* morbid or whining.

Nor did Percy seclude himself to await his inevitable end. To Walker Percy, his uncle was the best teacher imaginable, introducing him and his brothers to the rich cadences of Shakespeare and the heavy, mournful strains of Brahms and Wagner. And just as Walker Percy paid homage to his mentor, so *Lanterns on the Levee*, particularly in its early pages, is a remembrance of those who had guided Will Percy's own *Bildung*. What Will Percy seemed to remember from his various mentors, most of whom were solitary and eccentric, was a way of living with loneliness, a quiet courage which provided a heroic, but ultimately futile protest against an unfeeling world and death which presided over it.

Much of the power of *Lanterns on the Levee* and its elegiac ambience, which verges on but rarely succumbs to self-pity, lies in the barely suggested inner conflicts and the reticences which make themselves felt throughout the book. Though Will Percy has been scored, and rightly so, for his paternalism and racism, his own social and racial views were not without ambiguity. In *Lanterns on the Levee* he adverts repeatedly to the racial theme, as though he had to try to tell it again, so as to convince outsiders such as Powdermaker and Dollard and perhaps even himself. He laughs outwardly, but not inwardly, when his factotum, Ford, for whom Percy shows a quite condescending but real affection, informs him that the black tenants of his "Trail Lake" plantation consider Percy's automobile as "us car." When Percy asks him what they mean by this odd phrase, Ford replies that they think the car belongs to them, since it is their labor which has paid for it. That Percy would include such an incident in his book shows something of his inner doubts.

On sharecropping, Percy had opinions which jar our more enlightened sensibilities. It is, he says, a form of "profit sharing . . . the most moral system under which human beings can work together . . . I am convinced that if it were accepted in principle by capital and labor, our industrial troubles would be over . . . Sharecropping is one of the best systems ever devised to give security and a chance for profit to the simple and unskilled." Yet he goes on to admit that the "organic" relationship of planter and cropper is often, even generally, an occasion for rank exploitation and, in truth, depends upon the character of the planter. One suspects that even Percy knew that the personal factor had ceased to play a role, if it ever had, and that the system itself was exploitative.

When discussing race directly, Percy marvels at the existing peace and amicability between the races, since, he claims, they are centuries apart in intellectual and moral development. Yet this rather hackneyed judgment by the Delta aristocrat is balanced by the cogent observation that to live "habitually as a superior among inferiors . . . is a temptation to dishonesty and hubris and deterioration," an observation which shorn of its racial bias offers a truth that critics of colonialism have voiced. More than that,

Percy states quite openly another home truth which those of more liberal promptings, then and now, hear reluctantly: "the sober fact is we understand one another not at all." Again, though the important insight is compromised by the racial assumptions, such comments indicate that Percy was not quite the undivided self on race that we would have him be. This is not to say that Percy was a liberal *malgré lui*, only that he was sensitive to certain aspects of racial domination which other conservatives downplayed or ignored.

His discussion of "poor whites," however, was marked by no conflicting insights which signaled doubt or inner division. In *Lanterns on the Levee* Percy rendered no lip service to the egalitarian ideals of the 1930s and, unlike Cash, Agee, and some of the Agrarians, he saw no virtue in the common whites, past or present. Reflecting in part the peculiar demography of the Delta, Percy divided his South and that of his ancestors into three categories: the aristocracy, the poor whites, and the blacks. The poor whites were "intellectually and spiritually . . . inferior to the Negro." They were the corruptors of "civil" society, the mob, *Demos,* whose emergence into the public realm heralded the decline of quality not only in the South, but in Italy, Germany, and Russia. His unmitigated animus against the common whites reflected not only the traditional attitudes of his class; it was given added bite by his father's bitter senatorial campaign of 1911 against the champion of the poor whites, James K. Vardaman.

Thus Percy's protest against the world he never made assumed shape in his autobiography. First, he equated manners with morals; indeed he went so far as to elevate the former over the latter. The style was the man and the culture: "while good morals are all important between the Lord and his creatures, what counts between one creature and another is good manners." Manners were not, however, the exclusive property of the upper class, but could be found throughout the social system. This nod toward equality was only provisional, since manners were those habitual attitudes and actions which preserved the order of things and guaranteed that the bottom rail remained on the bottom. Percy not surprisingly felt that economics should mirror the social and political hierarchy; and thus his defense of sharecropping was part of a larger distaste for the cash nexus of capitalism and the leveling impulses of socialism. What was important was that the rational pursuit of profit be incorporated into an ethos of organic solidarity among the classes. Finally, Percy held that politics was an affair among gentlemen to whom the common whites should defer for enlightened guidance. Blacks were excluded altogether from the public realm and were to be governed by the time-honored precepts of family relationships as the "younger brother[s]" which he claimed they were. About women he felt much the same.

More generally, Percy's cultural vision embodied the "Delta ideal" and was linked in historical imagination with the early Virginia aristocracy and the feudal order of medieval Europe. The mood suffusing *Lanterns on the Levee* was one of cultural pessimism. He felt that he was presiding over the closing time of civilized life; most citizens had forgotten that it "is given to man to behold beauty and worship nobility." "A tarnish," Percy wrote, "has fallen over the bright world; dishonor and corruption triumph; my own strong people are turned into lotus-eaters; defeat is here again, the last, the most abhorrent."

How then can we characterize Percy and his vision of the Southern tradition? In his introduction to a recent edition of *Lanterns on the Levee*, Walker Percy castigates present-day critics for calling his uncle a "racist, white supremacist, reactionary, paternalist, Bourbon" and claims that in the Mississippi of the 1930s and 1940s, Uncle Will was considered a "flaming liberal" and a "nigger lover."[21] Though one can agree in the abstract with his animadversions against facile name-calling, Walker Percy seems guilty here of uncharacteristic obtuseness in rejecting these labels for his uncle. If it matters, Will Percy was all that his critics have claimed. But more important, all of the labels can be subsumed under the wider rubric of Catonism, which we have discussed earlier.

Aside from such intellectuals as T. S. Eliot and Henry Adams, the South, as we have seen, has clearly been the *locus classicus* of Catonist intellectuals. Pessimistic about the future, the Catonist looks with longing toward a past heroic age. In Nietzsche's terms he is a despairing "monumentalist." This vision has been relatively rare in America, whose dominant form of cultural nostalgia has been either Jeffersonian, a yearning for the return of a yeoman republic, or à hallowing of the Founding Fathers who, for all their Roman posturings, were not very good Catonists themselves. But the South has had in its cultural imaginings a period of aristocratic domination, a heroic war and an unjust occupation. Never discredited, but only defeated, the planters were fit subjects for twentieth-century monumentalizing on the part of Southern intellectuals. And though it would be unfair to call Percy an unqualified champion of militarism and anti-intellectualism, in most respects he fits the Catonist image quite well. With him, recollection led to a desire for repetition of the past. At the same time he realized that such a repetition was impossible.

To understand the inner, psychological dynamic of Percy's Catonism it is necessary to examine Percy's relationship with his father and his family, since for him, as for so many Southern writers of the 1930s, the father and the family became the mediating symbols by which he understood himself and his past. Percy came from an old Mississippi family (though, as is always the case in such matters, not that old), dating back to the 1830s. On the maternal side were French blood and the Catholic faith, while the paternal line reputedly traced back to the Percys of Northumberland. He was a member of the segment of Delta and black-belt planter class with Catholic or high-church Episcopal connections. Such families summered in the Virginia mountains or more often on Monteagle Mountain near Sewanee or at the north Alabama resort of Mentone. Typically their sons would be sent, as was Percy, to a college like Sewanee, where the Confederacy and Episcopalianism vied for top place, and then on to legal finishing school at the University of Virginia or Harvard. After graduation the sons would return to take over the family holdings or help their fathers manage them. Occasionally one of the returning sons would be infected with advanced ideas while "abroad" and acquire a reputation as the local liberal because he subscribed to *The New Republic* or *The American Mercury* and, like Faulkner's Gavin Stevens, mouthed traditional pieties in moderate tones. It might even happen that a returned son would choose the maverick's role, joining and perhaps even constituting the ACLU in the area or in the entire state. The lawyer portrayed by Jack Nicholson in the film *Easy Rider* is such a type, an alcoholic radical tolerated by family and friends in much the same way as the town looney or the crazy old lady who brandished her shotgun at children who trampled her flowers.

Implicit in this pattern, the staple of much Southern literature but nevertheless quite real, was the gradual decline in energy and will as generation gave way to generation. As Florence King has sardonically suggested, the Southern scion was urged by his mother "be half the man your daddy was," and the son took her injunction to heart."[22] The upshot was that, after three generations or so, the heroic age of the grandfathers who had fought the Yankees and driven out the carpetbaggers had given way to grandsons, pale copies of their fathers, and fallen prey to brooding, drink, or other destructive impulses. Colonel John Sartoris gives way to young Bayard Sartoris, hell-bent on self-destruction; General Compson is followed by the psychotic Quentin Compson.

Though lacking the dramatic flourishes, this pattern was at work in the Percy family; at least Will Percy felt it to be. All his life he felt small and physically unprepossessing beside his virile father and grandfather. Where they were resolute and heroic public men, he was a private versifier and full of self-doubt. It had been too much to live up to. Will Percy had to live in the shadow of a father he considered "the only great person I ever knew." "It was hard having such a dazzling father," he wrote of the man whose personal courage in facing down mobs and leading the fight against the Klan in the early 1920s was legendary in the Delta, "no wonder I longed to be a hermit."[23]

Such admissions come relatively rarely in *Lanterns on the Levee*. Clearly, however, the burden of being his father's son weighed heavily on Will Percy. Near the end of his memoirs Percy prefaces a discussion of the heroic efforts of his paternal grandfather—"Fafar" to Will Percy and "The Grey Eagle" or "Old Colonel Percy" to his acquaintances, a John Sartoris figure if there ever was one—in restoring white supremacy to Mississippi with the relieved comment that his great-grandfather, whose portrait also hung in the Percy house, had not been such a "demanding ancestor." This throwaway observation reveals some of the inner strain Will Percy must have suffered. Earlier, Percy admits that he and his father had not been close during his childhood and writes of fun he had fishing with one of his uncles in Virginia: "You walked along carrying the empty fish-basket and felt easy and liked his grumpiness." But then he follows with: "Of course he wasn't comparable to Father . . . ."

Never quite a hermit but always an outsider, Will Percy felt homeless where he should have felt most secure; and his constant travel betrayed an essential lostness and failure to gain purchase on a congenial reality. After college at Sewanee he had no clear sense of what he wanted to do and backed into Harvard Law after a lonely year in Europe. Then after law school he was again at loose ends; and Percy wondered in retrospect if his father hadn't yearned then for the younger son who had died early; he had been "all boy, all sturdy, obstreperous charm," everything Will Percy felt he wasn't. Though he enjoyed teaching a term at Sewanee, he eventually returned to Greenville to join his father's law firm and take up his bachelor's existence as sometime poet and fulltime assistant to his father.

Only with the onset of World War I and his service in combat did Will Percy for a time feel necessary. Out from under his father and family, some of his essential despair and isolation was alleviated; and he came alive. Thinking back on his war experience he writes: "Although you felt like a son of a bitch, you knew you were a son of God. A battle is something you dread intolerably and for which you have always been homesick . . . it somehow had meaning and daily life hasn't." Thus the war had great meaning for Percy and many Southern young men, for it represented a chance to prove themselves the equals of their heroic grandfathers and fathers—real and symbolic—who had risked their lives in the only war that had really counted. It became the great repetition, the chance to mirror the monumental deeds of the founders of the Southern tradition. Daily life, the keeping of accounts, and making a living were tedium itself. Even the cultivated and sensitive Percy was later to recall the contempt and irrelevance he had felt for art and conventional notions of beauty on the eve of facing death in battle. What he desired was not a moral equivalent of war, but something close to a military equivalent of culture.

The war did not last forever, and Percy returned to Greenville to resume his place in his father's shadow. He went through the Klan battles of early 1920s with him, but the central event of the decade for our purposes was the flood of 1927. Will Percy had been named chairman of local relief efforts and found agreement from his committee that the black population should be moved from the levee to better and safer quarters in Vicksburg. The local planters, however, feared that should their cheap black labor be evacuated, it would be lured north and never return to the plantation. As Percy relates it, his father agreed that he should not be intimidated, but did suggest that Will poll his committee again to make certain that there was still general agreement to remove the blacks. When the group reconvened, Percy was astounded to find that every member had changed his mind and recommended to a man that the black labor force be maintained on the Greenville levee.[24]

Later Percy discovered that his father had gone behind his back and personally persuaded the committee members to change their votes. Will Percy's authentic paternalism, uncomfortable as it may make us feel, had proved powerless before the commercial considerations of his father's kind of people. Even more startling —and telling—is that Will Percy could not bring himself to register the hurt and sense of betrayal he must have felt at the contempt his father had shown him.

The extraordinary reticence here only reminds us of Will Percy's absorption in the Southern family romance. Why the subtitle "Recollections of a Planter's Son" unless to remind us of his status as a latecomer, a minor planet in his father's orbit? In fact, Will Percy was every bit as much the planter as his father, who was primarily a corporation lawyer. Nothing points so much to the distorted view of his family's place in the Southern tradition as the continued reference to his father as a planter. In other circumstances a mother might have supplied the psychic and emotional resources to oppose the father and the collective weight of the tradition. But in the Percy family she did not or could not. Percy's mother remains a shadowy figure in *Lanterns on the Levee,* never really there for us, the readers, nor, one suspects, for Will Percy. We get a bare hint of his hurt only when Percy continues his description of the smile of his "undemanding" great-grandfather: it was "very shadowy and knowing, a little hurt but not at all bitter."

With his parents' death in the late 1920s Will Percy's "life semed superfluous." He took over the management of the family property and, as mentioned, became the man to see in Mississippi, an explainer of the region to outsiders. He spent the rest of his days traveling, reading, gardening, listening to Brahms and Wagner, and providing an education for three adopted sons who had been rendered homeless by their parents' suicide. Sharing himself generously with his sons, he became perhaps the father he would have liked to have.

Will Percy was also a poet, something one would scarcely learn from his autobiography.[25] During his lifetime three volumes appeared—*Sappho in Levkas and Other Poems* (1915), *In April Once* (1920), and *Enzio's Kingdom* (1924)—but after the mid-1920s the muse apparently departed him. Though his was a minor poetic gift, his poetry offers us a glimpse of his more private concerns, however refracted they may be by their expression in verse. The setting is generally in the past—medieval or ancient Europe and the Mediterranean; the mode is pastoral and bucolic; the tone, not surprisingly, elegiac. Blues, violets, and lilacs are the dominant colors of settings often populated by fawns, nightingales, and shepherds. There is little sweat or toil; and of his own time or region, Percy speaks little.

Three themes run through the poetry: the pathos of unrequited love, the deep conflict between physical desire and spiritual love, and the loyalty of son to father. The title poem of his first volume revolves around the love of Sappho for a "slim, brown shepherd boy with windy eyes / and spring upon his mouth!" and how this carnal love for a mortal cuts her off from Zeus: "And meeting him lost Thee!" Sappho's love is not without social and intellectual condescension, as when she observes of the object of her chaste desire that "His thoughts [were] the thoughts of shepherds." And though she dreams of kissing and being comforted by him, sexual passion is considered a form a "grossness." Still she desires him. The conflict of the spiritual and sexual is thematized again in "To Lucrezia," where Percy writes more strikingly and with less reticence of "some young god, / With blown, bright hair and filet golden, came, / And stretching forth the blossoming rod of beauty / Upon me wrought a pagan spell." The poem "Sublimation" in his second volume talks of locking "your sin in a willow cage / . . . Outside your good deeds cluck and strut / But small's the joy they bring."

In "Enzio's Kingdom" the central theme is the loyalty of son to father, a concern which obviously reflects the state of seige which Will Percy and his father experienced during the fight against the Klan and earlier against Vardaman. Enzio's father, Frederick II, has led a revolt against the Catholic Church and other European monarchs in the hopes of establishing a reign of universal peace in which the masses will be kept content, while the chosen few pursue the search for truth. Once his followers learn of his hard vision, Frederick is deserted and condemned. His father now dead, Enzio recalls their mighty plans and then how both grew as brutal and callous as the enemy they had been fighting. The climax comes when he exclaims: "There is no certain thing I can lay hold on / And say, 'This, this is good! This will I worship!' / Except my father."

A consideration of Percy's poetic concerns leads one back to *Lanterns on the Levee*. In writing of his year in Paris, Percy remembers how he was repulsed by a leering hermaphroditic statue in the Louvre and how he later learned that at one time the Greeks had "practiced bi-sexuality honestly and openly . . . It's a grievous and a long way you travel to reach serenity and the acceptance of facts without hurt or shock . . . By that time you are too old to practice your wisdom." And near the end of the book Percy casts back over his past to recall several fleeting and apparently unfulfilled homoerotic encounters. Thus Percy depicts himself, albeit obscurely, as a man divided within himself and unable to express openly his essential sexual desires.

Not only in love, if his poetry hints rightly, but in his family, Percy came to accept without self-pity that he "was never first place in any life." *Lanterns on the Levee* ends as Percy imagines his final confrontation with death, the "high God." "Who are you?" asks Death. Writes Percy: "The pilgrim I know should be able to straighten his shoulders, stand his tallest, and to answer defiantly: 'I am your son.'"

For all the positive influence of his father, Will Percy was in some fundamental way unmanned by him and by the tradition; and this foreclosed, I suspect, the full expression of his intellectual and creative capacities. The tensions and ambivalences which he so obviously experienced were never fully explored, either directly or indirectly.

Percy sensed that something was wrong but could never quite articulate his problem or say what it was and who was responsible. That block in his way was his father, who loomed over everything he did. Percy gave ample and authentic praise to his father and the tradition of the fathers, yet, if we know anything, it is that such over-valuations conceal resentments and bitterness. How else explain the rueful hints of awareness? And more deeply, why the explicit association of his father with death itself? Why else the forging of a life which was diametrically opposed to his father's style, if not partly by way of revenge as well as veneration? With his father's presiding presence always at hand, he could only blame himself—as weak and disappointing; or blacks —as irresponsible and inferior; or poor whites—as envious and barbarous—for the decline which had set in. No individual or group could match his father's heroic example.

Finally we can see in Percy what might be called a form of "cultural melancholia," which subsumes the Catonist label and the psychological relationship with his father. As with the melancholic, Percy could only blame himself for what in truth he should have directed at his father with whom he so closely identified, yet whose hold he surreptitiously resented. This is not to claim that all reactionary protests against the modern world are the issue of sons who have been overwhelmed by strong fathers and publicly bemoan what they unconsciously welcome. But in Percy's case, there was something like that at work. Overcome by the anxiety of his father's influence and the influence of a tradition which was so strong precisely at the moment of its demise, Percy could only obliquely register his protest. Set beside the moral as well as artistic achievement of his upstate neighbor, William Faulkner, Percy's efforts represent an important and fascinating failure. Indeed Faulkner, in his review of *In April Once,* noted that Percy was "like a little boy closing his eyes against the dark of modernity."[26] This is perhaps too strong. Still, Will Percy could only yearn for a world which was irretrievable, if it ever had existed, and which stood now under the sign of the father and of death.

5

Between Repetition
and Recollection:
Allen Tate
and William Faulkner

Among the Agrarians the sheer power of Allen Tate's mind was unmatched. Tate was born in 1899 in Kentucky, but lived for extended periods in northern Virginia and in Washington, D.C. The Tate family was constantly on the move; and following the failure of his business, the father lived apart from his wife and children. Later Tate would say that he resented his father's leaving and had felt humiliated by it. At Vanderbilt, Tate joined the Fugitives as an undergraduate and was by his own account an intellectually arrogant and sometimes insufferable young man.[1] Behind the arrogance, however, was a finely honed mind and a deep yearning for religious roots.

Tate was also the most cosmopolitan of the Fugitives. He defended literary modernism, especially the work of T. S. Eliot, against the doubts of John Crowe Ransom. From 1923 to 1929 he spent time in New York and Paris and was particularly close to Hart Crane, with whom he and his wife, Caroline Gordon, spent one cold winter. Yet Tate always felt a certain displacement in the modern world. As he wrote to Donald Davidson in 1928, "the quest of the past is something we all share, but it is most acute in me."[2] He quite consciously sought a tradition which would illuminate the inadequacies of the modern age and give form to his deep spiritual yearnings. Only in later years did he finally convert to Roman Catholicism.

It is ironic that Tate, one of the original New Critics, should have provided the essential explanatory framework for Southern cultural achievement. In "What Is a Traditional Society?" (1936), Tate offered an assessment of the modern cultural crisis. With the post-Renaissance disruption of the religious unity of Europe, the "historical imagination . . . myth-making . . . within the restricted realm of the historical event" became a dominant force in Western culture. But this historical imagination, which took classical Greece and Rome as its models, also exhausted itself; and modern man was left without any "forms of human action." The anachronistic uniqueness of the South consisted in its unity of "moral nature and livelihood," since "the economic basis of life is the soil of which all the forms, good or bad, of our experience must come."[3] Tate's literary and intellectual vocation became an extended assessment of the modern world's lack of a context for meaningful action.

In 1942, while writing about the Fugitives, Tate focused more sharply on the Southern experience. "After the war," he wrote, "the South again knew the world but it had a memory of another war . . . [it] meant not the obliteration of the past but a heightened consciousness of it; so that we had . . . a double focus, a looking two ways . . ."[4] This situation of being caught between two worlds, he claimed, was the precondition for the South's literary and intellectual flowering. A bit prematurely, Tate announced in 1945 that the literary Renaissance was over, but not before praising Faulkner as "the most powerful and original novelist in the U.S. and one of the best in the modern world," a judgment few shared in the mid-1940s and a testimony to Tate's critical acumen.[5]

Finally, in his "A Southern Mode of Imagination" (1959), Tate was to concur in Cash's assessment of the inadequacies of the Southern mind, a theme of his cultural-historical probings since his essay in *I'll Take My Stand*. The Southern mind, he noted, had been "an extraverted mind not much given to introspection" and characterized not by Emerson's "man thinking" but by "man talking." Consummate story-tellers and rhetoricians, ante-bellum Southerners had been incapable of "critical detachment" and blamed others for their plight. Robert E. Lee, Tate observed, had fought for a place and not an idea, thus revealing the mindlessness which so crippled the South.[6] Tate reiterated how important World War I had been in forcing the South to rejoin the modern world: "It looked round and saw for the first time since 1830 that the Yankees were not to blame for everything."[7] In invoking Yeats's "out of the quarrel with others we make rhetoric; out of the quarrel with ourselves poetry," Tate meant to capture the essential shift in cultural sensibility which produced major literature rather than strident polemics.

In Tate's biographies of Stonewall Jackson and Jefferson Davis and his novel, *The Fathers*,[8] he developed further the themes of his critical essays. The central concern of his writings on the Southern past (indeed of his entire work) was identical with what he saw in the life and work of Hart Crane as the modern romantic dilemma: the separation between thought and feeling, intellect and emotion, tradition and energy. It is a mistake to take Tate as a pure apologist for the ante-bellum South. Though he saw it as the nearest embodiment of the stable traditional order of medieval Europe, it contained all the contradictions which emerged in full force in the twentieth century.

An eloquent expression of the separation of past from present came in Tate's famous "Ode to the Confederate Dead" (1927; final version 1937). The less introspective Donald Davidson was disturbed by the poem and charged that the "Ode" was "not for the Confederate dead, but for your own dead emotion, or mine (*you* think) . . . its beauty is a cold beauty."[9] Though Richard Gray claims that the poem is about the creation of the vital myth of the past, the "Ode" seems to me much more about the failure of that monumental view of the past to retain any vitality in the modern world. "Ode" betrayed the influence of Eliot ("you shift your sea-space blindly / Heaving, turning like the blind crab") and thematized the sense of abandonment which overtook the observer unable to unite past energy and action with present self-consciousness. The heroic but dead soldiers serve only to "feed the grass row after rich row." For the onlooker "they will not last . . . Lost in that orient of the thick-and-fast / you will curse the setting sun." Autumnal images of desiccation and twilight images of time's inevitable passage render the ambience bleak and forbidding. "We shall say only the leaves" seems to leave the onlooker with no further meaning to be retrieved. All attempts to regain access are blocked by the self-enclosure of the narrator. The angel "stones the eyes"; and the panther devours himself narcissistically.[10]

In 1938 Tate offered the *reductio ad absurdum* of the New Criticism: an impersonal reading of his own "Ode." He typically urged that the reader not worry the question of why the poem was written nor try to identify the poet with the central consciousness in the "Ode." He then went on to suggest that "Ode" was about the "solipsistic" or narcissistic consciousness trying to re-engage a traditional past.[11] Even in the 1920s Tate was no optimist about the possibility of reviving the images or energies of the past. The loss of the Southern tradition was symptomatic of the loss of the larger tradition and the resulting disappearance of a common world.

Yet the severity of Tate's vision in "Ode" did not prevent him from further explorations of the Southern past. In 1928 he published a biography of Stonewall Jackson, which was, by his own admission, "due to a reversion to the romantic feelings of child-hood."[12] On the surface the despair of the "Ode" gave way to the monumental rendering of a Confederate hero. Yet even then there were strange ambivalences at work.

The style of *Stonewall Jackson* was a strange one—part Hemingway and part elementary school primer. If it was meant to be experimental, the result was a failure. Large chunks of the biography were devoted to Jackson's military exploits. Indeed Tate claimed that if Jackson had had his way and the Confederates allowed to invade Washington after the first battle of Bull Run, the South would have won the war then and there. The villain of the piece was Jefferson Davis, who fought an essentially defensive war, waiting for European support that never came.

Tate seemed strangely ambivalent and not a little condescending toward Jackson the man. Though Jackson was a first-rate disciplinarian and tactician, energetic and ready to carry the war to the Union, he was also "humorless, unimaginative," and "always obeyed orders." His mind was good, but not quick; and his ambition so great that "nothing specific could constrain it."

One might suspect that Tate's dead-pan style, which rendered Jackson a rather wooden figure, was intended ironically, that he set up Jackson this way in the pre-Civil War years so as to bring into sharper focus his great achievements during the war. Perhaps so. But from our vantage point Tate seems to be condescending to a courageous but essentially uninteresting man, the willing tool of a great cause. Indeed one might see in Jackson an example of Tate's later judgment that the ante-bellum South had been plagued by a lack of intelligence in other than military matters.

Stonewall Jackson also anticipated Tate's later concerns. At one point Tate described Virginia as a "feudal order" and spoke of the contrast between Northern and Southern culture. "In the South," he wrote, "the man as he appeared in public was the man: his public appearance was his moral life. The nearest equivalent to the 'inner life' were 'private affairs.'" The New Englander was mystical and religious; the Southerner practical and materialistic. Though opposed to slavery in the South, the Northerner was "a better slave; he would have the illusion of freedom." This rather quirky contrast came down ultimately to a contrast between the North, which was ahistorical and devoted to abstraction, a favorite Agrarian charge, and the Virginia-dominated South, which sought to preserve the compact of sovereign states. In this sense the aristocratic order of Virginia itself was the "hero" of Tate's work. Jackson himself was only its tragically short-lived servant.

In *Jefferson Davis* (1929), Tate was at his most "Southern"; but he admitted in a letter to Davidson that it was difficult to "be romantic about a politician."[13] Though the biography was much better written than his previous one (as Davidson tactfully observed), it was anything but a celebration of Jefferson Davis. If Jackson had been a figure of energy without intellect, Davis in Tate's hands showed a "curious separation of his intellect and his feeling" and was "emotionally undeveloped." Of the highest integrity but withal a martinet and political pedant, Davis pursued a "passive, defensive policy." But more importantly Davis failed to understand the new social forces which should have been harnessed in the ante-bellum South. Had Davis done this, the fate of the Confederacy might have been different.

Davis thus failed to lead the way in forging a new political and social vision. As Tate was later to write in his *I'll Take My Stand* essay, the South had been intellectually sterile. After secession it had adopted a constitution which essentially duplicated the federal Constitution: "The new impulse of that society was to be frustrated because their leaders could think only in politics—the politics of the U.S. Constitution." Neither moderates such as Davis nor Tate's beloved Virginians could grasp that the lower South was "pushing towards an empire, agricultural, slave owning and aristocratic." Tate granted that the deep South was certainly not aristocratic in origins, but its social vision (and structure) had been superior to Northern society in which "the classes are not so closely knit now." Though a form of "despotism," slavery was generally benevolent, from self-interest if for no other reason. For Jefferson, Tate substituted Chancellor Harper and Thomas Dew, the reactionary social theorists of the ante-bellum South, as ideological founding fathers of what had become a "distinct nation" on the eve of the Civil War. According to Tate this dynamic, hierarchical order in the deep South would have been the key to the development of a distinctively Southern culture.

In the Davis biography Tate also modified his assessment of the Virginia culture. The imperialistic slavocracy properly had little use for the Virginians, who were "a self-sufficient people, provincial to their very eyes; backward looking and contented to rest upon a mellow classicism." They had "no sympathy with the Lower Southern Dream of great empire." So much for the Old Dominion. As a man of the unimaginative and not so vital center, Davis was caught between the Virginia past and the lower South future. "He was neither a Cromwell nor a Caesar" and therein lay the Southern tragedy. If this were not a proto-fascist reading of Southern history, it came awfully close to it. It reminds us that fascism is essentially a form of political monumentalism, which, to be realized, must destroy the ethos which it claims to defend.

What emerged then from the biographies of Jackson and Davis and the cultural essays of the 1930s was Tate's vision of a traditional society, one in which "the artist was a member of an organic society."[14] The historical South had been but an inadequate exemplar of such an order. Indeed, Tate was less interested in the ante-bellum South per se than in the South as the last outpost of traditional European society. Southerners were the "last Europeans." But it lacked great writers, while the presence of black slaves had foreclosed the possibility of a genuine class society among whites. And when Tate sought to envisage such an ideal society, it assumed the form of a dynamic, expansionist, and authoritarian order, hardly a plausible context for the flourishing of the arts. Once again, energy and intellect, impulse and style seemed irreconcilable, not only in the South but in Tate's own mind as well.

Tate's Family Romance

In 1959 Tate asserted that the "center of the South . . . was the family," a notion which he had most forcefully expressed in *The Fathers* (1938).[15] In his only novel, the crisis in the Buchan family reflects and gives way to the crisis of the nation as it goes to war in 1861. At the center of the historical and cultural crosscurrents stands a young man, Lacy Buchan. Fifty years later, Lacy attempts to make sense of the way the world of his father and his family came apart. In comparison with the Davis biography, Tate's work of fiction is more sympathetic to the Virginia tradition; indeed, the novel is something of an elegy for a civilized way of life as it fell before the onslaughts of the untraditioned. And yet *The Fathers* achieves a certain tragic stature because Tate did not load the scales all on one side and make his version of the family romance a popular novel of the *Gone With the Wind* variety or an untroubled evocation of the plantation society as depicted in Stark Young's *So Red the Rose*. Though *The Fathers* was an elegy for a lost way of life, it was also a subtle but devastating dissection of the historical inadequacies of the Virginians.

"I have a story to tell," begins Lacy Buchan, "but I cannot explain the story." Though less agonizingly posed and explored

with the equanimity of maturity, Lacy Buchan's question is remarkably similar to Quentin Compson's central concerns: Who is
my father? What was the nature of the tradition whose heir I was
to be? Whose heir am I? Like Quentin, Lacy finds himself compelled to retell his past in the hope of laying to rest its disturbing
memories. Unlike Quentin, Lacy avoids the dismembering memories, the destructive repetitions, and the despairing recollections,
but the result is a certain dissociation from the past.

As the older Lacy remembers, the ante-bellum world young
Lacy Buchan inhabited was dominated by his father, Major Lewis
Buchan, one of the northern Virginia gentry. Less a personality
than a role, Major Buchan presides over an exquisitely static
world, simple on the surface yet complex in its orderings. In the
daily rounds and traditional forms of life—birth and death, meetings and marriages, peace and war—Buchan's world knows no
separation of private and public. It is a graciously impersonal
world, most like those evoked in *Lanterns on the Levee* or *So Red
the Rose*. As in Percy's world, it is not morality but manners which
are crucial; for, as Lacy retrospectively observes: "how could you
decide what people deserved? . . . So you came to believe in
honor and dignity for their own sake, since all proper men knew
what honor was and could recognize dignity; but nobody knew
what human nature was or could presume to mete out justice to
others." In the world of northern Virginia, civility is no ordeal but
rather the very essence of life. The Southern way of life, what
one character in *So Red the Rose* refers to as a "perfect academy
of memories" and another Buchan-like figure in Young's novel
takes to be "tradition, forefathers and a system of being," becomes
an end in itself. There is properly speaking no notion of morality
outside of the order and all particular shortcomings, even slavery,
must be measured in reference to the survival of that order. "They
did a great deal of injustice but they always knew where they
stood. . . ," thinks Lacy. Such an order was the only hope against
the "abyss."

It is important to stress that this world is not a prudish or
more than normally hypocritical world. Indeed, repugnance before the two great human experiences—sex and death—indicates

a lack of culture. If Tate's novel expresses the classic version of the family romance, it is not the Victorian version, with its emphasis upon gentility and repression which characterizes *Gone With the Wind*. The forms of life enable Major Buchan to carry on with poise at his wife's funeral which opens the story; George Posey cannot face death and must leave. Similarly, he is embarrassed by the copulation of animals. The "abyss" is not abolished by civilization; it is sublimated, dealt with in formalized ways.

In the world of Lewis Buchan time has been frozen, almost abolished, and replaced by the presence of tradition. This presence is symbolized in the portrait of the grandfather "looking down . . . upon the scene of death." "People," observed Lacy, "living in formal societies, lacking the historical imagination, can imagine for themselves only a timeless existence." This is Tate's theme from his essay in *I'll Take My Stand:* to live securely in a tradition is to live securely in the present and past. To become aware of time is to become aware of alienation from the tradition. It is the glory—and the fatal weakness—of the world of Major Buchan that it cannot imagine itself historically; that is, it takes itself as eternal. Faced with historical and familial crises, Major Buchan is helpless. In terms of the larger world, he is not very smart.

Counterposed against his father in Lacy's memory stands his brother-in-law, George Posey. A man of considerable energy and charm, George repeatedly violates the rules of the "intricate game," marries Lacy's sister, Susan, and eventually controls the Buchan fortune, such as it is. (Major Buchan has no head for business and has mismanaged his property.) Lacking a sense of the traditional order of things, he is above all "personal." Like Mitchell's Scarlett O'Hara or Faulkner's Thomas Sutpen, he has no rooted loyalties which transcend personal desire or ambition. Even his altruistic deeds are a violation. He sells the Buchan slaves and even his own half-brother as "liquid capital" to pay off the family debts. Yet, as Lacy suggests, George's commercial transaction is more "realistic," given the "fastidious self-indulgence" of Lacy's father. The tragedy of the situation, in Lacy's eyes, is that both were right—and wrong. Thus the split of civilization and energy, feeling and intelligence, the principled and the pragmatic.

George's sale of his half-brother, "Yellow Jim," illuminates Tate's version of the family romance. What is "wrong" in the transaction is not the enslavement and sale of a human being. Rather the violation lies in the separation of the slave from his black family and friends and, behind that, his separation from his white family. All of this is arranged by George, his brother. Family relationships should take precedence over commercial or abstract moral concerns. It is this one deed which brings on the destruction of the entire Buchan family.

Once the war begins, Lacy goes to live in the Posey home in nearby Georgetown, where he finds an assortment of strange and eccentric characters who live behind closed doors and read like Central Casting choices for a Faulkner novel. In that house "social acts became privacies," the inverse of the Buchan household. The novel charts the progressive descent into the private and the aberrant, the psychotic and the murderous. Susan goes mad after ruining the life of her sister-in-law and arranging the death of Yellow Jim in order to prevent another union between the two families. Thus George Posey's breaches of decorum, his violation of the social order, are mirrored in massive disruptions of the two intertwined families. Like Faulkner's Sutpen family, the Buchan family's torments mirror the nation's larger divisions. With the father (and the fathers) destroyed, the siblings engage in a fratricidal war.

And yet Lacy (and the reader) is drawn to the attractive vigor of George Posey in somewhat the same way that Nick Carraway in Fitzgerald's *The Great Gatsby* is drawn to that fascinating "innocent," Jay Gatsby. It is not, however, that Posey comes from "nowhere"; his family is an old Maryland family, one which is "more refined . . . but less civilized" than Lacy's. We learn significantly that George's father died early and that George was a "mother's boy"; and thus he lacked anyone to master his energies and give them form. He is always "elsewhere" and "without people or place." The result is that George inadvertently destroys whatever he touches, including his wife and his half-brother.

Still George becomes the "presiding face" in the Buchan home and wins Lacy's own personal allegiance. The fantasized judgment on George by Lacy's grandfather—"He does evil because he has not the will to do good"—is registered by Lacy but fails to change Lacy's heart. As his grandfather disappears, Lacy realizes that "I have nobody to guide me now." Major Buchan commits suicide—alone—when Northern troops order him off his farm. Susan "was mad." George disappears after killing his old enemy, a typically private act in the midst of the great public conflagration. Lacy is left without any presiding presence and returns to fight in the war: "If I am killed, it will be because I love him more than I love any man."

The Fathers is a finely wrought and exquisitely controlled achievement with no wasted motion or excessive emotion. But that is its problem as well. It is a mark of Tate's refined sensibility that he never depicted the aberrant or violent head-on. They come to us for the most part by report or glancingly. Thus the novel never threatens to become melodramatic or sensational as is often the case with Faulkner. But for that reason it remains rather cerebral and without passion, as though to have indulged in such scenes would have been to partake of the Posey spirit. The characters are closely observed and defined by their gestures, but rarely come to us with full force. We never experience Lacy's world in any but an intellectual way and his devotion to George remains a mystery. Likewise, Susan's descent into insanity seems in excess of what we know even of George's destructive power or their life together.

Indeed all this points to a wider fault of the novel: the culture which Tate depicts can hardly bear the weight of significance he claims for it. One doubts, for instance, that a deeply rooted culture would collapse so easily before the onslaught of alien forces. It might be objected, following my own analysis, that Tate is aware of the frailty of Virginia society and that its rapid demise was the point which he wanted to make. If so, the impact of the novel *qua* novel is lessened to make that point.

It is difficult, for instance, to take seriously the jousting tournaments which were favorite pastimes of the Virginia gentry. When

George Posey violates the rules of behavior expected at the tournaments, we are inclined to sympathize with him and see his breaches as trifles. The context cannot support the moral significance it is asked to illustrate. The fact is that Posey is much nearer our way of taking the world, is so much more familiar, that the chaos which he allegedly produces seems almost unfairly attributed to him. Again, this may be one of the points which Tate hoped to make with *The Fathers,* but in casting his novel in a realistic mode he invites disbelief.

The world Tate evokes also fails fully to engage us because it is so obtuse concerning individual and moral claims. With morality defined in terms of the preservation of traditional roles, there is little room in the world of *The Fathers* for private conscience, no way to challenge any particular or systematic aspect of the civilized society of Virginia. Nor in its ideal apotheosis is there any room for the artist's special angle of vision. Tate has constructed such a stylized society that most of the vitality, and in a certain sense seriousness, has been drained from it.

With all these doubts registered about the way in which *The Fathers* "works," aesthetically and morally, it is still an achievement of a high order. It is the closest any Southern writer of the Renaissance came to embodying the aristocratic *ideal* in convincing form. It also demonstrates that the artistic merit of Southern fiction did not depend upon adherence to modernist aesthetics or enlightened liberal morality.

The Fathers is finally firmly in the tradition of the family romance. Culture and civilization are seen as literally and symbolically *of* the father. Without an actual father—as is the case with George Posey—or the symbolically present culture of the fathers, society collapses into privatized anarchy, and the aberrant becomes the rule. The disruption of the family, most importantly the loss of the father, signals the destruction of an ordered world. Unlike some of the other Agrarians, Tate never blamed the loss of the world of the fathers on the North per se. The fatal flaw was there from the beginning, one which a Southerner such as George Posey could exploit. *The Fathers,* like *Absalom, Absalom!,* achieves the status of dialectic, not rhetoric.

But *The Fathers* presents no resolution of the conflict between past and present. Lacy, like the central consciousness in "Ode," can only evoke the past and turn away. By 1938 when *The Fathers* was published, the Agrarian cause had lost its momentum. The previous year Ransom moved to Kenyon College in Ohio; and in 1945 publicly renounced his Agrarianism. In 1938 Tate moved to Greensboro, North Carolina, to teach and the next year moved on to Princeton. Except for a short period in the mid-1940s when he edited the *Sewanee Review*, Tate was never to live in the South again. Left behind was Davidson, always something of a footman to the cause and increasingly isolated in his recalcitrance. Indeed, in the 1940s Davidson expressed a certain hurt at being abandoned, as his good friend Tate and others went on to positions of literary and academic prestige outside the South.

Perhaps then *The Fathers* was a fitting climax to the Agrarian enterprise. The Southern past had proven much more complex and more divided against itself than Tate or the others had initially thought. Caught between the static image of the Virginia ideal ("I am," he wrote in 1929, "emotionally, a Jeffersonian."),[16] the unchanneled energies of the expansionist lower South; and beyond that yearning for the fully traditional and ordered synthesis of medieval Europe, but never finding quite what he wanted or what was plausible, Tate moved on to other things. The turning away in quiet despair which had ended "Ode to the Confederate Dead" prophesied the ultimate outcome of Tate's search.

From Time to History:
The Lacerated Consciousness of Quentin Compson[17]

Until recently no Faulkner criticism had dealt adequately with Quentin Compson, the single most compelling of Faulkner's characters and the central consciousness in *The Sound and the Fury* and *Absalom, Absalom!*. Some have seen him as representative of the declining Southern aristocracy, driven to suicide by the vicissitudes of modernity and the collapse of the Southern tradition. Other readings stress Quentin's despair at the inhumanity of Thomas Sutpen. There are also those who moralistically accuse

Quentin of immaturity, of a failure to grow up, an approach which easily leads to an indictment of Quentin's parents as somehow inadequate and thus equally responsible for his demise. Still others have seen Quentin as a modern Christ-figure. A more general reading of Quentin's situation emphasizes his obsession with "time" and his attempts to escape its inexorable workings.[18]

Particularly popular of late has been the approach which makes Quentin an agonized Southern liberal, brought to grief not only by Sutpen's inhumanity but also by guilt over slavery and the oppression of blacks. Quentin's dramatic "I don't hate it" which closes *Absalom, Absalom!* thus becomes the classic expression of Southern liberal ambivalence toward the region. By extension Faulkner emerges as a liberal with a tragic sense, American literature's anticipation of Reinhold Niebuhr. Though there is something to be said for this reading of the Quentin texts, it tends to transform Faulkner's great works of the 1930s into elaborate, gothic façades behind which lurks the later Faulkner's tedious humanism of the Nobel Prize acceptance speech. Thus, after initial reactions to Faulkner as a backwoods nihilist and Southern rhetorician, a writer of genius but no talent, a political reactionary, even proto-fascist, he has been thoroughly domesticated and academized. Corncob pipe in hand and dressed rather smartly, he now gazes benignly into the middle distance, in the offices of countless teachers of American literature and Southern history.[19]

Yet one book has appeared recently to challenge these social, moral, and political readings of Faulkner: John Irwin's *Doubling and Incest/Repetition and Revenge*. Irwin's slim book is the best Faulkner criticism we have to date. It combines a close reading of texts with a deftly applied theoretical vision. Irwin's interpretation of Faulkner is informed by a reading of Freud, which in turn bears the mark of the French Freudians, particularly Jacques Lacan, and of the American critic Harold Bloom. Likewise hovering over Irwin's text is Freud's predecessor-contemporary and dark double, Nietzsche. Irwin insists, however, that his book is not "psychoanalytic criticism," by which he distances himself from psychoanalytic characterology and allegorizing. It is far from reductionist; it rather opens up and illuminates complexities.

For Irwin the central question posed by Quentin is "whether a man's father is his fate," a succinct expression of Irwin's more general thesis that what is at issue in Faulkner is "the struggle between the father and the son in the incest complex . . . played out again and again in a series of spatial and temporal repetitions, a series of substitutive doublings and reversals in which generation in time becomes a self-perpetuating cycle of revenge on a substitute."[20] This thematic focus is then elaborated by Irwin in terms of the relationships of shadow and mirror, doubling and incest, male and female, father and son, narrator and listener, repetition and recollection, and activity and passivity.

And yet Irwin's provocative reading of Faulkner and the Quentin "problem" suggests areas of neglect and misreadings of its own. In what follows I would like to examine *The Sound and the Fury, Absalom, Absalom!,* and *Go Down Moses,* using Irwin's analysis but going beyond it to suggest wider implications and different emphases which arise from reading Faulkner via Freud. Specifically, I will be claiming that the family metaphor implicates Faulkner's view of the history of the South as well as his rendition of the family drama; that the incest theme is closely connected with the problem of miscegenation; that both signal Faulkner's meditations on the nature of the cultural order, particularly as it threatens to collapse; and that finally Irwin's pessimistic reading of Freud's notion of repetition distorts his reading of Faulkner.[21] It is in *Go Down Moses* that we find the completion of the Quentin texts in the transformation of repetition into recollection.

As presented in *The Sound and the Fury* and *Absalom, Absalom!* Quentin's world lacks a matrix of meanings to demarcate past from present. Because past and present run together, he has no future. That Quentin lacks a future is reinforced by his sense of spatial entrapment and his lack of a viable location in place or time. We see Quentin in the process of psychic dissolution; he has lost any stable connection with a common reality. His narcissistic condition is reflected in his narrative confusion: he cannot tell his story or say what it is that he desires because he can find no one to whom he can tell it.

Yet Quentin's section in *The Sound and the Fury* presents the first of Faulkner's great transference situations, a proto-analytical free association between son and father.[22] Quentin attempts to tell his father that his essential desire is incest with his sister, Caddy, the relationship that culture does not allow. In *The Sound and the Fury* Quentin is obsessed with time as it is constituted and undermined by family disorders. Ultimately, for Quentin all that which participates in time is tainted and corrupt. His psychological revulsion against the workings of time reflects his revulsion against the social order embodied in the family, and this is underlain by an ontological revulsion against existence itself.

Like Benjy, Quentin has a "problem" with time: Benjy never becomes conscious of time, while Quentin is obsessed with it and wants to cancel it.[23] Where Benjy represents pure desire, unmediated by time, self, or concept, Quentin is desire canceled by the "idea" of time. What he objects to is less Caddy's actual sexual relations with other men than that they point to the fact that Caddy will leave the timeless realm of family relationships and enter the world of society and of change. Thus Quentin rejects Mr. Compson's claim that "It's nature is hurting you not Caddy." (Claude Lévi-Strauss observes that the "sexual is man's only instinct requiring the stimulation of another person.")[24] Sexuality is *au fond* social, and so is Quentin's problem. Mr. Compson comes closer to the truth about Quentin when he observes that "Time is your misfortune."[25] Quentin wants to isolate Caddy, who is the emblem of the pathos of time, "out of the loud world."[26] Thus, though Mr. Compson is presented in *The Sound and the Fury* as a world-weary, cynical alcoholic, he is essentially correct that it is not that Quentin wants to have sex with his sister but that he wants to stop time, a desire of which incest is the symbolic expression.

Quentin's section ends with a despairing exchange between son and father about time. By this point in his life Mr. Compson sees only the futility of human action or emotion. Tragedy is always "second hand," and hope is vanity. Quentin refuses his father's world-weariness by seeking to escape from the meaningless series of moments which makes up time. But behind both figures stands death. "It used to be," thinks Quentin, "I thought of death as a man something like grandfather a friend of his . . . Grandfather was always right."[27] Thus the presiding presence in the Compson family, the grandfather (or a "friend" who becomes Sutpen in *Absalom, Absalom!*), is death. The grandfather's presence in memory signals his absence in actuality. In Quentin's world the only truth is death, that is, time.

Quentin's own psychic instability is mirrored in his vacillation between an abstracted position outside of time and his entrapment within it. Rather than transcending his past he can only inadequately repeat it in the present. As he remembers fighting with one of Caddy's suitors, he wakens to find that he has attacked one of his college acquaintances. The little girl who "shadows" him as he walks near the river in Cambridge duplicates Caddy as the innocent "little sister," not yet subject to the corruptions of time and sexuality. Yet she is also "little sister Death," a reminder to Quentin that she is not Caddy and that his conception of Caddy is dead, destroyed by what he cannot accept.

Where Benjy is always literally himself and therefore not quite human, Quentin's body and his shadow move apart. He insists to Caddy that "You thought it was them [her suitors] but it was me," but he cannot make this literal identification with her suitors either. His claim is as hollow as his attempt to convince his father that he has had incestuous relations with Caddy. But his incest fantasy, his desire to stop time or to repeat it, becomes his reality, a sign of his madness.

Thus Quentin's is a psychotic vision. Having foreclosed reality, he re-establishes it in fantasy as Caddy's lover, a tortured way of replacing her lovers and replacing his father, her natural Oedipal partner. He peoples his world with versions of himself or extensions of himself, since in choosing Caddy he chooses a part of himself, one of his own "blood." He regresses to the stage of primary narcissism and thereby has no "world" except himself. Yet Quentin in his madness represents a higher level of awareness than Bayard Sartoris or Gail Hightower. He demonstrates the impossibility of psychic regression and the cancelation of time. His rememberings are dismemberings.

Aside from this descriptive account of Quentin's world, we

must deal with the question of what incest means in the Quentin texts. This is a question which transcends the question of Faulkner's intentions in *Sound and the Fury* or *Absalom, Absalom!*, for in writing "the author's intention and the meaning of the text cease to coincide."[28] As I have tried to establish so far, the desire for incest and the desire to stop or escape time are closely connected in Faulkner. But this crucial linkage must in turn be located in the context of the Southern family romance and the collapse of the cultural order. Though more fully and explicitly explored in *Absalom, Absalom!, The Sound and the Fury* marks Faulkner's initial presentation of the problem.

First, we must distinguish between the psychological meaning of incest, which varies from culture to culture, and the function of the incest taboo, which is one of the few cultural universals. Though we know of isolated historical instances where the taboo was systematically violated, these exceptions are restricted to certain special segments of the society in question; that is to say, the violation of the taboo is the exception which proves the rule and occurs in a context of adherence to the taboo. This is not to say that the incest prohibition covers the same relationships in all societies or even within the same society at different historical moments. Rather, as Lévi-Strauss has emphasized, there is no society in which there are *not* rules regulating marriage. The incest taboo constitutes (and is) the exogamous imperative, the requirement that one marry outside his own group, however that group may be defined.[29]

The two central discussions of incest came from Lévi-Strauss and from psychoanalytic theory via Freud and Otto Rank.[30] In *Elementary Structures of Kinship*, Lévi-Strauss notes the paradoxical quality of the taboo. Insofar as it is universal in human society, it seems to be natural and lawlike; yet insofar as it is an ordering rule which can be violated, it seems to be a social construct. Lévi-Strauss resolves the paradox by claiming that the incest prohibition is "at once on the threshhold of culture, in culture, and in one sense . . . culture itself."[31] The taboo against marriage among kin, however defined, is that which links and differentiates nature and culture: "It is less a union than a transformation or transition from nature to culture."[32]

Following Lévi-Strauss we can say that the incest taboo signifies that society has certain rights over the individual; indeed, it is the primary means of ordering society and ensuring its survival by linking a unit—the family or clan or whatever—with others through intermarriage. For Lévi-Strauss the incest taboo embodies not only a prohibition but also a positive injunction to move out into the world and into communication with other groups. The reciprocity necessary for individual and group survival originates in the exchange of women; social order triumphs over the randomness of nature. The child, who is the *natural* offspring of parents, becomes the means for establishing *social* alliances which are then perpetuated through biological unions. Thus, to "say" culture (or society) is to imply the incest taboo as constitutive. It is the prototypical cultural imperative. It orders society and thus generates time.

Freud's theory of the "historical" origins of culture and the individual inscription into culture via the Oedipal stage also places the incest taboo at the center of human, that is, cultural, life. The incest taboo is not only the most maiming repression, it is the absolutely necessary one.[33] We are only human in that we are repressed in our most fundamental desire. The son must give up the mother, an abnegation which is matched by the father's (or brother's) exchange of the daughter. No one may marry whom he originally desires.

I have made this brief excursion into anthropological and psychoanalytic theory in order to convey the absolute centrality of the incest taboo in cultural life. It is the primal social repression which the individual must accept, the anchoring prohibition in human history, and that which staves off the threat of regression to animality and forecloses the vain dream of superhuman status. In literature and myth, incest is generally associated with a status outside the human order or, in certain cases, as lying at the borderline between order and chaos. It is the mythological emblem of apocalypse and of "foundings," of the bestial and the superhuman, the disruptive as well as the constitutive. Its occurrence signals destruction and creation.

Seen in this light, Faulkner's *The Sound and the Fury* reveals a human order that is played out; the authority of the father is absent; and thus incest represents, on one level, the desire to be done with the whole thing. Incest is the great repetition which cancels the cultural order. It represents a move back to point zero "out of the loud world" and to the need for a new order which is not yet at hand.

Important here is another observation by Lévi-Strauss: "the incest prohibition is universal like language," and the sociologist and the linguist are concerned with "communication and integration with others."[34] It thus follows that in some societies the violation of the incest taboo is associated with the "misuse of language," since both are unauthorized forms of communication.[35] Clearly, Benjy and Quentin present examples of distorted and twisted discourse in *The Sound and the Fury*. Benjy lacks language altogether; and to address him violates the rules found in certain tribes against speaking to animals as though they were human.[36] His "noises" signify his desire to violate the human order.

Quentin obviously "has" language, but his discourse with others and himself is so distorted and so solipsistic, his thinking so abstract, that he is estranged from common reality. He is Benjy's mirror image, hovering above the human order in a realm of gnostic abstraction. To Quentin the world is "loud," one of the characteristics which Lévi-Strauss notes that some tribes associate with evocations of the violation of the incest taboo. Quentin's individual "problem" which prefigures the distortion in the cultural order is that his talk with his father is not therapeutic. Mr. Compson lacks the ability to clarify and order Quentin's world. Though he is Quentin's biological father and his discourse has a certain plausibility, he lacks the ordering authority which will anchor his words in Quentin's consciousness and structure it. He has neither a traditional nor a new "word" which can clarify memory and turn the desire for repetition into recollection and transcendence.

Though *The Sound and the Fury* does not explicitly thematize the destruction of the Southern tradition, it offers a specific example of a world in disarray as mirrored in the disorder of one Southern family. The power of the tradition as embodied in the grandfather is absent; there is no presiding presence. Thus Quentin's dilemma points toward the theme of Faulkner's last great work "The Bear": the search for a new father to replace the old, absent one. In *The Sound and the Fury* all Quentin can do is to fantasize incest with his sister. If incest, ultimately, is the desire to be one's own father, then his is a vain attempt to be done with the present social and temporal order and to found a new order of which he is the "father."[37]

Absalom, Absalom! continues Quentin's obsession with time, but in *Absalom, Absalom!* the obsession widens into a preoccupation with the Southern past. Quentin's historical consciousness is forced back to the origins of the tradition as he hears from Rosa Coldfield, an old woman (and Thomas Sutpen's sister-in-law), and his father the story of how Thomas Sutpen appeared out of nowhere one day in the 1830s with some twenty-odd slaves. Once in Jefferson, he buys land and proceeds to construct a huge plantation house. Sutpen then sets about finding a wife. By this wife, Ellen, he has two children, Henry and Judith. Later Judith falls in love with Charles Bon, a college classmate of Henry's and Sutpen's son by a previous marriage in Haiti to a woman of mixed blood. The Sutpen story ends with Henry killing Bon and then apparently disappearing. Thus Sutpen is deprived of the male heir to continue the line he has tried to establish. Quentin hears this story in the late summer before he departs for Harvard, where he commits suicide the next spring, the suicide which is at the center of *The Sound and the Fury*.

Absalom, Absalom! is arranged around a series of dialogues in which the recalled past overwhelms the present. The language continually threatens to break out of control; it is alternatingly sullen and hysterical, sober and florid. It is a "prison house."[38] Rosa and Quentin, Mr. Compson and his son, Grandfather Compson and Sutpen, Henry and Bon, Quentin and his college roommate, Shreve, talk feverishly with and at each other. Each is analyst and analysand in a whirl of transferences and identifications. Each tries out his or her interpretation of how and why "it really happened" and attempts to be quits with the past. Each spins out a past world in words which are both "his" and "not his." Each of the narrators in *Absalom, Absalom!* aims to get the story right, but none ever quite succeeds. The talking cure remains enmeshed in the sickness.

Or, perhaps more accurately, Faulkner never quite gets the story right. Though *Absalom, Absalom!* is almost unbearably dense and rich, finally it fails to cohere. There is a lack of fit between Henry's character and his action, between Quentin's agony and what we learn in the book itself. The psychologies of Rosa and Sutpen are generally clear, though even there are lacunae. But the mirroring actions of Henry's shot which kills Bon and Quentin's final outburst ("I don't hate it") seem somehow gratuitous. Something is in control of them (or the author) which makes it impossible to fathom exactly what is going on. Thus, on one level *Absalom, Absalom!* is about the failure to get the story (and history) right. The unresolved conflict at the heart of the novel mirrors the unresolved conflict at the heart of Faulkner's vision of the South and the impossibility of gaining purchase on an unmediated account of the past. There is no way "it really happened."

In *Absalom, Absalom!* Faulkner locates the origins of the Southern tradition in the banally Promethean ambitions of men like Thomas Sutpen. Faulkner seems to be saying that the destruction of the South came not from above the Mason-Dixon line or the rise of Snopsean humanoids, but from the Southern social order and tradition themselves.[39] To be sure Thomas Sutpen is a geographical and social interloper, but then so are all "founding fathers." As told by Rosa and Mr. Compson, his dramatic appearance on the scene takes on heroic (and demonic) proportions, worthy of the mythologizing of the past by Aunt Jenny in *Flags in the Dust*. As Mr. Compson describes the earlier times: "[They were] simpler and therefore, integer for integer, larger, more heroic and the figures therefore more heroic too, not dwarfed and involved but distinct, uncomplex who had the gift of living once or dying once instead of being diffused and scattered creatures drawn blindly limb from limb from a grab bag and assembled, author and victim too of a thousand homicides and a thousand copulations and divorcements."[40] In this passage Quentin's father reveals his nostalgia for the heroic past and a distaste for the

present, yet realizes, like Will Percy, that that past will never return. The heroic past stands in judgment over the present, just as
in an inverted way Rosa Coldfield's rendering of Sutpen is monumental in its demonization. For both Mr. Compson and Rosa,
however, it is not only their angle of vision but a basic lack of
information which prevent them from telling the story correctly.

If *The Sound and the Fury* presents the disorder within one
Southern family, *Absalom, Absalom!* forces Quentin to consider
the violations which attend the founding of the Southern order.
Sutpen is a "founder" and thus in a sense beyond good and evil,
a scandal to the good folk of the county.[41] Faulkner's account of
how Sutpen establishes his realm gives in miniature a picture of
the price paid for the founding of any order, whether traditional
or modern, revolutionary or restorationist.

Indeed there are two "founding" scenes in the novel. First,
there is the graphic image of Sutpen and his twenty-odd slaves
appearing on the scene, a backwoods version of Freud's primal
father with his horde of "sons" and one woman. Sutpen maintains
his domination by regularly engaging the slaves in hand-to-hand
combat, a fight to the death for mastery. In *The Phenomenology
of Spirit* Hegel posits the fight to the death for recognition as constitutive of self-consciousness, human society, and human history.
This, he claims, is not a fight for "mere" survival but for recognition of one's autonomy. The desire to survive characterizes the
animal world, while the desire for recognition marks the human
realm. It is not that Sutpen must fight his slaves to survive biologically or that he could not cow them with guns, but that for
him to remain master, an autonomous being over dependent beings, he must periodically take up this personal struggle. He does
not, however, kill the black slaves he defeats, since he is master
only under the condition of their recognition of his mastery.
Insofar as the master needs the slaves, he is paradoxically their
slave.[42]

In *Absalom, Absalom!* (in contrast with *Go Down Moses*),
blacks rarely take an active role in the story: they never defeat
the master or gain his recognition as equals. This avoidance of
direct confrontation bears on Charles Bon's story, since he never

forces the issue with Sutpen. He remains passive and never demands recognition.

We also learn that these struggles between Sutpen and his
slaves are witnessed by Henry and Judith Sutpen. Henry is the
"weaker" of the two, just as Quentin is weaker than his sister
Caddy. Yet Henry ends up having to kill his black half-brother,
Bon, while Quentin cannot kill his sister's suitors. The scenes in
the barn can also be seen as a homoerotic version of the primal
scene which, Freud claimed, is inevitably interpreted by the child
as a violent struggle. This "homosexual" theme runs throughout
the novel and suggests, among other things, that women in the
patriarchal order of the South played the subsidiary role of passive object, the reward to the victor in the homoerotic contest between black and white males.[43] All this is not to say that Faulkner
was rewriting Hegel or Freud, but it does suggest that the particular world which Faulkner constructed was founded upon a
complex skein of relationships of mastery and servitude.

Besides the master-slave relationship (which covers more
than just black-white relationships), there is another type of
recognition at issue: the Biblical one of the father's recognition
of the son. This relationship establishes the orderly succession of
power and inheritance in the family. Thus the social order is
guaranteed by the continuity of biological generations within the
family. The Oedipal conflict is resolved, and the incest taboo
upheld, by the promise of the father that the son will succeed him
rather than having to overthrow and destroy him. The Biblical-
familial recognition preserves the biological family and the social
order through the recognition of similarity and continuity. But in
the Southern social order the recognition of son by father is made
possible by the refusal of the white master to recognize the black
slave as fully human. What is at issue in *Absalom, Absalom!* and
Go Down, Moses are situations in which the father-son and master-
slave relationships coincide.

This is what Quentin comes to see: the family, the social
order, and the individual are founded upon domination and misrecognition. We learn with him that Sutpen only comes to realize
his social identity and that there is an "objective" structure within

which the individual is located, when he is turned away from the front door of a plantation house as a young boy in Virginia: "something in him had escaped and—he unable to close the eyes of it—looking out from within the balloon face. . . ." Sutpen's fall into self-consciousness, engendered by a lack of recognition from the black house slave who represents the upper-class whites, provides him with his essentially "imaginary" identity.[44]

After realizing that he is invisible to those above him (or their representatives), he returns home to observe his sister at work. He sees her (and himself) for the first time: "the very labor she was doing brutish and stupidly out of all proportion to its reward: the very primary essence of labor, toil, reduced to its crude absolute which only a beast could and would endure." Human history is revealed as the history of the "working slave."[45] This necessity of brute toil defines for Sutpen the difference between the human and the sub-human. To be human is to be recognized by others as master, as not-toiling. To labor anonymously without hope is to be sub-human, a beast: it is to be ultimately "black." By extension, then, the white South transformed a historically arbitrary relationship between black skin and bestial toil into a necessary relationship: social inferiority became biological inferiority.[46]

Sutpen's comprehension of his social status compels him to found a dynasty, his "design," but it does not lead him to seek to change the social order which failed to recognize him. Rather he seeks to join it. The irony of Sutpen's life is that to be recognized as not inferior he systematically denies such recognition to those whom his life touches. He abandons his wife and child (Charles Bon) in Haiti when he discovers that his wife is part-black. He fails to acknowledge his poor white tenant, Wash Jones, as an equal; and this is of course a repetition of what happened to him earlier. Wash's granddaughter, Milly, and Sutpen's sister-in-law, Rosa, are only potential breed-animals to produce a male heir for him. And Sutpen's denial that Bon is his son, his refusal to affirm the reconciliatory relationship of father and son, provides the key to the whole story, at least according to Quentin and Shreve.[47]

It is not that Sutpen is inhumane per se, at least no more so than any number of other slaveholders. Nor are his racial attitudes unusual or even particularly deeply rooted psychologically: Southern white racial consciousness is always about "something else" and needs to be interpreted. Rather his own experience, as situated in that specific historical context, tells him that "black" signifies non-recognition, that is, lack of humanity. To acknowledge his kinship with Bon is to taint his "realm of freedom" with toil and animality. This he spends his whole life refusing to do.

Finally, Sutpen seeks to repudiate his own past. But this is his doom, since what he repudiates returns to destroy him. Quite literally, Bon is the incarnation of Sutpen's past which returns to ruin his "design." This return of the repressed is also seen in the figure of Wash, who slays Sutpen with the scythe, the symbol of time's inexorable ways and the impossibility of denying the ultimate master, time. Sutpen's mistake lies in a misrecognition of time and in an attempt to deny it. This is his innocence.

From Mr. Compson, who tells what he has learned from *his* father, we also learn that Sutpen's attitude toward his own past was one of impersonal detachment, as though in telling his story he were talking of someone else: "he was not talking about himself. He was telling a story." In dissociating himself from his own past, Sutpen remains estranged from himself. It is not that he denies what has happened; instead, it is no longer his. The self he constructs for others has no commerce with the self he is or was for himself. In making others instrumentalities in the service of his "design," he becomes an instrumentality for himself. There is nothing personal in Sutpen's actions.

But if Sutpen's flaw (and the flaw of the entire social order) is a willed innocence of time and a misrecognition of others, Quentin's problem is how to comprehend all this, coming as he does at the end of a tradition which has turned on itself and pushed self-consciousness to the limits. He knows the structured relationships of class, race, sex, and the family which characterize the South, but cannot comprehend or assimilate them. He is born already knowing too much: "His childhood was full of them; his very body was an empty hall echoing with sonorous defeated names; he was not a being, an entity, he was a commonwealth.

He was a barracks filled with stubborn back-looking ghosts." That is, Quentin incorporates a complex mass of relationships which he cannot sort out. He confronts a bewildering variety of ways of remembering: the embittered memories of Rosa Coldfield, the despairing monumentalism of his father; and the dissociated and abstracted memory of Sutpen. Caught up in all of them, Quentin is unable to forge a point of view which will allow him to understand and then tell the story in its full significance.

Unlike Bayard Sartoris or Gail Hightower, Quentin realizes that a literal identification with the past is not only impossible but destructive. He identifies with Sutpen as the powerful and heroic grandfather who founds the tradition, yet he realizes that the tradition is flawed. Its flaw consists in its attempt to defeat time, Quentin's failed project on a much smaller scale. But his inability to mediate between past and present, recollection and repetition, difference and identity, in short, his extra-territorial position to the tradition, shows up in other mirrorings and duplications. The most obvious and central mirroring relationship is the one involving Quentin-Shreve/Henry-Bon, which Faulkner explicitly renders as a kind of *folie à deux* (*quatre*): "Where there was now not two of them but four." Even here, however, the pairs threaten to collapse back into a single figure: "It was Shreve speaking . . . it might have been either of them and was in a sense both: both thinking as one, the voice which happened to be speaking the thought only the thinking become audible, vocal. . . ." Shreve comes to assume the cynical, overripe voice of Mr. Compson as he pieces the story together. The collapse into identity points to the missing word, the absence of the paternal acknowledgment of succession (of similarity not identity) between Sutpen and Bon and implicitly Sutpen and Quentin, which would order the past and the present.

But the novel *Absalom, Absalom!* organizes itself finally around the positions of Sutpen and Quentin. Where Sutpen's historical consciousness refuses to acknowledge its own past, Quentin's is unable to establish difference: he is constantly forced toward psychic identity with the characters in the story. Quentin *is* the story he hears, yet it is not "his" story. Sutpen won't remember; Quentin cannot forget. Sutpen provides the action, while Quentin provides the self-consciousness.

Further, Sutpen's obsessive attempts to escape the "natural" echoes Quentin's own attempt to escape the taint of carnality; thus Quentin's fascination with Sutpen. Quentin's interest may also be engaged by the contemplation of Sutpen's heroic effort, amoral though it is, to define himself, to become his own father. Thus Quentin is not only repulsed by Sutpen; he is attracted by his example and envious of him. In learning who belongs in Sutpen's family, Quentin learns what Sutpen tries to deny by his whole life. Both Sutpen and Quentin remain slaves to the past. Quentin knows this all too well, while Sutpen refuses to recognize it.

Finally, *Absalom, Absalom!* thematizes the complex connections between the twin prohibitions which undergird the Southern family romance: the taboos on incest and miscegenation. They are the fundamental rules, one universal and one culturally specific, which shape the Southern tradition and lie at its center. The incest taboo in positive form provides the exogamous injunction: go outside the family (biological) for a sexual partner and mate (social). To choose incest is to attempt the primal repetition which culture forbids. It is to stop or reverse time, to undo what has been done, to unravel the social fabric, and to regress to the presocial. In *Absalom, Absalom!* incest is not only displaced from parent-child to siblings, but also from hetero- to homosexual relationships. The relationship of Bon and Henry is doubly incestuous: they are brothers and homosexuality is gender incest. It represents a muted hostility to the social order; and more specifically points to the hostility of male for female, the linkage which constitutes the possibility of the social order.

But the historically specific taboo underlying the Southern family romance is the taboo against miscegenation, the inverse of the incest taboo.[48] This taboo provides the injunction to endogamy, the command to marry within one's group, in this case determined by the pseudo-biological categories of the two races, and to shun marriage and the production of illegitimate offspring with those of the other race. The incest taboo forbids the identity relationship based upon repetition, while the prohibition of miscegenation forbids the relationship between the "different." The offspring of incestuous relationships are fancied to be biological enormities; the offspring of miscegenous unions are social outcasts and misfits.[49]

The miscegenation prohibition is the more complex of the two, at least in the context of the Southern family romance. In strict form it forbade sexual contact of any sort between the two races; yet, given the white male prerogative, it was relatively tolerated, even expected. The offspring of such a union were without legitimate social position: they did not take the "name of the father" and were of the mother. As Irwin points out, Bon is his mother's son. A socially sanctioned marriage between the two races threatened the purity of the white order. But the violation of both taboos represents in different ways the collapse back into nature and the destruction of the cultural order: incest via the reunion with the mother or mother surrogate and miscegenation via the union with blacks who signify the sexual, the realm of toil, the childlike, and the animal; in short the (pseudo-)natural. This analysis reveals as well the subterranean identity of women and blacks in the family romance. Both are taken to be hostile to culture as it is patriarchally defined. Sutpen's motives are comprehensible, but the relationship of Bon (black) and Judith (female) remains a mystery and opaque. It cannot be allowed.

At this point we must move back to a psychoanalytic reading to provide the dynamic for the structural reading of the family romance. The attempt—real or imagined—by a black male to usurp the white male prerogative and have a white woman violates both the taboo against incest and that against miscegenation. It is the son fulfilling the Oedipal desire to have the mother and abolish the father (principle) and thus it threatens the perverted patriarchal order of the South. The two taboos come to be identical in the specific historical context.[50]

Obviously, however, the social-cultural order is not individual psychology writ large. Because the family romance was so resolutely patriarchal, the "father" always had freer play in his sexual and social contacts. As long as it was the white male who "condescends," he elevated the black woman to his status, or at least avoided the absolute exclusion which a white woman would suffer or the absolute terror which threatened the black male. Since white women in a patriarchal society were seen as children of sorts, it was customary for the male-female relationship to include a defused component of the parent-child relationship. By extension the white male–black female relationship was drained of some of its incestuous affect. The incestuous affect was also minimized by the demotion of black women to less than human status. Put succinctly, individual psychological make-up comes close to being the social-cultural order writ small.

On this reading, then, *Absalom, Absalom!* is "about" the constitutive rules of the Southern family romance. Linked in the consciousness of one character, Quentin, the violations of these rules become emblems of the disorder at the core of the tradition and at the core of his psyche. It does not make sense for David Levin to claim that "In rejecting his heritage he [Quentin] rejects humanity, rejects himself."[51] Indeed, such a judgment would apply more to Sutpen than to Quentin. Quentin's problem is pre-moral: he can neither accept that the order is gone, nor can he duplicate that order in his present. In some ways both Quentin and Henry remain opaque to us. The context of the novel does not provide any clue as to why Henry would balk at miscegenation rather than incest and shoot Charles, as Quentin and Shreve think. Nor is Quentin's final and dramatic remark about the South "I don't hate it," earned in the context of *Absalom, Absalom!*. Both actions only begin to become comprehensible if we see the world of the novel as one dominated by repetition of roles and actions, a nightmare landscape of inescapable fate.

What we see in *Absalom, Absalom!* is the family romance decomposed into its constitutive opposites. There are no mediating structures, ideas, or individuals. Those figures who are racially "in between"—Charles Bon, his anguished son, Charles Etienne Bon, and Charles Etienne's idiot son, Jim Bond—are ultimately destroyed. Unable to locate themselves in a racial-social order, they internalize the split and are unable to locate themselves. Their social alienation mirrors Quentin's internal split between past and present. Things have fallen apart. The story will not let itself be told; recollection is overpowered by repetition which has become doom.

But not only can the story not be told within the novel. Faulkner himself seems to have run up against some unmastered aspect of his vision of the Southern past. At this point Faulkner had not quite gotten the story right either. As Irwin insightfully notes, Faulkner is a master of the "almost meaningful." We must new turn to *Go Down Moses*, where Faulkner finally makes his and the South's story meaningful.

6

Working Through:
Faulkner's <u>Go Down Moses</u>

Go Down Moses culminates Faulkner's exploration of historical consciousness which began with *Flags in the Dust*. With "The Bear" at its center, *Go Down Moses* represents a near perfect fusion of style, evocation of time and place, and attention to moral context, framed by the complexities of history and the rhythms of nature. All of Faulkner's prior fiction points toward this artistic and moral consummation; that which follows betrays a distinct falling off.[1]

    Go Down Moses is no recollection in tranquility, no equipoised and stylized vision; or at least not that alone. Faulkner sounds the agrarian elegy for a lost world, but never suggests that the Southern tradition is the cynosure of all virtue; nor does he surrender to the melancholy of his down-state neighbor, Will Percy, who died in the same year *Go Down Moses* appeared. *Go Down Moses,* like *The Unvanquished,* begins in a comic spirit and gradually moves to the tragic. The past discovered by Ike McCaslin is marked by violation, and the order he inherits is founded upon the enslavement of blacks and the insatiable exploitation of the land. If "The Bear" in particular seems to sound the Edenic theme so common in American writing, it speaks of a paradise already flawed. Unlike Quentin Compson, Ike McCaslin, the central consciousness of the novel, is not wrenched apart by the antinomy of past and present. By confronting, and working through, the past of his family and his region, he is able to transcend it, though not without cost.[2]

There are definite thematic linkages between *The Sound and the Fury, Absalom, Absalom!*, and *Go Down Moses.* In the first version of what was to become "The Bear," Quentin was the narrator, while Ike appeared as an old man. More important, Faulkner, in *Go Down Moses*, again scrutinizes the family romance, the power of the tradition of the fathers, and the tangled relationship of black and white as mirrored in the phenomena of incest and miscegenation within the structured opposition of nature and history (or culture). If the first two novels present the pathology of Quentin's historical consciousness, in "The Bear" we see Ike, having freed himself from the repetitive patterns of the past, able to make a moral choice.

It is crucial to read *Go Down Moses* as a whole.[3] Such a reading forces us to see that it is the history of the McCaslin family not of any one individual which stands for the history of the South. A genealogical reconstruction reveals that the family is composed of black and white members. Blacks are not only metaphorical children, blacks are literal children in the family—and also uncles and aunts, wives and husbands who exhibit all the strengths and weaknesses of their white kinsmen. In uncovering the origins and then narrating the development of the McCaslin family, Ike deromanticizes the Southern family romance.

The larger point is that Faulkner not only reveals the central place of blacks in the "family" but also, contrary to the conventional white Southern wisdom (and here one thinks of Will Percy), celebrates the endurance of the black family as symbolized in the "Fire in the Hearth." For the story of the McCaslin line revolves around the figures of Ike McCaslin *and* Lucas Beauchamp, the last remaining male descendants of the founder, Carothers McCaslin. In the story of Lucas and his family and in the story of the grief-stricken widower in "Pantaloon in Black," Faulkner renders black life with a careful complexity unmatched in his previous work. Gone are the wily but buffoonish retainers of *Flags in the Dust,* the wooden figures of virtue such as Dilsey in *The Sound and the Fury,* or the desperate mulattoes of *Light in August* or *Absalom, Absalom!.*

We learn of Lucas's raw courage when he confronts his "brother," Zack Edmonds, over whether Lucas's wife should remain with Zack after the latter's wife has died. In this "risk of life" Lucas wins recognition as an equal, as one "who had never once said 'sir' to his [Zack's] white skin"; and thus he refuses the master-slave relationship.[4] (His action does lack any collective, political implication, a problem we will take up later.) Indeed, Lucas rather than Ike inherits—that is, repeats—most of the traits of the family's founding father, Carothers McCaslin: "He's more like old Carothers than all the rest of us put together, including old Carothers. He is both heir and prototype simultaneously of all the geography and climate and biology which sired old Carothers and all the rest of us and our kind . . . nameless now except himself who fathered himself, intact and complete, contemptuous, as old Carothers must have been, of all blood, black white yellow or red, including his own." Thus in the end is the beginning.

But if familial piety is one of the informing values of the novel, it is hard-won and unsentimental. Ultimately, even the traditional form of recognition via the transmission of land from father to son is called into question. The sins of the fathers do weigh heavily on the sons. In "The Bear" we learn that in the 1830s Carothers McCaslin has refused to acknowledge his son by his incestuous union with his slave daughter; and a hundred years later, in "Delta Autumn," Roth Edmonds repeats the failure of his distant relative Carothers when he tries to buy his way out of a marriage to a woman who is distantly related to him and of mixed blood. Incest and miscegenation are the inseparable violations which mark the beginning and the end of the tradition. In "The Bear" their hidden complementarity becomes clear.

As in *Absalom, Absalom!,* Carothers's denial of recognition to his black offspring (except for money he leaves in his will) reveals the master-slave relationship which underlies the father-son relationship in the family. The young Ike McCaslin realizes what

Quentin had only sensed: the father-son relationship participates in the same dominative mode as the master-slave relationship. The Oedipal relationship remains tainted by enmity because the token of succession—the inheritance of land—is an illegitimate gift. The land does not belong to any one; and the fundamental crime is the will to possession: of land, of slaves, of sons. The family romance masks the history of domination which makes up the history of the family and the region.

For Ike, as for Quentin and Lacy Buchan, the central question is: who is my father and what is my tradition? Ike discovers his grandfather's crimes in the family ledgers, but, fortified by the virtues he has learned from his hunting mentor, Sam Fathers, who is an old man, part Indian and part Negro, Ike transforms the repetitive pattern of the family into an object of recollection and transcends the pattern by relinquishing his inheritance. Quentin can never discover the father or the tradition to order his world. Ike's actual father plays little part in his development, but his cousin, Cass Edmonds, who is "more his brother than his cousin and more his father than either," and his Grandfather Carothers play strong roles. But Ike finds in Sam Fathers a spiritual father worthy to impart to him a set of values, by virtue of which he can reject his family tradition.

The pattern of Sam's life is both repeated and reversed in Ike's life. Sam is denied the land which belonged to his father, an Indian chief, while Ike relinquishes his inheritance voluntarily when he discovers the taint on it. Sam's name means "Had Two Fathers," and this anticipates Ike's appropriation of Sam as a second father, the common experience of the mythological hero and a central theme of the family romance. In this new family romance the "colored" father replaces the white one. Further, Sam is forced to identify with the "out" caste, while Ike identifies with it voluntarily. When Ike travels to Arkansas to give a former slave, Phonsiba, the money left to her by Carothers (her grandfather as well), he asks her how she is. Phonsiba replies, "I am free." This in turn is Ike's response to his cousin Cass when Cass tries to argue Ike out of giving up his inheritance. And at one point in *Go Down Moses* Sam Fathers salutes a majestic buck as "grandfather," while at the end of "The Bear" Ike recognizes his complicity in the evil of the tradition by saluting a snake with the same greeting. This scene in which the son symbolically acknowledges the (grand) father is an assertion of a sort of spiritual mastery, a triumph over the father.

And yet Ike never completely escapes the repetitive pattern of his family. In their desire to be free and equal to whites, Phonsiba and her husband seem to be too much in a hurry to Ike. "Then your people's turn will come because we have forfeited ours. But not now. Not yet. Don't you see?," he says. These are the same words he repeats as an old man to Roth Edmond's mistress. Some day black and white will be able to marry—but not yet. The fact that neither Sam nor Ike leaves a male descendant points to the fragility of the countertradition Ike appropriates. Finally Ike's triumph is not so much an absolute separation from this collective past as it is the awareness, brought home to him by Roth's mistress, of how much he remains trapped in it.

Behind, yet caught in the historical world, stands the presiding presence of the bear, Old Ben. Though most readings of "The Bear" see Ben as the symbol of the wilderness that falls before the onslaughts of human progress, he functions much more ambiguously than that in the story. Early on he is described as moving through the wilderness like a locomotive, which later becomes an emblem of man's invasion and destruction of the wilderness. In this sense Ben represents the same kind of amoral force as old Carothers represents. Also the coincidence of the slaying of Ben and Sam's death indicates a kind of identity between the two: both are self-sufficient, haughty, and heedless of the normal world of men. Ike can only relinquish his heritage once Ben and Sam are dead, which reinforces the connection of Ben, Sam, and old Carothers: Ike's relinquishment slays his grandfather as well. This series of events becomes a metaphor for the murder of the primal father, the incorporation of his strength, and the identification with him. Ike's action both frees and maims him.

Thus in *Go Down Moses* the natural and historical worlds do not stand in contradiction so much as they mirror one another. The former has significance only insofar as man penetrates it. Its natural cycles are mirrored by the yearly ritual of the hunt. The nature of the historical tradition only stands revealed in light of the world of the woods and vice versa. To break the repetitious pattern of the tradition another order of repetition must be set over and against it.

Also, only with "The Bear" can we see the other aspect of Quentin's obsession with incest. Quentin's desire is not only for incest with his sister but for love for and from a father who is worthy to give and receive it. He lacks such a figure and must consequently attempt to become his own father. Ike finds his own father in Sam Fathers, but he is rendered heirless. He repudiates his inheritance in order that his son will not live under its curse, yet this abnegation costs him the love of his wife and hence a son. The remainder of his life is lived out in the increasingly meaningless yearly hunts, and he descends into nostalgic garrulousness.

But such a pessimistic reading neglects the power of Ike's emergence into historical self-consciousness. The occasion for Ike's relinquishment is his investigation of the family ledgers, the best example we have in American literature of the moral task of historical consciousness and the most graphic analogue of the psychoanalytic task of transforming repetitions into recollection. In deciphering the scrawled, nearly illegible entries of his semiliterate father and uncle, Ike, like the patient in analysis, learns to interpret the writing, the traces of past desires. Unlike Sutpen or old Carothers, Ike does not deny his past; and unlike Quentin he avoids the merging with those past desires. Ike literally "remembers" a past which belongs to him and his family. Once acknowledged and worked through ("He knew what he was going to find before he found it"), his past is transcended and becomes "other." He is free of it. According to Freud, we are not only our own individual past, but also the sum of our family's past.

Thus for the first time one of Faulkner's "rememberers" can tell his story to someone else. Ike assumes responsibility for his own story because he assumes responsibility for that which has been done in his family's name. It is this clear recognition of the determining force of the past which paradoxically constitutes the possibility for his saying, "I am free." And this possibility is achieved only by his inscription into another tradition. Only by recognizing another father can he acknowledge, yet be free of, his grandfather.

If it is by virtue of Sam's tutelage that Ike can confront his past, it is Cass Edmonds to whom he must tell his story and give his reasons. Cass's counterarguments are persuasive and rationally unimpeachable. He maintains, and Ike grants, that the Southern tradition is not all bad. Indeed, Ike is able in part to relinquish his inheritance because of what he inherits of old Carothers, "taking with him more of that evil and unregenerate old man" than he would like. When Cass reminds him of the weaknesses of blacks, Ike responds that those weaknesses derive from their enslavement and what they learned from the white man. Finally, Cass argues that whatever Ike wishes, he cannot be free: "No, not now or ever, we from them nor they from us." This is undeniable, but not to the point. Ike's only response is, "Sam Fathers set me free," by which he means not free from blacks, but free from the history of injustice.

But Ike's ultimate tragedy is that the virtues which enable him to relinquish his heritage are private virtues. His countertradition is finally a private and not a collective one. Moreover the space of its realization—the woods—has succumbed to the linear destructiveness of man's fabricated world. Indeed, as we have already noted, the principle of destruction was there in the woods all along.

Morality and Politics

The significance of Ike's relinquishment has been subject to much critical dispute. Positive readings of the "Ike stories" generally assume two forms. First, *Go Down Moses*, with particular emphasis on "The Bear," is seen as a modern rendering of archetypal human patterns, most prominent among them being the motif of the "initiation into manhood." Totemic symbols, mythological themes, and anthropological parallels abound; and Ike's story is meant to remind us of our primordial linkage to the natural world. If kept in proper perspective, this type of reading adds richness

to the novel. But it tends to undermine the powerful fourth section of "The Bear" by neglecting the specific historical and regional
themes in the work.

Another prominent approach to "The Bear" takes it as a story
of moral and religious significance in secular garb. R. W. B. Lewis
is eloquent in his claim that Ike's relinquishment is an act of religious atonement in the face of the evil of history.[5] According
to Lewis, Ike attains a sort of sainthood and thus re-acquaints the
secular reader with the Christian notions of suffering, penance,
and redemption. This view tempts one to see Ike as a Christ figure
and his life as a modern version of the passion. But to see Ike's
significance as religious in any but an ironic way is to confuse al-
lusion and analogy with identity, though it must be granted that
Faulkner trades a bit too willingly on Biblical rhetoric and parallels. Lewis avoids this sort of religious imperialism and is uneasy
about the isolation to which Ike's action leads him.

But there is another line of criticism which fails to be impressed by Ike's religious or moral stature. Richard Adams scores
Ike's arguments as illogical and unconvincing, while Herbert Perluck sees Ike's as the "story of a renunciation that fails."[6] In David
Stewart's words, Ike's actions provide him with "little more than
cheap satisfaction." In this view Ike emerges as socially irresponsible and a moral trimmer to boot, since he lives off the income
from the land he claims to relinquish. Indeed, Stewart includes
Faulkner among his accused by claiming that in *Go Down Moses*
Faulkner "induces a condition of paralysis and in this way per-
petuates the status quo."[7] Ironically, Faulkner was not adverse
to criticizing Ike. Though he did grant that Ike's vision gave him
"serenity and wisdom" but "not success," he was also later to say
in criticism of Ike that "what we need are people who will say,
this is bad and I'm going to do something about it, I'm going to
change it."[8] And in the novel itself, Faulkner destroys Ike's wise
old man persona.

A conservative critique of Ike (and Faulkner) would echo
this impatience with Ike's dithering. It would point to Cass Edmonds's enlightened paternalism as the more realistic and wiser
stance for the white Southerner of good will in the late 1880s.

But Cass's opposition is too "wise" by a half, too much the wisdom of Job's accusers. Though Cass is apparently a sensitive man and aware of the needs (or at least some of them) of blacks, like Will Percy he insists on their continued subordination. Like Percy, Cass affirms the authority of the tradition not only for its positive qualities but because it is the tradition.

Still neither of these positions seems persuasive. The radical and liberal critiques of Ike ignore the historical possibilities of a young white man in the Mississippi hill country circa 1890. Indeed, until the 1960s, Mississippi was in James Silver's phrase a "closed society." As late as the 1950s Southern moderates such as Mississippi's Hodding Carter, a man of considerable power and influence, continued to express their firm commitment to segregation and white racial purity and superiority, though all the while granting that glaring injustices existed.[9] In short, it is not all clear what sort of political action was possible for Ike in the context of the late 1880s. What was he supposed to do?

But here it must be granted that if Ike's gesture is a morally significant one (and I would insist that it is), it carries no political implication. The world which Faulkner creates and which Ike and Lucas inhabit offers no space of freedom for political or collective action. Indeed there is something to be said for tracing this to Faulkner's own apolitical nature. Despite his courageous pronouncements in support of the 1954 Supreme Court school desegregation decision, he was a States' Right Democrat insofar as he was a political man at all. To insist that he should have made Ike into a political activist is to misconstrue the possibilities of social change in Mississippi in the 1880s (or 1930s) and to misconstrue Faulkner's essential vision of politics and its importance. Still, flawed though it is by the impossibility of political embodiment, Ike's relinquishment is a form of moral triumph, despite what Francis Utley has called his later "backsliding."[10]

But to say that Ike's failure is ultimately a political failure (though not one for which he can precisely be blamed) is another way of saying that Ike's is a tradition of one. He lacks a way of translating this new mythos into a collective historical tradition to replace that of his grandfather, that is, the South's. Nor does it make any sense at all to say, with Olga Vickery, that Ike "evade[s] both the guilt of his grandfather and his own responsibility,"[11] for he confronts that guilt and responsibility more forthrightly than any of Faulkner's characters and most of Faulkner's contemporaries. Aside from Lillian Smith and W. J. Cash, it would be difficult to find a Southern writer, sociologist, or historian of Faulkner's era who so clearly identified and critiqued the essential foundations of the Southern tradition. But again it was the tragic fact of Faulkner's (and Ike's) world that historical consciousness and refusal to participate in the skein of injustice did not of itself lead to or suggest a way of translating moral gesture into political action. Though the burden of the fathers had been lifted, the shoulders from which it had been taken remained permanently bent. Only for later generations of readers would Ike's achievement be liberating.

The Costs of Creation

According to Harold Bloom, all modern creators want priority, to become the first in the series and hence found a new literary or cultural tradition. The way is blocked, however, by a tradition, embodied in literary precursors, whose very existence testifies to the fact that the individual artist is always already too late. The essential vision has been articulated, and nothing new remains to be done. This, according to Harold Bloom, is the anxiety of influence which diffuses the modernist literary enterprise and modernist culture generally.[12]

In his writings on the artist and creativity, Otto Rank anticipated much of Bloom's thesis when he asserted that the "will to immortality" was fundamental to the psychology of creation. "Liberated from God," the artist "himself becomes God."[13] Behind the artificed world lies the historicist anxiety, the will to originality, which is the complementary impulse to the will to immortality. This imaginary world is designed to withstand the ravages of time. The ultimate desire of the artist is to become his own father, to create himself, and thereby deny his father (Time) and all creative priority. Thus behind the artist's desire for immortality stands the fear of death. It is this fear of death, claims Norman O. Brown, which generates time and ultimately culture; but then paradoxically tries to escape them. This is another way of saying the modernist-romantic project is an impossibility. Art is not a way of escaping or stilling the anxiety but of expressing it.[14]

For Faulkner the confrontation with the Southern tradition, a literal historical entity and a fantasy structure, took the form of a confrontation with and critique of various fictional fathers and grandfathers. The various forms of historical consciousness which I have discussed were at the same time an exploration of the burdens of being a writer. This was expressed most centrally in the dialectic between weak sons and strong fathers in Faulkner's work. By *Go Down Moses* the unequal *agon* is inverted and the son triumphs over the father. But not without cost.

Put another way, in Faulkner's work and that of many of his Southern contemporaries, the desire to escape the looming presence of precursors is counterpointed with the desire to find a new father, a new force of tradition that will provide a way of continuing to live and write. This is a standard theme of much of this century's literature and particularly of some of Faulkner's most talented contemporaries and epigones. In Faulkner's work, however, we see the clearest expression of the interaction of these two impulses. For there we see all the essential "moments" in the movement of Southern historical consciousness in the 1930s and 1940s: from the monumentalist attitude of "O, that we could have it back again" to the despairing, anxiety-laden "We can't have it back again" and the even more tortured "Do we want it back again?" Repetition emerges as impossible and recollection alone remains possible. But this victory barely hides the desire to become one's own father. This is granted to Ike McCaslin, but only on the condition that he not become an actual father. In terms of the artist's project it means that the achievement of his vision comes at the cost of isolation and loneliness, for there can never be anyone to follow who will measure up.

Before pursuing this farther, the question of the mother must be raised: where is she? As we have seen in Percy's *Lanterns on the Levee*, she hardly makes an appearance, and Percy's life seems bereft of feminine presences. Tate's *The Fathers* opens with the death of Lacy Buchan's mother, while Lacy's sister is dangerous and destructive. In Lillian Smith's writings her mother remains opaque, and Carson McCullers's fiction lacks the stabilizing or energizing force of (white) female figures. And, indeed, in Faulkner the mother and women in general seem to move more and more to the periphery as we move from *Flags in the Dust* to "The Bear." When a woman makes an appearance she is the promiscuous sister or neurasthenic mother (*The Sound and the Fury*), the ethereal mother and mindless daughter (in *Absalom, Absalom!*), or the grasping temptress-wife in "The Bear." At best, she stands sexless and Cassandra-like on the fringes, passing judgment on the foolishness of men. But she is never at the center.

In the case of Faulkner, at least, we can make some interesting correlations with Freud, our other great critic of the patriarchal tradition. Both were ensconced in and tried to write their ways out of a patriarchal tradition which seemed powerful yet was on the verge of collapse. In both cases, women were conceived of as somehow impenetrable to masculine reason, both less and more than men, more in touch with the primal rhythms of life but also less "civilized" and thus a danger to the fragile cultural order. In both lives there existed a lifelong attachment to the mother, while the literal fathers appeared, against the mother, as weak and ineffectual.

This makes it all the more strange that for Faulkner, as for Freud, the father loomed so large while women were all but ignored in his writings. In placing the Oedipal situation at the center of individual and cultural life and thus making it the focus of his entire system, Freud underplayed the tremendous pre-Oedipal influence of the mother on the child, a neglect that only his followers have rectified.

Not only was Faulkner's mother a powerful force in his life, the desire for his future wife, Estelle Oldham, obsessed him during the 1920s when she was married to another man.[15] Both Faulkner and his biographer are tight-lipped on this matter, but by Faulkner's own testimony he was in the throes of "difficulties of an intimate nature" when he was writing *The Sound and the Fury;*

and one can safely guess that they had something to do with sexuality.[16] It is important to remember here that the occasioning image of that novel was "a little girl in muddy drawers" up in a tree, looking in the window of the family house at the death-bed of the grandmother. All the essential elements of this vision—the muddy pants, the tree, the witnessing of a forbidden scene, the connection of death with the bedroom—have to do with sexuality and its fatal lure, with the primal scene and the myth of romantic love. And surely Quentin's agonized but futile efforts to drive away Caddy's suitors reflect Faulkner's memories of his despair over Estelle's suitors and the one who finally married her. Sex, death, and women all seem somehow inextricably linked.

Thus we might speculate that neither Freud nor Faulkner did justice to women and in fact could never quite represent them as "complete" human beings because of the tremendous hold they exerted on each man's life and the powerful resentments each man harbored against their power. Their secret muses could never be acknowledged; the theory and the fiction respectively were "only" delays, ways of avoiding saying what they desired. Creation was a trope itself.[17] This was the anxiety of the mother's influence which underlay the more explicit anxieties that came from the ambitions directed against the fathers. Thus we can read the movement from incest to parricide both ways: the incest desire is the desire to destroy the father; the demystification (symbolic parricide) of the father conceals the incest desire. And this is another way of saying that the creative projects of both Faulkner and Freud, late romantics that they were, were finally unresolvable.

But most interesting, to return to the theme of the creator, is that in the life and work of Faulkner and Freud there was a continual juxtaposition of and vacillation between weak and strong, son and father. Freud, for instance, liked to think of himself as a "conquistador" and identified himself with or greatly admired Hannibal, Cromwell, Napoleon, and Moses. As the founder of a movement he insisted upon loyalty, felt nothing but bitterness and betrayal against those who went astray, and refused to acknowledge them once the break had been made. Yet Freud's theoretical and therapeutic focus was upon the weak and damaged sons and daughters who could not dispel actual or fantasized parental power. In the several fainting spells he experienced when confronted by what he read as signs of disloyalty from his "son," Jung, he displayed a deep fear of being overthrown and hence a vulnerability as a father. Nor is it accidental that the "story" of the murder of the primal father by the sons came in *Totem and Taboo* (1913), not long after his break with Jung. As the primal father of the psychoanalytic movement Freud could scarcely tolerate what he feared: the inevitability of a repetition of the revolutionary impulse at the origins of culture. It is no wonder that he was so taken with the notion that the Jews had slain their deliverer, Moses. To be a father was to be vulnerable and inevitably surpassed.

Though Faulkner was anything but the founder of a movement and remained as far as possible from organizational commitments, there is an analogous ambivalence in his fictional world. He was obviously fascinated with the fathers who were ruthless, cruel, and had founded an order—Sartoris, Sutpen, and Carothers McCaslin. As founders they assumed a certain amoral heroism and were beyond good and evil in any conventional sense. They were demiurges. But then so was the strong artist. Here we should remember that Faulkner labeled the map of Yoknapatawpha County as his: "William Faulkner, Sole Proprietor." This was an appropriately Sutpenian gesture and attached to *Absalom, Absalom!*, though undoubtedly with a hint of irony. At one point in 1939 he blurted out in a letter that "I am the best in America, by god."[18] A certain ruthlessness was revealed in his comment that "If a writer has to rob his mother, he will not hesitate; the 'Ode on a Grecian Urn' is worth any number of little old ladies." (Sutpen apparently felt the same way.) In addition, Faulkner sometimes expressed a feeling of profound detachment from ordinary concerns. For instance, he once said that he would like to be reborn as a buzzard: "nothing hates him or envies him or wants him or needs him."[19] And yet—all of these strong, commanding figures come to grief in acts of hubris which deny the humanity of others and exhibit a heedlessness of the reality: they cannot or do not take time into account. As with Freud this is the anxiety of the strong who know that strength will fade or be subject to challenge.

On the other hand there are the weak figures, the maimed sons rendered ineffectual by powerful fathers and grandfathers. They seem to stand for the other aspect of the artist's persona. In *The Unvanquished* the narrator writes that "those who can, do, those who cannot and suffer enough because they can't, write about it." Later Faulkner was to write to Malcolm Cowley of his passionate desire for anonymity, revulsion against his own existence: "It is my ambition to be, as a private individual, abolished and voided from history, leaving it markless, no refuse save the printed page . . . obituary and epitaph . . . : He made the books and he died."[20] The artist's act of creation was so presumptuous that, whatever hostile end he met, he should expunge himself from memory, leaving only the traces of his existence. Yet these marks of creation, the printed words, were also attempts to stop time which Faulkner saw as the artist's essential task. This was what lay behind his famous statement that he had tried "to get it all in one sentence."[21] If, as Richard Adams asserts (though too abstractly), Faulkner's central theme is the destructive effects of the attempt to stop time, this means that we must see Faulkner's characters who try to overcome time, whether weak or strong, as variations on the portrait of the artist.

This brings us to *Go Down Moses* with its two "sons"—Ike and Lucas. Lucas is a lineal heir of the Sartoris-Sutpen-McCaslin role. Like these precursors he is detached, amoral and indifferent to anything but what he chooses to take as his concern. Like Faulkner himself, Lucas changes his name as though to assert his uniqueness and make himself one of a type. In the latter stories, especially "The Bear," Sam Fathers and even Old Ben embody this same attitude. They are creatures utterly independent and self-sufficient who scorn normal human intercourse. Yet ultimately Faulkner seems less interested in this aspect of the artist than he is in the one represented by Ike, who is clearly a descendant of Quentin and even Gail Hightower and young Bayard Sartoris. Unlike them, however, he can endure the vision he possesses and can act, which is to say he can "say" it and by extension "write" it. With *Go Down Moses* Faulkner finally was able to tell the story he wanted to, or come close to it. For behind it had lain the task of forging "the conscience of his race." And conscience here should be taken to refer both to a new structure of moral perception and to self-consciousness. With this done, Faulkner's great moral and artistic task was essentially complete.

That Ike fails to become the founder himself and to pass on this moral (or aesthetic) vision to anyone else implies, finally, the impossibility of founding any tradition upon art. As with Ike, the artist's epiphanic experience and accompanying vision remain private or at least not compelling for the collectivity. They lack the authorizing power of the great religious visions, toward which Ike—and Faulkner especially later in *A Fable*—strain. Neither Ben (the cultural totem) nor Sam (the mentor) who presides over the moral and artistic "scene of instruction" survives except in the consciousness of one individual. The slaying of the fathers and the undermining of the tradition is finally a negative action. Like Freud's resolutely secular vision or Jung's quasi-religious one, Ike's can provide no basis for a new culture of communal symbolic significance. This is perhaps what Faulkner realized when he denied to Ike any offspring to perpetuate "his" tradition.

Finally, perhaps Faulkner was rendering in fictional form the artistic triumph and impasse, the personal achievement and frustration which he had reached by the early 1940s. Like Ike he was without a son, though he influenced many indirectly through his writing without assuaging his essential loneliness: "a widower now and uncle to half a county and father to no one." Isolated from his community, though he loved it deeply, and caught in a marriage which was anything but sustaining, he had become the old man he already felt himself to be when he wrote how he felt "on the verge of decrepitude" in 1929 at the beginning of his great design. Such were the costs of creation.

7

Narcissus Grown Analytical: Cash's Southern Mind

W. J. Cash's *The Mind of the South* is a quintessential expression of the regional self-scrutiny which marked the Southern Renaissance.[1] Published nearly four decades ago, the staying power of Cash's book gives it a rare place in American historical writing. Whatever its inadequacies on particular topics and whatever the vulnerabilities of its general thesis, *The Mind of the South* is one of those unusual works which improves with rereading. It is exciting and audacious and still compels even when it cannot persuade.

Cash's book has not been without its detractors. C. Vann Woodward has suggested, in an uncharacteristically caustic essay, that *The Mind of the South* for all its appealing qualities is wrong in its main contention and that it has hindered as much as aided an understanding of Southern history and culture. In his *The World the Slaveholders Made*, Eugene Genovese has made Cash responsible for the now unfashionable notion that the ante-bellum (white) South was plagued by guilt over slavery. The urgency of both attacks on Cash attests to the passionate reactions which *The Mind of the South* continues to elicit.[2]

How then explain the staying power of Cash's book? Part of

the reason lies in its skillful deployment of rhetoric. Behind the compelling narrative of *The Mind of the South* stands Cash's urgent attempt to make sense of the region's past, to come to terms with the Southern tradition and either to wrest from it what it still offered or be done with it once and for all. Thus, along with Faulkner and the Agrarians, Cash evokes the image of a man or a group of men furiously evaluating the Southern tradition of the fathers in search of a new pattern of significance: the Fugitive-Agrarians at Nashville; Quentin Compson and Shreve at Harvard; Ike McCaslin agonizing over the family ledgers; and finally Jack Cash, from his college years at Wake Forest on into the 1930s, always and endlessly bending someone's ear about the South and his work in progress. With these fictional and actual characters, and with Lillian Smith and Will Percy as well, it is the dialogue with the tradition, with others about the tradition, and with the self that makes them typically Southern and rather atypically American.

A reading of *The Mind of the South* quickly reveals the story-telling act at its core. Certainly not lacking art's hyperbole or healthy doses of sardonic exaggeration, Cash's book has drawn a charge from Woodward that he (Cash) was guilty of historical impiety and "Menckenian buffoonery." An examination of Cash's initial "The Mind of the South" essay in *American Mercury* in 1929 supports Woodward's charge. There Cash refers to poor whites as "peons," "peasants," and "lint heads," while blacks are occasionally called "coons" and "niggers."[3] The final product shows, however, that Cash not only freed himself from Southern romanticism and sentimentality, but that he also transcended the crude witticisms of his Mencken period. At best Cash gained from Mencken a heightened sensitivity to cant, a quality which Southern culture has traditionally lacked, and a propensity for phrase-making that went quite well with Cash's already fertile imagination and sometimes florid style.

Indeed, Cash's rhetorical range lifts *The Mind of the South* beyond a smart-aleck, sarcastic jape at the regional fathers. Unlike the conventional historian or sociologist, Cash continually intrudes by addressing the reader directly as "you" and refers to himself as "I," rather than hiding behind the scholarly "one." The sense of being addressed directly, of being compelled to listen, is heightened by Cash's habit of qualifying a point by his "but perhaps I labor the case" or "but let me take care not to exaggerate." His diction combines the colloquial ("busthead," "pone," "cracker," "hell of a fellow"), the arch allusions of the self-taught intellectual ("proto-Dorian," "more Tartarian than Tartuffe") with a veritable genius for the memorable label or phrase ("savage ideal," the "great Southern heart").

Moreover Cash is a master of concision. His short sketch of the rise of a yeoman to status and wealth (the model for this imaginary figure was Cash's great-great-grandfather) unites the broad generalization about the ante-bellum South with the cogent detail. And who could match Cash's amused scorn for Southern absurdities or his exuberant puncturing of Southern pretensions? Consider, for example, Cash's discussion of the construction of "skyscrapers" in the South around the turn of the century:

> What . . . if I told you they [skyscrapers] were going up in towns . . . which had little more use for them than a hog has for a morning coat . . . Softly do you not hear behind that the gallop of Jeb Stuart's cavalrymen? Do you not recognize it for the native gesture of an incurably romantic people, enamored before all else of the magnificent and the spectacular?

Besides the satirical thrust and the mock apostrophizing, Cash skillfully juxtaposes urban and the rural and links the New South gospel of commercial progress with Confederate derring-do. The comparisons are not merely rhetorical, however, since they unite separate historical contexts—1900 and 1865, urban and rural— and thereby clarify Cash's thesis on the essential continuity of the Southern mind.

One thinks also of Cash's marvelous evocation of the fickle Southern weather, its sullen languors and then sudden explosions into lightning and storms, mirroring and even shaping the Southern cast of mind. But all this is atmospherics and ornamentation compared with Cash's remarkable use of interior monologue in which he assumes the persona of the slave-owner or businessman or poor white. The following example concerns the Southern planter, fallen on hard times during Reconstruction, contemplating the fate of his poor white compatriots. Cash begins analytically, speaking as the omniscient narrator:

> They despised them now, as a rule, with an even greater doctrinal contempt than they had felt for them in the old days when they could not achieve rich lands and Negroes. Yet . . .

And then Cash moves *into* the psyche of the planter:

> . . . here they were, willy-nilly. Under our planter eyes. Men we have known all our days, laughed with, hunted with, and, in many a case, fought side by side with. Human. White. With white women and white children . . . Give them special advantages? We shall do nothing of the kind . . . We shall curse them roundly for no-count trifling incompetents who richly deserve to starve —always in our peculiar manner, which draws the sting of what we say. But look after them we must and will.

Thus, through modulation of style and tone, by detachment and then identification, Cash takes us into the mind of the upper-class Southerner. He presents the planter as sympathetically as possible, yet subtly underscores his limited social vision and all-pervasive racial consciousness. One would be hard put to find in the writings of the Agrarians or Will Percy (not to mention Mencken) so skill-fully rendered a feeling for the ideal of *noblesse oblige* under duress. All this from a writer Woodward accused of presenting only the "hillbilly" South.

Thus at his best, and that was quite often in *The Mind of the South,* Cash fuses the Southern capacity for rhetorical extrava-gance with the less typical capacity for satire and irony. The re-sult is a masterpiece of discursive prose, stylistically one of the most sophisticated works in American historiography.

But it is not merely Cash's literary sophistication and his un-common ability to write well, which explains the power of his book. In a decade of intense national and regional self-scrutiny, the South was overrun with sociologists, historians, journalists, film-makers, and photographers seeking to capture the essence of the place before it changed out of all recognition. What distinguished Cash's book from the common run was his root-and-branch analysis of Southern culture, one which was uncompromising in its insistence on discarding received wisdoms. Unlike, for instance, Virginius Dabney in his *Liberalism in the South* (1931), Cash scarcely mentioned Jefferson or the Jeffersonian tradition, which was rather unusual, since Southern liberals had traditionally repaired to the high ground of Monticello when in trouble. Cash implicitly recognized that Jefferson's real influence was rather minimal in the South of the Depression. Jefferson had become the champion of states' rights conservatives and the bulwark of timid moderation. He was, in short, of little genuine relevance.

Nor did Cash have much use for the effort to discover a vital, dissenting tradition in Southern history. Thus he avoided the special pleading of moderates such as Alabama journalist, John Temple Graves, or later the Mississippian, Hodding Carter, men who were always offering excuses for their all-too-small victories and their all-too-frequent defeats. Men such as these tried to perpetuate a tradition of Southern moderation founded upon such *soi-disant* Southern gentry virtues as civility. Cash certainly did not ignore the quiet graciousness which had marked the South at its best, but he gave himself (or his readers) few illusions that such qualities were still viable or could outweigh less attractive Southern characteristics.

In truth, men such as Graves, Carter, or Ralph McGill, editor of the Atlanta *Constitution,* reminded one of no one so much as they did of Faulkner's Gavin Stevens, the garrulous graduate of Harvard Law School who figures in Faulkner's later fiction. They were men of considerable intelligence, decency, and often courage, a credit to any region or community. And yet they were quite traditional Southerners finally, unwilling to cut loose from the strong constraints of their ethos. Perhaps it was their positions as newspaper editors, as partial "insiders," which held them back. They had to stay "in touch" and couldn't get too far ahead of their constituencies. Like Clarence Cason in *90° in the Shade*

(1935) they held that lynching for example, was an aberration, somehow not central to the Southern experience. This being so, they, like Gavin Stevens, felt that the South they represented could solve the region's problems without outside interference. "Just give us time; don't rush us" was their constant plea.[4] Cash knew better. As he noted near the end of *The Mind of the South*, though the masses made up the lynch mobs, the upper classes allowed them to perpetuate such horrors and were ultimately responsible. If anything was clear, as he noted in his review of Will Percy's autobiography, the course of Southern history was marked by the failure of the "better sort."[5]

But it was above all the lack of moral indignation which so compromised much of the efforts of Southern sociologists, historians, and journalists in the 1930s; and it was the presence of a profound moral (not moralistic) dimension in *The Mind of the South* which lent Cash's efforts a certain heroic quality. A reading of Jonathan Daniels's *A Southerner Discovers the South* (1938) brings this matter home.[6] Daniels's account of his travels throughout the South was thoroughly engrossing. Like Cash, Daniels stressed Southern distinctiveness and the often intimate links between black and white. He also ended his book with the cogent observation, later echoed by Cash, that the South had been failed above all by its self-appointed leaders.

Yet Daniels's work was all too anecdotal and lacked a compelling vision. For all his sensitivity to detail he could not quite bring himself to judge directly and harshly. He paid a visit to Will Percy, as so many others did, and observed that he "loved Negroes as another gentleman might love dogs." After noting the statue Percy had erected over his father's grave—"a marble figure of a knight in full armor"—Daniels wrote that Percy had "gone the way of other gentlemen out of action into intellectuality." Then, in the black belt, Daniels heard grisly stories of exploitation and murder of blacks. And yet he could never quite bring himself to believe the worst; he always opted for the judicious middle, rarely allowing himself sarcasm, much less outrage. Again, it is this spurious "even-handedness," aside from all other factors, which makes Daniels or Cason inferior to Cash.

It is also important to see Cash in relation to his contemporaries—the Agrarians, Faulkner, and the Chapel Hill Regionalists. Though Cash had little use for the Agrarians' monumental reading of the Southern tradition, he applauded their deflation of the ideology of progress and industrial development. He also approved the impulse of the Agrarians (at least some of them) to emphasize the central role of the yeoman in Southern history.

From their side, Agrarian Donald Davidson provided one of the few hostile reviews of *The Mind of the South*.[7] He scored the book for its lack of documentation, a criticism of some limited validity, but was far off the mark in claiming that Cash consistently underplayed the tradition of the small farmer. Davidson also took umbrage at Cash's "Menckenesque" tendencies, his hostility to religion, and his comparisons of the Southern mind to Fascism, Nazism, and Stalinism. Finally he criticized Cash for implying that blacks should be incorporated fully into Southern society. More generally, while granting that the book was "brilliantly executed," Davidson claimed that Cash had allegorized the Southern mind and then blamed it for real shortcomings: in short, all too often Cash "omits the history." What particularly irritated Cash was Davidson's claim, half in jest, that "Mr. Cash wrote that-there book for Yankees anyway."

Interestingly, Cash's analysis of the Southern tradition rather closely resembled Allen Tate's. Like Cash, Tate considered the essential weakness of the ante-bellum South to be a failure of intelligence and mind, an inability to escape received political and religious notions. Though Cash had little sympathy with Tate's vision of what might have been, their analyses were remarkably similar, a fact which Tate implicitly acknowledged in his essay of the late 1950s when he cited Cash to advance his own argument.

Cash was of two minds on Faulkner. As Cash's biographer, Joseph Morrison, indicates, Cash appreciated Faulkner's tremendous achievement but was troubled by his lack of social analysis. Like Lillian Smith and Paula Snelling, Cash was uncomfortable with the image of the South—the gothic pathology and florid decadence—which outsiders seemed to glean from Faulkner as the whole truth about the region. Thus Cash failed to read Faulkner whole and preferred fellow North Carolinian Thomas Wolfe. Actually *The Mind of the South* can be read as a gloss on much of Faulkner's work. Cash's discussion of the decline of Southern aristocracy after Reconstruction illuminates the history of the Compson and Sartoris families and the ethos from which Faulkner and Percy drew their sources. Writes Cash in near Faulknerian diction:

> Decay, as it came to them, came rather obliquely than directly; came, for long at least, and ironically, not so much through any even partial surrender to the demands made upon them as through the inevitable consequences of their failure and their refusal to surrender.

Further, Cash's central thesis about the frontier South and the lack of an authentic aristocracy in the old ante-bellum South echoes the Sutpen saga and the story of the founding of the McCaslin line. Partaking in as well as transcending the Southern ethos, *The Mind of the South* and "The Bear" represent the climax of a decade of memory seeking to come to terms with an otiose culture.

Consider Cash's relation, as well, to the Chapel Hill Regionalists under the leadership of Howard W. Odum, to whom Cash owed a profound substantive and conceptual debt. From Vance and Odum, Cash undoubtedly took the importance of the frontier and the elevation of the yeoman over the planter as the key figure in Southern history. Cash, along with Arthur Raper and Ira DeA. Reid in *Sharecroppers All* (1941), attributed the South's problems to its intense individualism, growing out of the frontier experience, and saw the need to devise new political and social strategies now that the frontier had disappeared.

Like the Regionalists, Cash focused on the social and economic background of the region; and like them he was scarcely tempted by Marxism or socialism. Yet, as we have noted, Odum and Vance were reluctant to stress the clearly exploitative aspects of the South or to say plainly what that relationship between the masses and classes had been. For Odum and Vance it sufficed to speak of the South's position as a colonial economy in general, a notion, which, though Cash alluded to it, failed to catch his fancy. Perhaps it seemed too much like special pleading, a way of blaming the Yankees for what properly was the South's responsibility.

Another similarity was the essential role which intelligence was to play in the future course of the South. Odum, over and over again in *Southern Regions*, stressed the importance of seeing "reality" clearly and acting upon that perception to change the South. "History," wrote Vance in his *Human Geography*, "not geography, made the Solid South."[8] In essence, Cash and the Regionalists sought to transcend the Southern tradition and to remake the South into a "rationally" coherent region. But the Regionalists were more optimistic than Cash.

This is not to say that Cash agreed in all particulars with Odum and Vance. He was generally more daring than they were; and he should be placed with the more radical of the Regionalists —Broadus Mitchell, Raper and Reid, Nixon and Woodward. Cash was less programmatically concerned than Odum, who seemed always to have an eye on the palatability of his analysis and proposals and thus avoided the pungent statement or the memorable phrase. His difficult and ponderous "Odumese," one suspects, was not all literary tone-deafness; rather, it cushioned, indeed at times substantially obscured, rather daring proposals. The "dual load of dichotomous education" might slip by the unwary or be softer in impact than the "burden of segregated schooling."[9]

Further, for purposes of analysis and planning, Odum wanted to divide the historical South into the Southeast and Southwest, thereby conceptually breaking the hold of the solid (historical) South. Cash focused on the unity and continuity of the Southern experience. Where Odum stressed the South as an integral part of the nation, Cash emphasized Southern distinctiveness. Where Odum saw Southern culture as immature rather than exhausted, Cash's notion of the savage ideal pointed to a repressive and ultimately obsolete cultural system. There were not two cultures, one retrogressive and one progressive, for him. Cash stressed the disastrous economic and social effect which white oppression had produced, where Odum tended to keep silent or to muffle any straightforward discussion of this issue.

But what of Cash himself? Near the end of *The Mind of the South* Cash describes the new Southern novelists such as Faulkner, Wolfe, and Caldwell and their feelings about the South:

> They hated it [the South] with the exasperated hate of a lover who cannot persuade the object of his affections to his desire. Or, perhaps, more accurately, as Narcissus, growing at length analytical might have suddenly begun to hate his image reflected in the pool.

The metaphorical references are significant. First, in identifying the South with a woman, Cash drives home his general point that the white woman had been closely identified in the Southern mind with the region as a whole. But the identification of the South with the Narcissian mirror image of the self takes on an even wider resonance. It recalls the solipsistic vision of Tate's "Ode," yet stresses the unwillingness, rather than the inability, to establish the identity of present and past. It also harkens back to Benjy's narcissistic existence in *The Sound and the Fury* and Quentin's death by drowning, but only to suggest a move beyond such a self-destructive vision. Narcissus as a seeker of engulfing identifications and Narcissus as a self-enclosed being demarcate the field of consciousness which Cash attempted to, and did, escape.

Further, both metaphors are organized by a figure who moves from attachment to alienation and thereby achieves a clearer vision of reality. As in all such motions of the heart the newly felt hate bespeaks the recently abandoned love; or, vice versa, as Quentin Compson showed in *Absalom, Absalom!*. In thus describing the new strain of self-consciousness among Southern writers of the 1930s, Cash recorded a similar transformation of his own feelings toward the region. For no one so much as Cash was the "exasperated lover," the "Narcissus" grown "analytical."

Joseph Morrison notes that until Cash went to college he was intensely sentimental about the South, devoted to the fundamentalist faith of his parents, and thoroughly committed to white supremacy. Indeed, as an adolescent he went so far as to refuse a Negro a seat beside him on the train. His favorite book was Thomas Dixon's *The Clansman*, from which the film *The Birth of a Nation* was made. Memory may have exaggerated his early commitment to the cult of Southern nostalgia, but he was later to write of his youthful enthusiasm in terms remarkably anticipatory of Faulkner in *Intruder in the Dust:*

> All of us learned to read on "The Three Little Confed-
> erates," all of us framed our hero-ideal on Stuart and
> Pickett and Forrest—on the dragoon and the lancer—ten
> thousand times, in our dreams, rammed home the flag in
> the cannon's mouth after the manner of the heroes of the
> Reverend Tom Dixon, ten thousand times stepped into
> the breach at the critical moment on that reeking slope at
> Gettysburg, and with our tremendous swords, and in de-
> fiance of chronology, then and there won the Civil War.[10]

Thus, when Cash later wrote of the sentimental romanticism, the legacy of white supremacy, the narrow and harsh religiosity, and the sectional chauvinism of the South, he spoke not only as a native but as a former believer.

Though Cash hoped eventually to write a novel, his life's work was *The Mind of the South.* Writing it was a long and arduous process. For long stretches at a time he failed to get anything down on paper. A moody and pessimistic man, Cash lived with his parents in the early 1930s and was the object of mockery and gossip as a ne'er-do-well and leech on his parents' meager resources. But by 1936 Cash came out of his funk, sent what were to be the first 160 pages of his book to Alfred Knopf, and took a position on the Charlotte *News.* According to Morrison, Cash's writing block could be traced in part back to his fear of offending his parents, since what he saw as so distressing in the Southern heritage constituted the very marrow of their lives. That Cash "worked through" this block suggests that the act of writing *The Mind of the South* was both the occasion for the emergence of Cash's Oedipal problems and a way of coming to terms with them. It was a form of therapy; if not a cure, at least an articulation of inner conflicts, which seemed marvelously successful—until his suicide in Mexico in 1941.

Of Cash's suicide there can be no definitive account. Morrison constructs a plausible case for "acute brain syndrome," an organic deterioration of the brain due to toxic agents, which manifests itself in paranoic delusions and auditory hallucinations. Suicide is often the result. I say "plausible" since Morrison is more convincing in clearing away the legends which grew around Cash's untimely death (especially that he was deeply wounded by the book's harsh reception; he wasn't because it wasn't) than he is in making his own case.

Indeed, Morrison too easily caricatures psychological explanations. Though Cash's recent marriage in late 1940 seems to have been a happy one (and it had laid to rest his fears of sexual impotence), Cash began to drink hard liquor more heavily after his marriage, a self-destructive course for a man notorious for not being able to handle alcohol. Perhaps like many writers, Faulkner being a case in point, post-publication depression was inevitable. Shortly after finishing *The Mind of the South* he visited Lillian Smith and spoke to her of being "drained and emptied." The train trip through the South to the University of Texas, where he gave the commencement address in 1941, was exhausting. Nor were matters helped, as Morrison notes, by the necessary adjustments to food, climate, and altitude in Mexico City.

The beginning of the end came with hallucinations that Nazi agents were plotting his death. But by the late 1930s whenever he drank too much, his "wholly rational fear of Hitler's evil intentions became . . . a mortal fear of Hitler the man." And once Hitler had begun his sweep through Europe, Cash would harangue colleagues at the *News* with a "violent and arm-waving oration of the menace to the United States of Hitlerism, which often resolved itself into the menace that Adolph Hitler personally posed to Cash." Thus the contents of Cash's paranoid delusions in Mexico were of a piece with past obsessions. They did not suddenly appear after physical debilitation in Mexico. Indeed, Cash makes the parallels between the Nazi mentality and the Southern mentality quite clear in the latter parts of his book.

None of this is to suggest an exclusively psychological etiology of Cash's psychosis and suicide. It does, however, suggest the complex and tangled psyche from which *The Mind of the South* grew. As A. Alvarez has written in connection with Sylvia Plath:

> . . . for the artist himself, art is not necessarily thera-
> peutic; he is not automatically relieved of his fantasies by
> expressing them. Instead by some perverse logic of cre-
> ation, the act of formal expression may simply make the
> dredged-up material more readily available to him. The
> result of handling it in his work may well be that he finds
> himself living it out.[11]

Catharses, if they come, come to the reader not the writer. Creation does not so much resolve conflicts as express them.

Approach

But what did Cash mean by "mind"? He referred, of course,
not to rational capability or intellectual expression but to a "fairly
definite mental pattern, associated with a fairly definite social
pattern—a complex of established relationships and habits of
thought, sentiments, prejudices, standards and values, and associations of ideas, which, if it is not common strictly to every group
of white people in the South, is still common in one appreciable
measure or another. . . ." In short, mind or perhaps better
"spirit" (*Geist*) was inseparable from social context. Further, Cash
was concerned with the white mind of the South and not black
modes of thought and feeling.

If Cash's figure of the "Man at the Center" is an essentially
literary device, taken from Odum's *American Epoch* (as Morrison claims), then Cash's "mind" is a Weberian ideal type. In this
limited sense Davidson was right in claiming that Cash's book
avoided "history." But the question to ask of an ideal type, one
which critics of Cash would do well to remember, is not whether
it is testable, but whether it illuminates the facts and makes sense
of them. It is an interpretive not explanatory concept. This is not
to say that Cash omitted assessment of causal forces; but his focus
was on how the Southern "mind" made sense of reality. As Cash
commented to Howard Odum: "My fictions will serve for the
getting at of at least part of the truth and that is the part that is
being pretty generally ignored." In sum, "mind" is a metahistorical
device.

It is also important to stress that any work which posits a collective mind will of necessity tend to be monolithic and stress continuity rather than discontinuity. Thus to claim that Cash should have emphasized conflict is to ask him to write a book other than the one he wrote. On the other hand, at no point did Cash maintain that the Southern mind was immutable or that it was racially grounded. It was theoretically possible, and historically evident to Cash, that typical Southern traits could change; and indeed that they were changing. But still he felt that the Southern past could best be seen in terms of unity and continuity.[12]

To an amazing degree, Cash's "mind" is almost pure "primary process." It is an impulsive force, operating according to the dictates of fantasy not reality: sensuality, concreteness, hedonism, aggression, and violence are its salient characteristics. It is also regressive and repetitive, heedless of the passage of time and forever trying to reconstitute former conditions. The Southern mind could only "feel" and not "think."

Indeed, Cash makes much use of quasi-psychoanalytic terminology and provides a veritable compendium of collective defense mechanisms. He sees the legend of the Old South as a "defense mechanism" to justify Southern treatment of blacks and to counter Northern claims to superiority. In noting the way in which the common whites identified with the planters, he describes what psychoanalysts refer to as "identification with the aggressor" and also anticipates Erich Fromm's essential thesis in *Escape from Freedom*. White Southern racial fears are clearly examples of projection, at least on one level; and the sexualization of black women and the desexualization of white women exemplify the mechanisms of splitting and overestimation. All of these unconscious ego defenses serve to foreclose a steady and accurate assessment of reality.

In claiming that the South had been unable to face "reality," Cash also implied that the South was caught up by a collective fantasy. One of the accepted truths about the Southern mind is that Southerners have displayed a "fear of abstraction."[13] Actually no section has been so mesmerized by an "idea" having so little connection with reality. To be sure, the idea of the South has not been an abstract one, articulated with philosophical consistency; it has rather been a sensuous image, a fantasy construct, grasped by feeling and not by thought. The result has been that the South, in its perverse quixotic romanticism, has always pursued chimeras —the "Old South," "White Purity," the "Lost Cause"—and ended, like the Knight of the Doleful Countenance, tilting with windmills. Just as Mr. Compson tells Quentin that "Sutpen's trouble was innocence," the South's problem, if one follows Cash, was innocence, nurtured by a strange inability to learn from its experience. As Cash himself points out, Southerners were not hypocrites, they were naïfs. Instead of learning from its rich historical experience, the South, like the infamous Bourbons, never learned, and never forgot, anything.

This tendency toward abstraction and monumentalizing of past tradition meant that the South, as Cash saw it, suffered from something akin to a collective repetition-compulsion, a cultural regressiveness bordering on a death wish. Its great authorizing figures were literally "losers" who found glory in defeat or death. The Southern mind, according to Cash, tended in times of crisis to hoist the banner of the "Lost Cause" and to revert to the trauma of the Civil War and Reconstruction. It attempted to undo its defeat and the workings of time and history. In making this attempt, however, only another defeat was ensured. Recollections served to bring forth further repetitions rather than transcendence of them.[14]

But it is important to stress that Cash, like Freud, raised to consciousness past traumas and their enslaving force in order that they might be mastered. Only by facing unfreedom could freedom be achieved. There is no better description of Cash's critical and ultimately therapeutic enterprise than Freud's "where id was, there ego shall be."

Cash's fundamental thesis was that there was cultural continuity between the Old and the New South. He undercut the notion that the Old South had originally been an aristocratic society, and then he destroyed the corollary notion that the New South, devoted superficially to industrial progress and the rule of commerce, was different in essence from the ante-bellum South. Thus he challenged those who claimed to see a new and enlightened South aborning. In this he was in partial agreement with the Agrarians, yet rejected the Agrarian notion that the South's troubles all stemmed from north of the Mason-Dixon line.

Cash's emphasis on the frontier as a crucial factor in the formation of the mind of the South turned Frederick Jackson Turner's thesis on its head, for Cash stressed the manner in which the frontier ethos hindered rather than encouraged genuine democracy in the South. Far from ushering in "the land of opportunity for all," the frontier(s) meant that the vices of "cunning, hoggery and callousness, brutal unscrupulousness and downright scoundrelism" had been most essential for survival and success.

The world-view of the quintessential Southerner, Cash's "Man at the Center," was marked by simplicity, extreme individualism, an innocence of "notions of class," a tendency to "boast, brag and violence," and, most crucially, "a capacity for unreality, romanticism and hedonism." But though Cash made him the central character in *The Mind of the South,* he by no means glorified the common Southerner to the denigration of the few genuine aristocrats or neglected the aristocratic code which, in certain of its aspects, did have a softening influence. With all that granted, to Cash's mind the Southern aristocracy was the yeoman farmer come on good times, hoked up in pseudo-romantic garb and quasi-feudal notions.

Although an individualist to the core, the common white came to identify his ego with the collective Southern destiny, which was in turn embodied in the planter class that exploited him daily. Cash explained this "hegemonic" relationship as follows: because the yeoman was so near the planter in origin and desires—they were members of the same "family"—he remained far from the controlling power of the section and the consciousness of what was actually taking place. Incapable of detachment, often illiterate and usually unschooled, fearful of threats from blacks below and Yankees outside, possessed of a Manichean world-view, and misled by political demagoguery, the "Man at the Center" fell right in line when Sumter was fired upon.

On reflection it is clear that Cash, in the first part of *The Mind of the South*, was trying to answer the question which all too few historians of the ante-bellum South have asked: Why was it that no substantial number of common whites ever mounted a successful challenge to the ideological or political hegemony of the planter class?[15] For Cash the pre-Civil War South lacked a rational political culture. Politics remained a matter of rhetorical posturing. Then, as later, sectional-racial unity won out over class solidarity. Cash was far from suggesting that the planter class consciously brewed-up a home-grown conspiracy to mystify its social inferiors. Ideology "works" effectively precisely when it is believed in good faith by those who stand to benefit from it. It is the great merit of *The Mind of the South* that Cash delineated, perhaps better than anyone else has (Eugene Genovese to the contrary notwithstanding), the way social control was maintained by ideological constructs and false consciousness.

As Woodward has noted, and as Cash himself stated in the preface, *The Mind of the South* dealt almost exclusively with the white Southern mind. In his discussion of the Old South, Cash devoted relatively little space to the black man or the institution of slavery. Cash did, however, point to the relationship between the two races as "nothing less than organic. Negro entered into white man as profoundly as white man entered into Negro—subtly influencing every gesture, every word, every emotion and idea, every attitude." Yet he never really developed this penetrating insight. Cash devoted some five pages to the effects of slavery on blacks ("inescapably brutal and ugly . . . it rested on force"). He charted its corrupting and brutalizing effects on the entire culture, its contribution to white guilt, and the concomitant elevation of white women to purity incarnate and the demotion of black women to sexuality incarnate. Unlike the Agrarians or even "liberal" historians such as Benjamin Kendrick and Alexander Arnett in *The South Looks at Its Past* (1935), Cash betrayed no hint of sentimentality about the institution nor did he try to pass it off as not substantially worse than the working-class environment of Northern or European workers; nor, finally, did he praise slavery as a "school for civilization." (How could it be, if the white South itself was bereft of a vital culture?) With all this said, Cash's primary focus remained the whites.

Still, at times Cash edged toward a vague, hazy sort of racism, especially when discussing black women and their supposed sensuality, an indication that Cash had not quite escaped his own earlier views. Describing the Negro as "in the main . . . a creature of grandiloquent imagination, of facile emotion, and, above everything else under heaven, of enjoyment," Cash also claimed that the black slave woman was "to be had for the taking," though he did acknowledge the effects of cultural disruption and commercial necessity in undermining conventional sexual morality. These, and other similar comments, do not constitute a full-blown theory of racial difference, but the implications were there. In defense of Cash it should be noted that, whatever critical remarks he offered about blacks he attributed the same or worse to whites, even to the point of suggesting that part of the white Southerner's incapacity for reality could be attributed to his Gaelic descent.

Cash was certainly aware of the acquiescent and demeaning roles the blacks were forced to play, but he failed to make the plausible move to the observation that the Negro, because he existed in two worlds, was far from the simple and uncomplex figure he was assumed to be.[16] Indeed, the slave had to learn to decipher the white world to a degree which was never required of whites vis-à-vis the black world. As Hegel claimed, the slave learns the fear of death (and the fear of the master) which is the beginning of wisdom, and represents potentially the more complex, more self-conscious of the two figures. Far from being a creature of impulse, the slave had to "learn" reality with far more diligence than the master.

Likewise, to jump ahead, blacks functioned in Cash's postwar South primarily as passive counters in the conflict between North and South. They became a sort of "given," an inherited part of the Southern cultural landscape that only negatively influenced white Southern culture. Blacks, like Yankees and modern ideas, were all transmogrified into one, vast, "generalized Other" which by definition threatened the Southern way of life. In much of this Cash was, of course, correct, yet he added scarcely a word about Booker

T. Washington or his central role in post-Reconstruction Southern race relations. Nor did Cash devote any space to W. E. B. Du Bois's *Souls of Black Folk,* the black counterpart of *The Mind of the South.*

In dealing with the social and economic realities of the twentieth-century South, Cash failed to do much better by the blacks. Sharecropping and tenancy came in for their share of discussion, but usually as they affected the poor white and yeoman. Cash also neglected the crucial, if limited, role that black farmers played in the Populist movement, as well as the emergence of disfranchisement and Jim Crow statutes in the first decade of the century. Poll taxes and literacy tests were discussed in reference to their effect on white voters. Cash quite acutely pointed to the lack of sustained class solidarity, the final deferral to the ruling class, and, in general, the existence of a surplus labor force, all of which doomed most strikes to failure. Yet here again Cash failed to stress sufficiently that it was often the existence of a black surplus labor force which made it possible for owners to break strikes.

Cash's biographer tells us that at one point Cash indicated to publisher Alfred Knopf that blacks would play a central role in his work. Why Cash abandoned this plan is not told us. One can only guess that in writing so personal a book and in creating a single central figure (the "Man at the Center") Cash found it impossible to enter into the thoughts and feelings of black Southerners, who, however complexly intertwined with whites, would tell a significantly different story.

Cash's second section, covering the years 1865–1900, charted the unprecedented institutional change and conflict in the South. Yet he contended that the characteristic ways of thought and feeling that had been formed in the pre-War years were only reinforced. Indeed, for Cash the four years of fighting and then the ordeal of Reconstruction bound Southerners of all classes together in a nexus of "common memories" which strengthened Southern individualism and lack of class awareness. The white Southerner increased his identification with the South. The "Lost Cause," the political hegemony of the Democratic party, white supremacy, a besieged Calvinism *cum* furtive hedonism, and the savage ideal grew apace. These years saw the vitiation of the aristocratic ideal, but also the emergence of the romantic myth of the Old South, a myth given credence in both South and North.

In his coverage of Reconstruction Cash was at his most biased. Like most other Southerners of his time, Cash resented the occupation and made this animus a central part of his historical vision. Liberals could be critical of unfettered capitalism yet remain with at least one foot in the Southern camp. Thus, along with other of his contemporaries, Cash tended in a pinch to grasp for a rather simple-minded economic interpretation to explain the "thievish" intentions of the "tariff gang," i.e. the Republicans. The entire process was best summed up, Cash felt, by a term taken from English history—"Thorough."[17] Beyond that there was really not much else to say.

Reconstruction and its aftermath saw the emergence of what Cash called the "rape complex." As Cash reminded the reader, there had always been a close identification of the South with the white woman. By the psycho-social logic of the situation, to attack the South was to attack her. Cash himself used the language of sexual violation—again signaling his participation in the mind he was dissecting—to describe Northern occupation: "Not Ireland nor Poland, not Finland nor Bohemia . . . was ever so pointedly taken in the very core of its being as was the South." Thus, if the Yankees raped the South economically and politically, the collective white mind feared a literal "rape" by the recently freed slaves.

But in Cash's hands the rape complex became more specific and more sophisticated. It ultimately derived from the fantasy vision of the Southern family and the South as family. Racial purity was absolutely central to the legitimacy of the white Southern society: "there was a final concern for the right of their sons in the legitimate line, through all the generations to come, to be born to the great heritage of white men." Black blood would deprive the male heir of the name of the father. And as Cash would also suggest, the rape complex was the underpinning for the later more commonly held notion that black political and social advances were covert ways of gaining sexual access to white women.

Thus what Faulkner did for incest, Cash did for miscegenation: he gave it wider social and cultural implication. To be sure, theories of the rape complex that emphasize psychological mechanisms—reversal and projection of desires: that black men must want white women because white men have desired and taken black women—are important. But Cash took the discussion of the rape complex out of the realm of guilt and projection and located its essential meaning in the context of the family romance and the white Southern obsession with purity of lineage. Cash's discussion of the rape complex revealed the way in which race and sex, psychology and social structure were so closely linked in the South and the way essential desires were translated and transformed into a vast array of articulations which became stable components of a culture.

The unanswerable question is how much Cash felt that he and his critical contemporaries were also violating Southern legitimacy and besmirching Southern purity. For, clearly, Cash both identified with the South and saw himself as one of its attackers. Given this ambivalence one can perhaps better understand how easy it was for liberal Southerners to accept the Reconstruction myth. By doing so they could at least give some public assurance of their *bona fides* as Southerners. More clearly the sexual issue was the final fallback for troubled Southern liberals (though not for Cash). On down into the 1950s and 1960s liberals could call for all sorts of reforms in the South provided they gave assurances that they would draw the line at true social, i.e. sexual, equality which would compromise the "integrity" of the two races. For, ultimately, the conservatives were correct. Once the notion that blacks were "children" in the larger Southern family was destroyed, once the family romance was demythologized, the incest/miscegenation taboo had to go as well.

Still, one cannot help but feel that Cash, for all his participation in the Reconstruction myth, correctly perceived that the War and Reconstruction created a collective psycho-cultural entity— the South—which loomed ever larger in the minds of white Southerners. The South's authorized tradition was created in the years of its demise.

Since the groundbreaking work of Woodward and other his-

torians in the late 1930s, Cash's charges against the Populists—
that they failed to focus on the economic and social realities of
tenancy and sharecropping, wasted their energies in attacking
Wall Street and the "Money Power," and ultimately capitulated
to the Democratic party—simply neglect too much and vastly
underestimate the importance of the Populists. Yet it is important
to consider Cash's critique. Indeed, Woodward noted that Populists such as Tom Watson drifted back to the Democrats and there
pursued a politics marked by a "psychology of frustration."[18] According to Cash, the leaders of the farmers' movement seemed
more interested in capturing the Democratic party machinery
(here he was thinking more of Ben Tillman than anyone else)
than in altering the power relationships within the South. Cash's
view tended to be that Populism was more an ideology of resentment than a set of coherent class or interest concerns.[19]

Further, though Watson remained an arch opponent of "New
Southism" and the Eastern Interests, he gradually came under the
spell of the "Confederate Creed" and worked for the "rehabilitation of the Lost Cause."[20] From a concern with who should rule
at home, the Populists moved to a preoccupation with home rule.
Sectional loyalties continued to take precedence over class and
interest considerations. It was this failure of Populism which Cash
saw as central, and thus he was highly skeptical of the staying
power of insurgent ideologies, a distrust which was undoubtedly
reinforced by the miserable record of later Southern demagogues.
Besides, for a man who was so sensitive to Southern anti-intellectualism and the region's hostility to new ideas—in short, the
savage ideal—the performance of the common whites was not at
all attractive, particularly after the Scopes trial.

It is certainly understandable that historians such as Woodward would find *The Mind of the South* inadequate in that it
neglected the discontinuities in Southern history, particularly in
the period between 1865 and 1914. Viewed in terms of institutional change, those who stress conflict have a point. Yet conflict
and discontinuity—the Populist insurgency and then its collapse,
black disfranchisement and the rise of Jim Crow—from a cultural-
psychological perspective can be seen as the expression of under-

lying, constant values. To argue as Woodward did in *The Strange Career of Jim Crow* that the rise of Jim Crow was a break in the continuity of Southern history is (arguably) correct in institutional terms, but finally misleading in terms of underlying white Southern attitudes toward blacks. Thus one vital component of the Southern mind—racism—took on a life of its own, and perhaps even increased in intensity, once slavery was abolished and slaves became freedmen. Cash's account of continuity is much more helpful here than interpretations that stress change and disruption.

Over half of *The Mind of the South* was devoted to the South in the twentieth century. There Cash spoke of a third frontier brought on initially by the development of the textile industry in the Piedmont South. He noted that the company town reproduced, with different external trappings, the paternalistic social and economic arrangements of the ante-bellum South. The common whites, drawn to the mill by comparatively higher wages and the promise of relief from the idiocy of rural existence, were again mystified, this time by the rhetoric of Progress, hitched to appeals to Southern chauvinism. The twin crusades of industrial development and education were the continuation of warfare against the North by other means. Clearly, such crusades were also forms of social control, ways of giving a little to keep a lot. This period also saw the emergence of a strong commercial middle class, speaking the language of the Rotary Club, yet paradoxically devoted to establishing its place in the Southern great chain of being.

Focusing on alternating periods of prosperity and depression, Cash charted the gradual demise of King Cotton and the rise of an industrial working class. While promising for the long run, these new social and economic developments seemed to lose most of the battles against inherited attitudes. As a close observer of the textile strikes in the 1920s, Cash noted that the workers, though often ready to strike at the drop of a wool hat, were just as easily brought back under control by appeals to sectional unity against such alien forces as Yankeeism and race mixing, which the unions supposedly represented. Incapable of a sustained battle, of institutionalizing their individualistic impulses: "they wilted much as the Populists had once wilted."

Other contradictory forces were emerging in the midst of social and economic change. The Southern demagogue, operating according to the principle of speaking loudly but carrying a small stick, became a standard figure in Southern politics. Except for Huey Long, whom Cash praised for his relative neglect of race-baiting (Cash even wanted to do a biography of Long), most of these men fell right into the Southern politics of rhetoric rather than of significant reform.

Likewise the 1920s witnessed a veritable flowering of cultural demagoguery. The savage ideal, which Cash likened to the prevailing ethos of Nazi Germany, Fascist Italy, and Stalinist Russia, took on new forms in the Ku Klux Klan revival, the Scopes trial, Prohibition, and other expressions of opposition to new ideas. Once more the Southern congeries of taboos was marshalled against the enemy. The common man, led on by his captains, essayed a "retreat upon the past."

And yet Cash characterized the 1920s as a period of new hope as well. Black education and pride showed signs of life; and a few Southern institutions of higher learning began their challenge to received ideas. This rise of a critical academic community, along with the tentative hope for a strong labor movement, the literary explorations of those "exasperated lovers" who went beyond the mint julep and magnolia school of Southern writing, all promised, though did not guarantee, a new critical spirit in the South.

Although Woodward has maintained that Cash had little appreciation for the tragic element in the Southern experience, the message of *The Mind of the South* was finally the South's tragedy of waste. Even if the Depression saw the rise of a critical intelligentsia, which the South had lacked before, "there was no articulation between the new intellectual leaders and the body of the South, and it is in this that the tragedy of the South as it stood in 1940 centrally resided." Caught between rabble-rousers such as Theodore Bilbo, Robert Reynolds, and Herman Talmadge and Bourbons such as Carter Glass, Harry Byrd, and Josiah Bailey, "the body of the South has inevitably been confirmed in complacency and illusion."

Thus, as Cash saw it, the mind of the South remained almost impregnable, resolutely ensnared in the repetitions of the past. If we remember that it is only analogy, it is not far-fetched to see Cash's Southern "mind" as neurotic, even pathological. As presented by Cash, the South monotonously returned to past actions and attitudes in times of crisis and embraced the very attitudes which had led to disaster in the first place. (What else was the Southern reaction to the Presidential Report on the South in 1938?) Its recollections remained governed by repetition, and it could never quite learn anything. Yet for all its faults, *The Mind of the South* records Cash's own personal liberation (though as with Ike McCaslin never complete) from the Southern tradition. Cash arrived finally at an insight into the complexities of the Southern experience: a collective mind so embroiled in the pathos of its own past that it failed to gain a tragic dimension.

Epilogue

The temptation is always great with a work such as *The Mind of the South* to bring it up to date, to measure its validity by how its thesis has stood the test of time. This is unfair to Cash (and to historians generally), since prediction is not their proper province. For instance, neither Cash nor anyone else, including Gunnar Myrdal in his *An American Dilemma* (1944), predicted that the major development in the post World War II South would be the enfranchisement and exercise of political power by blacks. One cannot help but feel that Cash's sense of irony would have been delighted by the emergence finally of two Georgians—Martin Luther King and Jimmy Carter—who spoke to the best rather than the meanest in their fellow Southerners.

And Cash would have been pleased and not a little surprised to find that the decade of his maturity—the 1930s—would be later marked as the heyday of the "Southern Renaissance." Like Tocqueville, who noted American cultural barrenness on the eve of the flowering of New England, Cash's own work and that of his contemporaries gave lie to the intellectual sterility which Cash saw distressingly evident in the Southern experience.

Cash's *The Mind of the South* was one of the first in a line of what has become a tradition of Southern liberal self-examination. This tradition was carried on in the 1950s through the 1970s by numerous writers such as James McBride Dabbs, C. Vann Woodward, Robert Penn Warren and, later, Pat Watters and John Egerton. By the 1970s Watters and Egerton, for instance, adopted a perspective that inverted Cash's. They saw the white South's shortcomings as the nation's writ small, and more graphically. The South had unfortunately adopted all the worst faults of the rest of the country. Still, Watters in particular echoed many of Cash's conclusions. Most central were the sheer waste of time and energy upon worn-out causes, the apparent inability of the South to think through its situation in any coherent manner, and, in an analogy which the Nazi-obsessed Cash would have felt profoundly, the evil of Southern innocence. As Watters expressed it: "Eichmann, not Simon Legree is the villain."[21] And the most consistent flaw that Watters detected in the contemporary South was the one with which Cash ended his book—the failure of Southern leadership.

Cash was a prophet perhaps, but only in the sense that the term refers to those imposing figures of the Old Testament—men who passed judgment upon their people and their times. Not only the "Interests," the "Bourbons," and the "Big Mules," but also the champions of the common white man have consistently failed to provide minimal leadership for the people of the South.

Indeed, Cash's analysis of the Southern mind suggests a pattern among non-aristocratic Southern leaders going back at least to Andrew Johnson. Johnson, one recalls, was an ardent Unionist, a champion of the common white and an avowed enemy of the planter class. Once President, however, he proceeded to mislead the South as to Northern intentions and vice versa, and eventually went over to a position of solidarity with his former enemies, the planters. Some historians have suggested that this was a move on Johnson's part to form a new national political party. Yet there seems to have been something else at work there, a psychological or intellectual weakness, which in time of crisis led Johnson to fall back in line with the essentials of Southern orthodoxy and betray his former position.

The same general pattern holds true, of course, for Tom Watson. As Woodward has written, the Georgia Populist, though no dirt farmer himself, originally spoke eloquently and courageously for the political and economic rights of the Southern yeoman, black and white. Yet after the debacle of 1896 and a period of political hibernation, Watson emerged to spend the rest of his public career mouthing the most scurrilous, racist, and nativist sentiments.

And there is George Wallace. Early in his career Wallace ran for circuit court judge against the scion of an old Confederate family. Wallace soundly trounced his opponent by blatant appeals to "populist" sentiments, such as, a vote for Wallace would be a vote for the "privates," whereas a vote for his opponent, who had been a colonel in World War II, was a vote for the "officers." Years later, after Wallace had ridden on the back of the Folsom organization to the governorship of Alabama, the Confederate flag flew defiantly over the state house in Montgomery. Again, section outweighed class. What we see in Wallace is the same ambivalence, the willingness in small things to sound like a cotton patch Karl Marx, yet, when it counted, to close ranks with the "officers" and the "Big Shots" and to elevate the South as romantic ideal and white supremacy as the chief article of faith to supreme importance over all else.

There is thus then, arguably, a pattern at work in Southern "populist" leaders who begin as insurgents but at crucial points betray their own interests and those of their followers. A nagging sense of personal, social and intellectual insecurity is accompanied by a deeply ingrained tendency to acquiesce to social and intellectual "superiors." With a President from Georgia who fancies himself a spokesman of the common people, it will bear watching to see if this disastrous pattern once more comes to the fore. Or perhaps it has been laid to rest. Cash is undoubtedly watching with interest.

8

From Therapy to Morality:
The Example of Lillian Smith

For Lillian Smith, as for W. J. Cash, the salient feature of the mind of the white South was denial of reality. Unlike Cash, she focused on race as the central reality of Southern life that white Southerners denied and distorted. Race was inextricably linked with religion and sexuality in the Southern psyche. "Sin, sex and segregation" thus constituted the "complex" that needed explication. Memory was to become the vehicle of therapeutic healing and the restorer of authentic morality.[1] Segregation became a metaphor for the estrangement and dehumanization of modern life.

In *The Inability To Mourn* Alexander and Margerete Mitscherlich discuss the failure of the Germans after World War II to face the enormities of the Nazi past and to "work through" that experience to the fundamental guilt which they had incurred.[2] For the Mitscherlichs, "remembering, repeating and working through" were necessary to come to terms with the past. But the Mitscherlichs note that this collective, moral-therapeutic process never occurred. Rather, denial characterized the Germans' attitude toward their past: some Germans denied knowledge of the evil deeds and genocidal policies of Hitler and his minions; others admitted knowledge but abjured responsibility for this knowledge. Not "we didn't know" but "what could we do about it, it was 'their' fault" was this claim. And finally there was the response of Eichmann and others who denied neither knowledge nor responsibility but rather guilt, itself: what they had done had been done under orders. Subsequent to the denial (which the Mitscherlichs differentiate from repression), Germans came to identify with the West and opposed alleged Soviet expansion. At the same time the Germans engaged in a "manic undoing" which expressed itself in "the huge collective effort of reconstruction."[3] Thus a clearly drawn confrontation with the past was avoided.

Though the differences between the German experience under Nazism and the Southern experience are vast, white Southerners have displayed similar reactions to the fate of blacks. And if Lillian Smith was anywhere near correct, the central psycho-social mechanisms involved have been denial and repression, the former directed against unacceptable aspects of external reality and the latter against drives originating within. Central in the denial process was, of course, the failure to recognize the full humanity of blacks. Beyond that respectable Southerners repeatedly denied that they were responsible for or even knew about lynchings and other gross violations of black rights. Enlightened Southerners addressed a form of "you-too-ism" to the rest of the country. It was granted that the South had its sins to account for, but the rest of the country was called to account for its treatment of the Indians; the North was as responsible for slavery as the South. Also many liberal Southerners denied not that there was a problem but that anything could be done about it. Pessimism provided the easy way out; the sense of the tragic complexity of the Southern racial situation an excuse for doing nothing.[4]

Lillian Smith was born in the small north Florida town of Jasper in 1897. (Jasper was divided equally between black and white.) Her mother's ancestors were rice planters in South Carolina before the Civil War, while her father's parents came from Scotch-Presbyterian, pioneer stock who fought the Indians and then acquired a bit of land and a relatively small number of slaves. She was to hear, and then later remember, the exciting tales told by her paternal grandmother, "Little Grandma," of life on the Florida and South Carolina frontier and that generation's dogged acceptance of life and death. For all the danger faced by her generation, it seemed at home in the world. Yet Smith came to see the inadequacy of Little Grandma's vision. This heroic and tough woman, who served as a sort of emotional "first aid station" for Lillian, believed that "nothing could win over life"; yet she lacked a sense of "inner" self or imaginative capacities.[5] What had been the answer for her on the frontier no longer served the sensitive young girl of artistic inclinations.

Lillian Smith felt closest to her father. Mr. Smith owned a lumber operation, a turpentine mill, a general store, and part interest in the water works and light plant in Jasper. He was born during the Civil War and was "hardheaded, warm-hearted, high-spirited,"[6] the solid provider for his family and a man of spirit, compassion, and fairness. Smith never fully delineated her mother; and one suspects a certain distance and lack of emotional connection between mother and daughter. She was, writes Smith in *Killers of the Dream,* "shy with words," and a "wistful creature." In contrast with Little Grandma, she lived a life of attenuated inwardness, a member of that generation of Southern women for whom the body had grown distasteful: "Her private world we rarely entered, though the shadow of it lay heavily on our hearts."[7] Of her brothers and sisters Lillian Smith says little. One brother, her father's favorite, apparently met an early death; and Smith notes of a younger sister that she was "more certain of her place in the family" than Lillian was.[8] Like Will Percy, Smith felt herself an outsider in her own family, revered her father and spoke sparingly of her mother, traveled widely, and never married. Yet, unlike Percy, Smith undertook the difficult task of analyzing rather than evoking her family romance and that of the South.

During World War I her father's fortunes took a turn for the worse, and the family moved to Clayton in North Georgia. After teaching in Tiger, Georgia, in 1918–19, Smith studied piano at Peabody Conservatory in Baltimore and then in 1922 went to China to teach for three years. She returned to help her father run a girls' camp near Clayton. There she lived until her death with her friend, Paula Snelling, directing the camp and in 1936 publishing a quarterly, *Pseudopodia*, which became the *North Georgia Review* in 1937 and then *South Today* from 1942 until its demise in 1945. Of her father's death in 1930 or her mother's in 1938, she wrote nothing.

Over the years she traveled extensively, particularly to South America and India, and lived for a few months at a time in New York. Some of her manuscripts were destroyed in a fire in 1944 and others in 1955, the latter fire having apparently been set by two young white men. In the late 1940s she wrote a column for the *Chicago Defender*, and over the years she contributed to liberal periodicals. In 1953 she discovered she had cancer and underwent breast surgery. From then until her death in 1966 she was in ill health. An early and ardent supporter of the 1954 Supreme Court decision and a member of the board of CORE, an admirer of Martin Luther King and Lyndon Johnson, she was a standing rebuke to more timid Southern liberals and moderates.[9] In refusing to become influential in conventional ways, she acquired a moral authority that far outweighed her institutional connections, which were always minimal.

Lillian Smith was one of that fascinating breed of Southern women with an iron will and moral courage far beyond what could be expected from a person of her rather conventional and privileged background. She recognized the contingency of personal fate in *The Journey* (1954), the companion volume to *Killers of the Dream*, when she profiled two couples from similar Southern backgrounds: one couple had become paranoic McCarthyites, while the other had developed moral and intellectual insight into the South's racial dilemma.

From another point of view, Lillian Smith reminds us that most of the important works of the Southern Renaissance came from white Southerners who remained in the South and resisted the attractions of the North. It was one thing for Northerners—or liberal Southerners gone north—to speak out against the evils and injustices of the South, but another for a woman like Smith to remain there and risk ostracism and even bodily harm for her beliefs.

Smith's intellectual achievement was matched by a moral witness to what she believed.

The Liberal Publicist

Smith's and Snelling's quarterly, *Pseudopodia,* was the most important and interesting liberal voice in the South from the mid-1930s to the mid-1940s.[10] Smith wrote a regular column "Dope With Lime" in which she ranged widely over contemporary issues, with special attention to the race question, the literature and social analysis of the contemporary South, and the coming of World War II. She often took time out from such weighty matters to talk of activities at Laurel Falls Camp and to celebrate the glories of the natural world on "Old Screamer," the mountain overlooking the camp. Smith also published sketches of life in China and excerpts from her novel-in-progress *Strange Fruit* and what was to become *Killers of the Dream.* Snelling reviewed almost all the fiction, and the two collaborated on several articles.

Readers were kept abreast of the works by Southern writers and works dealing with the South. Dollard's *Caste and Class in a Southern Town* was reviewed favorably, and Hortense Powdermaker contributed a biting attack on Donald Davidson's *Attack on Leviathan.* In an early issue of *Pseudopodia* Smith wrote that *Gone With the Wind* "wobbles badly like an enormous house on shaky underpinnings." It was "slick, successful but essentially mediocre fiction."[11] If there was a single object of their wrath, it was the Agrarians, whom Snelling accused of evading the "central truth" of the South—the relationship between black and white—and of encouraging a "retrograde Amnesia in the guise of Neo-Agrarianism."[12] Later, after the publication of *Strange Fruit,* Smith was quite angry that the Agrarians as New Critics would "sum up *Strange Fruit* with one hissing word 'tract' . . . ," although the judgment seems both inevitable and not entirely without merit. Her riposte was to observe that the Agrarians were among those "who love the South so much that they can't bear to live in it. . . ."[13]

Not surprisingly, Smith and Snelling overlooked the virtues

of their ideological enemies in their haste to expose their vices. While granting Tate's *The Fathers* a certain power, Snelling scored it for its unconvincing psychology and undue concentration on the life of the upper class.[14] Later, Robert Penn Warren's *At Heaven's Gate* received good marks because it seemed to mark Warren's liberation from his Agrarian past.[15] Smith was particularly biting on Will Percy and his fellow Greenvillian, David Cohn. In the spring 1940 issue of *North Georgia Review* she scored Cohn for purveying racist views much like Hitler's. And in a review of *Lanterns on the Levee* she characterized Percy's views as an example of "white arrogance" at the very moment America was fighting racism abroad. Indeed to Smith, Percy's genteel racism was "more disturbing . . . than a Georgia demagogue's cheap tricks."[16]

On the other hand, Smith and Snelling printed an excerpt from Cash's work in progress in an early issue of *Pseudopodia* and responded quite positively to the appearance of *The Mind of the South*.[17] Carson McCullers's *The Heart Is a Lonely Hunter* was lauded as a departure from the conventional modes of Southern fiction, but Snelling considered *Reflections in a Golden Eye* sophomoric, a falling off from McCullers's first work. Ellen Glasgow received measured praise for her "critical realism"; but in her case, as in Eudora Welty's *A Curtain of Green,* Snelling noted a failure to probe deeply and to lay bare the realities of the South.[18] In the same issue as the critique of Welty, James Agee's *Let Us Now Praise Famous Men* received one of its few reviews and a favorable one at that. Snelling noted its "grandeur and grandioseness" and went on to identify Agee as "as rich a talent and independent a mind as is functioning in American literature today."[19] She also praised Richard Wright's *Native Son,* but criticized Wright's resort to stereotypes.[20]

On Faulkner the editors were of two minds. Snelling lauded Faulkner and Erskine Caldwell for their probings of the inner life of the South. Yet, her ambivalence became apparent when she wrote that Faulkner was "both a symbol and a symptom of the ills of the South; and at the same time an intelligent and sensitive diagnostician of those ills."[21] Making loose use of psychoanalytic terminology Snelling held that Faulkner expressed the "subverted libido" of his region. Later in a review of *The Wild Palms* Snelling objected to the lack of fit between Faulkner's subject matter and the unconscious, emotional undercurrents which were at work in and threatened to overwhelm his stories. As in a dream, she claimed, Faulkner's fiction isolated and exaggerated a single characteristic and exhausted its possibilities.[22] Though this judgment failed to do justice to Faulkner's conscious artistry and craft, Smith and Snelling, unlike later critics, did Faulkner the honor of seeing in his work the driven man and not the comforting preacher of humanistic homilies. If they were too reductionist and defined realism a bit too narrowly, they did catch, albeit in a one-sided fashion, Faulkner's disturbing power. Faulkner was finally not quite political or liberal enough for their tastes. Nor were they sensitive enough to the sheer range of Faulkner's fictional voice, concentrating as they did upon what they saw as his excessive preoccupation with the pathology of the region. For, as Flannery O'Connor was later to claim, only the fantastic and the grotesque could in truth do justice to Southern reality.

But Smith and Snelling also addressed social and political issues in their quarterly. Smith was less interested in day-to-day or month-to-month events than she was in the moral and psychological implications of the region's past. She was one of the few Southern liberals in the 1930s who questioned the conventional Southern account of Reconstruction. In a review of three books on Reconstruction in 1937, Smith wrote caustically of Paul Buck's *Road to Reunion* that she doubted that "an intelligent Negro reading it would . . . share the author's bubbling pleasure in the 'miracle' of reunion"; and she noted how after Reconstruction "the North embraced with a great sob of pity the South, while the two mingled tears in a kind of ante-bellum love feast." In general, she questioned the bias of historians of Reconstruction against blacks, abolitionists, and egalitarianism.[23] When Southern senators opposed an anti-lynching bill in the late 1930s, she and Snelling detected the "compensatory mechanisms of Nordic bluster and paranoiac bluster."

Both Smith and Snelling were sympathetic to contemporary

reform movements in the South. Though missing the first meeting of the Southern Conference on Human Welfare in Birmingham in November 1938, Smith attended the rest of the meetings. To her, the 1939 meeting in Chattanooga was something of a disappointment, marked by behind-the-scenes machinations of the Communist party and the CIO and axe-grinding, lobbying, and pursuit of special interests.[24] The third SCHW conference in Nashville (April 1942) was a combination "reunion, rally, pilgrimage, revival." She had kinder words for labor, yet felt that more of the rank and file should have been represented.[25] In general, her analysis of these meetings revealed a decided lack of interest in economic concerns or the business of practical politics, even within the reform camp. Though generally favorable toward labor unions, she charged both business and labor in the South with immaturity. They simply were not her "issue," for all her insight into the social and economic needs of the region. Rarely if ever did one find in the magazine an analysis of the South as an economic colony. An excerpt from *Sharecroppers All* appeared, but nothing of that sort came from the pen of Smith or Snelling.

Besides the Agrarians, Smith had little use for Southern liberals more cautious and hesitant than she. Manifesting what Freud called the "narcissism of small differences," she lashed out at their timidity and complacency. The occasion for her most vitriolic attack came in the World War II years when liberals such as Virginius Dabney and John Temple Graves urged blacks to moderate their demands for equal treatment for the duration. Of Dabney and Graves she observed that they had inherited neither the power of the Southern planter nor the moral authority Southern clergymen once possessed. In times of minor crises men such as Dabney and Graves functioned ambiguously as buffers between the races, speaking softly for better treatment yet maintaining a fundamental commitment to "things as they are." Echoing Cash's charge of failure of leadership, she caustically observed that the Southern liberal "cannot bear not to think well of himself, nor can he bear for the world not to think well of him." The result of this division between the desire to maintain influence and wanting to do right was only to "sweeten the old segregation." For "fear of doing harm" nothing was done at all. Such was the ineffectual realism of her liberal contemporaries. It was a thinly disguised paternalism, another example of regression to traditional beliefs in times of crisis.[26] Neither they, nor those like them, during a free speech controversy at the University of Georgia with Governor Eugene Talmadge, would "publicly affirm [their] belief in democracy and in brotherhood of man in terms of their Southern reality."[27]

In the spring of 1942, *South Today* became, Smith later claimed, the first Southern publication to call for the "abolition of the poll tax, the white primary, discrimination in defense jobs, segregation in the armed services, in public buildings and conveyances and in our southern public education systems."[28] That is, she called for the end of the Jim Crow South. Indeed the call was somewhat anti-climactic, since all these positions had been adumbrated in one way or the other long since in the magazine.

Besides the South and its problems, the journal was most concerned with the prospect of peace and war. Before America's entrance into World War II, Smith was extremely skeptical of American moralizing against Nazi Germany, first because of the miserable record of the United States in the South, and second because the American allies—France and England—were the major imperialist powers in the world. Her three-year stint in China in the 1920s had made her extremely sensitive to the damage done to America's image abroad by racial oppression at home and support, tacit at least, of the imperialist powers. The issue of *South Today* in which she called for an end to segregation in the South also included a major section devoted to the question of the war effort and its relationship to black demands for civil rights and equality. Though she was reluctant for the United States to enter the war, she saw American intervention as an opportunity for significant reform at home and as a way to end colonialism abroad. In her writings in the postwar years she was to return continually to the international implications of racial segregation and the way it played into the hands of the Communists, for whom she had no use.

Though never an outright pacifist, Smith thought highly of Gandhi and Nehru. Before the war began, *North Georgia Review* offered prizes for essays exploring the roots of war. The autumn 1939 issue included an essay in which Gregory Nicola rejected the notion that the roots of war lay in economic conflict. In an essay which undoubtedly recommended itself to the editors because of its psychoanalytic perspective, Nicola traced the roots of war to man's cannibalistic urges and the deeply rooted desire to kill.[29]

Smith's own views on the roots of war were closely related to her views on the relationship between the sexes. Though no doctrinaire feminist and critical of women who emulated the opposite sex, Smith observed that women were perhaps less in love with death than were men and closer to the reality of life.[30] (She also expressed a biting skepticism of Hemingway's notion of women in a later issue.) But in the winter of 1941 she and Snelling addressed themselves to the twin problems of the roots of war and aggression and the relationship between the sexes. Because men felt an "unending enmity against women" they oppressed women. In addition aggression intended for women was often redirected against men in war. Anticipating a theme to which Smith would return in Killers of the Dream, the two noted that the male idealization of the woman was a way of "putting her always and forever in her 'place.'" Thus the Southern idealization of women was a particular example of a general male tendency.

Yet, women, they added, were far from guiltless. Women encouraged the repetition of the age-old patterns of aggression by only allowing favors on their own terms and by reducing men to little boys. Thus only by proving manhood in war could men recoup their lost prestige. "We are an oppressed group . . . But we have grown to love our chains," they wrote. Smith and Snelling agreed with Freud, provisionally at least, that women were "culturally stunted." In the future they would have to learn to live in the public realm as informed citizens, and reject the provincialism of their sex, in which they vacillated between being children and being Delilah-like temptresses.[31]

Whatever the overall validity of their analysis of the origins of war, the "Man Born of Women" essay was crucial in establishing the complex and subterranean relationships which bound the sexes together. Indeed, it was hard to see such a situation might be altered, if male resentment of women was so fundamental. Nor did Smith and Snelling suggest specific measures or structural reforms which would accompany or bring about change in this situation. The social, the psychological, and the ethical aspects of the issue were confused with rather than illuminating one another. In their work at the Laurel Falls Camp, the two women stressed the need for young people to become acquainted with their feelings and their bodies. A late issue of *South Today* was devoted exclusively to children. By not being allowed to play with dolls, for instance, little boys were unable to work through their own feelings of helplessness. Racial prejudice involved a distorted awareness of the body and had to be eradicated.[32]

In their general analysis of the "mind" of the South, Smith and Snelling most directly applied psychoanalytic theory. For it was to Freud, and American psychiatrists such as Karl Menninger, that the two looked for a way of analyzing and then changing the essential mind-set of the South. In several places Smith described how the campers would be led to explore their feelings regarding race and the sufferings that blacks had undergone. This was a way of countering what Snelling referred to as "amnesia," the forgetting of the Southern past, and a consequent lack of realistic insight into the South's fundamental problems. Furthermore, as indicated in the attacks on Southern moderates specifically and on the white South generally, Smith and Snelling saw the South as fixated upon the past, particularly the Reconstruction era. In crises, Southerners like neurotics tended to regress to traditional beliefs and ideals. At the core of the Southern tradition was white racial superiority and a general fear of change. They described this underlying conservatism as "resistance to recovery." "We [Southerners], their grandchildren," they wrote, "cling as compulsively to the past and its harsh, limited, stagnant way of life as did our grandfathers before us."[33]

With the psychoanalytic model in mind, one can grasp the range as well as limitations of the vision of Smith and Snelling.

They saw themselves, it is not hard to imagine, as therapists of the Southern psyche in their writings and in their work at the camp. What was required for change in politics, society, and even literature—for they were inseparable—was a realistic assessment of the situation. The Southern tradition was a composite of denial, avoidance, splitting, rationalization, idealization, resistance—the classic compendium of defense mechanisms which masked the past and present of the region and the self. Whatever the importance of economic and social change, it was equally necessary to dissect and then to transform the Southern mind. Until that happened collective pathology would eventuate in or be identical with moral blindness. Conversely, only by offering the therapeutic vision could the South become right with itself morally. Psychic health was synonymous with authentic morality.

In its decade of existence the number of subscribers to the journal that Smith and Snelling published grew from 27 to 5000. Many Southerners wrote to express their gratitude that the truth about the South was finally being told. Though never long on humor or satire, Smith and Snelling ventilated the seriousness of their venture with quizzes about the South; and "Dope With Lime" often provided an entrée to Smith's mind in her more relaxed moments. Once the war began, the focus of *South Today* became more general and less exclusively regional. Issues became rather thin in substance, often consisting of reprints of earlier articles or made up of extensive (and boring) responses from Southern clergymen about the role of the church in the South.

Pseudopodia began and *South Today* ended as a two-woman operation. Editorial and business matters for *South Today* had been handled by the two women; and as with all such heroic efforts, energies and interest eventually flagged. The chief weakness of their journal was the other side of its great strength: the unity of vision and focus inevitably led to a certain predictability. It never had the slick quality of a mass market periodical nor the sophistication of an academic quarterly. But in spite (or because) of that, it was a powerful and valuable voice for change in the Southern tradition.

The Family Romance:
The Two Mothers

Lillian Smith's was the small-town, rural deep South, the imaginative counterpart of the social context described by sociologists such as John Dollard. Its main fears were of the body, of blacks, and of death. Divided against itself, fearful of the self and the omnipresent black "others," the white South lurched between langorous summer days and nights and sudden explosions of violence, between the decorous, bloodless religiosity of church circle meetings and the powerful religious psycho-dramas of yearly revivals, between amicable contacts between black and white and then the dreaded lynchings. Behind it all stood "sin, sex and segregation."

Bargains long since made, the exact terms forgotten, shaped Southern society. As Smith wrote in 1942 (a piece which she later included in *Killers of the Dream*), the Southern polity was founded upon compact between well-off and poor whites: if blacks were excluded from any effective power in the society, poor whites would not challenge upper-class hegemony. Like Cash she traced the South's problems to a failure of leadership. Politicians roused racial fears to maintain white solidarity and their own power. Business and professional men (such as Smith's father), though decent, failed to question the racial or economic order. Clergymen preached the fear of eternal damnation and the sins of the body rather than the quest for justice and the joys of the senses; they sundered the message of spiritual equality from political and social equality, the message of individual responsibility from social responsibility. And finally there were the moderates who knew better, men such as newspaper editor Prentiss Reid in *Strange Fruit*, who was as cynical, even radical, in private as he was cowardly and acquiescent in public. In a world of family relationships, there was scarcely a public realm at all.

As I have noted, Smith's vision was essentially moral not historical. Still, a central aspect of that moral vision concerned the inadequacy of the tradition of the fathers and the grandfathers. Her books record the process of coming to see her parents, particularly her father, without idealizing him. For all their genuine kindness, her parents had passed on to her a compartmentalized and alienated existence: they "taught me to split my body from my mind and both from my 'soul,' taught me also to split my conscience from my acts and Christianity from the Southern tradition."[34] The effect of this split was a psychic and emotional confusion. The body and blacks were equated and subjected to repression. But Smith's indictment was more sweeping. Nothing of the legacy of the planter class was of much use: "Insight was not a quality their culture valued; nor intellectual honesty, nor self-criticism, nor concern for human rights; nor could they laugh at themselves."[35] Whatever moral authority it may once have possessed, the ruling elite of the South had long since lost it by the twentieth century.

In her autobiography, *Killers of the Dream,* Smith records one of those paradigmatic moments, a primal social scene, in the life of children of both races when they first become aware of race and try to puzzle out what color means. In an episode similar to one in Richard Wright's *Black Boy,* she tells of a young "white" girl, Janie, who mysteriously comes to live with the blacks. She is rescued from the black community by the "good" whites and goes to live with the Smith family. Further investigation determines, however, that Janie is "black" after all; and Lillian's playmate is sent back to the other world, once more an "other." The importance of this episode lies not only in the way it reveals the crucial significance of "color" but also in its revelation of the weakness of the adults who acquiesce in the tradition of white supremacy. And they were guilty as well as weak: "For deep down in their hearts, Southerners knew they were wrong."[36] Guilt was transformed into hate for those toward whom whites felt guilty; self-punishment was changed into aggression against the oppressed. Lillian Smith learned that the adults she respected and honored also exploited and were cruel to blacks. Not only the black world but also the white world was divided against itself.

Behind the social and cultural order stood the Christian God who "became the mighty protagonist of ambivalence."[37] In a strange way the guilt and weakness of the parents were masked by their religious submission to a higher cultural and religious power. Though God was all loving, he could also mete out punishment with terrifying quickness. "He was Authority,"[38] which in all its contradictions was not to be questioned, just as the social and cultural order was founded on contradictions and denials that were not to be questioned. The earthly counterpart of God as Authority was "They Who Make the Rules." The ambivalences of psychic and spiritual life were projected upon the social world. The body was denied, yet skin color was emphasized beyond all bounds. Sex and consumption vices such as smoking and drinking were strictly regulated, yet the children of the well-off were "sugar-tit children," coddled and spoiled.[39] Eating was of prime importance, yet its very prodigality was accompanied by the taboo against eating with members of the other race. To handle this mass of contradictions Southerners developed an extraordinary sensitivity to manners and decorum, to nuance and tone in social intercourse. Manners were not "mere" customs but the very emblems of a divided existence, protection against the violation of social taboos and protection against unwanted impulses.

At the heart of Smith's analysis was the family romance and the problem of the "two mothers." Of all the analysts of the South, Smith alone focused explicitly on women's role in the patriarchal tradition. According to her the key to race relations was the "mammy" tradition in the comfortable classes of the South. Among a relatively small but crucial segment of Southern society—the upper class and the relatively well-off middle class—young white children were commonly brought up and even nursed by black women who worked for white families.[40] Though lower-class whites did not experience this directly, they had over the years come to accept the great Southern family romance, "the official daydream that the Southern authoritarian system wanted the world to think our life was."[41] Poor white women envied the elevated status of better-off white women, and poor white men accepted the white upper-class male fantasies about black women. Thus the cultural tradition and its fantasized ideals pervaded white Southern society.

The chief victims were white women. Their idealization and

etherealization meant that husbands and children, particularly sons, looked to black women as the source of warmth and security, of sensuality and the pleasures of the body. In both *Strange Fruit* and *Killers of the Dream* Smith describes the paradigmatic moment when loyalties are transferred to the black mammy. Smith tells of how her "Aunt Chloe" chewed up food and gave it to her after she had refused to eat it as a protest against being replaced by a new child as the main object of her mother's affections. Aunt Chloe had literally saved her life while Smith's "real" mother had threatened it.[42] And in *Strange Fruit* Tracy Deen remembers a similar incident in his life. Indeed, throughout her work Smith repeatedly evokes the primal image of the black woman's breast and the desire to return to it, there to receive the warmth and sustenance which the white mother could not supply.[43] In *Strange Fruit*, Nonnie Anderson's mother remains a powerful force in the black community even after her death. As Sam, the black doctor, reminisces: "I see her reaching out and pulling everybody, everything, the whole world, to her, and sort of nursing it in her big lap—all of it, good and mean, its nastiness and its brightness, drawing it in against her breast."[44] By contrast Mrs. Deen is thoroughly unattractive and resentful, a grasping wife and mother. She barely tolerates her husband's sexual advances, has no use for her son Tracy, and is in the process of ruining her daughter Laura's life by condemning her artistic, sensual impulses. (One could safely guess that Laura is a stand-in for Smith here.)

White Southern women not only lost the loyalty of their children, but they were continually threatened by the rivalry of black women. For Smith, the white male desire for the black woman was founded on an incestuous desire for the (black) mother. She suggested that white men sought in black women the nurturing and sensual qualities which neither their mothers nor their wives supplied. But of course neither the nurturing union with the black mother nor the sexual union with the black woman could receive social recognition. Thus a "ghostly" aura surrounded essential relationships in the South. This desire for black women was denied in the casual exploitation and denigration of black women or reversed in aggression against them. In *Strange Fruit* Tracy, maddened by desire and grief, ends by beating his black lover, Nonnie Anderson. Though all-powerful in white fantasy, black women were vulnerable in reality. They received the hate which sprang from white male guilt and the resentment which arose from the powerlessness of white women.

It is important to unpack the implications here. First, as Smith noted, the "two mothers" situation made the normal Oedipal complications a matter of "simple adjustment."[45] With cultural and social approval denied to essential needs and desires, Oedipal impulses and identifications were only resolved with the greatest of difficulty. White males idealized white females and then suffered the consequences, while white women acquiesced in their progressive desexualization and turned away from their men and their own bodies to a religion which strengthened the sexual, psychological, and social order of alienation.

Thus Smith exposed the underside of the Southern family romance and attempted its ultimate demystification. Behind the idealization of white skin and social status, the fantasy of social and racial superiority in which every white child was a prince or a princess, lay a counter fantasy. According to Smith, the black mother, the kind "foster" parent, was the effective mother, though the white mother retained her official social role. At the same time the paternal principle was elevated out of all proportion; there was little to counter it. In much of the writing of male Southerners, men feel distinctly uncomfortable with female companionship and prefer that of other men and of animals. Sexuality becomes feminine, disruptive, asocial, and explosive. Any open acknowledgment of white female sexuality as normal is not tolerated. Masculinity is to be proved not so much with women as with other men.

Further, the realm of culture, the life of the mind and of sensibility, such as it was, became the province of white women. This was their consolation. Because it was identified with women, however, culture lacked prestige or public relevance and became crabbed, genteel, and sentimental. If we understand sentimentality to be "unearned" or "inappropriate" emotion, then official Southern culture was a sentimental one. Thus Southern cultural life was neither intellectually or emotionally mature.

Religion also became the province of women, as the evangelist Dunwoodie notes in *Strange Fruit:* it was the white female revenge upon white men, and thus the male resistance to its hatred of the body and its "civilizing" goal. God remained a powerful and vindictive father, as Smith pointed out, but she might have added that Jesus became feminized, the Protestant substitute for the Virgin Mary. He was the model of what women wanted to transform their men into—feminized, prissy eunuchs. In this form, however, he could never fully win over the men, since he was unsatisfactory as either a feminine or a masculine model. Thus, as Allen Tate observed, the South never developed a religion to match its social and cultural order. What Tate did not recognize was that it was the bifurcation of the maternal image which made a new religion impossible. Sexually and emotionally overestimated, the black woman remained socially without standing. The real mothers could never be acknowledged publicly. This was the ultimate denial at the heart of Southern culture.

How then are we to take Smith's analysis? Its general validity seems impossible of proof in any common meaning of the term. Clearly, there was a problem in making the hypothetical experience of a restricted number of Southerners valid for white Southerners as a whole. Yet from what we know from experience and from the literature, the individual and collective fantasies of white Southerners did point to a rough plausibility in her analysis. At best she offered a powerfully suggestive understanding of the incredibly complex vicissitudes of desire in the Southern cultural-social order.

Despite the fact that black and white women were her focus, Smith's analysis "works" better for men than women. Only rarely did she explore the desire of the white female for the black male. But more important, it is not clear how the white female desire for the black mother's breast was expressed. In most cases it was presumably repressed in keeping with the demands of the cultural imperatives. One might speculate that Smith's ersatz mother role as camp director and her insistence upon the importance of the body was a way of redirecting her unfilled desires. In championing the body and making it one of her central themes, she was undoubtedly trying to redress an imbalance in her own life.

Another problematic area was Smith's rendering of black life in *Strange Fruit* and *Killers of the Dream*. In *Strange Fruit*, the black characters do represent a range of types; and at one point Nonnie's sister, Bess, says, "I'm so tired of being two people," an indication that Smith understood the psychic burdens of being black. Yet her image of the black mother and her account of black life in *Killers of the Dream* edged toward a sort of inverted sentimentality. She spoke of the naturalness and "psychosexual" vigor of blacks and suggested that black mothers knew lessons of child-rearing which whites had forgotten or never learned. Being outside the "patriarchal-puritanic system" that "psychically castrated" women and children, the black mother could raise children with "a stability, a health, a capacity for accepting strain, an exuberance, and a lack of sadism and guilt that no Anglo-Saxon group . . . has ever known." Blacks were "sane at the core as neither a vengeful nor cringing people can be."[46] It was perhaps not accidental that the black world offered an appealing alternative to Smith's own experience as a white woman. The point is not so much that what Smith says is entirely wrong as that her picture of black life failed to do justice to the psychological and emotional damage that blacks had suffered.

Consequently, Smith underplayed the harmful effects of the close relationship of black mother to white child. In her emotional generosity, the black woman often spoiled the white child and taught him or her (particularly him) that gratification was his for the asking. Later, when immediate gratification was not forthcoming, as it never was, he exhibited that willfulness, the quick and mercurial temper, the cruelty, which observers as far back as Jefferson have seen as characteristic of Southern men. For the black child the tremendous gap between the remissive image of the black mother and the obduracy of the white world (which that same mother had to teach her child with often brutal blows) must have had effects which went beyond those caused by "mere" external oppression. The social order and the cultural tradition exacted a heavy price from both races.

About poor whites Smith had little to say except that their racism and proclivity for violence arose from a fear of loss of status, a stunted sexuality, and an emotional impoverishment. Still, she suggested that they possessed a toughness and vitality: "Most are not sick people nor cruelly perverse, they are starved. Most are conformists rather than idol worshippers."[47] But they remain undefined in her writings and only emerge in *Strange Fruit* to make up the lynch mob.

Thus Lillian Smith's fictional analysis of the Southern experience, *Strange Fruit*, was a sort of tract, replete though it was with acute observations of individual motive and social reality. The novel's faults lay in its unconvincing depiction of character and its lack of development. Though the mixture in Tracy Deen of genuine love for Nonnie and conventional attitudes toward blacks keeps him from becoming a liberal martyr, we never quite grasp what it is that drives him. Nor do we get much of a feel for Nonnie, his black lover. The plotting and the climax are a bit too pat, too mechanical, and never fully developed. Tracy's sister, Laura, hovers at the fringes of the novel and promises to be a more engaging character than Tracy; but we never truly enter her mind either.

Killers of the Dream, in truth, should be read with *Strange Fruit*, since it provides the personal and intellectual context for understanding the novel. Though *Killers of the Dream* is an autobiography of sorts, or better a meditation upon the intersection of personal and regional experience, there is much that is left out. Smith's later companion volume, *The Journey*, and her story for children, *Memory of a Large Christmas*, provide us with more information on her formative years and her intellectual career, yet her autobiographical writings are strangely silent on her personal relationships and vague on the texture of family life, which might have rendered her accounts more compelling. Her humanity and compassion, her wide-ranging mind and spirit are fully evident, but the personal dimension remains unexplored. Smith always strikes for the general lesson, the abstract moral of the situation, what one must learn from experience in order to survive as a human being. But the illuminating detail or experience is rarely there. Her voice lacks the range (or humor) of Cash's, and her focus is much narrower.

In the aftermath of the Supreme Court decision of 1954, Smith wrote in a short volume *Now Is the Time* (1955) that the integration of schools would be a great opportunity for America to show the rest of the world, particularly those areas of Asia which were under communist domination or threat of domination, that America opposed racial discrimination. As always the main obstacle to implementation lay in the psychological and moral realm. Again she spoke of the failure of Southern leadership. Thus, the answer to the deeply rooted psychological complexities of race relations remained strong public leadership and a willingness to face anxieties. Ultimately, hearts and minds would have to be transformed.

Indeed, the underlying assumption running throughout her work was that therapeutic insight leads to proper moral action.[48] Growth in awareness was *ipso facto* a moral process and a moral progress. Pathology was a refusal to face reality and a regression to the traditional. To open up and to go forward was to become more moral. Thus her vision, like Cash's, rejected the monumentalizing tendencies of the human mind in general and the Southern mind in particular. If the Southern mind seemed flawed to the core, this knowledge was the key to transforming it into something different and better. It was not, finally, the white fathers and their tradition, but the less obviously influential black mothers to whom the South should look for guidance.

Thus the analysis of the patriarchal tradition had come full circle. The Southern family romance had been decomposed. Not white but black, not fathers but mothers were to be the source of future strength. The cultural super-ego was to be replaced or at least augmented by a cultural remissiveness. From intellectual, moral, and cultural inferiors, Smith elevated blacks to superiors, those from whom Southern whites would have to learn in order to survive in a humane order. That, for her, seemed the core of a saving tradition to replace the fathers'.

9

From Theme to Setting:
Thomas Wolfe, James Agee,
Robert Penn Warren

Historically, the North Star has marked the path out of the South, for the ambitious as well as the poor and excluded. As the stereotypical province—rural, underdeveloped, culturally backward, yet possessing an exotic appeal—the South has admired and despised, embraced and spurned the characteristics of the developed, sophisticated, cosmopolitan, and "liberal" North. Not a few émigré Southerners have been driven by literary ambitions. By the 1920s New York, the center of the publishing world and the site of the nation's largest Bohemia—Greenwich Village—had become the place to go. For the Southerner with cultural ambitions, New York and the North represented a more fertile ground for intellectual and cultural exploration, an oasis of free thought and advanced ideas outside the "Sahara of the Bozart." Ambition and ideals dovetailed conveniently.

If the North signaled all that was *not* home and was treasured for that, young Southerners still found it hard to shake their Southerness. Carson McCullers's pungent comment that she returned periodically to the South to "renew her sense of horror" was probably representative in its mixture of attraction to and repulsion from the South.[1] And it often happened that the North would not let Southerners forget who they were, since the metropolis needs the province explained to it, piquing curiosity here and being assured there that the province is backward, if charmingly so. Some Southern writers who went north in the 1940s and 1950s —McCullers, Truman Capote, and Tennessee Williams in particular—seemed bent on perpetuating the image of decadence that careless readers of Faulkner and Erskine Caldwell in the 1930s had taken to be typical of things south of the Mason-Dixon line. Later, the civil rights struggle of the 1960s saw white Southerners attempting to explain the region's sins and shortcomings to a puzzled nation. Most prominent among them were historian C. Vann Woodward, novelists William Styron and Robert Penn Warren, and Willie Morris, and the young writers Morris drew to *Harper's* in the late 1960s.

Behind this stood the two archetypal émigrés of the Southern Renaissance years—Thomas Wolfe and James Agee. Unlike the Agrarians, who went north toward academic homes at Minnesota, Yale, or Kenyon, Wolfe and Agee were anything but academics. They were redskins, not palefaces.

Wolfe and Agee came from the up-country South, having been born nine years and approximately a hundred miles apart on either side of the Smoky Mountains.[2] Though both grew up in the moderate-sized Southern cities of Asheville and Knoxville, respectively, their families were of rural origins and possessed relatively little status or wealth. Their South had traditionally resented the black-belt hegemony in Southern affairs, and large pockets of Union sympathizers in the mountain South made life difficult for the Confederacy during the Civil War. The mountain yeomanry traditionally had equal distaste for planters, slavery—and blacks. Natives of the up-country South might dislike the Yankee, but not much more so than they disliked the Southerner of aristocratic mien or pretensions. If the typical Southerner was known for his rhetorical capacities, the Appalachian Southerner was as often as not laconic. All this is a way of saying that the mountain South lay outside the heartland of the tradition of the family romance. It was not that the family was unimportant; clan loyalties notoriously took precedence over all others in a fiercely local culture.

But, in the absence of the paternalistic cultural ethos of the plantation South, the family in the up-country never took on the wider cultural symbolism it possessed in the deep South.

Besides sharing similar origins, Agee and Wolfe both "lost" their fathers at an early age. In 1915 when Agee was six, his father was killed in an automobile accident; and at the same age Wolfe went with his mother when she left her husband to run a nearby boarding house and manage her properties. This early experience of loss must have had something to do with a theme common to their work: the search for self-definition, or as Wolfe put it clearly in *The Story of a Novel,* the "search for the father." Agee's biographer states that he lived "under the sign of his absent father."[3] Both men, particularly Wolfe, spent much of their lives searching for someone or something to order their chaotic lives and tame their considerable but erratic talents and energies. Unlike Faulkner, Percy, Tate, Cash, Smith, and the Agrarians, Agee and Wolfe were not trying to come to terms with the Southern cultural tradition of the fathers. They never experienced its full sway—or its loss. Rather, they were caught between trying to find a tradition to which they could belong and attempting to escape determinations of whatever sort. Their personal fatherlessness was mirrored by the lack of a tradition to which they could belong or which had shaped them.

Agee was close to his high school mentor, Father Harold Flye, with whom he corresponded all his life.[4] But this tie was not nearly so crucial as Wolfe's with Maxwell Perkins, his editor at Scribners, who, Wolfe himself realized, was Wolfe's spiritual and literary father. It is surely significant that in the long letter declaring his independence from Perkins, Wolfe spoke of Perkins's "castration of my work."[5] Allen Tate's description of George Posey in *The Fathers* could apply to Wolfe and to a lesser degree to Agee:

> George Posey was a man without people or place; he had strong relationships, and he was capable of passionate feeling, but it was all personal: even his affection for his mother was personal and disordered, and it was curious to see them together: the big powerful man of action remained the mother's boy . . . George was a man who

received the shock of the world at the end of his nerves. As to all unprotected persons, death was horrible to him. . . .[6]

If Wolfe and Agee escaped any strong, early influence of the Southern family romance, their adolescence and young manhood ensured a further distance from the Southern ambience. At age sixteen Agee entered Phillips Exeter Academy and went on to study at Harvard. He kicked around the Luce *Time-Life* organization at *Fortune* in the 1930s, wrote important film criticism for *The Nation* and *Time* in the 1940s, and fulfilled his life's dream of writing for Hollywood at the end of his life. Aside from occasional visits and the two-month stay in Alabama in 1936, Agee never returned to the South to live. Yet, he affected a rustic manner and apparently felt a vague disquietude, a sense of guilt over his betrayal of his Southern mountain roots, which he closely identified with his father. But as W. M. Frohock wrote of Agee: "Much as he liked to think of himself as hill-born in Thomas Wolfe's sense, he [Agee] moved north too early in life and acclimated himself too thoroughly to go down as a version of Wolfe's alien and unreconstructed hero. By preference, he spent his vacations in New York."[7]

Wolfe studied drama at Harvard after his receiving his bachelor's degree at Chapel Hill, and spent the rest of his life in New York City or traveling abroad, except for a not very satisfactory summer in the North Carolina mountains near Asheville in the 1930s. Unlike Agee, who was part of the emerging, predominantly Jewish intellectual elite, Wolfe was always the provincial in the metropolis, the overly sensitive rube who was fascinated and repulsed, often simultaneously, by the polyglot variety of Gotham. At one minute he could sound like Whitman, at the next like a fastidious conservative bemoaning the revolting masses. Both men expressed vaguely left-wing sympathies during the Depression, but Wolfe's *ressentiment* issued at times in ugly anti-Semitic opinions and actions; and, unlike Agee, he displayed little sensitivity to blacks. But after a visit to Nazi Germany, Wolfe gave signs of discarding his prejudices.[8] Wolfe was overly sensitive to criticism, particularly from "high-brow" intellectuals, and was forever in-

veighing against their obtuseness, while assuring himself that
their opinions hardly counted. In *The Web and the Rock*, for instance, he writes acidly of the intellectuals' modish deification of
Charlie Chaplin, one of Agee's favorites.

What marks the absence of tradition most clearly is the obviously self-referential nature of both men's work. This is a cliché
of Wolfe criticism. But with Agee, who turned a *Fortune* assignment of social reportage in Alabama into an extended and moving
piece of self-exploration, it was much the same. His late fiction—
The Morning Watch and *A Death in the Family*—pushed his own
self-exploration back to the unfinished business of dealing with his
father's death. Put another way, Wolfe and Agee were writers by
vocation who found it difficult to discover an essential theme beyond their own questing.[9] They swung between extremes of ela-
tion and melancholy, activity and inertia, a belief in their own
innocence and the holiness of all things and a sense that they had
violated the order of things and were guilty of some inexpiable
sin. Both found it hard to imagine that "middle distance," between
the extremities of experience, and to create characters and settings
which came alive in their own right. They were part of what
Quentin Anderson has called the tradition in American culture of
the "imperial self." They were, in that sense, less Southerners than
Transcendentalists.[10]

Thomas Wolfe and the South

Thomas Wolfe was born *in*, yet was not *of* the South. More than
any other major Southern writer, his reputation has gone into decline. In his lifetime critical opinion was divided over his achievement, though rarely over his genius. The criticisms of Wolfe—a
woeful inconsistency, the lack of differentiation between authorial
voice and protagonist's sensibility, the unwillingness to discriminate between the essential and the trivial, the failure to tell the
reader very much about his protagonist, Eugene Gant–George
Webber, and the shallow emotional and narrow intellectual reach
of his fiction—all seem to me essentially just.[11] Sympathetic observers would have it that Wolfe achieved a new maturity and

stability near the end of his life (after his break with Perkins); and Wolfe himself promoted this notion quite avidly.[12] But like the legendary Southern Bourbons, with whom he otherwise shared so little, Wolfe never really learned or forgot anything. He was always starting over again. Even his moments of isolation were noisy; and he was never able to halt that inexorable march through his own experience or to control his desire not just to experience everything, but to devour it.

Those who have written on Wolfe have stressed his rhetorical gifts and excesses, which he allegedly shares with Faulkner, Agee, and, following Cash, Southerners generally. A reading of Wolfe reveals, however, that his voice was less Southern than it was nineteenth-century English romantic. Where Faulkner's voice at full pitch was terribly compressed, self-lacerating, and seeking to say it all in one sentence, Wolfe's rhetorical flourishes were rather stagey, comprised of experiences and emotions strung out over paragraphs, seeking to force quality out of sheer quantity. His rhetoric was metonymical not metaphorical, and verged on "fine writing." This stylistic difference between the two is reflected in the relative lack of density in Wolfe's work: the past is thinned out rather than thickly textured.

Further, for all Wolfe's assertive claims to confront experience head-on, he was remarkably (and distressingly) "literary."[13] Some of the late stories in *The Hills Beyond*, such as "Chickamauga," along with scattered examples elsewhere, testify to Wolfe's keen ear for varieties of voice and character; but he came nowhere near Faulkner's protean capacity for shifting voice and mood. Wolfe was a "talker," while Faulkner was a "listener." To be the latter implies others to whom one is willing to listen and to whom others are willing to tell stories. Wolfe seems to have had little of this essential capacity for listening. He could satirize and parody, but only rarely did he render the other in a straightforward, disinterested way. Wolfe lacked a feel for independent reality, which is to say that he lacked imagination. His angle of vision was willed rather than imagined.

Wolfe's fiction makes relatively little use of the Southern context as such. "The hold," as Louis Rubin notes, "of the Southern community upon his characters is not very real."[14] Altamont or Libya Hill could as well have been in the Midwest as the South. They are of the "province," and the experiences peculiar to a Eugene Gant have little to do with where they take place. One searches for resonant sentences in Wolfe to match Faulkner's "It was a summer of wisteria" or Agee's "The lights were out all over Alabama," which express the very essence of a place and a time. His prototypical cry was "Oh, Lost!" and that makes all the difference.

This is not to say that Wolfe was unconcerned with the South or his origins there. In *The Web and the Rock* Wolfe captures the excitement of provincial Southern boys loose in the big city for the first time and their rather stagey but endearing Southern chauvinism. The narrator comments insightfully that such young men would do anything "for dear old Dixie except to return permanently to live there." And then he notes harshly that some did return to the South to boast and defend white supremacy and to scorn the way the arts were corrupted in the "rootless" North. (Certainly Wolfe had the Vanderbilt Agrarians in mind here, though in 1937 after he met several of them in Richmond he wrote that "I did almost everything except become a Southern Agrarian myself.")[15] But such passages were generally discursive and often polemical, set pieces, not scenes integrated into the action of the story.

Wolfe even tried to match the traits which his protagonist took from mother and father with what he considered the essential differences between South and North. But this effort remained formulaic and thoroughly conventional: South and North; feminine and masculine; soft and hard; web and rock; entrapment and autonomy. He could be quite biting about Southern meretriciousness. In *Look Homeward, Angel* Eugene Gant says of the South that it was a "barren spiritual wilderness" given to a "cheap mythology . . . it occurred to him that these people had given him nothing. . . ." In *The Web and the Rock* George Webber feels the pull of the North against the South of "cruelty and hurt." It was "the curse of South Carolina and its Southernness—of always pretending you *used* to be such, even though you are not now."

By contrast the people of western Catawba (North Carolina) were "plain people" and thus not given to such nostalgic moonshine. In *The Hills Beyond* Wolfe could satirize the Confederate pretensions of a family ancestor; and he took jabs at the New South spirit of speculation and boosterism off and on throughout his work. But one rarely senses that the indictment was directed at something which had once been held dear and was now abandoned. Away from his native state and region, Wolfe could wax fondly eloquent over them, yet even then this was more the young man-on-the-make's sentimental remembrance of his roots rather than anything specifically to do with the South. Thomas Wolfe and his stand-ins, not the South, were problematic in his fiction.

Certainly no one could accuse Wolfe of romanticizing the family. His father was a man of boisterous and often drunken eloquence, a sometimes lovable but more often tiresome blusterer. Nor did Wolfe's mother, a petty bourgeois Scarlett O'Hara, offer much material for romantic delineations. But the family was less an entity with which Gant–Webber had to come to terms than a complex skein of forces and emotions which he had to escape, only then to seek in different forms thereafter. In a strange way, the family itself became the emblem of a rooted and domestic existence. And Wolfe spent his life (and his fiction) trying to exorcize his experience in the family.

And yet if ever a life was marked by unconscious repetitions, the desire to rediscover lost time, it was Wolfe's. Wolfe's search for the father led him repeatedly to romanticize male mentors, and then just as repeatedly to grow disenchanted with them. An even more obvious repetition was Wolfe's romance with Aline Bernstein (Esther Jack in the fiction), a woman some eighteen years older than Wolfe. Though Wolfe's novels are remarkably reticent concerning sexual matters or even expressions of tenderness, they are quite voluble on Wolfe's love of eating. Esther Jack and George Webber don't make love when they are together; instead, she feeds and comforts him, providing the softer Jewish mother to replace the less nurturing Protestant one he had to leave.[16] Indeed, the Wolfean protagonist's characteristic "being-in-the-world" is marked by a vacillation between devouring and being devoured. At Harvard, Eugene Gant seeks to devour all the books in Widener Library just as he devours experience generally. His heroes are always hungry and thirsty, wanting to be taken care of. In a remarkably revealing letter, written in 1932, Wolfe wrote: "I want you to remember that I was not a man who starved to death, but a man who died of gluttony, choking to death on an abundance of food, which surpassed everything but his hunger."[17]

It is perhaps this overpowering orality which marks Wolfe's essential narcissism, his swings between a desire for union and oneness and a deep suspicion of others, his inability to maintain stable ties, his lack of interest finally in the autonomy of the people and objects in the world that fascinated him, the shallowness of his sensibility. It was all for *him* and not for itself. One searches his fiction for the measured and calm discourse with friends or acquaintances from whom nothing is demanded. His fictional world fails to remain in our memory as does Faulkner's; rather what we remember is a central figure moving through a world which exists only insofar as it has to do with him. Unlike Faulkner's characters who are plagued by too much, Wolfe's never get enough. Recollection leads only to repetition.

It is important also to emphasize the frightening, hostile place the world was for Wolfe and his protagonists. Though the provincial is always suspicious, Wolfe's suspicion of the other, especially Jews and women, and his imputation to them of dirtiness, penury, and lasciviousness (particularly hard to credit coming from Wolfe) point to more than conventionally held prejudice. Having barely escaped a mother who weaned him at three-and-a-half years and with whom he slept until he was nine, Wolfe feared whatever called his sense of himself into question, whatever might reveal the inner chaos. And yet he was fascinated by the other as well. But somehow these contrary stances were never integrated. What is at issue here is not Wolfe's personal opinions and prejudices so much as that he could never quite create a fictional world which could argue against his own beliefs. Perhaps this is another way of saying with Louis Rubin that Wolfe, the author, was never able to distance himself from Gant–Webber, the protagonist. Wolfe was too much *in* his writing, too given to special pleading.

This brings us back to the problem of Wolfe and the South, Wolfe and culture generally. His search for a father represented a recognition of the need for stability, for equipoise, for something to change his world from an extension of himself to something which had independent existence. In *The Story of a Novel* Wolfe spoke of the personal and cultural dimensions of this problem. The search for the father was "not merely the father of his flesh, not merely the lost father of his youth, but the image of a strength and wisdom external to his need and superior to his hunger, to which the belief and power of his own life could be united." And then, near the end of that book, he returned to the theme at a general level when he spoke of the difficulties confronting American writers. Reversing the cultural optimism of Emerson and Whitman, who had called for liberation from Europe's courtly muses, Wolfe bemoaned the lack of a tradition for the American writer: there was "no antecedent scheme, no structural plan, no body of tradition that can give his own work the validity and truth it must have . . . he must make somehow a new tradition for himself."[18] What Wolfe testified to here was not the sense of being overshadowed by a tradition, but the absence of one; his was the anxiety of no influence, the burden of self-creation. And in moving so typically from the lonely, isolated individual to an all-embracing communion with the American ethos itself, Wolfe lacked what might have mediated the two—a regional tradition that would have ordered his efforts, even as he rejected it.

This is not to deny that Wolfe saw rightly, at least from his vantage point, the uselessness of the decaying Southern ethos. His tragedy was that he lived beyond any cultural tradition except that which he could piece together on his own. It was not a matter of believing or not believing in a religious faith or sharing certain ideas and ideals or manners. Wolfe was no different from many others there. The problem rather was that he had little sense of what had been lost and what might have once provided coherence. Like Jay Gatsby, Wolfe could finally only believe in the "green light," the world of infinite possibility.[19] As a result he was continually re-creating his innocence. The protagonist of his later work could not have been "Eugene Gant," since the late fiction was less an elaboration than a repetition of the early novels. To be sure, emphasis was shifted and new episodes introduced, but nothing much developed. It was a replay. Had Wolfe actually gone back home earlier, he might have realized that he could not "go home again," could not retrieve it all in memory and relive it. This might have given him the necessary distance to let the present and past world be, and to let others come alive.

James Agee: Intruder in the Dust

If Thomas Wolfe's reputation has waned since his death in 1939, James Agee's has grown remarkably. Until his posthumously published *A Death in the Family* received a Pulitzer Prize in 1956, Agee was little known beyond the readership of *Partisan Review* and those who followed his film criticism in *The Nation* and *Life*. *Let Us Now Praise Famous Men* received high marks from Lionel Trilling, Paul Goodman, and a few others when it appeared in 1941. The 1930s were over, however, so Agee's unclassifiable documentary *cum* autobiography went generally unnoticed.

Agee has rarely been considered a major figure in the Southern Renaissance. Though his major writings are generally set in the South, his name is hardly mentioned when Southern cultural and literary achievements of the post-Depression years are assessed. Except for laudatory words from Paula Snelling in *South Today* and George Marion O'Donnell, most Southern writers ignored *Famous Men* when it appeared. Clearly, neither it nor the author quite matched the conventional notion of literary Southernness. Agee had no academic or (Southern) literary affiliations, and was not associated with any established Southern institutions. Though not political in any strong sense, Agee associated himself with the anti-Stalinist Left at the *Partisan Review,* an allegiance that few other Southern writers or intellectuals found congenial, to say the least.

In the 1940s, and previously, Agee's keen interest in film, photography, and popular culture set him apart from those of Agrarian and anti-modernist sympathies, who considered such phenomena symptoms of cultural decline not of creativity. Whereas

Faulkner loathed writing for Hollywood and had only a casual interest in the movies, Agee loved both.[20]

Here it might be well to discuss Agee's film criticism briefly, since it reveals his essential notions about art and even some of the problems he had faced in writing *Famous Men*. Agee's reviews and essays for *The Nation, Time, Life, Partisan Review*, and *Sight and Sound* were informed by a unified sensibility (though not theory) which over time transformed his film reviews into a body of film criticism.[21] As much as anyone, Agee was responsible for creating this new field of critical activity; indeed, in his case the stature of the criticism generally outweighed the object of critical address.

In keeping with the democratic and avant-garde commitments in his life and art, Agee saw film as both popular and high art. If a choice had to be made, then Agee seemingly preferred the genuinely popular appeal of the cinema. In a review of Carl Dreyer's *Days of Wrath*, Agee asserted that "there is only one rule for movies that I finally care about: that the film interest the eyes, and do its job through the eyes." D. W. Griffith's greatness lay in "his power to create images; he was a 'great primitive poet.'" And it is no accident that Agee's best-known essay on film, "Comedy's Greatest Era," was in praise of those masters of the silent film— Harold Lloyd, Harry Langdon, Buster Keaton, and, above all others, Charlie Chaplin. Their language of gesture expressed the highest achievement of the medium. The "eye" of perception and its technological extension, the camera, were the crucial aesthetic tools.

Image and gesture were central to the popularity of great film. In a *Life* essay on his friend John Huston, Agee claimed that Huston was "a born popular artist . . . he operates largely by instinct, unencumbered by much reflectiveness or abstract thinking, or any serious self-doubt." Huston "honors his audience" by making pictures which demand that the eye "work vigorously; and through the eye they awaken curiosity and intelligence. . . ." This was central in "good entertainment" and in "good art." One suspects Agee here of both a bit of condescension and not a little envy. For his praise of Huston encompasses everything Agee was not as an artist in his extreme self-consciousness and self-criticism. In fact he added that Huston lacked "that intense self-critical skepticism" necessary for great art.

Still, Agee's approach seems an essentially sound one, and in retrospect a more generous one than the strict distinctions urged by his friend Dwight Macdonald in the debates about mass culture in the 1950s. For Agee, both popular and high art were hostile to the pretentious and the "arty," the self-indulgent and the self-righteous. Though his standards were almost perversely high, he could ferret out of the most unlikely movie a redeeming gesture or image which gave him and, he hoped, the viewer the excitement, first visual and then intellectual and moral, so central to good art of any sort. And though he was suspicious of "message" films, he was an incessant moralist about the film's obligation to itself and its intentions: all that could reasonably be demanded of a film was that it do what it set out to do.

In reading his film criticism one also finds hints of the problems he had faced in and the attitudes that had shaped his Alabama book. An essay in 1944 attacked black artists Hazel Scott, Paul Robeson, and Louis Armstrong for succumbing to the lure of meretricious "pseudo-folk art." Agee had a standing suspicion of attempts to depict the "people" faithfully, probably a remnant of the anti-Stalinist Left's distaste for popular front sentimentality. All too often the results were grotesque, condescendingly folksy or self-consciously and pretentiously simple, as in the pseudo-Biblical diction of American Indians or primitive peoples. As we shall see, Agee too faced this problem in *Famous Men;* and his statement that "finding a diction proper to the so-called simple folk is one of the most embarrassing, not to say hopeless, literary problems we have set ourselves" illuminates his reasons for largely avoiding a direct rendering of the speech of the three tenant families.

One film in particular seemed to address the same problems he had faced in his Alabama book, Jean Renoir's *The Southerner.*[22] Agee praised it for avoiding political preaching or exposé and for its "poetic, realistic chronicle of a farm year's hope, work, need, anxiety, pride, love, disaster, and reward. . . ." But he took the film to task for missing the language and work, the movement and gesture, the "posture and speech and facial structure" of its subjects. The review ended with Agee wandering a bit afield, obviously casting back in memory to his own experience. If, he wrote, "you don't see or appreciate or understand your subjects as well as you think you do, you stand likely therefore to be swamped by your mere affection or respect, and so perhaps should give up the whole idea." One wonders to what extent such musings were retrospective self-criticism.

Finally, and rather unexpectedly, Agee explained away D. W. Griffith's egregious racism in *The Birth of a Nation,* a charitable gloss that comported ill with the sensitivity on matters of race displayed in *Famous Men.* It may have been that because he was so bent on making Griffith the founding father of film he could not grant that, to put it mildly, the film maker had been "anti-Negro." Rather, Agee defended Griffith for going to "preposterous lengths to be fair to the Negroes as he understood them, and he understood them as a good type of Southerner does. I don't entirely agree with him . . . but Griffith's absolute desire to be fair, and understandable, is written all over the picture." Thus in his zeal to ward off Comstockery from the left as well as the right, Agee fell into the trap of defending the indefensible because it came in tandem with the great and innovative, and was "sincere."

Roughly a decade separated Agee from Faulkner, Wolfe, and the Agrarians. And, perhaps more than any other Southern writer of his time, he felt the full impact of literary modernism. His sensibility was shaped not only by Eliot and Joyce—the standard modernist pioneers—but also by Kafka, Malraux, Céline, and the cinematic innovations of the Russians. Like the Agrarians, he was fond of the metaphysical poets, and his high-church Episcopalian upbringing might have inclined him to a devotion to ritual and tradition. But the Agrarian creed and its Southern chauvinism were foreign to Agee. In fact, a satiric poem published in *Partisan Review* in the late 1930s poked fun at the Agrarians, and apparently offended Allen Tate. The middle two stanzas go:

When the world swings back to sense
(But the world is so damned dense)
An indisputably Aryan
Jeffersonian Agrarian
Will be settin' on the ole rail fence.

Swaying slightly with a hot cawn bun,
Quoting Horace and the late John Donne,
He will keep the annual figures
Safe from the prying eyes of niggers,
And back his Culture up with whip and gun.[23]

In sum, Agee was committed to democratic visions as well as to the elitist assumptions of modern literature. This mixture of cultural radicalism and literary modernism led him to see art as highly dangerous and subversive if attended to properly, a far cry from the ostensibly apolitical and culturally conservative intentions of the Agrarians. Unlike Wolfe, who aimed for a broad audience, or Faulkner, who seems to have written for himself, or the Agrarians, whose poetry and criticism sought to preserve an aristocracy of vision against the leveling impulses of the age, Agee explicitly sought a democratic, high art. It was not the only apparent contradiction that marked his life and his work.

More than is usually the case, Agee's life and work are impossible to separate. He endlessly complicated the injunctions of the New Criticism. Particularly in *Famous Men* a (perhaps *the*) central concern was an investigation of his own motives and intentions. There was clearly no straightforward way to separate the dancer from the dance. Whereas Faulkner hid his private concerns with mulish obstinacy, and Wolfe told much while revealing little, Agee was bent on a lacerating, probing, self-examination. Utterly uncompromising with himself and his motives, he ultimately became his own most important topic. Unlike Wolfe, Agee was less interested in limning the portrait of the artist as a young (and not so young) man than he was in revealing the person behind the artifice. His concern with self took on the trappings of a secular quest for justification—by what right may I write and pretend to articulate the truth? Not the creation of a world but the discovery of the truth of his vocation and of *the* world in which he found himself obsessed him. In this Agee manifested a higher degree of self-awareness than any other Southern writer of his time.[24]

Despite—or perhaps because of—his self-consciousness, Agee never quite got untracked. In 1930 at the age of twenty-one he wrote to Father Flye that it was difficult "to decide what I want to write."[25] He was consumed not only by the movies but by music; and his Guggenheim application of 1937 proposed enough projects to keep any five artists working a lifetime. (Needless to say, his application was rejected.)[26] Agee seemed to sabotage his own efforts with his melancholy, self-pity, and self-contempt. Already aiming to be the best before he had even been very good, he wrote in 1932: "I am simply not capable of being the kind of person, of doing the kinds of things, which I want to be."[27] One must contrast this with Faulkner's quiet labors from the mid-1920s to the mid-1940s, and his quite genuine (and moving) sense of amazement when, pondering what Malcolm Cowley had put together as *The Portable Faulkner*, he wrote to Cowley: "By God, I didn't know myself what I had tried to do, and how much I had succeeded."[28] Faulkner knew that he was good; Agee had heard that he could be.

Other contradictions marked Agee's life and work. He was strongly attracted by the Blakean vision of the holiness of things; yet Agee was fascinated by the bizarre and the grotesque, and often displayed a mordant cynicism about human worth and motive. One might attribute the latter to his strong Christian upbringing, except that Episcopalianism has rarely been noted for its strenuous spiritual demands or moral rigor. More likely Agee's own self-contempt and masochism were at work here. Another set of contrarieties was revealed in Agee's tender, excruciating consideration for others, which was underlain by a violent streak that brooked no control. Indeed, according to T. S. Matthews, his collaborator, photographer Walker Evans eventually broke off close contact with Agee because of Agee's violent tendencies.[29] In his writings, particularly *Famous Men*, Agee addresses and assaults his reader, stakes out the widest claims for his work, yet doubts not only his good faith but even his capabilities. If it works, it has failed; if it doesn't, it likewise has failed.

But it was never a problem of laziness. Everything was of the utmost importance, and thus relatively little got done. A cover story for *Time* was labored over with the same assiduousness as his own work. Agee was, it seems, unable to discriminate between the essential and the superfluous. This was "the discrepancy" his last wife Mia observed "between the talent and the tasks to which it was put."[30]

Since Agee's death there has been an extensive and by now tedious debate as to the nature of Agee's "failure." As several have noted, Agee would have been the last to blame the spirit of the times or the depredations of mass culture, or even the need for money, for his failure to write more about what most interested him. Agee himself claimed that his swings between feverish activity and melancholy betokened a "weakness of the will," though he wrote to Father Flye that his wife Mia "struck much closer, with self-pity. . . ."[31] Indeed, when he was twenty-five he wrote to his former mentor that he was faced with the problem of "how to become what I wish I could when I can't" and spoke of his need for "guidance, balance, coordination."[32] Later, Dwight Macdonald would observe of Agee that he was "born in the wrong time and place . . . American culture was not structured *enough* for Agee's special needs." Unlike Faulkner in Hollywood, "Agee didn't have this kind of toughness and shrewdness."[33] And Louis Kronenberger was onto the same thing when he wrote that Agee "had magnanimity but not, I think, strength . . . not something flabby, but just not sufficiently firm."[34]

But why call Agee a failure at all? He left behind a novella, *The Morning Watch*, an unfinished novel, *A Death in the Family*, several short stories and fables, a prize-winning book of poetry, a considerable body of film criticism, and one unclassifiable work, *Let Us Now Praise Famous Men*.[35] Though *Famous Men* will be our focus here, it might be well briefly to mention the others. As for the verse, Dwight Macdonald's claim that Agee's best poetry is scattered throughout his prose seems to me essentially just. *The Morning Watch* is too cloying and obvious in its symbolism; it

needs ventilation, some modulation in tone. In short, it is too pre-
cious and "written." It is all the more surprising that *A Death in
the Family*, which was done at roughly the same time in the
late 1940s, is a minor masterpiece, a moving work which combines
tact and feeling to near perfection. Agee's ear and eye are master-
ful in capturing nuance and detail. It is one of the few works by
an American writer (and certainly a Southern one) which depicts
family life as more than a chamber of horrors, a breeding ground
for psychoses. But for all that, *Famous Men* is the work which will
define Agee's status and which stands as a landmark in Southern
writing of the 1930s and 1940s.

Let Us Now Praise Famous Men

In 1936, the twenty-seven-year-old Agee and photographer Walker
Evans spent two months in Hale County, Alabama, on assignment from *Fortune*. After receiving the manuscript, the editors at
Fortune realized that Agee's experience had led him to something
other than what they wanted or what their readers expected from
the magazine. The material was released to Agee and Evans, who
found and then lost (over editorial policy) one publisher, Harper,
and finally found another, Houghton Mifflin, which published
Famous Men in 1941.[36]

Agee composed several pieces in the late 1930s while working
on the Alabama book. In one unpublished fragment Agee spoke
of his need to "restore . . . such of my lost life as I can . . . This
book is chiefly a remembrance of my childhood, and a memorial
to my father."[37] Here Agee was shaping his conception of what
would become *A Death in the Family*. Just as importantly, this
attempt at recovery of his lost life, the effort to tell his own "story"
and locate himself in the context of his family, was at the center
of his Alabama project as well.

Agee realized the precarious nature of his effort at restitution. In the same fragment he talks of his tenuous connection with
his family's past: ". . . my ancestors, my veterans. I call upon
you, I invoke your help, you cannot answer, you cannot help; I
desire to do you honor, you are beyond the last humiliation. You

are my fathers and my mothers, but there is no way in which you can help me, nor may I serve you."[38] To exist, he says at the conclusion of the fragment, means to be eventually forgotten, to be expunged from human memory. But as if to counter this "fact," Agee was to memorialize those "famous men" in his Alabama book and give them—and himself—a lasting place. If the monumental form of Southern historical consciousness invoked the heroic and collective past (as in Tate's "Ode to the Confederate Dead"), Agee offered a kind of inverted monumentalism, the hallowing of the obscure and the "private." Thus his *Famous Men* was to be a counter-heroics, more in the tradition of Emerson and Whitman than Tate and the Agrarians.

Then in his piece "Knoxville: 1915," published in *Partisan Review* in 1938 and later placed at the beginning of *A Death in the Family*, Agee sounded the "search for identity" theme. "Knoxville: 1915" creates the mythic, almost Edenic still-point which constituted the possibility and the necessity of his art. In richly sensual terms, it pictures the family together at twilight after summer supper. Adults talk on the porches; fathers water lawns; the clanging of trolleys echoes in the background. It ends with a blessing upon the family. But then Agee follows with the note of estrangement: "[they] will not, oh, will not, not now, not ever; but will not ever tell me who I am."[39] This sense of alienation indicated the distance Agee had traveled since that summer of 1915 just before his father's death. A similar movement from "at-home-ness" to estrangement will recur in *Famous Men*.

Finally Agee's application for a Guggenheim Fellowship in 1937 ("Plans for Work: 1937") included a preliminary and remarkably straightforward statement of his Alabama project. Already he sought to distance his effort from "art" by considering it "as exhaustive a reproduction and analysis of personal experience, including the phases and problems of memory and recall and revisitation and the problems of writing and of communication, as I am capable of . . . to tell everything possible as accurately as possible; and to invent nothing."[40] Here it is important to emphasize "recall and revisitation," for they will come to refer not only to his month in Alabama, but also to his early life. The process of recalling his Alabama experience was a way to return to his own childhood. The return to the South was the "spatial" analogue of his temporal regression,[41] an attempt to find out who he was and where he belonged. What he sought, then, was a recovery of that period before the death of his father, before the fall into time, awareness, and estrangement.

Rather than analyzing *Famous Men* in terms of its overall structure (for example, as following the sonata form) or discussing its dominant imagery (night/day, dark/light, wet/dry, sea/land), it is most profitable, I think, to see the book as concerned with three things: 1) the development of an epistemology and aesthetic which will enable Agee to 2) capture and convey the lives of three tenant families and 3) ultimately to find his way "home." Agee's experience with the three families was an occasion for developing the other two concerns. The result is what Faulkner would refer to elsewhere as a "splendid failure," a work which ranks with the best creations of the Southern Renaissance.

The Aesthetics and Epistemology

For Agee epistemology is aesthetics: to perceive is to perceive beauty. In *Famous Men* the aesthetic is founded upon two assumptions: first, the superiority of consciousness to imagination, and, second, the inadequacy of language for the task Agee sets himself. According to Agee, the camera and the "unassisted weaponless consciousness" are the means by which "immediacy" and "human actuality" can best be rendered. Since the connection between words and things is arbitrary, however, Agee questions the ability of words to convey what he wants about reality: "Words cannot embody; they can only describe." They are pointers, not the things themselves. Were it possible, Agee claims that he would have offered: "photographs; the rest would be fragments of cloth, bits of cotton, lumps of earth, records of speech, pieces of wood and iron, phials of odors, plates of food and of excrement . . . A piece of the body torn out by the roots might be more to the point." What Agee was attempting was an Emersonian vision, but one that denied itself the central romantic and modernist power: the imagination.

These notions need a bit of unpacking. At one level Agee located himself in a traditional American attitude of suspicion toward art and artifice. While artifice is a sign of corruption and decadence, the showing of function and display of craftsmanship are desirable.[42] But though this suspicion of "artiness" was present in *Famous Men*, Agee meant more by his objection. A powerful motif running throughout *Famous Men* was the dangerous, explosive potential of art to change lives. The conventionally educated person emasculated art and rendered it thoroughly safe; but that was not a fault inherent in works of art as such.

Nor did Agee object to works of the imagination because they diverted political consciousness into safe channels. The arrangement of the elements in *Famous Men* suggests a Brechtian attempt at "alienation"—one is never allowed to settle into a conventional way of reading or ready set of responses. Excerpts from *King Lear* and Marx are followed by a page from an elementary school primer. But this alienating effect is also intended to distance the reader from conventional liberal or left-wing political responses. In an age that saw the flat-footed politicization of art, Agee stood Brecht on his head.[43]

Agee objected most strenuously to the deification of the imagination because he felt that art obscured more than it clarified reality. Ultimately, art could not be taken seriously (rightly so by implication) because it involved a "willing suspension of disbelief." Over and against art stood reality or "nature," by which Agee seemed to refer to all that which is not consciously crafted for aesthetic effect; a meaning reminiscent of Emerson's in *Nature* where "nature" refers to all that is "NOT ME": "Everything in Nature, every most casual thing, has an inevitability and perfection which art as such can only approach . . . a contour map is at least as considerably an image of absolute 'beauty' as the counterpoints of Bach which it happens to resemble." And later: "It is simply impossible for anyone, no matter how high he may place it, to do art the simple but total honor of accepting and believing it in the terms which he accepts and honors breathing, lovemaking, the look of a newspaper, the street he walks through."[44] In the final analysis, if art could not be taken literally, it could not be taken seriously. But if Agee's aesthetic registered the influence of a decade that had grown suspicious of the conservative implications of literary modernism and of a culture that was suspicious of artifice, he was too strongly influenced by modernism to have come to his view without considerable doubt and self-division. Using the techniques of literary modernism, he sought to forge a type of sophisticated realism that would in turn avoid the dangers involved in a naïve attempt to mirror reality. No matter how unfortunate we might judge his overly simple dichotomy between imagination and consciousness, art and reality, Agee had earned the right to this view.

The implications of Agee's privileging of reality over art were crucial in what followed in *Famous Men*. Agee's aesthetic of the "unassisted consciousness" is an example of what Jacques Derrida has called the "metaphysic of presence" which stands behind the Western philosophical and artistic tradition.[45] That metaphysic holds that on principle unmediated access can be gained to God, Truth, the Good, the Absolute, Reality, or whatever might serve as the "god-term" in a religious or philosophical system. According to Derrida, such immediacy is impossible, and we find "only" traces of a former persence: absence is "already always there." By implication we can never return to a time of unalienated origins, nor can we reach the end of history. That we only succeed in discovering the "trace" results not from insufficient rigor or faulty rationality, bad faith or moral shortcomings. It is in the nature of things. Furthermore, Derrida's critique of the metaphysic of presence speaks most clearly against the phenomenological effort to gain access to essences by bracketing normal assumptions and against the anthropological nostalgia, running from Rousseau down through Lévi-Strauss, that seeks to discover man before his "fall" into written language. Agee's *Famous Men* bears a certain family resemblance to both such efforts. Also, Agee's suspicion of writing and his strong desire to present objects in their immediacy illustrate the valorization of visual over linguistic communication, and the demotion of "writing" to a necessary evil in communicating the truth about the lives he observed.[46] The objects he wished to include in lieu of the text were not for him the signs of absence, but were marks of presence, of immediacy.

But Agee's aesthetic involved him in a crucial contradiction.

He assumes, for instance, that actuality is "a universe luminous, spacious, incalculably rich and wonderful in each detail, as relaxed and natural to the human swimmer, as full of glory, as his breathing." Whether one traces this view to the Joycean epiphany in which beauty is "in" things rather than imposed upon them or invokes the Emersonian "transparent eyeball" which attempts to bring the "axis of vision" and the "axis of things" into congruence or claims with Blake that "everything that is is holy," Agee's notion of consciousness includes characteristics which are not deducible from the operations of the unassisted consciousness or from actuality itself. Moreover, with this theory of perception and of beauty, Agee has difficulties dealing with the existence of pain, suffering, or evil. If suffering is a "natural" phenomenon or evil is a part of perceived reality, then consciousness can hardly imply an aesthetic capacity for discrimination or a capacity for moral judgment. If everything that is is holy, then pain and suffering are illusory or, what is worse, potentially beautiful. Finally, Agee has it every way: truth is beauty is actuality is holiness, a thoroughly Emersonian notion.

There is yet another implication of Agee's aesthetic. If we follow Derrida's line of thought, we can see that Agee's efforts to empty his consciousness of imaginative artifice, to see things directly without mediation, inevitably must fail. Agee's frustration comes through in his constant moralizing throughout *Famous Men*, the double-binds he imposes on the reader (if you criticize the book, you are reading it the wrong way; if you like it, you are a philistine who fails to register its full power), and the violence he does against himself and his effort. He tries to establish his moral right, his epistemological purity, and his aesthetic immediacy by paradoxically confessing his failing in each of those realms. If I admit my faults, he seems to reason, I can achieve the proper vantage point, which is not a vantage point at all but the status of a "bodyless eye," a term reminiscent both of Emerson and of the aesthetics of the camera. But the problem is that he has transformed an ontological condition—that of our belatedness, our existence in a world of "traces" of absent presences—into a condition following from his (and our) failure. And we can see this in the language he uses to describe himself: he is a "spy," a sort of voyeur. But if he is going to capture the lives of the three families, he must necessarily intrude into and "violate" their lives. He is caught in a double-bind: not to violate is to forgo access to actuality; to enter their lives is to commit a moral fault.

At times in *Famous Men* Agee drops his impossible claims and allows the resulting complexity of interaction between himself and the families to emerge. One of the book's most powerful sections comes when Agee admits his sexual attraction to Emma Woods, speculates that she understands and reciprocates it, and writes of the resulting complications, hesitations—and communication.[47] It is so powerful precisely because Agee represents himself as an embodied I not a "bodyless eye." And Emma emerges as fully human, a desiring subject whose desire is reciprocated, rather than as something "holy." It is not "immediacy" which is represented, for there is no such thing. Rather we grasp the mediations of time and place, education and status, culture and power, and sexual desire within which Agee, Evans, and the families are caught. But Agee rarely allows himself this freedom.

Here we must go back and take up the second central aspect of Agee's aesthetic—his theory of language and representation—and its relationship to Walker Evans's photographs. Evans, like Agee, was suspicious of artiness and commercialism and began his career by rejecting the former quality in Alfred Stieglitz and the latter tendency in the work of Edward Steichen. Though, according to John Szarkowski, Evans's work was informed by the notion that "nothing was to be imposed on experience; the truth was to be discovered, not constructed,"[48] his photographs are highly stylized and clearly posed. Unlike the photographs of Margaret Bourke-White, which are so obviously aimed at eliciting a stereotyped response from the viewer and are so artificially "natural" in their attempt to capture the subject in an "unguarded" moment,[49] Evans's are stylized to the point of artlessness, or at least give the illusion of being so. They are "denotative" but only weakly "connotative"—or again not connotative in the expected ways.[50] They don't do the thinking and feeling for the viewer, and are thus rarely "kitschy." As Susan Sontag has pointed out,

Evans (like Agee) falls within the Whitman tradition which finds beauty or significance in the plain and commonplace, even in what is generally taken to be ugly or distasteful.[51] The larger point here is that this is a cultural convention that makes use of artifice, device, and values of its own.

In a sense Evans's photographs work against the grain of Agee's prose. In their spare, austere, even classical quality, they come much closer to Agee's aesthetic than do the writer's romantic sensibility and literary style, which is dense, convoluted, and often extremely self-conscious and "written." Indeed, the last thing which could ever be said of Agee is the apt characterization Sontag gives of Evans's photography—"noble reticence."[52]

There is yet another quality of photography that connects it with Agee's aesthetic and with his personal quest: it is an "elegiac art."[53] It represents a past time and place that have been frozen and can be re-evoked in the present. At least with photography, the age of mechanical reproduction has served, contrary to Walter Benjamin's speculation, not to destroy the "aura," the sense of distance and even mystery, but to augment it.[54] Photographs become icons that both imply and negate time. If we keep this in mind we can see why Agee was so fascinated by the camera: it could stop time. It returned an absence to presence, and this was what he was seeking in Alabama.

Unlike most books containing a text and images, the photographs, at least according to Agee, are "not illustrative" of the text, nor does the text serve as a relay point linking the pictures. Their arrangement does not tell a story.[55] Very few of the photographs are referred to directly in the text; and as Agee would have it: "They, and the text, are coequal, mutually independent and fully collaborative." This is a case where Agee's intentions seem to be fully consonant with the effect of the text. And these intentions also illustrate another aspect of the book's strategy: the effort to involve the reader in the production of meaning rather than providing it for him.[56]

But the photos also presented Agee with an insuperable challenge: how to do the same thing with words that Evans had done with the photographs? The fundamental problem facing Agee was that Evans's photographs are iconic or analogic messages, while human language is a digital mode of communication.[57] Of course the photographs are not the objects they represent, but they stand in a "motivated" relation to those objects. One does not need a code to translate or transform the photograph into what it represents.[58] By contrast, words, as Agee well recognized, have no connection by resemblance (of any sort) with what they stand for: the relationship is arbitrary or conventional. More specifically Agee notes that words can falsify through "inaccuracy of meaning" and "inaccuracy of emotion"; and they cannot "communicate simultaneity."[59] Here Agee was onto what contemporary students of communication, such as Gregory Bateson, have emphasized: it is not just that the two modes communicate the same thing in different ways (one picture is worth a thousand words) but that they communicate different things in general (a thousand words still wouldn't necessarily communicate what a picture does). "Words," Agee writes, "like all else are limited by certain laws."

It is for this reason that Agee wanted to reject "naturalism." In his exhaustive description of a particular scene or experience the naturalistic writer conveys everything but what that scene is like. The description "gathers time and weightiness which the street [the scene described] does not of itself have; it sags with this length and weight." What is achieved is "the opposite pole from your intentions." Or to shift the metaphor, a naturalistic description resembles the situation of a person who in order to tell a joke must spend his time with an explanation "fifteen times the length of the joke." Agee leaves the matter unresolved, but adds that it is also a law of language that words attempt to be more than words. "Human beings may be more and more aware of being awake," that is, they use language according to its law of separation of word and thing, "but they are still incapable of not dreaming." Through our use of words we seek to bridge the gap between words and the objects they describe. Thus, Agee in *Famous Men* attempted to transcend the "languageness" of language via language, even though he knew the attempt would be futile. Where Faulkner attempted to overcome *time* by "saying it all in one sentence," Agee tried to overcome that mythical *space* between signifier and signified, between words and the objects they describe. Finally, the human capacity for language is a sign of that original separation from the source. The separation is a spatial one (in birth), but more importantly a temporal one involved in our being *in* time and being constituted by time. Agee's impossible aesthetic project, which pushed him to the limits of consciousness and language, mirrored his attempt to recover his own lost past, to overcome the spatial and temporal gap separating him from that still-point in his own life.

The Three Families

William Stott's contention that *Famous Men* transcended the documentary conventions of the 1930s reminds us that the Depression decade marked the coming of age of the documentary as a way of exposing poverty and suffering, on the one hand, and celebrating American life and culture, on the other. It was the decade of the WPA state and local guidebooks, the popularity of the newsreel and the photomagazines (*Life, Look*), the recrudescence of regionalism and Popular Front evocations of the "people," and the social science writing of the Lynds, Dollard, and Powdermaker, which went beyond statistical analysis to make use of participant observation.[60]

Yet Agee strenuously objected to the ways journalists, photographers, and politicians distorted the lives of those they investigated. For him journalism was a way of lying, while the political efforts of well-meaning liberals and radicals were wrong-headed. Where imaginative efforts offended reality by their artifice, the conventional documentary *à thèse* ended by patronizing, peddling quaintness and pity in the guise of objectivity.

Only if one remembers what Agee was reacting against, for example, a book such as Erskine Caldwell's and Margaret Bourke-White's *You Have Seen Their Faces*, can the extremity of his rhetoric and his often self-serving attacks on others be provisionally understood. Instead of assuming a detached posture of superiority, Agee made problematic his own reactions to what he saw and his efforts to figure out how to convey them. He wished to "live into" the lives of the poor. From this point of view it is easy to sympa-thize with Agee's desire to avoid conventional statistical analyses or lengthy excursions into the origins of Southern sharecropping. Such exercises diverted attention from the actuality of the lives in question. Like "Adam on the first day," Agee attempted to clear a space among his contemporaries from which he could see the lives of the Gudgers, the Woods, and the Ricketts clearly, and see them whole. To jettison the overlay of conventional expectation and assumption would perhaps make this possible.

Inevitably Agee arrived at a vantage point every bit as "in-terested" as those of his journalistic and literary counterparts whose mistakes he wanted to avoid. Agee's descriptions of the grain and texture of buildings, the embedded toil and sweat ap-parent in the clothing, the excruciating monotony of the daily round make up some of the finest writing in the book. Like Tho-reau, Agee took common things, routines, and necessities and in-vested them with the luminosity of the most conventionally poetic object. But in doing so he by no means forswore the devices of the imagination. To convey what *is*, which was his goal, it was necessary to make comparisons of a metaphorical nature. For in-stance, he likened the color of worn overalls to "some of the blues of Cezanne" and the intricate patchwork of George Gudger's shirt to "the feather mantle of a Toltec prince." The clothing was ut-terly functional yet Agee charged it with symbolic import and ironic significance.

Indeed, Agee succeeded much better in re-creating the ambi-ence of the three families than he did their lives as human beings.[61] We rarely hear them speak in their own voices or get a feel for the way they articulate their lives. Agee feared that, if he in-cluded more direct discourse, *Famous Men* would be taken as a repository of quaint dialect at which his readers could smile con-descendingly. Also at work, however, was Agee's suspicion of the spoken word, a self-defeating position for one who hoped to cap-ture something of the lives of the creatures who speak—human beings. More generally, Agee depicts his hosts as "poor naked wretches," utterly without that which would make them human— culture. As Robert Coles has observed, Agee mentions nothing of their religious life;[62] nor do we hear them at song or telling stories and we rarely see them in other than commercial relationships. We learn that members of two of the families are kin, but we never see the three families as part of any social context. They have no politics or art, and no future.

It is possible that Agee was essentially accurate in his depiction of these particular lives. But it is not so much his empirical observations of their lives that disturb as his refusal to grant them any space of freedom. In comparison with Faulkner's *As I Lay Dying* or even Erskine Caldwells' fiction, Agee's depiction of "poor whites" fails to begin to do justice to the complexity of their lives. As one critic has suggested, this may have to do with the fact that Agee didn't stay around long enough actually to enter the lives of his subjects fully. By comparison with Faulkner, "Agee . . . seems the mere visitor or the native away too long, ..."[63] Which he was.

Besides comparing the tenants with helpless and defenseless animals throughout *Famous Men*, Agee also sees them as innocents, crucified by the world and crippled by its murderous intentions. This was what Lionel Trilling meant by Agee's lack of "moral realism."[64] Agee does not deny their hatred of and cruelty toward blacks and livestock, but claims that "you must reckon them 'innocent' even of the worst of this." They are finally not responsible, since "by their living and by their education, they are made into hopeless and helpless cripples" and are not as "well equipped as domestic and free animals." But not only do they lack political or class consciousness, they also have little or no sense of beauty or aesthetic consciousness:

> I would say too that there is a purity in this existence *in* and *as* "beauty," which can so scarcely be conscious of itself and its world as such, which is inevitably lost in consciousness, and that this is a serious loss.
>
> But so are resourcefulness against deceit and strangling; and so are pleasure, and joy, and love: and a human being who is deprived of these and of this consciousness is deprived almost of existence itself.

Here, however, Agee's text and Evans's photographs argue against his own assertion. There are innumerable places in the book where one of their subjects shows some feel for decoration and attempts to make beautiful what is "only" commonplace. It is as though in denying himself the uses of the imagination, Agee intends to deny it to his subjects. And as William Stott notes of Evans's photography: "Rather than show how simple the poor are, how feeble, how limited, he shows them to be complex, strong and pervasive." Not only defeat but pride and affection show through as do (again in Stott's words) "these people's sense of form, balance and symmetry, and their fierce hunger for order."[65] These are vital ingredients in an aesthetic self-consciousness.

But even Stott, much as he admires the book, points out that Agee and Evans "commended the full humanity of their subjects, but did not fully disclose it."[66] As an example, he reprints an Evans shot which appears in neither edition of *Famous Men*. It shows a well-scrubbed, freshly combed-and-brushed Gudger family with George Gudger standing cockily in the middle of the back row, his arms spread expansively around his wife and sister-in-law. The interesting thing about the photograph is that it shows the Gudgers in a different light from what we would have expected from Agee's agonized depiction of them. (Evans told Stott that he would include this photograph in *Famous Men* if a new edition were ever printed.) Its importance lies in the way it shows "the Gudgers honestly yet as they really want to be seen";[67] that is, it shows a part of their reality that Agee (and to a lesser extent Evans) all but ignored in *Famous Men*.

In some ways, then, it was no wonder that Agee felt so intrusive: he did not allow subjects with capacities equal to his to emerge and to comprehend what he wanted to do. For Agee, the white tenants are proto-human and lack any significant measure of self-consciousness. They labor rather than work, and are immersed in and shaped by the brutal natural cycle of sheer survival.[68] Agee's failure to grant them recognition as subjects (except occasionally) turns him into a master, benevolent and well-meaning though he may be, to their slave-like existence. They exist at his sufferance. To have allowed them to speak, so that they might have spoken back to him in anger or disagreement, would have called into question the prelapsarian state of innocence imputed to them. As it was, all mediations between them and others—speech, love, argument, politics, religion, song, and story—are denied to them. This was Marx's idiocy of rural life with a vengeance.

The most glaring example of Agee's patronizing attitude toward the three families comes in the "Education" section. Agee goes on at some length about the miserable education the children receive (though he never observed instruction, since he was there in the summer). But it is not so much the lack of training or the inadequate equipment that is so scandalous; rather, it is the fact that the schools are part of "the world's machine," and even good teachers are "servants of unconscious murder." Changing the curriculum would make no difference. And he adds that his Harvard education is "by no means an unqualified advantage." Here Agee edges toward sheer impertinence. No doubt any education is inadequate, but some are more so than others. And certainly a Harvard education presents its own problems. But Agee's judgment does not go down well coming from one who was in a position to make the discriminations between a Harvard education and some other kind precisely because of his educational advantages. Finally, it is difficult to understand how Agee could depict the sharecroppers' lives as bleak and with practically no redeeming features, yet condemn liberal or radical attempts, clumsy and manipulative though they may have been, to change the conditions under which these families lived. As it stands, Agee can have it both ways: he can rail against the powers and principalities, but then repair to aesthetic contemplation when solutions are called for.

It is also important to make explicit the relationship between Agee's aesthetic and his depiction of the three families. If actuality is beautiful and holy *in itself,* there is no imperative to bring about change. Consciousness triumphs over analysis or action. Why, for instance, would one want George Gudger to have new overalls when they would lack the epiphanic potentialities of the old ones? On the other hand, given this aesthetic, it is difficult to see how Agee can consistently indict the soul murder which he saw in Alabama. Second, holiness or beauty are not qualities most readily associated with human beings. In fact they are more easily perceived in inanimate objects and non-human life than in humans, who are often perversely unholy. Finally, to have "housed" his subjects in culture would have implied that Agee himself was perceiving through complex mediations rather than "immediately." Indeed, Agee admits the role of mediating structures when he discusses the way in which beauty is class-determined. The mistake he makes is in confusing class-determined styles of beauty with the aesthetic capacity itself, which is found throughout human and animal life.[69]

At this point several objections might be raised. Alfred Barson objects to Trilling's critique (and by extension mine) by asserting that "Agee is not writing fiction but fact; his emphasis is on the mystery, not the evocation, of what is."[70] And according to Peter Ohlin, Agee's purpose was not to make the tenant families come alive as characters, but to assume that and not betray it.[71] These defenses of Agee ultimately derive from Agee's own self-justification when he writes that, in contrast with fiction, which owes its reality to the writer, the people and place in *Famous Men* "exist, in actual being . . . and as no character of the imagination can possibly exist." However true this was for Agee, because he had lived with the families, it is not the case for the reader, who gains access to them only through Agee's re-presentation of them. Because Agee claims a different status for the world rendered in *Famous Men* does not mean that it is so.

Besides Barson's flat-footed distinction between fact and fiction, it makes little sense to claim that Agee is more interested in mystery than evocation. His comments on "Education" and "Work," for instance, are explicit about the nature of tenant existence; and he certainly tries to evoke, in however peculiar a way, the quality of the tenants' lives throughout *Famous Men.* Nor is it enough simply to assume that Agee's subjects come alive, as Stott recognizes as well. I have tried to indicate why I do not think that they do.

A second response to criticism of *Famous Men* is voiced by Ohlin when he claims that "journalistic, sociological, political or artistic grounds" provide no valid bases for a critique of Agee's effort. Rather, only criticism from the standpoint of "philosophy, morals, history, psychology" is admissible.[72] Behind this position lies Agee's own distinction between the first collection of activities and that which is to be taken "seriously." Provisionally, one understands Agee's polemical thrust against convenient pigeon-holing; but ultimately this distinction is a rhetorical one. (One might also wonder how to separate politics and morals.) Further, if Ohlin argues that *Famous Men* demands a response, then one such response might be political. Ultimately Ohlin's distinction assimilates too easily to Agee's tactic of foreclosing criticism by discrediting its source.

Finally, *Famous Men* is not obviously political, except to its detriment and perhaps even to the lives involved in it. For one who knew and admired Malraux's *Man's Fate*, Agee's suppression of possibility is very strange. But perhaps the reason lies in Agee's own life history. As Barson, Ohlin, and W. M. Frohock contend, *Famous Men* is, above all else, autobiographical. It is Agee's actuality that is successfully rendered in the book; and to it we will now turn.

Search into Lost Time

To say that *Famous Men* is highly personal understates the case considerably. If the usual documentary included no theory of aesthetics, it most certainly did not record the personal, idiosyncratic reactions of the author either. For that reason the autobiographical and personal sections of *Famous Men* are all the more innovative, an altogether stunning achievement. In the light of Agee's stated intention of conveying the lives of three tenant families, these autobiographical sections may seem self-indulgent to some. Indeed, they do to me. But they also flow from the aesthetic that Agee develops and the rendering he gives of the lives of the Woods, the Ricketts, and Gudgers. With these two tasks accomplished, Agee establishes a field within which he attempts—but in vain—to recapture what he had lost at an early age.

The central themes of Agee's self-revelations are identity, love, and death, the three crucial poetic "crossings" that Harold Bloom assigns to American romantic writing. As we have already seen,

one of the most powerful sections in *Famous Men* records Agee's sexual desire for Emma Woods, something inconceivable in the documentaries or the sociological studies of the 1930s, and matched perhaps only by Lillian Smith's *Killers of the Dream*. Agee also recounts his experience of finding himself alone in the Gudger house, and how this recalled his adolescent experience of the "cold reptilian fury of the terror of lone desire which was upon me" when in his grandfather's house. Agee becomes the voyeur of his own lust.

Crucial for understanding Agee's personal quest is the way he establishes his close identification with the Gudgers as the book unfolds. On awakening the first morning there he remembers how it was to awaken as a young boy at boarding school, and that "it is in no beauty less that the gestures of a day here begin." But the sun is an enemy of the tenants, depleting the energies which the dark of night has replenished. Earlier, Agee tries to convey through a series of imagined discourses the sense of entrapment which marks the stunted lives once, he imagines, so hopeful. "How did we get caught? Why is it things always seem to go against us . . . I'm so tired it don't seem like I could ever get rest enough. . . ." The rhetorical query of "how were we caught" recurs periodically, and the section ends with "(How was it we were caught?)." Agee is also asking this question of his own life.

As *Famous Men* progresses, Agee works backward in time, to his first days in Alabama and to his early life. The climax of Agee's self-exploration and identification with the Gudgers comes in the "Inductions" section. He records his desperate need to escape to Birmingham and the desire for a woman which overtook him on his return to Hale County. The Sunday is a scorchingly hot one, and Agee captures something essential when he writes of "the desperateness of sunday . . . this sunday deathliness in whose power was held the whole of the south. . . ." And a few pages later, he writes of "this damned south spread under and around us, miles and hundreds of miles, millions and millions of people, in this awful paralysis of sunday, and the sense of death." This is the world of intense heat and Southern sun that bleaches the very life out of the landscape and the people who inhabit it. A diffused

eroticism reminds him of death rather than of life. It is a kind of hell, a rural wasteland, devoid of life or sustenance.

Almost unhinged by the heat and desire and despair on the trip from Birmingham, Agee asks, "Who the hell am I?" He flirts with the idea of ramming his car into a tree, an action which would have repeated his father's death in a car accident. He considers the damage he does to his wife either by staying with her or by leaving her. He then launches into a vituperative attack upon himself, art, and just about everyone:

> you never live an inch without involvement and hurting people and - - - -ing yourself everlastingly and only the hard bastards come through, I'm not born and can't be that hard, apparently, and - - - damn Genius and Works of Art anyway and who the hell am I, who in Jesus' name am I.

After rejecting the notion that anything will change, he ends with "Just an individualizing intellectual. Bad case of infantilism. And - - - - you, too."

As he returns to the Gudgers, he goes deeper within himself and further probes his own shortcomings. At this point Agee either experiences or fantasizes two incidents that relieve his feverish mood. In the first he stands in a much welcomed downpour "mouth wide open to take its falling" and finds relief. The second finds him lying on the ground "prostrating myself as upon a woman" within an enclosed springhouse. It reminds him of a similar site at his grandfather's, a place of calm and refreshment. But he looks up to see a huge bullfrog with "his silver larynx twitching constantly with scarcely controllable outrage." Thus, Agee's approach "to the heart and heart's blood of my business and my need."

The account of these two experiences prepares the way for meeting the Gudgers. He becomes fond of them as they wait out the storm together, but he decides not to stay the night with them. He must return, however, when his car gets stuck in the deeply rutted, red-clay road. They offer Agee food, and he reluctantly accepts, not wanting to offend or cause extra trouble. As George and Annie Mae Gudger sit and watch him eat, they all talk. At this point Agee arrives at the emotional center of his proj-

ect: the return South to Alabama and his quest into his own past come together:

> the feeling increased itself upon me that at the end of a wandering and seeking, so long it had begun before I was born, I had apprehended and now sat at rest in my own home, between two who were my brother and sister, yet less that than something else; these, the wife my age exactly, the husband four years older, seemed not other than my parents . . . and all that surrounded me was familiar and dear to me . . . and that this was my right home, right earth, right blood, to which I would never have true right. For half my blood is just this; and half my right of speech . . . I am robbed of a royalty I can not only never claim, but never properly much desire or regret . . . there is so keen, sad and precious a nostalgia as I can scarcely otherwise know; a knowledge of brief truancy into the sources of my life, whereto I have no rightful access, having paid no price beyond love and sorrow.

As in the "Knoxville: 1915" passage, Agee establishes his "at-home-ness" in this family circle which he has sought his entire life, but then undercuts it. He can never feel at home, because of some unnamed inadequacy. For a moment, Agee identifies his "real" parents as members of the excluded group, an inversion of the family romance. Not identification "upwards" in fantasy, but down and back to earlier, more "primitive" and less sophisticated times characterizes his fantasy. But reality intrudes.

One wonders then if Agee's rendering of the Gudgers, Ricketts, and Woods as "innocents" was not an attempt to cancel the disruption in his own life—the death of his father—that marked his fall from innocence into awareness. If they are innocents and he is their "child," then he was also once innocent and can perhaps regain that innocence. The prelapsarian state that he imputes to them marks *his* distance from them and the extremity and inescapability of his own weakness and despair. The consciousness of time and, ultimately, death will not allow a final identification with the still-point of the family triangle.

But Agee's sense of guilt and intrusion, of being alien even in his own "place," must also be explained. Though speculation on such matters is highly risky, one cannot help but wonder if the guilt Agee bore throughout his life did not have something to do with the feeling that he had been responsible for—or at least desired—the death of his father. It is surely significant that the death took place when Agee was six, still perhaps embroiled in his desire to have his mother and be rid of his father. What was worse, his desire came true. In *The Morning Watch* young Richard identifies his father with Christ, who is crucified for all our sins. When Richard later kills a snake after momentarily wanting to save it (on Good Friday), the mixture of sorrow, pity, and violence is clear, and would seem to point to analogous feelings toward his dead father. Not only does the young boy worship his father and his memory, he hates his father for having abandoned him. Where Will Percy's problem seemed to have been a father so "present" as to block any independence, Agee was overwhelmed by the absence of his father. In neither case could a realistic assessment of the ambivalent feelings be carried out; and guilt and aggression, turned upon the self, did their corrosive work. Reverence and violence existed uneasily together.

Here we must also recall the springhouse scene, which is full of erotic suggestion. Besides Agee's description of his prone position, the enclosure is where butter, milk, and cream are kept. It is the source, the mother, with whom he is engaging in symbolic intercourse. The bullfrog becomes the father who looks on with "outrage" at the son's usurpation of his place. As he had intruded upon the frog's territory to take the mother (the earth and the spring), his own desire as a young boy had come between his father and his mother. No wonder Agee felt the sense of intrusion and violation throughout his life.

Finally, then, Agee's search in *Famous Men* was for the restitution of the family triangle prior to his father's death, before the fall into time. The only way he could articulate this was to render the Gudgers as innocent animals, without future or past. Caught in the round of biological existence, yet holy, they are both less and more than human. They lack the burden of self-consciousness which plagued Agee and which he wanted to escape.

But Agee also knew that it would never be possible to return to this mythical state, as he knew that he could never use language to transcend language. Lacking a cultural tradition to house his own life and a real father whose life (not death) could have provided a framework for existence, he lived exposed and on his own. He had only the myth of the doomed, rebellious, and subversive artist to guide him, an *imago*, which stood in the service of the death-drive. Only by eventually committing suicide, as he in truth did,[73] could he both repeat his father's strange glory and find his way back—or forward—to the innocence which he had lost so early. For only at death can one be what and who one is, receive deliverance from the dividedness that marks human life, and find oneself at home.

From Politics to Psychology: Warren's All the King's Men

More than any other Southern novelist, Robert Penn Warren has been concerned in his writing with exploring ethical and philosophical issues.[74] Indeed, Warren's weakness as a novelist has been a proclivity to preach at his characters and at his readers, and to philosophize. As Roger Sale has asserted, the conflict between Warren's talent for story-telling and his interest in striking off profundities compromises the quality of his fiction.[75] This judgment is not confined to outsiders and non-Southerners. No less than John Crowe Ransom voiced similar misgivings when he wrote to Allen Tate about *World Enough and Time* that Warren's world-view led "him to philosophize sententiously about Truth, Innocence, Justice and what not."[76]

Such a comment is particularly ironic in light of the Agrarian animus against "abstraction" and Warren's own insistence that Southerners display a deep-seated suspicion of "abstraction."[77] By abstraction the Agrarians referred, first, to the scientific-technological vision of reality and, second, to the efforts of political liberals and radicals to run roughshod over human nature in the name of social change. Warren preserved the spirit of this double-barreled critique of abstraction, but by the post-World War II years his attacks on the spirit of abstraction fit easily into the dominant cultural mood, which stressed the non-ideological and non-doctrinaire nature of the American experience as an antidote to the dogmatic rigidity and ideological horrors of Stalinist Russia. Closer to home, for Warren (and C. Vann Woodward) the South was to play America to the North's "Russia." The South exemplified a sort of historical reality principle that might keep the nation on an even keel. This was a Southern version of the end-of-ideology thesis that appealed so to many chastened liberals in those years.

The philosophical underpinnings of Warren's writing combine existentialist themes and vaguely psychoanalytic motifs.[78] Prominent among them are the search for identity and self, the problem of human freedom, the complex relationship of past and present, with the saving power of the *deus ex machina* "love" thrown in for good measure. For Warren, man's chief end is knowledge of the human condition; and it is this knowledge, as expressed in poetry and fiction, that reconciles man to his fate and returns him to a union and communion with nature and others. Thus, there is in Warren's view a movement from alienation from self and others through trials and tests to a reconciliation with self and others, a self-acceptance and hence acceptance of others. This pattern of secular salvation, a moral therapeutic and modern mythological heroic, provides the conceptual underpinning for all of Warren's fiction. But because Warren's stories must conform to this procrustean conceptual schema, the moments of insights and reconciliations at the climax of his novels often seem willed and unearned in the context of the story.

Warren was one of the pioneering practitioners of the New Criticism. More important, Warren championed Faulkner as early as 1930; and his lengthy review-essay of Malcolm Cowley's *The Portable Faulkner* in 1946 helped mightily to rehabilitate Faulkner's reputation.[79] Warren's essay was marked by the desire to claim for Faulkner more than "regional" significance. The Mississippian was clearly, for Warren, a writer of universal import. "The legend," he wrote, "is not merely a legend of the South, but is also a legend of our general plight and problem. The modern world is in moral confusion." More important, there was in Faulkner's

work a "constant ethical center . . . to be found in the glorifica-
tion of the human effort and human endurance."[80]

Several things need to be said about Warren's reading of
Faulkner. First, it says as much about Warren's intentions as a
novelist as it does about Faulkner's. Second, Warren's "ethical"
reading of Faulkner increasingly carried the day in the critical
rediscovery and rehabilitation of Faulkner in the 1950s. In his
essay Warren took several swipes at left-wing critics, particularly
Maxwell Geismar, who considered Faulkner a reactionary and
proto-fascist. In that sense Warren's defense-*cum*-appreciation
was a valuable corrective. But, it went too far in the other direction and read back into Faulkner's great work of the 1930s what
was barely emerging in *Go Down Moses*. Warren's ethical and
universalizing reading comported all too well with what was weakest in Faulkner, something the publication of *A Fable* revealed.

Faulkner's verdict on Warren's *All the King's Men* revealed
a proper suspicion of striving for the large effect. After reading
the galleys of Warren's soon-to-published novel, Faulkner responded (to Warren's publisher) that the "Cass Mastern story is
a beautiful and moving piece. That was his novel. The rest of it
I would throw away."[81] (In the novel Jack Burden was once a
graduate student working on a doctoral dissertation in history. For
his project he must read through the letters of Cass Mastern, a
distant relative of his father's. The story he pieces together from
the surviving documents concerns Mastern's affair with a close
friend's wife, the friend's suicide, and Mastern's subsequent effort
to expiate his "sin" by freeing his slaves and taking responsibility
for what he has done. Mastern dies in the Civil War in 1864.)
Though Faulkner's judgment is too harsh, it still displays a certain
cogency. In telling the Mastern story, Warren allows the implications to emerge on their own rather than telling the reader how to
interpret it. (The same judgment applies to *A Fable*; the embedded story of the jockey is a small masterpiece, vintage Faulkner, but the rest could have been discarded.) Thus in his desire
to be a worthy successor of Faulkner, Warren misread Faulkner
to bring him into line with his own proclivities and constitute him
as a precursor of Warren's own concerns.

Though one of the original Fugitive-Agrarians, Warren was

the youngest and least tied to Agrarianism as a creed. From early on he ranged more widely than most of his Vanderbilt colleagues and has by now important work to his credit in almost every literary genre. Coming as he does from south-central Kentucky, Warren had ties, like Wolfe's and Agee's, much more with the up-country South and the hard-scrabble world of the small farmer than with the black-belt or the aristocratic legacy of the old South. There is little nostalgia in Warren's work for the culture of the family romance, at least in any specific historical sense. And though the father-son theme is central in his work, it lacks the historical-cultural resonance found in Faulkner or Tate.

Warren's *All the King's Men* belongs with V. O. Key's *Southern Politics* and C. Vann Woodward's several works as major efforts to explore the cultural implications of the "revolt of the rednecks" against the conservative Democratic hegemony, the repository, albeit a highly compromised one, of the tradition of the family romance in Southern politics. Admittedly, though not exclusively, modeled on the career of Huey Long, the novel was organized around a fictional situation remarkably similar to the one so vividly (and bitterly) described by Will Percy in *Lanterns on the Levee*.[82] In both cases the old order of commercial, industrial, and agricultural interests, overlain with a patina of aristocratic prestige, faced a challenge from the poor farmers and the hill people.

But unlike the Delta aristocrat, Warren's sympathies did not lie exclusively with the forces of order and stability. Though one can scarcely identify the ideological sympathies of the novelist (particularly a good one) with any certainty, Warren's fictional treatment of Willie Stark is by no means hostile. In fact, some early reviewers of *All the King's Men* claimed that Warren had whitewashed Stark (whom they saw as a thinly disguised Huey Long) and thus glorified a home-grown form of fascism. Whatever the faults of *All the King's Men*, its superiority to the rest of Warren's fiction lies in the genuine though not uncritical sympathy which Warren shows for all his main characters. In other of his novels, especially *Night Riders* and *World Enough and Time*, Warren seems deliberately to load the dice against his protagonist, who is usually a blind idealist, possessed by an *idée fixe,* and over his head in the sea of history. As a result the central figures lack a certain life of their own and fail to compel our interest.

Though Jack Burden eventually rejects Stark's strong-arm tactics and the atmosphere of intimidation which he encouraged, even thrived on, Jack does attempt to understand the personal and political forces that made Willie run. Willie wants to do "good"; and indeed he had. But besides doing good, Stark wants power for its own sake, not merely to defeat opponents but to humiliate them. This is perhaps his main flaw. But the flaw is made comprehensible in the political context of the book: it is "earned." Nor does Warren make Stark a figure of energy and charisma without intelligence. Stark knows what he wants to do with his power and knows how to go about doing it. His sheer intelligence is more than a match for that of any of his enemies or his friends.

Warren's treatment of Stark also anticipates V. O. Key's contention that Southern politics has more often than not been a contest of personalities rather than of principles. Stark's political movement is based on an impulse rather than any very coherent ideology. This is not to deny that Stark has principles and a program of sorts. But the Stark machine is built on no coherent ideology shared by his lieutenants and his followers. It rather depends on Willie's personal qualities and his ability to tap the emotions of his supporters. That Jack Burden, whose sympathies initially lie with Willie, could so easily abandon his cause indicates the ideological vacuum and the lack of staying power of Southern middle-class liberalism. Neither Willie nor Tom Watson was an educator as well as a leader. But unlike Watson, Stark makes no appeal to racism and nativism. Such impulses are not central to Stark's (or Long's) appeal; and he "luckily" dies before he might have been tempted to use them. *All the King's Men* was thus the first attempt by a Southern novelist to treat a Populist-type movement and its leader sympathetically and evenhandedly.

The question must also be raised as to the extent to which *All the King's Men* is importantly a Southern novel as opposed to being a novel set in the South. The brilliant opening pages of the work show Warren's ability to render a mood and ambience in full and startling concreteness. The atmosphere is *echt*-Southern; of that there can be no doubt. But, unlike the fiction of Tate, Faulkner, or Lillian Smith and like the writings of Agee and Wolfe, the South as an historical-cultural entity is not thematized in any clear-cut way. To be sure Judge Irwin is, for example, a representative of the old planter class, a figure much like Leroy Percy in his combination of Old South manner and New South connections; but his significance in the novel does not depend upon these characteristics. Neither his life nor death raises questions of regional import; the decline of the old way of life and the triumph of the new commercialism are only mutedly introduced as themes. Richard Gray has asserted that *All the King's Men* is typically Southern in its concern with the way past and present are inextricably linked.[83] That is certainly a central theme of the novel, but that is precisely the problem: its generality. Surely all sorts of works in modernist literature are organized around this theme without thereby making them uniquely Southern.

Thus in *All the King's Men*, and in most of Warren's fiction, the South serves as a setting rather than a theme itself. More important, Warren's dominant concern in *All the King's Men* is less an evaluation of the collective Southern past than, first, an exploration of the problem of power and political insurgency and, second, of self-definition and identity. This latter concern is closely related to Warren's standing concern with the relation of past and present. But in *All the King's Men*, unlike *Absalom, Absalom!* or "The Bear," this crucial relation is problematic for an individual, Jack Burden. It is *his* problem and not that of the region as a whole. The wider symbolic resonance is simply not there.

The central concerns of *All the King's Men* are closely linked to a vexing formal problem in the novel: the status of Jack Burden's narrative and the credibility of what he says. Early critics of *All the King's Men* too easily confused Burden's first-person, retrospective narrative with Warren's own point of view; and defenders of the novel properly warned against such an identification. Yet, as Sale observes, Warren seems to want it both ways. Clearly, for instance, Jack abandons his "great twitch" view of human action and responsibility for a position that makes the individual ultimately responsible for his own actions and the implications of those actions—the "spider web" view. He comes to see this as the meaning of the Cass Mastern story. His discovery of the story as a graduate student in history and his working through the letters and extant documents parallels his later, less disinterested attempt to dig up dirt on Judge Irwin. What Jack learns from the Cass Mastern episode eventually enables him to transcend his past and live in the future. Only when he absorbs what the Cass Mastern story has to tell him can he complete the job of writing up the story. Finally, Jack's use of the Cass Mastern story as a moral touchstone repeats Ike's and Quentin's obsession with the pasts of their families. But, again, the regional implication is absent in Jack's case.

There is, one cannot help feeling, a certain anti-climactic quality about Jack's rebirth into moral responsibility at the end of the novel. Jack takes no action as a concrete token of his responsibility, at least none that matches Cass's freeing of his slaves. Intellectually and emotionally he acknowledges his responsibility in the complex of events that leads to the deaths of Irwin, Stark, and Adam Stanton; and through his conversation with his mother he comes to accept his own past. But this recognition and acknowledgment lead to no wider responsibility nor do they demand anything of him. Unlike Ike McCaslin, who abjures his land and loses his wife, Jack, like Job, gets everything back: he gains a wife and an inheritance of money and property.

For most of the novel Jack is a cynical, know-it-all, pseudo-tough-guy who sounds more like a character from Hemingway than Faulkner and whose flip posturing is meant to signal his alienation from others and himself. Because he cannot solve the riddle of his own past and discover the significance of the Cass Mastern story, he lacks a future. Still, as narrator, Jack gives us clues all the way through that this is his pre-enlightened incarnation. It is Jack himself who dissects his own values and action. This in itself helps Warren avoid some of the faults of his later novels.

Jack's birth into insight comes when he learns who his real

father is. At the beginning Jack plays a pliable but aware son to Stark's strong father. As with the Quentin-Sutpen connection in *Absalom, Absalom!* consciousness and action, passivity and activity are divided between two characters, a device that mirrors the central spiritual problem of the novel: the alienation of self from self, of past from present, of father from son. Jack's distasteful political task of blackmailing Judge Irwin leads to the suicide of the Judge. Jack then learns from his mother that the Judge, not the weak Ellis Burden, is his father. The price of such knowledge is always high, though always necessary as well, in Warren's work. As Jack says: "Well, I had swapped the good, weak father for the evil, strong one . . . I had dug up the truth and the truth always kills the father . . . and you are left alone with yourself and the truth, and can never ask Dad, who didn't know anyway and who is deader than a mackerel." Within the action of the novel, the son slays the father and gains insight; the wiser narrator Jack kills off his earlier incarnations; and the author rewards Jack as God rewards Job.

The implications of this passage are crucial to understanding the novel, but their effect is weakened by a certain confusion and lapse in tone. To find the truth about one's own past, Warren says, often involves suffering and even violence. The father possesses or stands for what one must know, and the knowledge wrested from him leads to freedom and responsibility. Only by acquiring this knowledge of his family's past and learning the true feelings of his mother can Jack acquire a future, which is to say a self that can act freely. Jack's (pseudo-) ancestor, Cass Mastern, had caused the suicide of his friend when the friend discovered the affair between Mastern and his wife. Mastern's acceptance of responsibility leads ultimately to his ostracism and death. Jack causes the death of Judge Irwin, who cannot acknowledge the action in his own past that had led to the suicide of the man he replaced in the American Electric Power Company. Irwin's suicide in the present sets in motion Jack's understanding of the past, the death of his old self and the emergence of a new one.

This pattern of not merely the interaction of present and past but of repetition echoes the trap of the Faulknerian historical consciousness. "Perhaps the only answer," Jack reminisces, "was that by the time we understood the pattern we are in, the definition we are making for ourselves, it is too late to break out of the box . . . To break out of it, we must make a new self. But how . . . ? At least that was the way I argued it back then." And it is precisely Jack's change of heart which weans him from this bleak view. But Jack's conversion seems gratuitous; and neither it nor the novel's upbeat ending is quite convincing. Parricide, insight, and reversal are all present as in the Oedipal drama and its private modernist version, the psychoanalytic context. Yet what Jack "learns" is both too abstract and too sentimental. What he has done or desired does not have to be paid for; rather the lessons he carries away are the typical apolitical virtues of love and individual responsibility.

There is also a problem with the tone of Jack's narrative. In the "mackerel" passage quoted above, he lapses into a voice reminiscent of his earlier, cynical self. The flip use of "Dad" and the "mackerel" reference are too "in character" to suggest any new hard-won insight, and they undercut the seriousness of the passage rather than heightening its impact, as Warren had suggested the creative mixture of types of language would in his essay "Poetry—Pure and Impure." This failure of tonal control betrays, I think, the implausibility of Jack's rebirth into a new self.

There is another problem that demands resolution on both the personal and the political level—that of power and the relation of ends and means. Before Jack's conversion, and after he has talked with Willie about the problem of power, Jack meditates on the "theory of historical costs" and the way good intentions can lead to evil and vice versa. This is a view which Warren seems to have considerable sympathy for in later works such as *Brother to Dragons* and *Band of Angels*. Through Jack in *All the King's Men* Warren suggests the difficulties involved in judging past or present action and the necessity for a complexly ironic view of history.

The status of this view of history becomes problematic by the novel's conclusion. *All the King's Men* ends with the lone and scarred survivors, Jack and Anne Stanton, together; and Jack suggests that he will return eventually to politics to work for Hugh Miller. This evocation of Miller is bewildering, since he makes a brief appearance early in the novel as Willie's well-meaning but weak-kneed Attorney-General who resigns because he can't stomach Stark's methods. If Jack (and Warren) accept the theory of historical costs, then it would seem that working for Miller is a repudiation of this philosophy of politics and power, a way of soothing one's conscience at the expense of political effectiveness. If Jack, however, repudiates the theory, then he would seem to work against the grain of Warren's own position. And this seems implausible since the novel ends on an upbeat note, notable more for its sonority than its clarity: ". . . soon we shall go out of the house and out into the convulsion of the world, out of history into history and the awful responsibility of Time."

I must confess that I have no idea what these last lines mean. Warren does seem to want it both ways; and this, I think, makes up part of the contradiction that lies at the heart of the novel. Indeed, there is another contradiction of sorts at the end. Warren sets forth a view of freedom and responsibility that is gained through the costly confrontation with past and present reality. Jack Burden seems to have escaped the repetitious pattern of history. Yet Jack notes the irony of living in Irwin's house and writing about Cass Mastern. It is, he thinks, "a situation . . . too much like the world in which we live from birth to death, and the humor of it grows stale from repetition." This would suggest that Jack still suspects that he is caught in the process of time marked by repetition not freedom: entrapment not freedom is his fate. But his observation is followed immediately by the brave words of the ending.

I suspect that the confusion in *All the King's Men* has something to do with the fact that the relationship between the two stories—Willie's and Jack's—is never satisfactorily worked out. *All the King's Men* begins as a political story of a poor boy who rises to power, his attempts to break the "interests," and the personal, political, and moral costs involved.[84] As seen through Jack's voice this would have made a fine and rather unique Southern (and American) novel. Yet *All the King's Men* gradually becomes the story of Jack Burden's search for his father, i.e. the search for knowledge of his own past that will free him for the future. The two stories are only tenuously connected, and the linking device— Willie's desire to find incriminating information about Irwin—is not entirely convincing. By the end the Stark story has become a backdrop for Burden's quest and Stark's death a way of precipitating a resolution of the quest. One might argue that the two stories mirror one another: Jack and Willie both do harm in the process of doing good. And both win through to insight, though Willie perishes. Yet the insight Jack attains is "only" personal and fails to illuminate the historical, ethical, and political issues raised by the Stark story. A political leader's use of bad means to achieve good ends is not finally in the same universe of moral discourse with the similar actions of an individual that have only circumscribed implications.

Thus what promised to be a profound political novel ends by being swallowed up by a private quest for identity, a form of secular salvation. In C. Vann Woodward's analysis of Tom Watson and the Populist movement, we can see some of the reasons for the failure of Watson and the Populist movement. But with *All the King's Men* it is difficult to discover what we are to learn from Willie Stark's story. It is less a matter of complexity or ambiguity here than that Warren seems to lose interest in the political issue altogether. Paradoxically, then, where Faulkner's *Absalom, Absalom!* and *Go Down Moses* begin as private quests of apparently limited implication and end by engaging the "awful responsibility of Time" and the question of responsibility for one's individual and collective past, *All the King's Men* begins with the wider political world and ends by withdrawing from it into the rhetorical resolution of a private quest. Consciousness defeats action; the private vision, the public involvement; the ironic son, the strong fathers.

10

The New
Southern Liberalism:
V.O. Key, C. Vann Woodward,
Robert Penn Warren

After 1930 there developed an important reassessment of Southern political culture. Beyond the florid rhetoric and political posturings, Southern politics was, as V. O. Key insisted, serious business. It had been a form of self-defense, a sort of regional jiujitsu allowing the weaker South to stave off the thrusts of its more powerful but clumsier Northern opponent. Perhaps for that reason, among others, it tended toward extravagance and a certain unreality.

Yet, politics within Dixie had also been about race and class, the preservation of upper-class and white hegemony. Sometimes the class (or "interest") conflict was obvious. Still, however much U. B. Phillips's central theme of white supremacy must be nuanced, Southern politics had been dominated by the race question. Historically, racial hostility functioned to discourage alliances across racial lines that might have threatened the existing political dispensation.

In very general terms this was the situation facing Southerners who wanted to alter the political landscape after 1930. During the Depression most Southern politicians supported the economic liberalism of the New Deal and occasionally enlivened it with the language of agrarian insurgency.[1] Louisiana had its Huey Long and Alabama its Hugo Black. In North Carolina, business and academic progressives provided a certain "moderate" influence. But the fact remains that during these years there was no mass challenge to the political and social order in the Southern states. Political participation had been low since the early years of the century. While blacks had been largely disfranchised, the mass of white voters showed increasingly less interest in voting or participating in the political life of their states.

During the Depression a thoroughgoing scrutiny of the Southern political tradition was begun. Increasingly, academics and intellectuals devoted more attention to the Populist heritage, the only post-Civil War movement to challenge the hegemony of the Democratic party. In the 1940s there were modest increases in black political participation and a new willingness of liberal and moderate politicians to court, however timidly, the black vote. By the late 1940s the prospects for the emergence of a two-party South were discussed widely. As Alexander Heard noted in his A Two-Party South? (1952), most concerned Southerners agreed that the Democratic hegemony over Southern politics was unhealthy and that the monologue should be replaced by a dialogue. Conservatives felt that the national Democratic party had grown too liberal; moderates were disturbed by the lack of dialogue itself; and progressive forces looked to a realignment of political parties to remedy the social, economic, and racial problems which had accumulated over the years.[2]

And yet there were contradictory forces at work. A measure of prosperity in the post-World War II years led many Southern politicians to grow more conservative on social and economic issues. Moderate intellectuals such as John Temple Graves and Virginius Dabney moved rightward, with Graves going over to the Dixiecrats in 1948. Though historians and political scientists were rapidly rediscovering the importance of Populism, the social bases for an agrarian liberalism combining the New Deal program with the Populist spirit were rapidly disappearing. The new Southern intellectual liberalism was a mood without a movement, a vague ideology without social roots. The usable past it sought to discover lacked contemporary resonance.

Indeed, the post-1954 realignment of Southern politics would proceed under a conservative and/or racist dispensation. The Republican party, the conservative Democrats, and third-party (chiefly Wallacite) splinter groups would grow, while Southern liberalism would all but disappear. From 1954 until the early 1970s the politics of regional recalcitrance would carry the day. Southern political liberalism would ironically be revived not by white agrarian sources or from a new industrial working class but from the once-excluded black voters.

Groundwork

The patriarchal culture, white racial psychology, and politics were closely linked in the Southern mind. Yet those writers who offered critiques of the tradition of the fathers and of white racial attitudes rarely engaged political issues directly. For instance, Cash ended his *The Mind of the South* by bemoaning the lack of contact between the South's intellectual and political leaderships; but concerned as he was with the cultural nexus from which politics issued and preoccupied with Hitler's advance across Europe, he made no further suggestions. Though Cash spoke highly of Huey Long, he underestimated the importance of the Populist movement. For Cash, the Populists had not been tough enough and had finally succumbed to the savage ideal and proto-Dorian convention. Mencken's influence had undoubtedly helped keep him from anything approaching adulation of the rural masses. They were the enemies of free and enlightened thought. Rather, Cash saw the forces for political change arising from the Southern working class and the critical spirit of the universities. For Howard Odum, eager as he was to paper over conflict of any kind, the Populists undoubtedly seemed too radical. Thus Cash and the Regionalists were simply not that interested in the contemporary political implications of their rehabilitation of the yeoman strain in Southern history.

Not surprisingly, the Vanderbilt Agrarians were less than enthusiastic about rural insurgency, past or present, or about mass politics. And they generally shied away from a class analysis of

Southern society, with one exception: Herman C. Nixon. By the end of the 1930s Nixon's writings increasingly emphasized class conflict and the exploitation of poor whites and blacks by black-belt planters and business interests. In addition, Nixon was a leading figure in the Southern Conference on Human Welfare, the nearest thing to a popular, liberal movement for change in the region.[3]

In *Possum Trot* (1941) and *The Lower Piedmont Country* (1946) Nixon focused on that subregion of the South containing Chattanooga, Atlanta, and Birmingham as its three urban centers.[4] Contrary to received opinion, asserted Nixon, "the South is inherently neither solid nor completely right wing," though he granted that "conservative or reactionary elements exercise an undue and unfair share of power."[5] According to Nixon, this subregion had challenged black-belt and lowland domination in the past and might serve as a source for a new, more liberal South. Chattanooga and Birmingham were industrial centers, and the TVA had revitalized much of the subregion. Nixon admitted that in the area the Klan's roots were deep and that white supremacy and anti-union sentiment were firmly entrenched as well. In fact, the crucial term in the quotation above was "inherently." Though the South had been conservative, Nixon hoped that subregions such as he described would provide the social and economic bases for a new Southern politics.

The other Agrarian who showed consistent interest in the yeoman South was historian Frank Owsley. In *Plain Folk of the Old South* (1949) he shifted his sights to the ante-bellum years. Echoing Cash without acknowledging him, Owsley contended that the pre-War South had been no simple three-class society of planters, poor whites, and black slaves. Rather, the "plain folk"— the "landowning farmers and herdsmen"—comprised the bulk of the Southern population.[6] Written from a Turnerian perspective, *Plain Folk* claimed that Southern yeomanry had occupied much of the best land in the South (on this point he parted company with Cash) and that the upward path from yeoman to planter status had been relatively easy to negotiate.

Owsley's book was only superficially at odds with the aristocratic tradition. For Owsley, the white Southern population was a "genuine American folk," united by race, language, custom, tradition, and history.[7] Explicitly "not class conscious," the yeoman farmers admired their less plain brothers and sisters and assumed that they, too, "could make it."[8] This indicated the "sense of unity between the plain folk and the aristocracy."[9] Unlike Cash, Owsley celebrated the lack of class consciousness in the ante-bellum South. The planter class maintained its hegemony by "personal and local" ties rather than through physical or economic coercion.[10] The ideal society was not an egalitarian one, but a unity of diverse classes welded together by a common folk spirit. Of the Populists he said little.

Aside from voices such as Nixon's, the rediscovery of the Populist tradition and agrarian insurgency came from younger Southern academics. Rooted in the experience of the 1930s, this largely academic movement exemplified clearly the way in which the past was pressed into the service of the present. An older tradition was exhumed and "re-membered" so as to provide the markers for a new departure in the Southern political culture. Forgotten alternatives were resurrected. In Nietzsche's terms, the academics of the 1930s and 1940s combined critical and monumental history: the politics of the Solid South was analyzed and rejected, while the politics of the forgotten or ignored Populist heritage was taken as a guide to future action. But however intellectually important and promising, the intellectual rediscovery of Populism proved to be a political dead-end.

The One-Party South: Myth or Reality?

If academics led the way in reshaping the contours of the Southern political past, the liberal political scientists were concerned primarily with demonstrating the possibility of a two-party South. (In this they showed the impossibility of separating political science and history.) Historical research was pressed into the service of present concerns. In complementary fashion, the efforts of the historians concentrated upon the Populists and bolstered the argument for a two-party South in the present. If meaningful political divisions had marked Southern politics in the past, then the monolithic politics of the contemporary South was no unalterable fact.

In this area as in others, studies by outsiders anticipated and paved the way for analyses by native Southerners. In *Race, Class and Party* (1932) Paul Lewinson rejected the "solid South" notion,[11] and asserted that one-party domination after the Civil War had masked the real divisions in Southern society. The South, Lewinson claimed, was riven by conflict between border and deep South states, urban and rural areas, black and white, rich and poor. Still, the case Lewinson set forth undermined his thesis as much as it supported it. First, he confused the existence of a solid political South with the fact of social divisions within the South. And he was hard put to explain why, even after the final disfranchisement of blacks in the 1890s, the Democrats failed to divide along ideological and interest lines in any consistent fashion. Instead, the politics of personality and of race continued to cancel prospects for meaningful political divisions.[12]

The importance of Lewinson's book lay in the fact that it showed the way for later political analysis to establish the historical foundation for rejecting the one-party South in the present. In essay after essay in the next two decades, historians and political scientists emphasized the "other" Southern political tradition of liberalism and democracy against the tradition of aristocratic, black-belt hegemony.[13] "Objectively," it was clear that the South, past and present, was marked by all sorts of economic, social, and political divisions. But those who emphasized a certain unity and consensus in the Southern experience were to have the better case. Whatever the experts thought should be the central issues in Southern politics, the bulk of (white) Southern voters, small and racially exclusive as that bulk was, rather consistently thought otherwise. Put more pointedly, when it came down to race as the central theme in Southern politics, whites would continue down into the 1960s to vote their prejudices and not their "interests." If other issues predominated, then divisions could and did take place along fairly "rational" lines.

Lewinson's *Race, Class and Party* also pioneered in marking the 1890s as the key decade in post-Civil War Southern politics. Unlike C. Vann Woodward, who would later try to demonstrate discontinuity, Lewinson saw the disfranchisement of the black Southern voter as a fairly continuous process after 1876. But he did note that both Democrats and Populists vied for the black vote in the 1890s; the Democrats, he claimed, were generally more successful. He recognized that opposition by rural insurgents to certain types of disfranchisement measures was based on the fear that such efforts might be turned against themselves as well as against blacks. But after the mid-1890s methods became more sophisticated and were made more color-sensitive.

In his *American Dilemma* (1944) Gunnar Myrdal covered much the same ground.[14] Though differences with Lewinson were not glaring, Myrdal stressed the solidity rather than complexity of the political South. For him as for Marian Irish, upon whose essay "The Southern One-Party System and National Politics" he drew heavily, white supremacy was the central motif in Southern politics.[15] Like Lewinson, however, he saw a general and continuous disfranchisement process at work after 1876. Initially illegal and surreptitious, suffrage restrictions were written into the state constitutions by the 1890s. Along with Jim Crow measures this legislation "solidified the caste line and minimized the importance of class difference in the Negro group."[16] In other words, the discriminatory legislation of the 1890s in the South ratified a *fait accompli*.

Of equal interest were Myrdal's observations on Southern politics. He first observed that Southern conservatism was unique in "being married to an established pattern of illegality."[17] Conservatives had the power, but not the (national) law; liberals had the law, but not the power. Second, Myrdal noted that, with the exceptions of the Klan, the Prohibition movement, and the Populist insurgency, the South had seen no mass political movements: it had a "low level of political culture."[18] Related to this observation was his insight that the South "lacks nearly every trace of radical thought."[19] Unlike Latin American republics or the European societies in which the left and the right vied for power over the not so vital liberal center, the South lacked a left or even much of a liberal center.

Myrdal showed critical sympathy toward Southern liberalism, which lacked a mass base and depended upon the largesse of the federal government and the philanthropic foundations for its survival and what little leverage it exercised.[20] In effect colonial intellectuals, Southern liberals were discredited before the fact and forced to nibble around the edges of the Solid South, "cajoling, coaxing and luring the public into giving in on minor issues."[21] With men like Dabney and Graves in mind, Myrdal claimed that Southern liberals "do not . . . demand social equality . . . and they declare against 'inter-marriage.' "[22] The South was not a fascist political culture, but a strange combination of "a stubbornly lagging American frontier society with a strong paternalistic tinge."[23] All this was Myrdal's way of saying that the South's political culture was pre-modern: there was no rational correlation between class and politics nor consistent adherence to the values underlying the American political system in general, i.e. the American Creed.

Still, Myrdal was ever optimistic. With his tendency to see the best in an apparently hopeless situation, he claimed that the New Deal and World War II had undermined the "legal foundations for Negro disfranchisement."[24] This optimistic note was joined with a thinly veiled prediction of worse things to come if change were not initiated. Prudent conservatives as well as liberals should begin to re-enfranchise blacks, and he questioned the folkways/stateways dictum by urging a challenge to Jim Crow laws.[25]

The Southern Dilemma

Two years after Myrdal's massive work appeared, V. O. Key and his assistants began a comprehensive study of Southern politics, which was to be another blow aimed at the midsection of the solid political South. Financed by the Rockefeller Foundation and based in Tuscaloosa at the University of Alabama, Key and his associates set to work on a considerable task involving 538 interviews and fifteen months of work. In 1949 Key, a native of Texas and a professor of political science at Johns Hopkins, published *Southern Politics;* and three years later his chief assistant, Alexander Heard, published a spin-off work of his own, *A Two-Party South?*.[26]

Southern Politics belongs with Cash's *Mind of the South* and Howard Odum's *Southern Regions* as a major attempt by a native to take the measure of Southern distinctiveness—and backwardness. Like Cash's work, *Southern Politics* wasted little time with the pieties about the Jeffersonian tradition or soothing noises about the heritage of Southern politics, as least as conventionally conceived. Though never matching Cash's vivid and often powerful prose, Key's book was much better written and more lively than the massive volumes of Odum or Myrdal. *Southern Politics* also marked a shift away from the 1930s' emphasis upon economics and reflected the centrality of politics in the decade preceding the 1954 school desegregation decision. Though economic backwardness was still obvious, there were signs in the post-World War II world that the South was slowly catching up with the rest of the nation.

Key's study ranged over a staggering variety of topics, from colorful political history to dry technicalities of party financing. For our purposes, however, two matters assume prime importance: Key's analysis of the historical and social origins of modern Southern politics and his normative theory of two-party politics. Key used the latter to take the measure of the former. Later Key would call himself a moderate New Deal Democrat, and in *Southern Politics* the bias showed. At the core of his normative theory was the assumption that a two-party system encouraged the meaningful democratic politics which the South had historically lacked. Like Myrdal, Key used an external standard—in his case the American two-party system—to throw into bold relief the idiosyncrasies of Southern politics.

Closely related to a preference for the two-party system was Key's belief that the rational or logical bases for a political party were "sectional, class or group interests." The (restricted) competition between interest-based political parties would, in Adam Smith fashion, generate a healthy politics. Or more accurately, Key's notion of limited competition reflected the New Deal ideology of regulated capitalist economics and the newly emerging pluralist, interest-group ideology. As of the mid-1940s, however, Key contended that the South not only lacked a two-party system, it lacked a political party system altogether. Whatever it had once been, the Democratic party in the South had degenerated into a "holding company for a congeries of transient squabbling factions."[27]

As Key negotiated his way through the thicket of Southern state politics, he revealed the pernicious implications of the lack of genuine political conflict in the South. In states such as Alabama, politics was dominated by localism, what Key called "friends and neighbors" politics. The next step up from localism were regional alliances within a state, a form of political organization that made little rational sense, based as it often was on historical allegiances, as in Republican East Tennessee. Southern state politics also reflected a heavy emphasis on personality. And of course racial politics was a time-tested way of gaining the voters' attention. Finally, Key observed, on occasion, intra-state political struggles might center on class or economic divisions and thus assume a certain rationality. For this reason Key homed in on the Populist revolt of the 1890s as the first (and last) time that Southern politics displayed a healthy concern with economic issues.

From his catalogue of political irrationality, Key drew the following lessons. Festooned as it was with factional instability, state party-politics in the South exhibited little or no continuity. Without continuity there was no accountability or responsibility. Issues and answers shifted from election to election. Elected officials who betrayed their promise were seldom, if ever, disciplined by the party or removed by voters. New leadership was repeatedly thrown up, only more often than not to prove incompetent. Politics, for Key, was clearly more than winning elections. Key suggested that in the long run the shapelessness of Southern politics hurt the "have nots." Without planning or ways of rewarding or punishing, no consequential programs could be devised or implemented. And without clear differences between candidates, the voter could never be sure for whom or what he or she was voting.[28]

Key's forays into the region's political history touched upon the "Solid South" problem and the search for an alternative to the Bourbon political tradition. Southern political life had been dominated by the coalition of black-belt planters and large industrial and financial interests. But the fact that Southern politics had been shaped by this coalition did not imply that political, social, or economic conflict had been absent among Southern whites. In state after state Key found opposition to planter control based on the up-country regions, the historical centers of early Republican and then Populist strength. Louisiana was a classic case: Huey Long's center of strength in northern Louisiana had also been the stronghold of Louisiana Populism. In his assessment of future prospects, Key hoped that the dormant rural insurgency would ally itself with the emerging industrial and urban working class and together provide a solid social base for a more liberal Southern politics. He emphasized several times that it was not the yeoman and poor whites who were responsible for political exclusion and domination of the black vote; it was the upper-class black-belt interests. The Democratic party, he felt, would move leftward in the coming years; its more conservative elements shift into the Republican party, which would in turn lose its up-country and mountain support (as in East Tennessee and western North Carolina) to the Democrats.

To explain the black-belt domination of Southern politics, Key devoted a chapter to the Populists and the disfranchisement movement of the 1890s. Key's discussion was highly qualified, even muddy, at times, but like Myrdal and Lewinson he saw the disfranchisement legislation as the culmination of a steady process that had been gathering steam since Reconstruction. It had been a *fait accompli* by the 1890s. He did, however, emphasize the competition between conservative Democrats and Populists for the black vote and observed that the impetus for actual disfranchisement came from counties with a high percentage of black population.[29] More generally, he suggested that the group which had power—whether conservative or insurgent—tended to support black disfranchisement.[30] Since conservative Democrats tended to be the entrenched power, it followed that they were primarily responsible for eradicating the black vote once and for all. This case was strengthened when one remembers that voting restrictions such as the poll tax and literacy tests affected poor whites as well as blacks. But whatever the particular justification, enough whites agreed to black disfranchisement to push through the measures in Southern state legislatures, though not without considerable up-country opposition.[31]

Thus, by eliminating the black vote, whites had supposedly sanitized Southern politics and enabled whites to divide without the specter of the black swing vote. But as things turned out, the 1890s was the last decade for any open and rational, i.e. "interest," politics in the South. Political and social issues were fought out in muted and refracted form within the Democratic party—both more than and less than a true party. Having lost their potential black allies, the up-country whites were diverted into the politics of race and personality and the grab for temporary benefits based on transient coalitions. Still, Key was relatively optimistic about the future. Industrialization and urbanization, the out-migration of blacks, and an alliance of rural insurgency with the labor movement promised a new rationality in the political culture.

It was—and is—difficult to take issue with Key's judicious, thorough, and engrossing study, which has been the model for a host of books on Southern politics since then. Still, questions can be raised about the concept of the party system and the concept of interest-group politics. Put succinctly, the connection between the two is less obvious than Key was willing to grant.

First, according to W. G. Carleton, Key's study lacked convincing comparative data on the superiority of two-party to one-party politics.[32] Coming at Key from the other direction, Cortez A. M. Ewing charged Key with presenting "an apology for bad democratic politics" and with underestimating the need for a new political party that appealed to blacks and poor whites.[33] Though overstating Key's apologetic intentions, Ewing's point was well taken. It called attention to Key's assumption that a two-party system was inherently more responsive to "real" issues than either single- or multi-party systems. Indeed, were politics to be a contest among interest groups, then Key's thesis suggested the desirability of a multi-party system as strongly as it did a two-party one.

Though Key can hardly be blamed for misreading the course of politics in the 1950s and 1960s, the emergence of the Republican party in those decades in fact reinforced the general conservatism of Southern politics. Thus neither "two-partyism" nor interest-group politics guaranteed "rational" politics; like the Texas of Key's study, the emergence of a Republican party gave conservatives two bases of operation in Southern states. Put another way, Key, along with most other advocates of modernization, from Odum on, overestimated both the short-run liberalizing effects of social and economic development and rural support for liberal measures, while underestimating the resistance to black suffrage in the deep South and the weakness of the labor unions. Both Key and his chief assistant Alexander Heard were too quick in passing off the Dixiecrat revolt of 1948 as a failure, for its politics of race, state's rights, and economic conservatism was to permeate Southern politics after the 1954 Supreme Court decision.

*Nor was the proper relationship of party organization to interest groups clear. Key's interest-group notion of politics implied a Madisonian notion of factional competition, while the two-party system in practice envisaged political parties as *coalitions* of factions. This raised the question as to whether the American party system could provide a normative model for Southern politics. While Key implied that the two national parties were qualitatively different, one could have considered the national parties in pretty much the same light as Key saw the Democratic party in the South. Neither national party was unified by interest or ideology. Finally, as Theodore Lowi has pointed out, a pluralist politics could operate without including blacks as one of the legitimate contending forces. Interest-group politics has conservative as well as progressive implications and encourages the maintenance of the status quo by established groups. That is, the American party system, made up of two umbrella organizations of competing factions, tends to neglect the interests of some groups in the process of meeting other group expectations. Some groups are more equal than others.

There was also a problem with Key's equation of rationality with pursuit of "sectional, class or group interests." By highlighting "interest," Key elided the matter of whether there might not be a conflict between, say, sectional and class interests. More important, Key never indicated why economic issues or class interests were to be seen as more rational than psychological, historical, or even racial ones. For example, the white South seemed firmly united in opposing racial integration. Here the cultural-historical psychology of racism overrode particular class interests, particularly those of the poor whites. If the white Southerner "thought" or "felt" in *völkisch* terms, if that was his dominant political concern, then it was rational for him to insist on the maintenance of racial apartheid.

Yet, even on economic grounds, the notion that interest politics embodies a higher rationality is not that self-evident. It has been a cliché of Southern liberals and radicals that the true interests of the common whites and blacks lay in political and social cooperation, not in competition and conflict. But why? Given a depressed, underdeveloped economy with a surplus labor force and the lack of ideology proposing a radical restructuring of the economic and social system, it is far from clear that the economically rational course for marginal, struggling white farmers or white industrial workers was to support equal competition for their jobs by blacks. Only in the long run did such cooperation make rational sense, but, as Myrdal pointed out, there was no radical movement in Southern politics to express such a long-range vision.

Key's pluralist vision was based on rather shaky intellectual foundations, welcome though it was as an alternative to Southern politics as carried on in the past. Key neither adequately justified nor developed his concept of political rationality. It was manifestly of little empirical use in explaining past Southern politics and, at best, failed to do justice to the complexity of individual or group political behavior. Moreover, though Key's theory was clearly normative in some aspects (the primacy of two-party politics and of "interest" considerations), it lacked a moral component that would guarantee social and political equality, all interest-group considerations aside. One might argue that Cash had measured Southern politics against a similar rational standard and found it wanting. Still, Cash had anchored his notion of political irrationality in Southern history extending back to the ante-bellum days, where Key was hard put to explain why the Populists had not been more successful, since they had pursued a rational politics. Like Odum, Key hoped that the South would abandon the dictates of past tradition and embrace the higher rationality of self-interest. But like Odum, and unlike Cash, he was a bit too sanguine about this possibility. In sum, what Key articulated in *Southern Politics* was the political complement of Odum's trickle-down theory of economic development as the solution to the South's ills.

The Rediscovery of Populism

At a meeting of the Southern Historical Association in November 1969, C. Vann Woodward delivered an uncharacteristically harsh attack on W. J. Cash. Woodward had reviewed Cash's *The Mind of the South* when it appeared in 1941, mixing general praise with caveats about Cash's neglect of conflict and discontinuity in the Southern experience.[34] The tone of the review was rather friendly if a bit condescending, in the manner professional historians tend to adopt toward outsiders who try to do history. Little did anyone know at the time that Cash and Woodward, and their differing views of the Southern past, would come to represent two conflicting readings of Southern history.

According to Woodward's misreading of Cash, Cash was a zealous reformer whose thought betrayed a shallow grasp of human affairs, a lack of appreciation for the "tragic theme in history."[35] Genuine if limited insights about the culture of the South had been so obsessively followed as to become ridiculous. Of course, one could not help remember that Cash hit Woodward where it hurt—the Populists. Woodward's biography of Tom Watson in 1938 had been an important landmark in the resurrection of the Populist tradition, but Cash was unimpressed by the immediate importance or lasting impact of Populism. At some point Cash and his influence had to be dealt with, and in a manner not unlike the one which Woodward claimed Cash had displayed toward the mind of the South. Woodward's essay, which was an important and often insightful critique of Cash, also revealed much about Woodward's own career as a historian and as a Southern liberal.[36]

If a single figure has dominated the Southern historical writing following the Depression it is C. Vann Woodward. A native of Arkansas, Woodward attended Emory University as an undergraduate and, after receiving an M.A. at Columbia, took a Ph.D. at Chapel Hill in 1937. After World War II, Woodward taught at Johns Hopkins until the early 1960s, when he moved to Yale. Thus there is in Woodward's career a rather typical pattern traced by many successful Southerners: a rise in professional esteem and prestige in tandem with a geographical move northward.

Between 1938—when his dissertation, *Tom Watson: Agrarian Rebel*, was published,—and 1955—when *The Strange Career of Jim Crow* appeared—Woodward revolutionized the established views of Southern history from the end of the Civil War to World War I. The core of his historiographical achievement was in *Origins of the New South, 1877–1913*, which appeared in 1951 along with a closely focused and highly detailed study of the Compromise of 1877, *Reunion and Reaction*. When the dust had settled, a new way of looking at Southern history had emerged, a new paradigm was established. With these works, all basically the product of the same research, Woodward's view of post-Reconstruction Southern history prevailed.[37]

This is not to say that Woodward worked in an intellectual or historiographical vacuum. He had been active in the early 1930s in the defense of Angelo Herndon in Atlanta and was strongly influenced by Odum and Vance at Chapel Hill.[38] In the 1930s Woodward was not averse to offering a class interpretation of the South which reflected not only the radical spirit of time but the historiographical vision of Charles Beard and of Woodward's mentor at Chapel Hill, Howard K. Beale. Unlike the Beardians, however, Woodward was attuned to the importance of race in Southern history. The dissertation on Watson and the ensuing studies in the 1950s would be dominated by this focus upon economics and race, class and caste.

Woodward's historiographical revisionism was accompanied (and aided) by numerous books and essays by other historians in the 1930s and 1940s. Besides Woodward's biography of Watson, these years also saw biographies of Robert Taylor, Ben Tillman,

and Leonidas L. Polk and numerous articles on Populism and the
origins of the Jim Crow system.[39] For instance, in 1937, Daniel
Robinson published a measured defense of Southern demagogues in
the two-year-old *Journal of Southern History*.[40] According to Robinson it made no sense to view the Tillmans, Bilbos, and Longs as
bizarre symptoms of the degeneration of the region's political culture. The more conservative and decorous political tradition had
been idealized out of all just proportions. Rather than condemning
the demagogues, Robinson tried to understand the context in
which inflammatory and extravagant language was effective; and he
traced their anti-black rhetoric to the fact that the conservatives
had the black vote sewed up. Once in office the "redneck" leaders
had been rather moderate and progressive leaders, neither as radical as conservative opponents feared nor as empty of achievement as
liberals had asserted. Robinson also identified the 1890s as the
onset of black disfranchisement. Thus Robinson's essay and others
like it provided Woodward with the materials for his new interpretive schema.

Here it would be well to keep in mind what Woodward was
working against as a historian of the South. As late as the 1930s
Southern history tended to be an exercise in hagiography, in monumentalizing and devoted antiquarianism.[41] Its dominant mood
was celebratory and/or defensive. Neither the institution of slavery nor the beneficent influence of the planters was scrutinized
with any skepticism. Regrettable as it was in the abstract, historians
such as U. B. Phillips viewed slavery as a school for civilization, the
cornerstone of a graceful and valuable way of life.[42] Responsibility
for the Civil War was generally laid at the feet of the North or
attributed to inept leadership on both sides. About Reconstruction
there was little argument. Academic historians, as well as popular
ones, felt the South had been justified in resisting what they considered the misguided racial and economic policies of the North.
The later more radically inclined Beardian emphasis upon economic factors would inadvertently support this view of Reconstruction. Nor were things much different in accounts of the post-
Reconstruction South. Little work was done in the New South or
Populist periods, nor was much attention paid to the rise of dis-

franchisement and segregation. A perusal of the pages of the *Journal of Southern History* between 1935 and the early 1950s reveals a decided concentration upon the sectional conflict, then the War and Reconstruction. The periods on either side of this great divide were historiographical no-man's-lands.[43]

Still, there were signs in the 1930s that standard opinions were being revised. Following Du Bois's *Black Reconstruction in America, 1860–1880* (1935), F. B. Simkins and Howard K. Beale openly questioned the conventional accounts of Reconstruction horrors, particularly the allegations of ineptness and corruption among the freedmen and their white allies. Unlike Cash or Lillian Smith, these historians were less interested in the cultural psychology of racism than they were in its political and economic roots. Gradually it became clear that the standard version of post-Reconstruction Southern history stood in need of considerable modification. Who profited from disfranchisement and under whose aegis had it in fact taken place? Who held political and economic power in the New South? Were the men who controlled the "Redeemer" governments the same men, or same type of men, who had led the South into war? Once these questions were raised, Southern historiography could never be the same. The person most responsible for raising and answering them was C. Vann Woodward.

Tom Watson: Agrarian Rebel contains or at least anticipates the rest of Woodward's major historiographical revisions. Its subject was a Georgia politician who, prior to Woodward's biography, was considered one of the most colorful—and vicious—practitioners of rabble-rousing in Southern history. In Woodward's hands Watson emerged in full dimension and with a certain tragic aura. Though unmistakably sympathetic to Watson, Woodward's account was no exercise in hagiography. To the thirty-year-old biographer, Watson's life was "in many ways the tragedy of a class, and more especially the tragedy of a section."[44] Or perhaps Marx's oft-quoted dictum conveys the contradictions of Watson's life, as presented by Woodward, even better: "Hegel remarks somewhere that all facts and personages occur, as it were, twice. He forgot to add: the first time as tragedy, the second as farce." The first part of Watson's life was in many ways tragic. His misfortune was to get a second chance in Southern politics; and his politics degenerated into a farcical copy of what they had once been.

In his biography of Watson, Woodward established the thoroughly "untraditional" nature of the post-Reconstruction leadership in the state of Georgia, a thesis he later expanded to cover all the Southern states in *Origins of the New South.* The so-called Redeemer governments had been headed by men who often cooperated with the Republicans during occupation and had been ante-bellum Whigs. Moreover, they were thoroughly committed to industrial development of the prostrate agrarian economy. Older and authentic agrarians such as Robert Toombs and Alexander Stephens were shoved aside: commercialism was added to class rule and racism to make up the new dispensation.

Second, as Woodward set forth Watson's involvement in Democratic party politics, his growing dissatisfaction and his move to form a third party, he made clear that Populism in the South was better organized and more radical than its Western counterpart, which up to that time had attracted the most attention from historians. Watson never fell for the free-silver issue which William Jennings Bryan championed as a panacea in 1896 and which helped destroy the Populist party. Watson was a "middle of the roader," contrary to the sound of it, the more uncompromising of the Populist factions.

Woodward's third major historiographical advance emphasized Watson's attempts to forge a coalition of white and black farmers to challenge the New South industrialists and the conservative leaders of the Democratic party. It was on this point that Watson appeared particularly radical, considering his later reputation as a racist without equal. In the midst of the Depression of the 1890s and only a couple of decades removed from Reconstruction, Watson dared challenge the suffocating hold of the Democratic party and white supremacy upon Georgia politics. Here was a genuine exponent of the two-party South and of "interest" politics.

This third point has been subject to considerable misinterpretation. Part of the problem lies in the fact that a skillful historian, especially one as attentive to complexity as Woodward, writes with sufficient ambiguity to allow various implications to be drawn from his work. Later readers of *Tom Watson,* particularly in the 1950s and 1960s, would see Woodward's Watson as a civil-rights advocate before the fact and the Populist party a model for the beloved community of interracial harmony and political unity. Southern liberals wanted (and needed) heroes. They would remember Watson's forthright early opposition to lynching and the convict lease system, his courting of the black vote and defense of black supporters, and his willingness to speak from the same platforms as blacks. Nor did Woodward exactly discourage such glosses when he wrote: "Never before or since have the two races in the South come so close together as they did during the Populist struggle."[45] But the inattentive reader tended to slide over Woodward's qualifying remark that Watson had advocated political, *not* social equality. Advanced though Watson's political strategy may have been, his racial views were not atypical in his historical context.

Woodward's biography, like Watson's life, divided into two parts. The second charted the devolution of Watson to hard-shell racial and religious bigotry of the most phobic "competitive" sort. In the 1890s, race had been Watson's constant "nemesis" (as it had been in Southern politics generally). When Watson returned to active political life in 1904 after eight years of semi-retirement, he fervently embraced his old nemesis. During his moratorium, Watson came close to insanity, drank heavily, and constructed "Hickory Hill," a big house reminiscent of Andrew Jackson's "Hermitage," on the nine thousand acres (with 44 tenant families) he owned. In his new incarnation Watson had not completely shed his Populist sympathies, at least on economic and social issues; but besides the racism and nativism, he became an ardent defender of the "Confederate Creed" and saw his role as one of rehabilitating the "Lost Cause."[46]

In depicting Watson as a colorful, if not entirely typical, representative of Southern progressivism, Woodward used Watson to sound a theme he would expand in *Origins of the New South*— the thoroughly racist nature of the Progressive movement south of the Mason-Dixon line, where "progressive" political reform often meant the removal of blacks from political life. This stood in ironic contrast with the early promise of Populism. The "rednecks" came off looking no worse and at times better than their middle-class successors. Watson remained a committed agrarian, whatever else he became, and heaped scorn on New South advocates and the South's own Woodrow Wilson, whom he judged a canting hypocrite. He considered the South the Ireland of the Western Hemisphere; and he violently opposed U.S. involvement in World War I, was instrumental in getting Leo Frank lynched, loved and supported Socialist Eugene Debs, and welcomed the Bolshevik takeover in Russia. What Richard Hofstadter was to call the paranoid style of American politics received new meaning with the later Watson.

If there is a major weakness in Woodward's engrossing biography of Watson, it is his failure to explain, as opposed to describing, the metamorphosis of Watson's racial beliefs and his conception of the role of blacks in Southern politics. Certainly, as Woodward claimed, the frustration of defeat, fraud, and violence met by Watson and the Populists played a major role. Yet Woodward's reluctance to engage in psychological probing, speculative though it would have been, left a wide gap between Watson's experience and his reaction to it. Indeed, throughout his writings Woodward has shied away from psychological probings, preferring rather to focus on "external" forces.

But Woodward does supply at least some of the raw materials for such speculation. From early on Watson had been rather unstable emotionally, a brooder and great hater, a vindictive and violent man, given to suspicion of others. There was also in him an "irrational core of nostalgia for a lost paradise of childhood"; and Woodward quotes a passage from Watson's writings in which the Georgia leader evokes in loving terms his "stately, self-contained, self-reliant" grandfather on the "old Southern homestead . . . How sound, sane, healthy it appears even now . . . ."[47] Here we have again the evocation of the heroic grandfather, while of his own, less admired, father Watson had little to say. Watson's later decision to build a sumptuous plantation house, to install one of his father's old black retainers as a reminder of former days, and to assume the role of the lord of the manor testified to a deep nostalgia in Watson.

Nor was Watson's longing for the past confined to personal musings or his private life. Indeed, Woodward observed that the Georgia Populist avoided attacks on the old ante-bellum agrarians, since his Populism was shaped by the agrarianism of Robert Toombs and combined with a "tough minded realism."[48] Thus the materials are in *Tom Watson* for interpreting Watson's agrarianism as in part a reactionary ideology. (Richard Hofstadter was later to see the entire Populist movement as such.) In short, Watson was a prisoner of the Southern family romance that lay at the core of the Southern tradition. The veneration of the arcadian ante-bellum ethos and the heroic grandfather, the ambivalence toward industrial progress, and the sense of decline, even the fond memories of a virtuous "black mammy," were all present.

Indeed, a convincing argument has been made that the transformation in Watson's racial attitudes was not that great at all.[49] Whatever the exact case, Watson's psyche contained the raw materials for the virulent racism that surfaced after 1900. This racism was anything but "conformist," anything but the expression of perfunctory obeisance to traditional attitudes. Watson's anti-Semitism and anti-Catholicism of a scurrilous, pornographic sort indicated his emotional commitment to a phobic view of the "other." The most vicious ideological components of the culture resonated with some fundamental weakness in Watson's psychic structure. Given to personal paranoia, he came to pursue a paranoic politics. He would seem to fit rather well the ideal type of the authoritarian personality.

Though an "agrarian rebel" and always a maverick of sorts, Watson was not without a Napoleonic streak, and in fact wrote an admiring biography of the French leader who betrayed the democratic promise of the French Revolution. (Watson had earlier written a study of the French Revolution which praised the militancy of the Jacobins.) This attraction to a figure of great power, combined with Watson's attraction to the trappings of planter aristocracy, point to a central problem in Populism: the extent to which it was an expression of envy and resentment. Sheldon Hackney has suggested that these aspects of Populism were dominant in Alabama.[50] Populists wanted less to change the "system" than they wanted to be cut in on the take; or, at best, they were reacting to a historical experience in which an agrarian ethos was fast disappearing and their ambitions were to reinvoke and reinstate that lost order. Either of these facts helps explain why later agrarian leaders so often sold out their followers once they gained office, or proved ineffectual. They had no substantive ideology, only a "gut" feeling that power helps satisfy.

Though *Tom Watson* suffered from lack of psychological probing and a reluctance to speculate, the biography was skillfully done and fascinating, as well as being thoroughly researched. But *Tom Watson* also established another tendency in Woodward's work: a fascination with failure, with frustrated dreams and blasted hopes. There was no way to read Watson and Populism as anything but failures; and Woodward's treatment of Watson suggested that a man and a cause can only be judged failures, if they have offered a hope worth considering.

In the same year that *Tom Watson* appeared, Woodward also delivered the Phi Beta Kappa lecture at the University of Florida. His address, "The South in Search of a Philosophy," revealed a bit more about the young man who was to revolutionize the historiography of the region.[51] The first part of his speech recapitulated the essential message of the Watson biography. The Redeemers and New South boosters came in for rough treatment, while the Populists were praised for championing " 'political equality' for the Negro."[52]

More interesting were Woodward's comments on contemporary Southern life. He scored the Vanderbilt Agrarians for having lived off stocks and bonds in Paris before returning as converts to Agrarianism after the 1929 crash.[53] Their romanticization of the past mirrored Henry Grady's roseate view of the future for an industrial South. Not yet a champion of Faulkner, Woodward was of the opinion that the Mississippi novelist "seemed to draw most of his subjects out of abandoned wells"; strange times, he suggested, produced strange fiction.[54] Woodward reserved his praise for Regionalism, a vision committed to "facts." Only by following the "hard narrow path of realism . . . the only one that really leads out of the maze" could the South escape a future as bleak as its past had been.[55] The Phi Beta Kappa address revealed a taste for the sardonic that would later become modulated into the irony and judiciousness Woodward so cultivated.

But the ironic vision emerged in full force in Woodward's magisterial *Origins of the New South, 1877–1913* (1951). There he surveyed the decades between the end of Reconstruction and the assumption of the Presidency by Woodrow Wilson. On the surface these years had seen the recovery of a defeated and prostrate South. The region had made strides toward modernization; and the election of a Southern-born President in 1912 seemed to signal the triumphant reintegration of the South into the nation.

Yet, beneath the surface, the more things had changed, the more they had stayed the same. In some cases they became worse. Behind the boasts of New South advocates and Southern Progressives, Woodward detected economic and racial exploitation. Behind the trumpetings of Southern progress, he detected colonial exploitation by outside industrial and financial interests. The sectional ideology of the period and reality were at wide variance. Woodward's ironic realism—the vision that things are rarely as they seem or turn out the way one hopes—was a perfect instrument for identifying the complex entanglement of appearance and reality in those years. On guard against the monumentalizings of conservatives or the vain optimism of Southern boosters, Woodward expressed the new realism that Cash had hoped for in *The Mind of the South*.

Woodward began *Origins of the New South* by examining the Southern state governments that, in displacing the Reconstruction regimes, had reputedly "redeemed" the South. He showed, as he had for Georgia in *Tom Watson*, that in state after state the "Redeemer" governments had been dominated by a corrupt oligarchy of railroad, lumber, iron, and commercial interests. Though granting due obeisance to regional pieties, both past and present, the Redeemers had set about turning the South into an economic colony of Northern and European business interests. In short, the Bourbons differed from New South advocates in emphasis only; and neither did much more than rake the profits off the top of the region's economy, while continuing to herald a new order of progress for all the citizens of the South. This industrial order, like its agricultural predecessor, was in thrall to outside interests and run by a small home-grown elite. Like many of the Regionalists, Woodward saw the South as an economic colony.

The other focus of *Origins of the New South* fell upon the conflicts in Southern society that came to a head in the Populist insurgency in the 1890s. According to Woodward, the events of that decade gave lie to the notion of the Solid South.[56] But here it is necessary to examine more closely the idea of the Solid South which was so central in the writing of Southern history and politics in the 1930s and 1940s and one which rests at the heart of the Cash-Woodward debate.

If one takes the term "Solid South" to refer to politics, then Woodward was certainly correct to be skeptical of its usefulness for the ante-bellum South, where Jacksonian Democrats and Whigs vied for control.[57] Nor did Woodward neglect the potential political conflict in the post-Reconstruction years, which came to fruition with the Populist movement. In short, the continuity in Southern politics referred to the presence of conflict. On the other hand, Woodward's thesis in *Reunion and Reaction* (1955) was that Democratic party domination had emerged out of the Compromise of 1877. This hegemony successfully met the Populist challenge of the 1890s, adjusted to the Progressives' efforts, and, except for the election of 1928, lasted into the 1950s, where Woodward again detected the stirrings of resurgent Republican party.[58] Thus, in Woodward's account, political conflict, expressed in party struggles, was always incipient, but emerged openly only in the 1890s. Though Cash judged the Populists less important than Woodward, there is no great disagreement otherwise. To be sure, Cash had not emphasized party divisions in the ante-bellum years. But then he had not stressed politics much at all.

Second, if solidity (or "unity" as Woodward put it in his later critique of Cash) refers to economic and social divisions throughout Southern history, there is no argument between Cash and Woodward, as Woodward himself granted. What they disagreed on was the importance of the political expressions of this social conflict. But, as we shall see, Woodward ended by substantially agreeing with Cash on the powerful hold the Democratic party exerted over Southerners.

Third, if "Solid South" refers to a unity of values and attitudes, particularly those on race, then Cash would seem to have the better case. Woodward vacillated on the significance of Populist racial dissent, but his case for a vital white dissenting tradition on race was not a strong one at all. He cited Lewis H. Blair and George W. Cable as opponents of segregation.[59] But two examples hardly make a case, particularly when Blair reverted to advocacy of white domination later in life and Cable was also a believer in white supremacy.[60] Woodward also later pointed to pre-War Southern dissent on slavery but he could not instance anything approaching a mass movement or politically significant opposition. He had a stronger point when he called attention to important intellectual activity in the ante-bellum South that Cash had ignored, but his point was vitiated when one observes that the figures Woodward mentioned were generally intellectual defenders of slavery and aristocratic hegemony.[61] Cash undoubtedly (and understandably) was indifferent to the intellectual merits of the ideology of cultural reaction.

In the matter of institutional discontinuity, Woodward had the better of the argument. But it should be kept in mind that Cash's attention fell upon the cultural psychology in which Southern institutions were grounded, while Woodward was almost exclusively concerned with observable forces, movements, and institutions. In this sense, Cash and Woodward simply talked past one another; they were interested in different things. Finally, however, Cash's thesis seems to be more cogent and complex: a unity of cultural values kept economic, social, and political conflict in check despite the disruption of Southern institutions.

Still, Woodward's conflict view of Southern history opened up new perspectives on Southern history, particularly in the period in which conflict was most apparent. By the early 1950s he was also fruitfully out of step with developments in American histori-

ography. By that time American history had come to be dominated by the "consensus" approach. Beard, Turner, and Parrington,
class consciousness and conflict, radicalism, and sectionalism were
out of fashion. American history was being rewritten from a point
of view that stressed the unity of American cultural experience,
general prosperity rather than economic disparities, a political
culture of liberalism rather than one of reaction or radicalism.
Tocqueville, not Marx, seemed the most appropriate guide to the
American past. In the face of all this Woodward generously acknowledged his indebtedness to Charles and Mary Beard in the
second edition of *Reunion and Reaction,* a gesture that was all the
more becoming since Charles Beard had fallen out of historiographical and political favor.[62]

But while Woodward stressed conflict and discontinuity in
Origins of the New South, the story he told was not the progressive tale of the ultimate triumph of good over evil, of the "people"
over the "interests." Having perhaps registered something of the
waning of radical hopes since the 1930s, the Cold War atmosphere, and the rise of the Dixiecrats, Woodward had taken a
sober second look at agrarian insurgency in the South. *Origins
of the New South* emphasized the correlation of agrarian dissent
and anti-black legislation, the rather limited extent of black-white
cooperation, and was more dubious about the Populists' emphasis
upon the reconciliatory powers of economic self-interest. "It should
be added," he wrote, "that those gains [political cooperation between races] were limited and that their significance is easily exaggerated." Tom Watson hardly appeared in the pages of *Origins
of the New South;* in retrospect his efforts at inter-racial cooperation appeared idiosyncratic rather than typical of Populism. Still
Woodward preferred the Populists to the middle-class liberals of
the period, since the former, though apparently less enlightened
on matters of race, focused on class and economic issues.

If *Tom Watson* was flawed by Woodward's failure to explain
his protagonist's reversion to racism as a political tool, *Origins of
the New South* saw Woodward shy away from a complete explanation for the failure of the Populist movement. The challenge had
been offered by Cash when he asserted that the Populists had

"wilted" when under pressure, thus confirming his view of the supremacy of the cultural tradition over self-interest. At one point in *Origins of the New South* Woodward rather darkly suggested that "the controlling forces in America would be no more reconciled to a Populist South than they had been to a planter-Confederate South or a Carpetbagger-freedman South."[63] Perhaps not, but such a wide conspiratorial net, which included in one catch a reactionary slave regime and a democratic-egalitarian one, was hardly convincing. More convincing on the failure of Populism were his discussions of the lack of effective leadership among the Populists, the manipulation of votes, particularly black ones, and fraudulent election practices by conservative Democrats.

Later, in *Origins of the New South,* he seemed to attribute the final demise to the confusions engendered by the election of 1896. The Democrats stole the silver issue and made it into the major issue of the campaign. Moreover, "with the agrarian radicals in alliance with the party of big business and the party of white supremacy in combination with Negroes against lower-class whites, it was little wonder that the masses lost confidence and became apathetic."[64] In addition, the disfranchisement measures affected poor whites in some cases as much as they did blacks.[65]

Still, something more was needed. (Woodward did note the economic upturn in the later years of the decade.) Why were the masses so apathetic and confused? To evoke such explanations is to beg the question of what engendered these feelings. Surely the failure of leadership and weakness in organization played a role. Nor was there much to the Populist ideology beyond fulminations against the interests and frenzied protests against falling prices. And the fusion issue of 1896 surely reflected an ideological soft spot; it was less that fusion had occurred than that it led to collapse. Woodward's tendency to blame external forces was a significant part of the story, but surely not the whole story.

In his chapter on Southern progressivism, Woodward observed that after the turn of the century the reform impulse found expression *within* the Democratic party and thus could not be discredited by the third party label and all that it implied. But if reform could only gain wide support within the Democratic party, this would certainly indicate the deeply rooted symbolic hold of the party over the classes *and* masses. And what else is this but Cash's notion of the proto-Dorian bond among Southern whites— racial unity against blacks and sectional unity against outside ideas or organizations as expressed in a united political front?

Origins of the New South was a thoroughly scholarly work addressed primarily to other historians. But with *The Strange Career of Jim Crow* (1955) published soon after the revolutionary Supreme Court decision of May 1954, Woodward aimed at a wider audience. Woodward had contributed background material to the NAACP as it prepared its argument against school segregation before the Supreme Court, and was thus not only involved as a historian but as a participant, tangential though his role may have been.[66] *The Strange Career of Jim Crow* has undoubtedly been Woodward's most read book, even by early civil rights workers. In it Woodward moderated his usual skepticism a bit and produced a work that, in pointing to "forgotten alternatives" in the past, suggested possibilities for the present and future.

The Strange Career of Jim Crow covered the same historical terrain as *Origins of the New South*, but with an eye on race relations. This time, though, Woodward developed some of the observations of *Origins of the New South* into a full-fledged thesis. *Origins of the New South*, for instance, included a chapter on the disfranchisement of blacks called "The Mississippi Plan as the American Way." Woodward was unique, however, in his account of racial politics between Reconstruction and the 1890s, for, unlike Lewinson, Myrdal, and Key, he stressed the discontinuity between 1877 and 1890. Disfranchisement was no *fait accompli* by 1890. *Origins of the New South*, moreover, had included relatively little discussion of the rise of legal segregation in the South. It was upon this issue that the main emphasis of *The Strange Career of Jim Crow* was to fall, ironically so since there was a much weaker case to be made for discontinuity in segregation than in disfranchisement.[67]

As with Watson's interracial politics, *The Strange Career of Jim Crow* could be read two ways. The "tough" version had it that the legal-constitutional underpinnings of segregation emerged in the South only in the 1890s and were not completely established until the end of the first decade of this century. Woodward never denied that in practice segregation had existed before the 1890s or that blacks had been prevented from voting. Nor that integrated public schools or churches had ever been the rule, except in New Orleans, where schools were integrated for a short time. What he wanted to stress was the institutional and legal discontinuity between 1865 and 1890; more generally for his 1955 audience he wanted to show that neither segregation nor disfranchisement was historically inevitable or part of a firmly established Southern tradition. Segregation had a relatively short history; and if it had been consciously instituted (as it had), it could just as consciously be abolished. Stateways did not necessarily follow folkways. The reverse was as often the case. And, contrary to Myrdal's and Key's *fait accompli* thesis concerning disfranchisement, suffrage restrictions were drastically accelerated, diminishing political participation rather than ratifying what already was the case. Thus Woodward's tract was clearly addressed to his native region in an attempt to demythologize the existing social and legal institutions that regulated race relations.

There was, however, a "sentimental" version of his thesis that Woodward helped encourage. It suggested that the underlying racial attitudes (the folkways) of white Southerners had for a time possessed a certain flexibility. Travelers and natives observed widespread "race mixing" in the post-Reconstruction years. The obvious corollary was that white Southern attitudes in the 1950s might not be or did not have to be as rigid as one might expect. In *The Strange Career of Jim Crow* Woodward returned to a more sanguine view of the Populist interracial experiment, with Watson as his focus, and asserted that "the radicals went further in the direction of racial integration than did the conservatives."[68] Though this rather rosy view was heavily qualified, the eager reader might not unreasonably have seen it as warrant for hope.

Yet Woodward's assertion is quickly divested of much impact when one considers that to best the conservatives was not going very far at all. As he was the first to admit, conservative Democrats openly courted (and won) the black vote. Here Woodward, like other champions of the Populists, tended to embrace a moral-political double standard. When the Bourbons supported the black franchise, they were acting from cynical self-interest and blatant paternalism; when the Populists sought the black vote, something more than mere political calculations was at work. Second, it is questionable whether the term "racial integration" meant anything at all in the setting of the 1890s, since Populists, including Watson, did not support social equality. In fact, Southern liberals such as George Washington Cable and Lewis Harvey Blair came much nearer to advocacy of such a position. Here it seems that Woodward, as he would later admit, decidedly overemphasized the enlightenment or radical nature of Populist thinking in such matters.[69]

The Strange Career of Jim Crow also neglected two areas that demanded attention. In such a short work it would scarcely have been possible to expand upon *Origins of the New South,* but Woodward might have reminded his readers a bit about the lack of economic power that underlay the political and legal vulnerability of blacks in the South. The tunnel vision of *The Strange Career of Jim Crow* made it easy for the reader to forget that segregation and disfranchisement took place in the context of black economic subordination, a legacy of the failure of Reconstruction. Related to this was Woodward's neglect of blacks themselves in *The Strange Career of Jim Crow* and in all of his works. To be sure one of his main achievements was to focus on those policies and practices that affected black life; but rarely in his work, except for his chapter on Booker T. Washington in *Origins of the New South,* do we see individual blacks, or groups, in action. One would like to have known, for instance, why a greater number of blacks did not support the Populists in the 1890s. Were there conflicting voices among black leaders in the South on this issue? With this information missing, blacks became in effect passive respondents to the white world. Undoubtedly this reflects in part the situation they found themselves in, but one doubts this was the whole story.

Though not exactly central, there is another aspect of Woodward's writing that deserves attention, since Woodward is a historian of and from the South: his clear though measured rebuke to the North for abandoning its political and racial ideals. Woodward concluded *Reunion and Reaction* by scoring the Republican party for dropping its moral idealism, capitulating to industrial and commercial interests, and entering into a tacit alliance with conservative Southern Democrats. This was a new and creative twist on the Beardian notion of Reconstruction. And in *The Strange Career of Jim Crow* Woodward blamed Northern capitulation to racial imperialism, the rise of nativism, and sheer indifference to the fate of blacks for encouraging the full-fledged emergence of the caste system in the South in the 1890s. Here was a new type of Southern response, which chided the North not for its radicalism but for its timidity.[70]

Since the early 1950s Woodward has abandoned the scholarly monograph for the essay. At his best, Woodward is a master of the genre, applying his ironic vision with rapier-like subtlety and leaving wounds that only later begin to bleed. At its worst, Woodward's ironic vision becomes a way of avoiding clear judgments. Though always a graceful writer, he often so disguises the intent of his prose that definite judgments are almost undetectable. For instance, in his defense of the Populists in "The Populist Heritage and the Intellectuals" (1959), Woodward admitted that the Populists "may have been bitten by status anxieties"; but, if so, the fear of declining status was no major factor, since "there was not much further downward for most Populists to go."[71] This later judgment slides over two facts: that many Populists were middling farmers who, though on the brink of disaster, did have somewhere "downward" to go; and second, that Southern farmers had grown up in a culture that had idealized the agrarian life. Not only was their economic plight bad—and it was certainly that—their social and cultural values were under attack. Then, several pages later in the essay Woodward granted that "they [the Populists] took refuge in the agrarian myth, that they denied the commercial character of agricultural enterprise and sometimes dreamed of a Golden Age."[72] This would seem to contradict what he had asserted earlier—that the Populists could hardly have been influenced by a decline in status. Yet, it agreed with the heavily qualified admission that they might have suffered from status anxieties. This was not so much complexity of judgment as it was an unwillingness to make one at all.

Woodward's best-known collection of essays is *The Burden of Southern History* (1960), in which he shifted his concern from internal economic and political conflicts to Southern distinctiveness. That is, Woodward came to stress the unity and commonality of the Southern experience, a particularly ironic move, since he was later to attack W. J. Cash for having done the same thing in his *The Mind of the South*.[73] Woodward added cultural history to his concerns by devoting an essay to the Southern writer's view of history and one to Herman Melville and Henry Adams. Woodward became less the Populist sympathizer and chronicler of rustic radicalism than the chastened liberal of the "realist" variety, applying Niebuhrian strictures against American arrogance as mediated by his reading of the Southern historical experience. This was the ironist as moralist.

An indication of where Woodward was heading came in his "Irony of Southern History," the presidential address he delivered to the Southern Historical Association in November 1952. There Woodward advanced his own interpretation of the central theme of Southern history, a favorite game of Southern historians since U. B. Phillips. According to Woodward, the South's experience was that history, to paraphrase Arnold Toynbee, had happened to it. In a nation that had enshrined prosperity and success and attributed them to unique virtue, even innocence, Woodward felt the South illustrated a quite different experience. And this experience placed the South nearer, he claimed, to the common experience of mankind than to the rest of America.[74]

Further, Woodward asserted that the historical experience of the South had something to offer the country at large. In the midst of the McCarthy era (though he failed to mention the Senator by name), scapegoating, looking for villains to explain national difficulties, made no sense. In the 1850s a similar intellectual iron curtain had descended between North and South. It should not be repeated; and the critical spirit of the 1930s should be encouraged rather than stifled. Also, the South's experience of having extravagant hopes dashed by defeat should teach the nation that its goals, well meaning though they may be, could not be relentlessly imposed on the rest of the world. Realism, not messianism, was the best guarantee of a sensible foreign policy.

The central problem with Woodward's eloquent essay was that it was difficult to detect which Southerners gave evidence of having learned from the region's unhappy history or at least of having learned what Woodward wanted them to learn. In this sense Woodward's essay was addressed as much to the South as it was the rest of the nation, and expressed a hope for what Southerners might come to believe in the future as much as it described the present state of Southern historical consciousness. As a prescription, it was eloquent and valuable. But as history and psychology, it made little or no sense, then or in the ensuing years after the 1954 decision. On this issue Cash's emphasis upon the repetitive pattern in the white Southern mind was of more value: in times of crisis, the South fell back upon old ways of resisting and upon self-exculpation and manifested a blindness every bit as marked as the nation at large. What Woodward's essay showed was what Woodward himself had distilled from his career as a historian: the ironic complexity of human hopes and desires. Things rarely turn out as planned. Second, and here the appeal to Southern pride entered, the defeated and scorned South had something to teach the more confident and self-righteous North. Thus the essays were both a call to principle, based primarily on the negative strictures of historical irony, and an appeal to the South (and the nation) to learn from its historical experience.

Interestingly, Woodward's ironic historical consciousness fit into none of the Nietzschean categories. Though always sympathetic to the forces of reform, Woodward avoided monumentalizing them. One could learn from failure as much as from success. Yet, neither was Woodward's view exactly a "critical" one. Though certainly acknowledging the shortcomings of the past, his message was not one of progress over a benighted past. Indeed, he implied in *The Strange Career of Jim Crow* and *Tom Watson* that crucial possibilities had been embraced in the past which could instruct the present.

Woodward must be seen as a representative of the second generation of the Southern Renaissance. The figures from whom he sought guidance and from whom he distanced himself—in the former case, Faulkner and Warren, and the latter, Cash—were central to the initial stages of the Renaissance. That is, Woodward's shaping tradition was not so much the Southern past of the pre-1930s period as the tradition of critical consciousness that emerged in the 1930s. Put another way, Woodward's rise to pre-eminence marks the rapprochement of Chapel Hill and Nashville. With its emphasis upon irony and complexity, his sensibility was congenial to that of the Agrarian-New Critics at their best.

Yet in Woodward this has not been the sort of easy posturing to which the Agrarians all too often fell prey.[75] For there are two kinds of irony: that of the Agrarians tended to be too easily skeptical of all change, even hostile to it. This was irony on the cheap, a sophisticated form of gloating, or "I told you so." But the Woodward of *Tom Watson* and *Origins of the New South* displayed an ironic vision which was "earned," at least by historical contemplation. It honored historical efforts at change and warned only against self-righteousness and overinflated hopes that could never be fulfilled. Woodward's work suggests that the crudities, the violence, and the fanaticism of those who attempt to change things had to be seen in context of the repressive structures surrounding them.

Also Woodward avoided the self-righteousness of the Agrarians' version of innocence. If Woodward's works taught anything, it was that the South had been exploited not only by the machinations of Yankee capital but also by its home-grown elites. With Cash, he emphasized that the South's problem could not be solved by blaming outside forces or villains exclusively. Unlike the Agrarians, or the Regionalists, Woodward was quite sensitive to the race as an omnipresent factor in Southern history. It had divided the exploited against themselves and been as responsible as anything else for that fictitious folk unity of (white) classes and masses which Owsley and others so celebrated. The historian's work provides no plan for action, but in Woodward's critical detachment and unwillingness to accept the received myths about

the Southern past, his work, as of the mid-1950s, was a fitting tribute to the critical consciousness that Cash saw emerging during
the Depression decade.

"North Toward Home"

Woodward and Robert Penn Warren are the crucial transitional
figures linking the first generation of the Southern Renaissance
with the post-1954 South. Warren left the South (in 1942), going
first to Minnesota and then to Yale in the early 1950s. Joined there by
Woodward in the early 1960s, their personal and intellectual coming together in the North signaled the rapprochement between
Nashville and Chapel Hill. It also marked the consolidation of a
Southern intellectual liberalism which had little direct relationship
with Agrarianism, Populism, or the social planning ideology of the
Regionalists and liberal modernizers, though it had learned from
each of these positions. Indeed, this new liberalism was less a political program or a coherent theoretical position than an attitude,
a way of seeing the world. In their detachment from specific interests or institutions in the South, Woodward and Warren articulated a transcending vision of the Southern past but at the price
of a certain thinness of feeling. In relation to Faulkner, Tate, Ransom, Odum, even Cash, they were latecomers and survivors. In
this sense they "knew" more than their predecessors; and thus, I
think, the central place that irony, the wisdom of latecomers, assumes in their thought.

It is fitting that the Agrarian who wrote explicitly on race in
I'll Take My Stand should make most explicit his departure from
that earlier position and urge compliance with the Supreme Court
decision of 1954. Written while he was a Rhodes Scholar at Oxford, Warren's "Briar Patch" essay in *I'll Take My Stand* was an
updated version of Booker T. Washington's separate-but-equal
stance.[76] Even at that it was a bit too much for a diehard like
Donald Davidson to swallow.

From today's perspective Warren's essay represents an arrogance few would now dare in trying to fathom the complexities
of race relations or the needs and desires of black Southerners.

Yet one cannot too readily dismiss Warren for the extremity of his opinions. As he later claimed, no one in the South, at least no white person, was calling for an end to segregation in 1930.[77] Howard Odum had said much worse of blacks earlier; and he had said it more explicitly. In *The Mind of the South* Cash had allowed himself a few comments that could be called racist. Nor was Warren alone in his reading of Southern history, particularly of the horrors of Reconstruction and the way in which the behavior of the freedman during that difficult time had "badly impaired the white man's respect and gratitude,"[78] as though the black man should have apologized for desiring freedom. Warren's praise for blacks in those days was at best back-handed. For instance, in *John Brown* (1929) he contended that, in contrast with Northern fanatics, "the slave . . . was more realistic and more humane; he never bothered his kinky head about the moral issue . . . [He possessed] no great reservoir of hate and rancor . . . ."[79] Blacks were good-natured children to be treated benevolently but firmly.

And yet Warren can also be excused too easily, despite his self-apologetics. Odum and Vance openly questioned black racial inferiority in the early 1930s, and Cash made clear the decidedly unbenevolent nature of slavery in his book, something Warren could not bring himself to do in *John Brown,* in "The Briar Patch," or in anything else he wrote until the 1950s. Though Warren spared his readers such egregiousness as the "kinky head" characterization, "The Briar Patch" was an essay divided against itself. If offered progressive suggestions coupled with assertions of black inferiority and a blindness to the deeply insulting aspects of segregation. Warren, for instance, held that a black professional who wanted to sleep in a white hotel, even though a comparable one for blacks existed (the ludicrousness of the situation was obvious on the face of it), exhibited a "defect in self-respect" and was "doctrinaire."[80] Such was the standard litany of the Southern moderate on into the 1950s. "Extremists" on both sides were denounced even-handedly. The Klan and the NAACP were equally at fault. One took a position in the "responsible" middle, no matter where the extremes might be located. Thus the superior humanistic vision of the Agrarian ideology.

Even Warren's more generous suggestions were undercut by his conventionally racist and reactionary views. He called for vocational education for the black masses without denying the need for higher education for a black elite, urged equal civil rights, equitable application of political rights, black economic independence, and even the unionization of the black labor force to undercut the depredations of industrial capitalism and foreclose the competition between poor whites and blacks. Yet the essay ended with a fond glance toward the past. Warren claimed that by "temperament and capacity" the Negro belonged in the small towns and farms, and that tenantry and "the rural life provide[s] the most satisfactory relationship of the two races." "Let the negro sit beneath his own vine and fig tree," waxed Warren rhetorically. "[T]he restoration of society at large to a balance and security," which was disrupted by the industrial order, was the most desirable course to pursue.[81]

Between 1930 and the publication of *Brother to Dragons* (1953), Warren had little to say about race, either in his own voice or in his fiction and poetry. *Brother to Dragons* was an imaginary dialogue between the present, as embodied in "RPW," and the past, as embodied in Thomas Jefferson and the various principles in a murder case in Kentucky in 1811. Warren took an actual historical event, constructed a story around and from it, and used this to draw both personal and universal implications. Though near the end of *Brother to Dragons* Warren delivered himself of a few moralizing paradoxes, *Brother to Dragons* is an engrossing and moving work. In it RPW's own opinions could be countered by others and thus his looser pronouncements did not go undisputed.[82]

At the center of *Brother to Dragons* was a consideration of the nature of human nature: whether man is basically good or contains a mixture of good and evil. Within the story, it was hardly a debate at all, since Thomas Jefferson, who was to speak for man's essential innocence, had already abjured his "enlightenment" views and swung to the opposite pole of despair and cynicism.[83] Jefferson refuses to acknowledge that Lilburn Lewis, the brutal murderer of the slave George, is part of the Jefferson line and that he

(Jefferson) too might have been capable of or a participant in such an evil. The message of Jefferson's sister (Lilburn's mother) and of RPW is that we must take responsibility for our complicity in evil rather than deny it: Lilburn's "face is only a mirror of your possibilities." At the end, Jefferson, like Jack Burden, has won his way through to insight: "For without the fact of the past we / cannot dream the future."[84] As in *All the King's Men,* until we accept the past we will have no future.

The other theme, one that framed the historical tale, concerned the relationship of father and son and the need for reconciliation between the two. What one learned from the Lilburn Lewis story prepared for what one learned about the relationship of father and son. The visits of son and father to the site of the brutal murder touch off the poet's ruminations on the relationship of generations. On the one hand "the only / Thing in life is glory" yet to be happy is:

> To be reconciled to the father's own reconciliation.
> It is most difficult because that reconciliation
> Costs the acceptance of failure.

Acceptance of the father is the acceptance of time and the realization that time defeats us and our desire for glory. Yet it seems a way of making a virtue out of a necessity: "What is wisdom and what the dimming of faculty? / What kindliness and what the guttering of desire?" And yet, RPW concludes, "We must believe in virtue." Virtue comes when vanity and desire for glory are transcended.

Warren seemed to be saying that the urge for glory and the desire to escape oblivion constitute our common condition, as does the need for reconciliation with one's father that marks the opposite impulse. This paradox can only be resolved in knowledge, a kind of quasi-Hegelian movement, as expressed in literature: "All is redeemed / In knowledge." Thus, as in *All the King's Men* and anticipating his essay "Knowledge and the Image of Man," Warren makes self-knowledge and, what amounts to the same, knowledge of the past into the central task of being human. To deny evil or deny time (which is the essence of the desire for glory) is to deny the essential knowledge of what it means to be human. RPW ends by being prepared, like Jack Burden, "To go into the world of action and liability."

Brother to Dragons was an important expression of the new Southern liberalism because it rejected once and for all the optimistic Jeffersonian heritage. But in a wider sense Warren's verse-drama was a call for America to transcend the shallow view of human nature which Warren saw at the heart of the country's culture. Like Woodward he was implicitly claiming that the South had something to teach the rest of the nation. But this effort put RPW in the position of romanticizing, even excusing, Lilburn Lewis's brutal action by a bit of psychological and metaphysical legerdemain: "All's one in common collusion" and ". . . that's the instructive fact of history / That evil's done for good, and in good's name . . . ." Lilburn's act was "final evidence for the existence of good." At this point in *Brother to Dragons* Jefferson responds with what is surely an appropriate rebuttal: "And if that's all / Why not say evil is evil, and not sweeten / Your slobber with any pap of paradox?" RPW admits that he's had thoughts of this sort as well.

Thus, as in *All the King's Men,* Warren seems to want things both ways. What is further disturbing is that Warren sees Jefferson's failure to acknowledge man's capacity for evil as the main problem rather than focusing on Jefferson's specific violation of humanity as a slaveowner. For the sin of conservative historicism, the refusal to pass judgment on the past and its institutions (for example, slavery), is a denial of human possibility as serious as Jefferson's denial of man's capacity for evil. What Warren was doing here fit the dominant intellectual mood in post-World War II America. The tendency in political and social analysis of that period was to theologize political and social concerns, an inversion of the Marxist tendency to reduce conflicts to social or economic self-interest. This is to say that Warren's thought lacked social and cultural mediation or any way to bridge the gap between individual knowledge and universal implication. What Lionel Trilling called a "culture's hum and buzz of implication" was neglected.[85]

This is not to say that Warren did not pay any attention to slavery. In the persona of RPW he criticizes Jefferson for having lived off slavery while projecting a vision of future innocence. But by concentrating on the brutal murder of one slave, he distracted attention from the daily indignities of the institution. Slavery in short was wrong not so much (or not only) because slaves could be murdered with impunity, but because the institution daily denied the slaves' essential status as human beings. Further, the Thomas Jefferson of *Brother to Dragons* lacked historical authenticity. To load Jefferson with responsibility for philosophical innocence and for having ruined his nephew's (Meriwether Lewis) life came close to absurdity. Though Jefferson may have been complicit in a metaphysical sense, he was neither guilty of Lilburn's murder nor responsible for Lewis's suicide. Thus the historical setting never really functioned in a compelling way.

Warren's tendency to abstract his works from historical reality emerged in full force in *Band of Angels* (1955). Amantha Starr, the central character, is a "white" girl who suddenly discovers she is a "black" slave when her father dies. The novel is set in the South during the War and Reconstruction, but slavery as an institution or as the shaping force in the lives of those who are enslaved is less important in *Band of Angels* than Amantha's efforts to establish her identity. Though one of the problems in discovering who she is involves race, it is finally less important than Amantha's general refusal to take responsibility for her life, a standard theme in Warren's fiction. The "tragedy of the mulatto," a common theme in American and Southern literature, is transformed from a social or even psychological into an almost metaphysical condition.[86] For all of Amantha's agonizing search for identity, she never actually registers what it is like to be a slave. At the end she takes responsibility for her life—another one of Warren's climactic conversion scenes—and realizes that no one can set her free but herself, but this takes place in a figurative (and almost literal) void, the West. To be free is not to identify with a social group, in this case blacks, and not to engage in the struggle for group liberation. Freedom is to be found rather in an individual act of spiritual resolution.

Band of Angels sounds other of Warren's standard themes. Rau-Ru, a slave whom Hamish Bond has "rescued" from Africa and made a quasi-son, ends by killing his slave-master "father,"

Bond. Amantha's search for identity is embodied in a rejection of male figures because of the unresolved anger she feels toward her father whom she thinks has abandoned her. Miscegenation and quasi-incestuous sexuality abound, but they are to little purpose in the context of the novel. Only when Amantha accepts her husband, Tobias, a former idealist and now a drunk and ne'er-do-well, as a flawed human being and not another protective father can she accept herself and acknowledge responsibility for her own life.

Like other of Warren's protagonists, Amantha Starr is an unappealing and exasperating creation. She is snippish and spoiled, lures people in and then rejects them; she wants it both ways. And more so than in *All the King's Men* or *Brother to Dragons,* the historical and the private fail to work together. *Band of Angels* exhibits the worst fault of the historical novel as a genre: the imposition of contemporary (or authorial) concerns upon an early historical context in which they seem implausible and anachronistic. For Amantha's fate seems to follow less from the logic of the historical context or even from her character than it does from Warren's pursuit of the identity-responsibility-freedom theme. Again, as in *Brother to Dragons,* this is not to say that Warren does not understand the pressures of slavery upon slave or master. It is rather that they do not seem particularly relevant to Amantha's quest or Warren's interests. In slighting historical reality Warren succeeds only in creating metaphysical melodrama.

Warren's *Segregation* (1956) tells us much more than its author intended, as well as sounding his usual themes.[87] In this small volume, a first version of which appeared in *Life,* Warren announced his support for Southern compliance with the desegregation order of the Supreme Court. The book is an account of his visit to the South in the wake of the *Brown v. Board of Education* decision and of his conversations with whites and blacks. His conclusion that there was a variety of attitudes on both sides of the racial lines is scarcely surprising. If the South could come to terms with the race problem, according to Warren, it might achieve a unique moral identity, an echo of Woodward's hope that the South might have something to teach the rest of the nation.

But in a real sense *Segregation* is a muted confession of self-betrayal and of betrayal of the region. Warren starts by explaining that "I went back, for going back this time, like all other times, was a necessary part of my life." Then late in the book he registers relief at finally leaving the South: "Yes, you know what the relief is. It is the flight from the reality you were born to." These two passages indicate a startling division in Warren's own life as a writer and as a Southerner. As a novelist (and moralist) Warren's message was the necessity for the individual to come to terms with reality and accept responsibility for it. He speculates in *Segregation* that black and white Southerners share an "instinctive fear . . . that the massiveness of experience, the concreteness of life will be violated: the fear of abstraction." This was the old Agrarian suspicion of abstraction now attributed to Southerners themselves. And yet the book ends with Warren's turning away from the reality he was born to and returning to the North. What he registers is a sense of relief not betrayal. Thus, though Warren confronted the public and moral issue facing the South in *Segregation,* he failed to engage the issue of loyalty to roots by not returning to the South to live and work.

About *Segregation* otherwise there is relatively little to say. As Paul Goodman observed, the book was embarrassingly written in places, full of breathless endings, and at times incomprehensible.[88] For instance, with Goodman one can only wonder what Warren can possibly mean when, after hearing a young white at Fort Nashborough express his hate for "niggers," he adds melodramatically, ". . . somehow the hallowedness of that ground he [the young man] stood on had vindicated, as it were, that hate." And though one may find it difficult to imagine General Lee shaking hands with Orville Faubus, one can imagine the Confederate leader shaking hands with Nathan Bedford Forrest. Informing Warren's account was the notion that, somehow, the Confederate cause had been a noble one, led by noble men, unlike the unseemly resisters of change in the South of the 1950s.

In *Segregation* one is told the not very surprising fact that blacks resent segregation's assaults on their dignity, yet are divided as to how best proceed against it. They, claim Warren, must learn the difficult virtue of "magnanimity." The white problem is explored in more detail. According to Warren, whites are faced with the "fact of self-division." In the white Southern psyche there is a "deep exacerbation of some failure to find identity." By resisting desegregation the white Southerner denies time (change) and the right of blacks to exercise the individuality which white Southerners claim for themselves. Thus, we have the return of another of Warren's central concerns: inner alienation and the search for moral identity.

The larger problem with Warren's analysis is conceptual. Again, as Goodman noted, Warren presents the white South's problem as a psychological one, yet applies the rhetoric of moral dilemma to it. He confuses the tragic and the pathetic.[89] This same dual level of analysis can be found in Lillian Smith's work. Yet, she was clearer in distinguishing the two levels and implied that only when the psycho-cultural problem was resolved could the moral decision be made.

Indeed this confusion of the psychological and moral lies at the root of Warren's entire literary project and the world-view informing it. Jack Burden's problem seems so elusive because, though his symptoms are psychological—the lack of affect and an inability to feel, withdrawal from involvement with others, a willingness to be used—Warren "solves" the problem through a moral conversion, a (William) Jamesian willing to will. Love serves as the *deus ex machina*; it is at once a psychological and morally informing force.

Similarly, Warren resorts to "love" as an explanation for Lilburn Lewis's murder of the slave George. But this merely confuses the issue. There is no moral issue involved in Lilburn's action; or, better, the action involves no moral conflict. It is the act of a psychotic. And use of the historical case as an occasion to debate man's essential goodness or evil is a misguided one. To have considered slavery and the proper way for "moral" men and women in the ante-bellum South to confront it would have been one thing. But the murder of George by Lilburn is a psychological problem. Warren suggests that Lilburn desired "contact with something . . . real/For all we all ask in the end is that:/Reality." If this is Lilburn's desire, then he truly is psychotic. The philosophical debate with Jefferson is in the context an irrelevance.

Thus we have the moral therapeutics that lie at the heart of

Warren's work. "For forgetting is just a kind of remembering," says one of the characters in *Brother to Dragons*: but the implication in Warren is that this is a moral not psychological problem. Warren to the contrary, psychological explanation is not a way of making "all history . . . a private alibi-factory" but a way of understanding the constraints of apparently "free" and responsible action. It is not that the language of morality or language of psychology can be jettisoned. Rather, both are necessary, but not to be confused. There is an obligation to accept responsibility for understanding that which one had no control over in the past. And once this is understood, there is a responsibility to take responsibility for this knowledge in the present.

The question must be left open as to whether Warren's own self-division is moral or psychological—or both. But much of Warren's moralizing rhetoric seems to be a cover for something else, a fundamental fear of appearing moral or committed to a cause or group beyond the individual. Does his standing suspicion of those who display commitment to a supra-individual idea or cause betray a desire for such in his own life? For despite Warren's moralizing, it is those who are skeptical of human possibility as much as those who are innocent of the potentiality for evil who need to explain themselves. With the past hopelessly ambiguous and the present confused, Warren leaves the individual aware of the ironies of the past and the tragic consequences of action. Resolving these conundrums in thought, not in action, the individual is left as an ironic, knowing, but lonely observer.

Conclusion

In this study I have traced in a rather small group of Southern writers and intellectuals between 1930 and 1955 a progress in self-consciousness. The term "progress" itself carries optimistic connotations; and the metaphors I have used through the study are organic ones of growth, emergence, flowering, and (re-)birth. The new replaced the old. An exhausted tradition gave way to the possibility of a revitalized Southern present and future.

And yet a counter movement is at work as well in this study. I have traced the way in which an illusion was unmasked, a romance de-romanticized, a mystery de-mystified. At first glance this would seem to present no problem. To create something new, the old must be destroyed. The ground must be cleared for new growth to appear. Still this unmasking/unmaking action at work in the figures I have discussed carries a certain sober, chastened quality. The history of the South becomes a burden in a new way. For most of the writers we have examined it was the content of the tradition—the family romance—which was the burden to be thrown off. But for some of the same writers, especially the Faulkner of "The Bear" and Will Percy and perhaps even C. Vann Woodward, it was historical consciousness itself that was burdensome. If the tradition of the fathers had been naïve, heroic, and relatively unself-conscious, those who came later were worldly-wise, cautious, and self-aware.

With these apparently conflicting moods—optimism and world-weariness, growth and destruction—in mind, the problem of historical irony must be pursued a bit further. Put succinctly: the destination of ironic historical consciousness is a superior knowledge and insight, but a lesser ability to act upon that awareness. In *The Use and Abuse of History* (1877), Nietzsche claimed that, in a culture dominated by historical consciousness, action had become all but impossible and the dominant feeling was that "we are late survivals, mere epigoni."[1] Recollection led only to repetition rather than heroic transcendence. But as Hayden White has pointed out, Nietzsche did not want to "deny the past and himself as he was in the past, but to forget it."[2] Only he who could remember could also learn the "power, the art, of forgetting."[3] Rather than to decrepit and jaundiced epigoni, Nietzsche wanted life to belong to the living.

But the unmasking of illusions and ambitions is not the exclusive province of the ironic consciousness. The monumental form of historical consciousness can demystify present realities in the name of past greatness. The Agrarians showed that quite well. And the critical view of the past exhibited in the work of the Regionalists, Cash and Smith, demystified past claims to achievement by showing their inadequacy measured against the needs of the present and future. What is different about the ironic historical consciousness is that it dissolves certainty, questions achievements, in the name of consciousness itself. A certain detachment becomes an ideology itself rather than a strategy in the service of some higher value.

Nietzsche foresaw what was coming in the culture generally, and his anticipations have been echoed more recently. For most collectivities throughout history tradition has been essential to survival. The actions of the group and its leaders, the lives of exemplary heroes, the cautionary tales about the impious and disloyal, the piety of the holy and the devotion of the saintly made up the collectivity's past tradition. This tradition provided the

standards by which the present was measured; it was public property and preserved for collective purposes.

Yet in this century the past is no longer "there" in the way it
has been previously. In *Cosmos and History* Mircea Eliade has
explored the background of this fundamental shift in historical
consciousness in the West. According to Eliade, "archaic man,"
saw "life as the ceaseless repetition of gestures initiated by others."[4] In traditional societies, time was a burden which ritual,
purgation, and celebration periodically relieved. All history was
cyclical and sacred. But with the advent of Christianity came a
fundamental reorientation in historical awareness. History came
to be seen as a linear process toward a goal. Christ had entered
history, and all the demi-gods and heroes were destroyed. Until
Christ's return, history was essentially man's realm and potentially
secular. Coming at the end of a long unfolding and exhausting
of historical consciousness, Western man now finds himself the
possessor but also the prisoner of "historical consciousness." For
those—and they are most—who see no redeeming event at the
center or end of history, no *kairos* or *telos,* the question now becomes: "how can the 'terror of history' be tolerated from the view-
point of historicism?"[5] There are no models or redeeming repetitions, no satisfactory theodicy.

Indeed, there are signs that professional historians, usually
the last to get the word, are beginning to grasp this fundamental
re-visioning of history and its uses. Writing in the early 1970s,
J. H. Plumb contended that the "past" was dead.[6] Where Eliade
emphasized the religious and mythological functions of historical
consciousness in traditional societies, Plumb focused on the way
ruling elites throughout history have used the past to strengthen
their social and political control. But unlike Eliade, Plumb was
not so worried by this death of the past. In fact, he ended by calling for more of the same. "History," the more or less critical survey of the past informed by the ideal of objectivity, was now free
to tell the "story of change" and how reason had been applied to
human affairs in the name of progress. Despite Plumb's optimistic
noises, what united him with Eliade was the awareness that the
past no longer seemed to have the power to compel or to comfort.

Hayden White has repeated these assessments of the historical awareness of the modern West. For White, the modern historical consciousness is aware principally of its precarious position
and that of all renderings of the past. White, writing in the "Ironic
Mode," claims that the ironic vision of the past is based on the
"ultimate inadequacy of consciousness to live in the world happily
or to comprehend it fully." It is aware "of its own inadequacy."[7]
Yet, White speculates, the ironic is only one position vis-à-vis the
past, and contrary to its claim, has no more privileged status than
any other position. Still there are no other compelling ways of
construing the past now available; and thus the modern observer
must rest uneasily with his position of pseudo-superiority.

Put in another and more direct way, the ironic historical consciousness operates in the name of no positive community or symbols of commitment. In this it is joined by the historical vision
that is expressed in Freud's "analytic" attitude.[8] The individual is
left to cope, to make do primarily with and for himself. It is in this
same sense that Max Weber claimed earlier that the inevitable
destination of the rationalization of the world would be its disen-
chantment. Put in a wider social and historical perspective, modernization (in the non-Communist West) implies the ironic form
of historical consciousness. Precisely at the moment when new
forces are released from the dead hand of the past, there is no
longer any clue as to what the new energies might be used for.

At this point it is necessary to take up the political question,
which has been implicit in this study. In a situation such as the
South's after 1930, when the Southern tradition was being dealt
a death blow, irony could have radical political import. The status
quo was revealed to be useless and hollow, no longer viable or
effective. Yet to be consistent, irony must also be directed at the
forms of action and belief in the present and the future, whether
they be radical or conservative. This was less than apparent while
the destruction of the family romance was under way. For that
romance was built around the fundamental valorization of difference and hierarchy. Past was superior to present; parents to children; male to female; white to black; rich to poor. To destroy the
power of this model seemed to strike for equality. And it did.

But the kind of vision of equality which emerged in Southern thought in these years after 1930 was a uniquely "modern" one. If Weber, and more recently Benjamin Nelson and John Murray Cuddihy, are correct, modernization in the cultural realm undermines particularistic loyalties and values that weld together the family, tribe, clan, and caste. Modernization aims for the formal and legal equality of all members of the society. This is what John Dollard had in mind when he claimed that modern society, including the South, needed a population of "functionally interchangeable" members.[9] In Nelson's words, Western society has moved from a position where some are "brothers" and the rest are "others," to a situation in which "all become *equally* rather than *differentially* others."[10] This, in short, is the vision of the liberal society of equality before the law.

Yet on one matter conservatives such as Will Percy and the Agrarians and Lillian Smith in her later religious incarnation were correct to be worried.[11] For the modern liberal society lacks any compelling vision to unite its members beyond the dictates of self-interest. That is to say, it lacks a positive vision of action or community. Once the older cultural, political, and social structures have been discredited, there is nothing left to take their place except momentary desires or temporary goals. There is no public realm in the normative sense, no notion of the common good, whether religiously or politically defined. Howard Odum's planning ideology and V. O. Key's political pluralism reflected this lack of positive community, as did Woodward's ironic treatment of the Southern past and Warren's suspicion of large-scale abstractions. The destination of historical consciousness in the South circa 1955 was a Southern version of the end of ideology. In the regional context it seemed to be "progressive," but in reality it offered nothing but a negative critique.

It is for this reason as well that I must question Garvin Davenport's linkage of the ironic vision of Woodward and Warren with the positive vision of Martin Luther King, Jr., in his *The Myth of Southern History* (1970).[12] For missing in the visions of Woodward and Warren was a source of values or a goal beyond history (as in Christianity) or at least a communal vision which transcended the immediate historical experience (as in Marxism). The tantalizing promise of King's vision of non-violent change was what Nietzsche saw as the antidote to ironic historical consciousness: a capacity to "learn to forget." This movement of consciousness involves forgetting in two senses. First, it refers to the ability to forget the impossibility of ever doing anything new or anything different from the past. For, as Nietzsche pointed out, if one fully remembers, he can never do anything. It has all been tried and accomplished—or failed—before. Second, forgetting involves wiping from memory the grievance against the past, a much more difficult accomplishment than the first sort of forgetting. Otherwise the history of change becomes a history of attempts to "get even." But this is also ultimately impossible and can destroy any vision of a positive community in the future.

Still, we know the fate of the Civil Rights movement and have placed too much of a burden on it anyway. Certainly the retreat of men such as Allen Tate to Catholicism offers no general solution. And neither Faulkner's sonorous but empty stoic humanism nor Smith's cosmic evolutionism, taken from Teilhard de Chardin, seems very promising. Nor considering what it replaced should be the vision—and the imperfect reality—of the South as a modern, liberal society be scorned. It is by most indices a better place to live, to carry on daily life, than the South in 1930 or 1830.

The writers and intellectuals we have examined took up the historical-cultural problems confronting them; and, as Marx said, that is all we can demand of anyone or any age. But the South, and the modern world which it has finally, albeit reluctantly, joined, must now deal with a new cultural situation. The value of the work of a contemporary Southern writer such as Walker Percy is that he recognizes that the tradition of the fathers is gone forever, as are the heady days of the Southern Renaissance. The fathers and Faulkner must both be transcended.

Finally, it should not be forgotten that Nietzsche speaks not only of forgetting but also of "learning." Only someone who has learned the past, engaged in that repetition, recollection, and working through, and made the past his own can transcend and thus truly forget the past. "All" the history of recent Southern culture after 1930 has to offer are several examples of men and women who attempted this difficult task. Standing as we do at the point of ironic contemplation of their efforts, we can see their shortcomings. But it was their efforts that provide us this vantage point.

Notes

1 A Southern Renaissance

1. C. Vann Woodward, "Why the Southern Renaissance?" *Virginia Quarterly Review 51*, No. 2 (Spring 1975), 222-39.

2. *Ibid.*, p. 222.

3. Raymond Williams, *Marxism and Literature* (London: Oxford University Press, 1977), chapter 9.

4. Lewis Simpson, "The Southern Recovery of Memory and History," *Sewanee Review 82* (1974), p. 5.

5. *Ibid.*, p. 9.

6. *Ibid.*, p. 13.

7. Friedrich Nietzsche, *The Use and Abuse of History* (Indianapolis: Bobbs-Merrill, 1957); Hayden White, *Metahistory* (Baltimore: Johns Hopkins University Press, 1973); and *Tropics of Discourse* (Baltimore: Johns Hopkins University Press, 1978).

8. A complete cultural history of the Southern Renaissance would also have to deal with the region's drama and poetry, legal and religious thought, and its music.

9. John Irwin, *Doubling and Incest/Repetition and Revenge* (Baltimore: Johns Hopkins University Press, 1976).

10. Frederick L. Gwynn and Joseph L. Blotner (eds.), *Faulkner in the University* (Charlottesville: University of Virginia Press, 1959; Vintage, 1965), p. 268.

11. Louis Hartz, *The Liberal Tradition in America* (New York: Har-

court, Brace and World, 1955), chapter 6; and C. Vann Woodward, *American Counterpoint* (Boston: Little, Brown, 1971), chapter 4.

12. Edward Shils, "Metropolis and Province in the Intellectual Community," *The Intellectuals and the Powers and Other Essays* (Chicago: University of Chicago Press, 1972), pp. 355–71.

13. Allen Tate, "Aeneas at Washington," *Collected Poems, 1919–1976* (New York: Farrar, Straus and Giroux, 1977), p. 69.

14. Virginius Dabney, *Liberalism in the South* (Chapel Hill: University of North Carolina Press, 1931).

15. In *Democratic Promise: The Populist Movement in America* (New York: Oxford University Press, 1976), Lawrence Goodwyn stresses the educational efforts of the Farmer's Alliance and Populism generally. Whatever the effect of these efforts, they seem to me relatively short-lived in the South and nothing like the educational efforts of working-class movements in, say, England.

16. The phrase "introspective revolution" is taken from Fred Weinstein and Gerald Platt, *The Wish To Be Free: Society, Psyche and Value Change* (Berkeley: University of California Press, 1969). It refers to the pre-World War I revolt against the bourgeois family and the father in which Freud and Kafka are central figures. My thesis is that the South witnessed something similar in the 1930s and 1940s.

17. In *The Great War and Modern Memory* (New York: Oxford University Press, 1975), Paul Fussell traces the emergence of the modern ironic vision from the experience of the Great War as reflected in poetic diction. Yet Southerners such as Faulkner or Tate certainly felt no compulsion to temper their rhetoric nor is their rhetoric meant exclusively ironically.

18. For the relationship of Mencken to the South see Fred Hobson, Jr., *Serpent in Eden: H.L. Mencken and the South* (Chapel Hill: University of North Carolina Press, 1974); Edward Shapiro, "The Southern Agrarians, H.L. Mencken and the Quest for Southern Identity," *American Studies 13,* No. 2 (Fall 1972), 79–92; and Joseph Morrison, "Colonel Mencken, C.S.A.," *Southern Literary Journal 1,* No. 1 (December 1968), 42–59.

19. The late Benjamin Nelson called my attention to Joseph R. Levenson's *Confucian China and Its Modern Fate* (Berkeley: University of California Press, 1966), which discusses how a tradition became a "tradition." Much the same happened to the Southern tradition in the 1930s.

20. Allen Tate, "Remarks on Southern Religion," *I'll Take My Stand* (New York: Harper & Bros., 1930; Harper Torchbooks, 1962), p. 162.

21. Donald Davidson, "Sequel of Appomattox," *The Fugitive Poets,* ed. by William Pratt (New York: E.P. Dutton, 1965), pp. 78–79.

22. In his novel *The Last Gentleman* (New York: Farrar, Straus and Giroux, 1966; Signet, 1968), Walker Percy sets forth this four-generation sense of decline from heroism to irony (pp. 15–16), which

obviously bears on Percy's own relationship to the Southern tradition and to his family, particularly to the life and work of his adoptive father, William Alexander Percy.

23. Hannah Arendt, *Between Past and Future* (New York: Meridian, 1961), pp. 91–141.

24. See Freud's *Civilization and Its Discontents* (New York: W.W. Norton, 1962), for a general discussion of the full meaning of the reality principle. According to Paul Ricoeur in *Freud and Philosophy* (New Haven: Yale University Press, 1970), reality is ultimately synonymous with necessity or *Ananke*.

25. Ricoeur, *ibid.*, p. 299.

2 THE SOUTHERN FAMILY ROMANCE AND ITS CONTEXT

1. See Immanuel Wallerstein, *The Modern World-System: Capitalist Agriculture and the Origins of the European World Economy in the Sixteenth Century* (New York: Academic Press, 1974), for the concept of the "periphery"; and André Gunder Frank, *Capitalism and Underdevelopment in Latin America* (New York: Monthly Review Press, 1967) and *Lumpenbourgeoisie: Lumpenproletariat* (New York: Monthly Review Press, 1972), for the concept of "underdevelopment."

2. See Eugene Genovese, *The World the Slaveholders Made* (New York: Pantheon, 1969); and also Rollin Osterweiss, *Romanticism and Nationalism in the Old South* (New Haven: Yale University Press, 1949; Peter Smith, 1964); William R. Taylor, *Cavalier and Yankee* (New York: George Braziller, 1961; Anchor, 1963).

3. C. Vann Woodward's *Origins of the New South, 1877–1913* (Baton Rouge: Louisiana State University Press, 1951) is still the most comprehensive discussion of post-Reconstruction Southern economic development.

4. Paul Gaston, *The New South Creed* (New York: Knopf, 1970).

5. Woodward, *Origins,* p. 309.

6. George Tindall, *The Emergence of the New South: 1913–45* (Baton Rouge: Louisiana State University Press, 1967), chapters 2 and 4.

7. The standard accounts of race relations in this period are Woodward's *Origins,* chapters 12 and 13, and his *The Strange Career of Jim Crow,* 2nd rev. ed. (New York: Oxford University Press, 1966), chapters 1–3.

8. Barrington Moore, *Social Origins of Dictatorship and Democracy* (Boston: Beacon Press, 1966), pp. 438, 425, 442.

9. Woodward, *Origins,* chapters 7, 8, and 9; Lawrence Goodwyn, *Democratic Promise: The Populist Movement in America* (New York: Oxford University Press, 1976).

10. Woodward, *Origins*, chapter 12; and J. Morgan Kousser, *The Shaping of Southern Politics: Suffrage Restriction and the Establishment of the One-Party South, 1880–1910* (New Haven: Yale University Press, 1974).

11. See Tindall, *Emergence*, chapter 7, and also his *The Persistent Tradition in New South Politics* (Baton Rouge: Louisiana State University Press, 1975) and *The Ethnic Southerners* (Baton Rouge: Louisiana State University Press, 1976), chapter 7.

12. As a "favored colony" the South's economically subordinate position was marked by a "low rate of income convergence" with the North. That convergence had become a divergence by the 1920s and 1930s. Such a favored colony is, observes Joe Persky, "in an excellent position to receive the spin-off of older industries from the metropolitan center, but not to generate or quickly partake in the dynamic phases of innovative cycles." Persky, "The South: A Colony at Home," *Southern Exposure 1*, No. 2 (Summer/Fall 1973), 14–22. For more recent discussions of the South's economic situation see: Tindall, *Emergence;* William H. Nicholls, *Southern Tradition and Regional Progress* (Chapel Hill: University of North Carolina Press, 1960); and John F. Kain and John R. Meyer (eds.), *Essays in Regional Economics* (Cambridge: Harvard University Press, 1971).

13. Quoted in Richard Hoggart, *The Uses of Literacy* (New York: Oxford University Press, 1957; Beacon Press, 1961), p. 133.

14. Besides Taylor and Osterweiss, see Paul Buck, *The Road to Reunion: 1865–1900* (Boston: Little, Brown, 1937); Francis Pendleton Gaines, *The Southern Plantation: A Study in the Development and Accuracy of a Tradition* (New York: Columbia University Press, 1924; Peter Smith, 1962); and Lawrence J. Friedman, *The White Savage* (Englewood Cliffs, N.J.: Prentice-Hall, 1970), chapter 4.

15. Besides Cash and Genovese, see Bertram Wyatt-Brown, "The Ideal Typology and Ante-Bellum Southern History: A Testing of a New Approach," *Societas 5*, No. 1 (Winter 1975), 1–29; and Paul Conner, "Patriarchy: Old World and New," *American Quarterly 17*, No. 1 (Spring 1965), 48–62.

16. Sigmund Freud, "Family Romances," *The Sexual Enlightenment of Children*, ed. by Philip Rieff (New York: Collier Books, 1974), pp. 41–45.

17. Otto Rank, *The Myth of the Birth of the Hero,* ed. by Philip Freund (New York: Vintage, 1959), p. 9.

18. In her *The Ego and the Mechanisms of Defense* (London: Hogarth Press, 1976) Anna Freud gives examples from case histories in which animals serve as stand-ins for the father and reverse the negative perceptions of him: they become friendly and helpful. Slaying the dragon or frightening the beast is a variation on this theme in fairy tales.

19. Taylor, *Cavalier and Yankee*, p. 124.

20. *Ibid.*, p. 126.

21. *Ibid.*, p. 283.

22. Hortense Powdermaker, *After Freedom* (New York: Atheneum, 1968).

23. Buck, *Road*, p. 213.

24. Gaston, *The New South Creed*, p. 170.

25. Bruce Clayton, *The Savage Ideal* (Baltimore: Johns Hopkins University Press, 1972), p. 3. Clayton concentrates his attention on the following men: writers—Walter Hines Page, William Garott Brown, Thomas Nelson Page; academics—William P. Trent, John Spencer Bassett, Edwin Mims, W. E. Dodd, John Kilgo, Edwin Alderman, Samuel Chiles Mitchell, James Kirkland; and Edgar Gardner Murphy, A. N. McKelway, and Woodrow Wilson.

26. *Ibid.*, p. 207.

27. *Ibid.*, p. 41.

28. *Ibid.*, p. 20.

29. *Ibid.*, p. 5.

30. Kousser, *The Shaping of Southern Politics*, p. 251.

31. Lawrence J. Friedman, *The White Savage;* and George Fredrickson, *The Black Image in the White Mind* (New York: Harper and Row, 1971; Harper Torchbook, 1972).

32. Friedman, *White Savage*, pp. 26, 22.

33. Fredrickson, *The Black Image*, p. 285.

34. Pierre van den Berghe, *Race and Ethnicity* (New York: Basic Books, 1970). Paternalistic racists see blacks as human, but barely; competitive racists see them as sub-human. This is another way of saying that the Southern family romance was a way of expressing the nature/culture distinction in Southern society.

35. The grandson-grandfather alliance is implicit in the family romance. As Ernest Jones notes in "The Significance of the Grandfather for the Fate of the Individual" and "The Phantasy of the Reversal of Generations," *Papers on Psycho-analysis* (London: Ballière, Tindall, and Cox, 1918), pp. 652–57, 658–63, the grandfather can serve as the heroic substitute for the demoted father. In his "Reflections on American Identity" in *Childhood and Society*, 2nd rev. ed. (New York: W. W. Norton, 1963), Erik Erikson observes how American mothers often hold up their fathers to their sons as figures of power and integrity while subtly rejecting their husbands (pp. 312–14). Thus to break the hold of the family romance it was not the father alone, but the grandfather as well, who had to be demystified.

36. This phrase comes from Anne F. Scott, *The Southern Lady; From Pedestal to Politics, 1830–1930* (Chicago: University of Chicago Press, 1970). See also Carroll Smith-Rosenberg, "The Hysterical Woman: Sex Roles and Role Conflict in 19th Century America," *Social Research*

39 (Winter 1972), 652–78; and Barbara Welter, "The Cult of True Womanhood: 1820–60," *American Quarterly 18* (Summer 1966), 151–74.

37. Scott, *The Southern Lady*, p. 218.

3   MODERNIZERS AND MONUMENTALISTS:
SOCIAL THOUGHT IN THE 1930S

1. Information on Odum's early life and subsequent career is taken from George B. Tindall, "The Significance of Howard W. Odum to Southern History: A Preliminary Estimate," *Journal of Southern History 24*, No. 3 (August 1958), 285–307; Wayne D. Brazil's "Howard W. Odum: The Building Years, 1884–1930," Ph.D. dissertation, Harvard University, 1975; and Marshall Sosna's *In Search of the Silent South* (New York: Columbia University Press, 1977), chapter 3. Brazil's dissertation is exhaustive and a bit more critical than most writing on Odum, but it ends just when things become interesting.

There is relatively little secondary literature on the Regionalists. Marian Irish's "Proposed Roads to the New South, 1941: Chapel Hill Planners vs. Nashville Agrarians," *Sewanee Review 49*, No. 1 (January-March 1941), 1–27, is an early attempt to compare the two groups, while Dewey Grantham's "The Regional Imagination: Social Scientists and the American South," *Journal of Southern History 34*, No. 1 (February 1968), 3–32, is a useful overview of the historical, political, and intellectual context of the development of Regionalism.

2. Brazil, "The Building Years," p. 602.

3. Howard W. Odum, *The Social and Mental Traits of the Negro* (New York: Columbia University Press, 1910), p. 52.

4. Tindall particularly is much too lenient on Odum. The thrust of Odum's study and the material I have cited indicate that Tindall's claim that Odum "did not specifically define the sources of his [the Negro's] differences" (p. 287) is well off the mark. A couple of years later Odum conducted a study of black children in Philadelphia to justify segregated public schools there. It should be said, however, that Odum and Guy Johnson made major contributions to the preservation of black folklore and thus exhibited a concern with black life certainly not found among the Agrarians.

5. Brazil, "The Building Years," pp. 232, 235–36.

6. Tindall, "Significance . . . ," p. 287.

7. Howard W. Odum, "The Duel to the Death," *Social Forces 4*, No. 1 (September 1925), 189.

8. Brazil, "The Building Years," p. 560.

9. Howard W. Odum, *American Epoch: Southern Portraiture in the National Picture* (New York: Holt, 1930).

10. *Ibid.*, pp. 132–34.

11. *Ibid.*, p. 248.

12. *Ibid.*, p. 267.

13. *Ibid.*, p. 341.

14. Rupert Vance, *Human Geography of the South* (Chapel Hill: University of North Carolina Press, 1932, 1935).

15. *Ibid.*, pp. 19, 22.

16. Howard W. Odum, *Southern Regions of the United States* (Chapel Hill: University of North Carolina Press, 1936).

17. Vance, *Human Geography*, p. 76; Odum, *Southern Regions*, p. 227.

18. Vance, *Human Geography*, p. 274.

19. Odum, *Southern Regions*, p. ix.

20. Vance, *Human Geography*, pp. 462–63.

21. Odum, *Southern Regions*, p. 19.

22. Tindall, "Significance . . . ," p. 295.

23. Odum, *Southern Regions*, p. 487.

24. *Ibid.*

25 *Ibid.*, p. 521.

26. *Ibid.*, pp. 187–91. Sosna notes that Odum felt he had been unduly neglected by Roosevelt's New Dealers. Though Odum was not on the panel which drew up the famous *Report on Economic Conditions of the South* (1938), the report was essentially inspired by Odum's analysis in *Southern Regions.* Its central theme was the South's colonial economic status, but not race nor civil rights nor the burden of maintaining a dual school system was mentioned. As it was, the report aroused a storm of opposition in the South.

27. Howard W. Odum and Harry E. Moore, *American Regionalism,* (New York: Holt, 1938), p. vi.

28. *Ibid.*, p. viii.

29. Odum, *Southern Regions*, p. 131.

30. Howard W. Odum, *The Way of the South: Toward the Regional Balance of America* (New York: Macmillan, 1947), p. 204.

31. Rupert Vance, "Rebels and Agrarians All, Studies in One-Party Politics," *Southern Review 4,* No. 1 (Summer 1938), 26–44.

32. This is certainly implied by his emphasis on expert planning.

33. Vance, "Rebels . . . ," p. 21.

34. Howard W. Odum, *Race and Rumors of Race* (Chapel Hill: University of North Carolina Press, 1943), p. vii.

35. Broadus and George Mitchell, *The Industrial Revolution in the South* (Baltimore: Johns Hopkins University Press, 1930), p. 114.

36. *Ibid.*, p. 146.

37. Arthur F. Raper and Ira DeA. Reid, *Sharecroppers All* (Chapel Hill: University of North Carolina Press, 1941).

38. *Ibid.*, p. vii.

39. *Ibid.*, p. 244.

40. All other factors aside, it undoubtedly helped that Reid was black.

41. W. T. Couch, "An Agrarian Programme for the South," *American Review 3*, No. 3 (June 1934), 313–26.

42. Herman C. Nixon, *Forty Acres and Steel Mules* (Chapel Hill: University of North Carolina Press, 1938). Nixon's book was intended to counter what Nixon considered the distorted picture of Southern tenants in Margaret Bourke-White's and Erskine Caldwell's *You Have Seen Their Faces*, (New York: Modern Age Books, 1937).

43. C. Vann Woodward, "Hillbilly Realism," *Southern Review 4*, No. 4 (Spring 1939), 679.

44. Nixon, *Forty Acres*, p. 5.

45. *Ibid.*, pp. 31–33.

46. *Ibid.*, p. 81.

47. *Ibid.*, p. 93.

48. *Ibid.*, p. 96.

49. Twelve Southerners, *I'll Take My Stand* (New York: Harper & Bros., 1930; Harper Torchbooks, 1962). I have not directly discussed the companion volume (and successor) of *I'll Take My Stand*, Herbert Agar and Allen Tate (eds.), *Who Owns America?* (Boston: Houghton Mifflin, 1936). It is less explicitly about the South and generally benefits from the wider focus. It also articulates a position based on the small producer and the centrality of private property (with occasional nods toward farm cooperatives), an ironic repetition of the Republican ideology of the 1850s. In a strange way it is nearer the ideology of Hinton Helper than George Fitzhugh and draws very little on the plantation tradition.

The critical literature on the Agrarians is all too vast. John L. Stewart's *The Burden of Time* (Princeton: Princeton University Press, 1965) is the most complete and most cogent critical work, while Louis Rubin's *The Wary Fugitives* (Baton Rouge: Louisiana State University Press, 1978) is more sympathetic. Alex Karanikas's *Tillers of a Myth: Southern Agrarians as Social and Literary Critics* (Madison: University of Wisconsin Press, 1966) claims that the ideal of the Agrarian South was a smokescreen; the "true ideal was the Middle Ages" (viii). As far as I can tell he unfairly tars the Agrarians with the brush of anti-Semitism due largely to their (or at least Tate's) connection with Eliot. Richard H. Pells's *Radical Visions and American Dreams* (New York: Harper and Row, 1973) and R. Alan Lawson's *The Failure of Independent Liberalism* (New York: Putnam, 1971) put the Agrarians in the context of American regionalism of the 1930s; while Lawson, as well as Garvin Davenport in *The Myth of Southern History* (Nashville: Vanderbilt University Press, 1970), stress the Jeffersonian and yeoman dimension of the Agrarians' ideology. Richard Gray's *The Literature of*

Memory (Baltimore: Johns Hopkins University Press, 1977) focuses on the split between the planter and yeoman elements and rightly, I think, takes the Southern component of Agrarianism as more than a smoke-screen. As I try to make clear, the dichotomy between yeoman and planter ideals is certainly there, but ultimately reconcilable in the vision of a hierarchical society. Clearly they are not reconcilable if one takes the Agrarians to be egalitarians, even if "for whites only."

50. Barrington Moore, Jr., *Social Origins of Dictatorship and Democracy* (Boston: Beacon, 1966), pp. 491–96. See also John R. Harrison's *The Reactionaries* (New York: Schocken, 1966) for a discussion of the anti-democratic aspects of literary modernism. In many of its central figures modernism represented a linkage of aesthetic experimentation with political and cultural reaction. Of all the Agrarians Tate probably came closest to this position.

51. Louis Rubin, "Fugitives as Agrarians: The Impulse Behind *I'll Take My Stand," William Elliott Shoots a Bear* (Baton Rouge: Louisiana State University Press, 1975), p. 163.

52. John Tyree Fain and Thomas Daniel Young (eds.), *Literary Correspondence of Donald Davidson and Allen Tate* (Athens: University of Georgia Press, 1974), p. 79.

53. *Ibid.*, pp. 191–93.

54. John Crowe Ransom, *God Without Thunder* (New York: Harcourt Brace, 1930).

55. *Ibid.*, p. 95.

56. *Ibid.*, p. 124.

57. William Knickerbocker, "Theological Homebrew," *Sewanee Review* 39, No. 1 (January-March 1931), 103–11. Knickerbocker concluded wryly that a better title for the book would have been "Thunder without God."

58. Fain and Young, *Literary Correspondence*, p. 255.

59. *Ibid.*, p. 251. The information about Tate, Lytle, and Warren comes from Davidson's *"I'll Take My Stand*: A History," *American Review* 5, No. 3 (Summer 1935), 315.

60. John Crowe Ransom, "Reconstructed But Unregenerate," *I'll Take My Stand*, p. 14.

61. Frank Owsley, "The Irrepressible Conflict," *ibid.*, p. 62.

62. Allen Tate, "Remarks on Southern Religion," *ibid.*, p. 166.

63. *Ibid.*, p. 168.

64. *Ibid.*, p. 172.

65. Wendell Berry, *A Continuous Harmony* (New York: Harcourt Brace Jovanovich, 1972), p. 66.

66. Andrew Lytle, *Bedford Forrest and His Critter Company*, rev. ed. (New York: McDowell and Obolensky, 1960).

67. *Ibid.*, p. 15.

68. *Ibid.*, p. 36.

69. *Ibid.*, p. 149.

70. *Ibid.*, p. 384.

71. *Ibid.*, p. 385.

72. Frank Owsley, "The Soldier Who Walked with God," *American Review 4*, No. 4 (February 1935), 437–59.

73. Frank Owsley, "Lucius Quintus Cincinnatus Lamar," *American Review 5*, No. 4 (September 1935), 503.

74. John Crowe Ransom, "Sociology and the Black Belt," *American Review 4*, No. 2 (December 1934), 153.

75. Robert Penn Warren, "The Second American Revolution," *Virginia Quarterly Review 7*, No. 2 (April 1931), 284. As Warren's review indicates, the Beard thesis in Southern hands lent itself to all sorts of conservative and racist twistings.

76. Frank Owsley, "Scottsboro, The Third Crusade: The Sequel to Abolition and Reconstruction," *American Review 1*, No. 3 (June 1933), 285.

77. Allen Tate, "A View of the Whole South," *American Review 2*, No. 4 (February 1934), 424–25. In an essay in the previous issue Ransom could breezily refer to blacks as the "darkey" ("The Aesthetics of Regionalism," *American Review 2*, No. 3 (January 1934), 308).

78. Donald Davidson, "Still Rebels, Still Yankees," *The Attack on Leviathan* (Chapel Hill: University of North Carolina Press, 1938), p. 142.

79. Donald Davidson, "Gulliver with Hay Fever," *American Review 9*, No. 2 (Summer 1937), 164, 167.

80. H. L. Mencken, "The South Astir," *Virginia Quarterly Review 11*, No. 1 (January 1935), 55.

81. Davidson, "Gulliver," p. 170.

82. Davidson, "Dilemma of Southern Liberals," *Attack*, p. 267. This was an expanded version of an essay in *American Mercury* in 1934.

83. *Ibid.*, pp. 283–84.

84. Davidson, "Howard Odum and the Sociological Proteus," *Attack*, p. 298.

85. Donald Davidson, "The Class Approach to Southern Problems," *Southern Review 5*, No. 2 (Autumn 1939), 268, 270. Davidson also accused Woodward of smearing the Agrarians by claiming that they had adopted the myth of the Old South. Rather, Davidson asserted, they had emphasized the "little fellow rather than the big fellow" (p. 265). In this essay Davidson distanced himself from a defense of the aristocracy and even on occasion had kind words for the Populists. But neither Davidson nor Owsley ever really attacked the planter class or plantation slavery nor did they ever really attempt to resurrect the Populist example.

86. Allen Tate, "Notes on Liberty and Property," *American Review* 6, No. 5 (March 1936), 598–99. This essay was Tate's contribution to *Who Owns America?*.

87. Richmond Beatty and George M. O'Donnell, "The Tenant Farmer in the South," *American Review* 5, No. 1 (April 1935), 81.

88. Frank Owsley, "The Pillars of Agrarianism," *American Review* 4, No. 5 (March 1935), 532.

89. *Ibid.*, pp. 529–47; Davidson, "Federation or Disunion: The Political Economy of Regionalism," *Attack*, pp. 121–22.

90. As will become clear, I am not interested in a full-blown discussion of the historical origins or the philosophical underpinnings of the New Criticism. The New York critics—Trilling, Kazin, Howe, Rahv, Rosenberg—were always wary of the New Critical hermeticism. See, for instance, Kazin's *On Native Grounds* (New York: Harcourt Brace, 1942) in which he charges both Marxist and Formalist criticism with rigid dogmatism. In the 1960s the New Criticism came in for considerable battering from "New Leftish" literary men. See Louis Kampf's "The Scandal of Literary Scholarship" and Richard Ohmann's "Studying Literature at the End of Ideology," in *The Dissenting Academy*, ed. by Theodore Roszak (New York: Pantheon, 1968). One of Trilling's colleagues at Columbia, Quentin Anderson, scores the New Criticism for its isolation from "the messiness of lives and the incoherence of history" in *The Imperial Self* (New York: Knopf, 1971; Vintage, 1972), p. 35, while Eugene Goodheart in his *Culture and the Radical Conscience* (Cambridge: Harvard University Press, 1973) and Gerald Graff in "What Was New Criticism?" *Salmagundi*, No. 27 (Summer-Fall 1974) offer more balanced, though still critical, assessments of the impact of the New Criticism.

91. The biographical information comes from Thomas Daniel Young's *Gentleman in a Dustcoat* (Baton Rouge: Louisiana State University Press, 1976), which is a long, surprisingly interesting but totally uncritical biography of Ransom. See also Young (ed.), *John Crowe Ransom: Critical Essays and a Bibliography* (Baton Rouge: Louisiana State University Press, 1968). Ransom's critical writings are in *The World's Body* (Baton Rouge: Louisiana State University Press, 1938), *The New Criticism* (Norfolk, Conn.: New Directions, 1941), *Beating the Bushes: Selected Essays, 1941–1970* (New York: New Directions, 1972), and *Poems and Essays* (New York: Vintage, 1955).

92. Ransom, "Wanted: An Ontological Critic," *Beating the Bushes*, p. 44.

93. Ransom, "Poets Without Laurels," *World's Body*, p. 57.

94. Ransom, "Criticism, Inc.," *World's Body*, p. 347.

95. *Ibid.*, p. viii.

96. *Ibid.*, p. xi.

97. Ransom, "The Tense of Poetry," *World's Body*, pp. 247, 250.

98. Ransom, "Forms and Citizens," *World's Body*, pp. 29–31.

99. Ransom, *The New Criticism*, pp. 140–41.

100. Ransom, "Art and the Human Economy," *Beating the Bushes*, pp. 128–35.

101. Ransom, "Empiric in Politics," *Poems and Essays*, pp. 135–45.

102. Tate's essays can be found in *Essays of Four Decades* (Chicago: Swallow Press, 1968) and *Memoirs and Opinions, 1926–74* (Chicago: Swallow Press, 1974). Radcliffe Squires has written *Allen Tate: A Literary Biography* (New York: Pegasus, 1971) and edited *Allen Tate and His Work* (Minneapolis: University of Minnesota Press, 1972). I will deal more directly with Tate's essays on the South in Chapter V.

103. Tate, "Men of Letters," *Essays*, p. 3.

104. *Ibid.*, p. 27.

105. Tate, "Three Types of Poetry," *Essays*, p. 196.

106. Tate, "Emily Dickinson," *Essays*, pp. 281–84.

107. *Ibid.*, p 288.

108. *Ibid.*, pp. 294–95.

109. Tate, "Yeats' Romanticism," *Essays*, p. 305.

110. Tate, "Hart Crane," *Essays*, pp. 313, 315.

111. Tate, "The Profession of Letters in the South," *Essays*, p. 534.

112. Quoted in Thomas Daniel Young's *Ransom* (Austin: Steck-Vaughn, 1971), pp. 27–28.

113. Cleanth Brooks, *Modern Poetry and the Tradition* (Chapel Hill: University of North Carolina Press, 1939), pp. 45–48.

114. Robert Penn Warren, "Pure and Impure Poetry," *Selected Essays* (New York: Random House, 1958), pp. 27, 30.

115. Brooks, *Modern Poetry*, p. 203.

116. *Ibid.*, p. 95. Brooks used this phrase to characterize Tate's poetry particularly.

117. Tate, "Men of Letters," *Essays*, p. 15.

118. Dudley Wynn, "A Liberal Looks at Tradition," *Virginia Quarterly Review 12*, No. 1 (1936), 69.

119. Or perhaps what is as disturbing, it showed how easily the premodern tradition lent itself to anti-democratic impulses.

4 REPETITION AND DESPAIRING MONUMENTALISM: WILLIAM FAULKNER AND WILL PERCY

1. The biographical information on Faulkner is taken from Joseph Blotner's two-volume *William Faulkner* (New York: Random House, 1974) and his "The Falkners and the Fictional Families," *Georgia Review 30*, No. 3 (Fall 1976), 572–92. The essay in particular should lay

to rest any notions that Faulkner simply transcribed his family history into his fiction. In *The Unwritten War* (New York: Knopf, 1973), Daniel Aaron makes much the same point about Faulkner's ambivalent attitude toward the Southern cause in the Civil War.

2. William Faulkner, *Intruder in the Dust* (New York: Random House, 1948; Signet, 1960), pp. 125–26.

3. Blotner, *Faulkner*, 1:531–32. The passage itself was written two years later in 1928.

4. William Faulkner, *The Unvanquished* (New York: Random House, 1948; Signet, 1961), p. 173.

5. Blotner, "The Falkners," p. 574.

6. Joseph Blotner, *Selected Letters of William Faulkner* (New York: Random House, 1977), p. 212.

7. Blotner, *Faulkner*, 1: 90.

8. *Ibid.*, 2: 1516.

9. *Ibid.*, 1: 117. Blotner also notes that Phil Stone, Faulkner's hometown mentor and friend, thought the close ties of the Faulkner boys to their mother may have explained William's "animosity towards women" (p. 631).

10. In his *The Prison House of Language* (Princeton: Princeton University Press, 1972), Fredric Jameson observes of fiction read through Structuralist glasses that we learn a new sign system, a "surplus of signifiers" which "re-articulate . . . a new system of relations" (p. 133). This is another way of saying that in Faulkner we find a new world which is separate from historical reality (it is not "history") yet illuminates that world.

11. Gene Wise, *American Historical Explanations* (Homewood, Ill.: Dorsey Press, 1973), p. 13. For all the literary attention devoted to *The Sound and the Fury*, I find Wise's discussion of Benjy the most valuable and enlightening.

12. See Suzanne Langer's *Philosophy in a New Key* (Cambridge, Mass.: Harvard University Press, 1942) and Walker Percy's *The Message in the Bottle* (New York: Farrar, Straus and Giroux, 1975) for a discussion of the linguistic and cultural significance of the Helen Keller story.

13. Wise, *Explanations*, p. 13.

14. All quotations are from *Flags in the Dust* (New York: Random House, 1973; Vintage, 1974).

15. Faulkner was involved in a tragic repetition linking his fiction and his life. Late in 1935 his young brother, Dean, was killed while flying. Since Faulkner was an avid pilot and had been instrumental in interesting his brother in flying, his grief was compounded by guilt over indirect responsibility for Dean's death.

16. All quotations are from *Light in August* (New York: H. Smith and R. Haas, 1932; Modern Library, 1950).

17. William Alexander Percy, *Lanterns on the Levee: Recollections of a Planter's Son,* introduction by Walker Percy (Baton Rouge: Louisiana State University Press, 1973). All quotations are taken from this edition of *Lanterns on the Levee.*

18. For first-hand accounts see David Cohn, "Eighteenth Century Chevalier," *Virginia Quarterly Review 31,* No. 4 (Autumn 1955), 561–75; Hodding Carter, *Where Main Street Meets the River* (New York: Rinehart and Co., 1953), chapter 6; and Hortense Powdermaker, *Stranger and Friend* (New York: W. W. Norton, 1966). Phinezy Spalding's "A Stoic Trend in William Alexander Percy's Thought," *Georgia Review 12,* No. 3 (Fall 1955), 241–51, is a rather uncritical defense of Percy, while James Silver's "William Alexander Percy: The Aristocrat and Anthropologist" (unpublished) is quite critical. Professor Silver was extremely helpful in preparation of my discussion of Percy which was presented in an earlier version (along with Professor Silver's paper) at the meeting of the Southern Historical Association, November 1975, in Washington, D.C.

19. Walker Percy, *The Message in the Bottle* (New York: Farrar, Straus and Giroux, 1973), p. 4. Will Percy was not actually Walker Percy's uncle. He was a cousin of Walker Percy's father and thus Walker Percy's cousin, once removed. Upon the death of their parents, Walker Percy and his two brothers were adopted and brought up by Will Percy. Since Walker Percy generally refers to his cousin (and adoptive father) as "Uncle" Will, I will follow that usage.

20. Cash's review of *Lanterns on the Levee* appeared in the Charlotte *News,* May 10, 1941, and is reprinted in Joseph Morrison's *W. J. Cash* (New York: Knopf, 1967), pp. 290–94. In David Madden (ed.), *Remembering James Agee* (Baton Rouge: Louisiana State University Press, 1974), David McDowell recalled how fond Agee was of *Lanterns on the Levee* and speculated that the review in *Time,* March 24, 1941, was Agee's (p. 96). The review is poorly written, unstinting in praise of Percy, and registers not a single objection to Percy's views of sharecropping. It is hard to see how Agee could have written the review, but if he did, it represents the clearest case imaginable of the corrupting influence of the Luce publications.

21. Percy, *Lanterns,* p. xiii.

22. See Florence King's bracingly irreverent *Southern Ladies and Gentlemen* (New York: Stein and Day, 1975), chapter 12. Early in his *The Last Gentleman,* Walker Percy charts this generational decline from the men of action of irony and finally to the "passive" Will Barrett. In a very general way Percy's fiction had been about the difficulties of living in the untraditioned world which his uncle saw aborning. Though his irony and wit have been turned against this new dispensation, Percy's view of the world is by no means his uncle's. It arises rather

from a continual dialectic with Will Percy's world-view. Walker Percy is much more of a Southern novelist than he or the critics have allowed.

23. In his "William Alexander Percy and the Bourbon Era in the Yazoo-Mississippi Delta," *Mississippi Quarterly 26*, No. 1 (Winter 1972–73), 71–88, Will Holmes takes Will Percy to task for "help[ing] to perpetuate a mythical view of the Bourbon leaders," including his father. Holmes also makes clear in his biography of Vardaman, *The White Chief* (Baton Rouge: Louisiana State University Press, 1970), and in his essay that the political conflicts involving Leroy Percy were less a clash between high principle and low demagoguery than between two contending elites for power. Whatever his impressive personal qualities, the elder Percy's probity, Holmes notes, has not gone unquestioned. Leroy Percy was primarily a railroad and utility lawyer and was allied with Vardaman at one time.

24. See Pete Daniel's *The Shadow of Slavery* (Urbana: University of Illinois Press, 1972), pp. 152–57, for a full discussion of the controversy aroused by the flood relief program in Greenville. I am not concerned here with presenting an overview of the events of the spring and summer of 1927 but with analyzing Will Percy's own account of events.

25. Quotations are taken from *The Collected Poems of William Alexander Percy*, foreword by Roark Bradford (New York: Knopf, 1943).

26. William Faulkner, *Early Poetry and Prose*, ed. by Carvel Collins (Boston: Atlantic Monthly Press, 1962), p. 72.

5   Between Repetition and Recollection: Allen Tate and William Faulkner

1. Biographical information comes from Allen Tate, *Memoirs and Opinions, 1926–74* (Chicago: Swallow Press, 1975); Radcliffe Squires, *Allen Tate: A Literary Biography* (New York: Pegasus, 1971); and (ed.), *Allen Tate and His Work* (Minneapolis: University of Minnesota Press, 1972).

2. John Tyree Fain and Thomas Daniel Young (eds.), *The Literary Correspondence of Donald Davidson and Allen Tate* (Athens: University of Georgia Press, 1974), p. 212 (letter of April 12, 1928).

3. Allen Tate, "What Is a Traditional Society," *Essays of Four Decades* (Chicago: Swallow Press, 1968), pp. 551, 554, 556.

4. Tate, "The Fugitives, 1922-25," *Memoirs and Opinions*, pp. 32–33.

5. Tate, "The New Provincialism," *Essays*, p. 545.

6. Tate, "A Southern Mode of Imagination," *Essays*, pp. 581, 584, 587.

7. *Ibid.*, p. 592.

8. Quotations are from *Stonewall Jackson* (New York: Minton, Balch, 1928; Ann Arbor: University of Michigan Press, 1965) and *Jefferson Davis: His Rise and Fall, A Biographical Narrative* (New York: Minton, Balch, 1929). Tate's two biographies have been neglected, particularly as they relate to his cultural criticism and his novel *The Fathers*. In my discussion I will be concerned with evaluating their place in Tate's thought and not with judging Tate's assessment of Confederate military or political strategy; for example, Tate's claim that if Davis had allowed it, Southern armies could have captured Washington after Bull Run.

9. Fain and Young, *Literary Correspondence*, p. 186 (letter of February 15, 1927).

10. Richard Gray, *The Literature of Memory* (Baltimore: Johns Hopkins University Press, 1977), p. 84; Allen Tate, "Ode to the Confederate Dead," *Collected Poems 1919–1976* (New York: Farrar, Straus and Giroux, 1977), pp. 20–23.

11. Tate, "Narcissus as Narcissus," *Essays*, pp. 248–62.

12. Fain and Young, *Literary Correspondence*, p. 215 (letter of April 12, 1928).

13. *Ibid.*

14. Tate, "Profession of Letters in the South," *Essays*, p. 519.

15. Quotations are from *The Fathers* (New York: G. P. Putnam's Sons, 1938; Swallow Press, 1960). Strangely, *The Fathers* has received little critical attention; or at least not the attention it deserves. The tendency reflected in Arthur Mizener's essay (which introduces the 1960 edition) and Richard Gray's discussion in *The Literature of Memory* is to place Tate's sympathies with the public world of Major Buchan. Yet the novel (and Tate's vision of the ante-bellum South) is marked by a deep ambivalence toward both Buchan and Posey as representatives of two distinct ways of life. In her "The End of the Old Dominion" in *Allen Tate and His Work,* Janet Smith notes the weakness of the old Virginia way of life, as does Walter Sullivan in "Southern Novelists and the Civil War," *Death by Melancholy* (Baton Rouge: Louisiana State University Press, 1972). Only Louis Rubin in his discussion of Tate in *The Wary Fugitives* has bothered to mention why "the Fathers" of the title is plural rather than singular.

16. Fain and Young, *Literary Correspondence*, p. 231 (letter of August 10, 1929). This self-characterization is preceded, however, by the suggestion that the tradition of Jefferson be repudiated, which it was in the biography of Davis.

17. See Jean Hippolyte, *Genesis and Structure of Hegel's Phenomenology of Spirit* (Evanston: Northwestern University Press, 1974), where he writes, "the lacerated consciousness is, against the unhappy consciousness, consciousness of the end of a certain world . . . it is also, generally, the final consciousness of every culture" (p. 414).

18. All of these critical positions are straw men, but they convey, I think, the range of attempts to deal with the "Quentin problem" in the "Quentin texts." I single out the liberal interpretation since it represents a view of Quentin which I long held. Nor is it completely absurd. But it does seem to me an excessively imposed interpretation of the texts.

Because the critical literature on Faulkner is so voluminous, I am reluctant to add to its volume. Yet the publication of John Irwin's *Doubling and Incest/Repetition and Revenge* (Baltimore: Johns Hopkins University Press, 1976) confirmed me in the approach which I had been formulating at the time I read the book. Irwin's superb book thus both sharpened my focus and allowed me to strike out in new directions. Since one of my general themes is the problem of the precursor's influence, a variation on a theme by Harold Bloom, I may as well own up to a bit of influence anxiety of my own vis-à-vis Irwin's book. My review of Irwin's book "Faulkner and Freud," *Salmagundi*, No. 36 (Winter 1977), 133–39, represents my initial assessment which has gone largely unchanged.

19. This is a (perhaps overly cryptic) reference to the picture of Faulkner on the cover of *Faulkner in the University*, ed. by Frederick Gwynn and Joseph Blotner (Charlottesville: University of Virginia Press, 1959; Vintage, 1965).

20. Irwin, *Doubling and Incest*, pp. 110, 157.

21. Irwin's view is that the therapeutic process—repetition, recollection, and working through—is also a form of revenge and fails to escape the closed circle. Granted that there is no notion of complete cure in Freud, still something can be gained in the process which incorporates, preserves, and yet transcends the past. In this sense Irwin's reading of Freud—and Faulkner—is overly pessimistic.

22. Quotations are taken from *The Sound and the Fury* (New York: Jonathan Cape and Harrison Smith, 1929; Signet, 1959).

23. I use "cancel" here to refer to the denial and abolition of time.

24. Claude Lévi-Strauss, *Elementary Structures of Kinship*, rev. ed. (Boston: Beacon Press, 1969), p. 12.

25. It is important to remember that time is not a neutral container of human action but is constituted by the social order, specifically by the succession of generations. Hence a disturbance in the family and between generations will be mirrored in distortions of temporality.

26. As Malcolm Cowley once observed, in Faulkner's writing sexual perversion often points to social disorder, rather than vice versa. To anticipate, I would say that the sexual and social are inseparable and can be "read" both ways.

27. In *Doubling and Incest* Irwin uses Faulkner's comments on the failure of Grandfather Compson to support his reading of Quentin's

attempt to escape the family's endless repetition of failure. For example, in *Faulkner in the University*, Faulkner says in an interview in 1959 that "There was a basic failure before that . . . It was the basic failure Quentin inherited through his father or beyond his father" (p. 3). This, clearly, is Faulkner glossing Faulkner, and I prefer to trust the original texts of *The Sound and the Fury* and *Absalom, Absalom!*.

28. Paul Ricoeur, "The Model of the Text: Meaningful Action Considered as Text," *Social Research* 38, No. 3 (Autumn 1971), 534. Because of this gap between intention and meaning, interpretation is both necessary and possible. Though I have alluded to the meaning of incest in the previous pages of Quentin, what follows is an attempt fully to interpret what it means, using other texts to illuminate this Quentin text.

29. Lévi-Strauss, *Elementary Structures*, p. 9. There is of course considerable anthropological and psychoanalytic literature on the problem of incest and the related matters of exogamy and endogamy. My account here basically follows Lévi-Strauss and Freud. Nikolaus Sidler's *Zür Universalität des Inzesttabus* (Stuttgart: Ferdinand Enke Verlag, 1971) accepts Lévi-Strauss's position while discussing historical instances where the taboo was systematically violated. In his *Death and Sensuality* (New York: Walker, 1962; Ballantine, 1969), Georges Bataille accepts the nature-culture dichotomy as constituted by the incest taboo, but claims that Lévi-Strauss neglects the fact that woman as "gift" represents an "effusion or celebration" (p. 205).

30. Freud's first anthropological-historical discussion of incest comes in *Totem and Taboo* (New York: Modern Library, 1939). Clearly for him, as for Lévi-Strauss, the incest taboo marks the onset of culture. This renders all reading of Freud as a biological determinist highly suspect. The instincts are always mediated in Freud's theory. Though Juliet Mitchell mounts a powerful defense of Freud in *Psychoanalysis and Women* (New York: Pantheon, 1974), she evades the fact that for Freud culture seems to be inescapably patriarchal, whereas for her it is "only" contingently so. See also Otto Rank's *Das Inzest-Motiv in Dichtung und Sage* (Leipzig und Wien: Franz Deuticke, 1912) for an exhaustive discussion of the mythological and literary occurrence of the incest theme. Rank also notes something which is relevant for *Absalom, Absalom!:* brother murder (e.g. Cain and Abel) is often linked with rivalry over possession of the sister. The basic psychoanalytic assumption is that sibling incest is a displaced version of parent-child incest.

31. Lévi-Strauss, *Elementary Structures*, p. 12.

32. *Ibid.*, p. 25.

33. Sigmund Freud, *Civilization and Its Discontents* (New York: W. W. Norton, 1962), p. 51.

34. Lévi-Strauss, *Elementary Structures*, p. 493.

35. *Ibid.*, p. 495.

36. *Ibid.*

37. See N. O. Brown's *Life Against Death* (Middletown, Conn.: Wesleyan University Press, 1959) and K. Colburn's fascinating "Hedonism, Incest and the Problem of Difference," *Theory & Society 2* (1975), 351–74.

38. *The Prison House of Language* (Princeton: Princeton University Press, 1972) is the title of Fredric Jameson's critique of structuralism and formalism.

39. Here I am obviously taking exception to the line of Faulkner criticism, represented by Cleanth Brooks, which sees Sutpen as an aberration, a sort of heroic Snopes.

40. All quotations are taken from *Absalom, Absalom!* (New York: Random House, 1936; Modern Library, 1951).

41. As J. G. A. Pocock has noted in *Politics, Language and Time* (London: Methuen, 1971), drawing upon Max Weber, the founders of a tradition fit into the tradition with considerable difficulty. Charismatic foundings and traditional orderings stand in tension with one another.

42. G. W. F. Hegel, *The Phenomenology of Spirit,* trans. and ed. by J. B. Baillie (London: Allen and Unwin, 1931), pp. 228–40. Lévi-Strauss's male exchange of women would represent his version of the initial master-slave relationship. That the master is the slave of his slaves is the contradiction at the heart of the master-slave relationship.

43. One wonders how Leslie Fiedler missed this example of his famous theme of male, interracial homoeroticism in American literature. By extension the American vision of male interracial harmony would be the ideological inversion of the master-slave relationship which dominated reality. The fights in the barn clearly foreshadow the Henry-Bon struggle and its ultimate "resolution"; and one should also note that, as Irwin emphasizes, the conflict of brothers is a displaced version of the father-son conflict. Finally, Henry and Judith in the loft rings an interesting change on the image of Caddy in the tree watching her grandmother die in *The Sound and the Fury*.

44. I use "imaginary" here in the sense used by Jacques Lacan, the French psychoanalyst. It refers to the aggressive, paranoic constitution of the ego in the early months of life which Lacan names the "mirror stage." See Jacques Lacan, *Ecrits* (New York: W. W. Norton, 1977), pp. 1–7.

45. Alexandre Kojeve, *Introduction to a Reading of Hegel,* ed. by Allan Bloom (New York: Basic Books, 1969), pp. 3–30.

46. In Hannah Arendt's terms Sutpen learns the meaning of "labor," the biological production of that which is consumed in order to survive in contrast with "work" and the realm of freedom. See *The Human Condition* (Chicago: University of Chicago Press, 1958), Parts III and IV. Put abstractly, racism represents the failure to see that society is a

system of relationships in which individuals (and groups) are defined by their place in the system rather than having fixed "essences." In the South, white and black become "natural symbols"; but false ones.

47. The Sutpen-Bon relationship is a version of the struggle between Jacob and the Angel in which the "weaker" one does *not* receive the blessing of the stronger. This reveals that the Biblical resolution of the master-slave (i.e. father-son) conflict is recognition which promises future succession.

48. In *Elementary Structures* Lévi-Strauss alludes at several points to the close proximity in certain societies, e.g. the U.S. South, of the incest and miscegenation taboos; see, for instance, pp. 10 and 46. In *Roll, Jordan, Roll* (New York: Pantheon, 1974), Eugene Genovese quotes Henry Hughes, a Mississippi planter, as saying: "The same law which forbids consanguinous amalgamation forbids ethnical amalgamation. Both are incestuous. Amalgamation is incest" (p. 418).

49. In *Absalom, Absalom!* Charles Etienne Bon's son is an idiot, which is to say both a social outcast and a biological enormity.

50. In *Caste and Class in a Southern Town* (New Haven: Yale University Press, 1937) John Dollard first pointed out this overdetermination of the taboo on interracial sex in the South.

51. David Levin, *"Absalom, Absalom!*: The Problem of Recreating History," *In Defense of Historical Literature* (New York: Hill and Wang, 1967), p. 125. Levin's is a prime example of the liberal reading of *Absalom, Absalom!*. I assume he is writing with tongue in cheek when he calls Bon "the first freedom rider" (p. 132).

6   Working Through: Faulkner's *Go Down Moses*

1. All quotations are from *Go Down Moses* (New York: Random House, 1942; Modern Library, 1942).

2. Again Irwin's approach leads him to a pessimistic reading of Faulkner, while I see in "The Bear" an escape from the repetitious patterns of the family and the region. Thus *Go Down Moses* not *A Fable* brings together the problems introduced and explored in *The Sound and the Fury* and *Absalom, Absalom!* (the Quentin texts).

3. Though this injunction follows Faulkner's intentions and enables a reading linking Lucas and Ike, *Go Down Moses* is rather uneven as a whole. "Pantaloon in Black" is sometimes taken to be the odd story, but it does add another moving dimension to Faulkner's treatment of black domestic life. Still its culminating irony is too heavy-handed. "Delta Autumn" has its powerful moments, but the symbolic linkage of the doe and Roth's mistress is made too obviously. The title story is a throwaway and points ominously to things to come.

4. It is also important to note that Lucas changes his name from

"Lucius" as though to be his own creator; as did William Faulkner when he added the "u" to his family name.

5. R. W. B. Lewis, "William Faulkner: The Hero in the New World," *The Picaresque Saint* (Philadelphia: Lippincott, 1956, 1961), pp. 179–219. Lewis's is by far the best of the religious readings of Faulkner.

6. Herbert Perluck, "The Heart's Driving Complexity: An Unromantic Reading of Faulkner's 'The Bear,'" *Bear, Man and God,* ed. by Francis Lee Utley, Lynn Z. Bloom, Arthur F. Kinney (New York: Random House, 1964), p. 303.

7. David Stewart, "The Purpose of Faulkner's Ike," *Bear, Man and God,* p. 332.

8. Frederick Gwynn and Joseph Blotner (eds.), *Faulkner in the University,* (Charlottesville: University of Virginia Press, 1959; Vintage, 1965), pp. 54, 245. The first of these two remarks was made in an interview in 1957; the second in 1958.

9. Hodding Carter, *Where Main Street Meets the River* (New York: Rinehart, 1953).

10. Francis Lee Utley, "Pride and Humility: Cultural Roots of Ike McCaslin," *Bear, Man and God,* pp. 233–60.

11. Olga Vickery, "Moral Order and Ike's Redemption," *Bear, Man and God,* p. 326.

12. Bloom's essential thesis is most clearly expressed in *The Anxiety of Influence* (New York: Oxford University Press, 1973) and *A Map of Misreading* (New York: Oxford University Press, 1975).

13. Otto Rank, *The Myth of the Birth of the Hero,* ed. by Philip Freund (New York: Vintage, 1959), p. 129. See also Malraux's *The Voices of Silence* (Garden City: Doubleday, 1953) for a similar thesis in the history of art.

14. This is Bloom's reinterpretation of the psychoanalytic theory of art which sees art as cathartic and therapeutic. An idea similar to Bloom's is expressed by Lévi-Strauss when he contends that myths do not resolve but rather express structural oppositions.

15. Joseph Blotner, *William Faulkner* (New York: Random House, 1974), vol. 1. Blotner writes that Estelle's first marriage was "deeply traumatic [for Faulkner] . . . Mixed with his feeling of loss was a reaction of bitterness toward Estelle" (p. 195).

16. *Ibid.,* p. 571.

17. See Peter Brooks, "Freud's Masterplot: Questions of Narrative," *Yale French Studies* (Literature and Psychoanalysis), 55/56 (1967), 280–300. For Brooks, and by extension for Bloom, all manifestations of creativity, i.e., Eros, are ways of defending against death, the ultimate desire at the heart of incest.

18. Joseph Blotner (ed.), *The Selected Letters of William Faulkner* (New York: Random House, 1977), p. 113.

19. Blotner, *Faulkner*, 2:1594–95.

20. Blotner (ed.), *Selected Letters*, p. 285.

21. *Ibid.*, p. 185.

7 NARCISSUS GROWN ANALYTICAL: CASH'S SOUTHERN MIND

1. All quotations are taken from W. J. Cash, *The Mind of the South* (New York: Knopf, 1941). Biographical information and observations are drawn from Joseph L. Morrison, *W. J. Cash: Southern Prophet* (New York: Knopf, 1967).

2. See C. Vann Woodward, "The Elusive Mind of the South," *American Counterpoint* (Boston: Little, Brown, 1971), pp. 261–83; and Eugene D. Genovese, *The World the Slaveholders Made* (New York: Pantheon, 1970), pp. 137–50. An attempt to counter Genovese on Cash can be found in Richard King's "Marxism and the Slave South," *American Quarterly* 29 (Spring 1977), 117–31. In the pages devoted to Woodward I take up again the Woodward-Cash controversy.

3. This essay is included in Morrison's biography.

4. In his *In Search of the Silent South* (New York: Columbia University Press, 1977), Martin Sosna stresses this aspect of Southern liberalism. As we shall see, Lillian Smith also saw quite clearly the vain hope that white men of "good will" in the South would take action.

5. The Cash review of *Lanterns on the Levee* is also reprinted in Morrison's *W. J. Cash*.

6. Jonathan Daniels, *A Southerner Discovers the South* (New York: Macmillan, 1938).

7. Donald Davidson, "Mr. Cash and the Proto-Dorian South," *Southern Review* 7, No. 1 (1941–42), 1–20.

8. Rupert Vance, *Human Geography* (Chapel Hill: University of North Carolina Press, 1932), p. 22.

9. Howard Odum, *Southern Regions of the United States* (Chapel Hill: University of North Carolina Press, 1936), p. 19.

10. One cannot help but notice the blatant sexual imagery in this passage, which can be found in Morrison, p. 12.

11. A. Alvarez, *The Savage God: A Study of Suicide* (New York: Random House, 1972; Bantam, 1973), pp. 36–37.

12. A more cogent criticism of Cash's monolithic emphasis might be taken from Erik Erikson's discussion of national character in *Childhood and Society,* specifically the opening pages of "Reflections on American Identity." Erikson asserts that national character is best described in terms of counterpointed tendencies rather than single characteristics. Even in light of this, Cash's "Mind" stands up well methodologically,

for he stresses the contradictions within the mind of the South between, for instance, individualism and identification with the South as a collectivity.

13. Robert Penn Warren, quoted in C. Vann Woodward, *The Burden of Southern History* (Baton Rouge: Louisiana State University Press, 1960; Vintage, 1961), p. 23.

14. In *Wallace* (New York: World Publishing Co., 1968) Marshall Frady refers to the South's "romance of defeat."

15. Stanley Elkins of course asked this question of blacks under slavery.

16. The classic text here of course is W. E. B. Du Bois's *Souls of Black Folk* (Chicago: A. M. McClurg, 1903), especially chapter 1.

17. "Thorough" was the name given to the repressive policies of the Earl of Stafford and Archbishop Laud during the reign of Charles I of England.

18. C. Vann Woodward, *Tom Watson: Agrarian Rebel* (New York: Macmillan, 1938; Oxford University Press, 1963), p. 331.

19. In his study *Populism to Progressivism in Alabama* (Princeton: Princeton University Press, 1969) Sheldon Hackney makes much the same point about Populism in Alabama: that it was more about power than principle or ideology.

20. Woodward, *Tom Watson*, p. 248.

21. Pat Watters, *The South and the Nation* (New York: Pantheon, 1969), p. 352.

8 FROM THERAPY TO MORALITY: THE EXAMPLE OF LILLIAN SMITH

1. My discussion of Smith concentrates on her writings and those of Paula Snelling in the periodical *Pseudopodia* (1936–37), which became *North Georgia Review* in 1937 and then in 1941 was renamed *South Today*. Helen White and Redding Sugg, Jr.'s *From the Mountain* (Memphis: Memphis State University Press, 1972), brings together selected essays and articles from the periodical and includes a valuable introduction. The three works by Smith which I focus on are *Strange Fruit* (New York: Reynal and Hitchcock, 1944), *Killers of the Dream*, revised and enlarged (Garden City: Doubleday Anchor, 1963), and *The Journey* (New York: Hillman, 1960).

Critical analyses of Smith's work are by no means numerous. Redding Sugg, Jr., "Lillian Smith: A Prophecy to *Strange Fruit*," *Atlanta 9*, No. 10 (February 1970), 40–44 and "Lillian Smith and the Condition of Women," *South Atlantic Quarterly 71*, No. 2 (Spring 1972), 155–64 are both helpful. Louise Blackwell and Francis Clay, *Lillian Smith* (New

York: Twayne, 1971) is a not very enlightening and often flat-footed literary biography, while Margaret Sullivan's "A Bibliography of Lillian Smith and Paula Snelling with an index to *South Today*, ed. by Joseph Riley," *MVC* Bulletin, No. 4 (Spring 1971), is quite useful. Morton Sosna's *In Search of the Silent South* (New York: Columbia University Press, 1977) includes a chapter on Smith entitled "Lillian Smith: The Southern Liberal as Evangelist," pp. 172–97, which stresses the religious dimension of her thought. Sosna and Thomas Krueger's *And Promises To Keep: The Southern Conference on Human Welfare, 1938–48* (Nashville: Vanderbilt University Press, 1967) provide background on white Southern liberalism and Smith's place in it.

2. Alexander and Margarete Mitscherlich, *The Inability To Mourn* (New York: Grove Press, 1975).

3. *Ibid.*, p. 28.

4. The tragic posture was one that troubled white Southerners found appealing, particularly in the post-World War II cultural context. It allowed them to parade their own moral perceptions without having to act upon them.

5. Smith, *The Journey*, pp. 71, 64.

6. Smith, *Killers*, p. 23.

7. *Ibid.*, p. 22. See Ann Douglas's *Feminization of American Culture* (New York: Knopf, 1977) for a discussion of this process in nineteenth-century New England.

8. Smith, *Killers*, p. 93.

9. In "Lillian Smith: A Prophecy of *Strange Fruit*," Sugg notes that the Atlanta *Constitution* and particularly Ralph McGill attacked Smith as a "zealot," as wearing a "hair shirt," and accused her of being given to "the pouring of ashes on her head and salt in her psychiatric wounds" (p. 42). Hell hath no fury like a Southern moderate whose hand had been called.

10. The periodical published by Smith and Snelling reminds one of Dwight Macdonald's *Politics*. Both ventures were understaffed and under-financed but their editors were pioneers in delineating the crucial moral and political issues of their time which other more "sophisticated" journals neglected.

11. Smith in *Pseudopodia* (Fall 1936) and collected in White and Sugg, *From the Mountain*, pp. 28, 30.

12. Paula Snelling, "Southern Fiction and Chronic Suicide," *North Georgia Review* 3, No. 2 (Summer 1938), 6.

13. Smith, "Dope With Lime," *South Today* 8, No. 2 (Winter, 1944–45), 7.

14. Snelling, review of Allen Tate's *The Fathers*, *North Georgia Review* 3, Nos. 3-4 (Fall and Winter 1938–39), 31–32.

15. Snelling, "A South Against Itself," *South Today* 8, No. 1 (Spring-Summer 1944), 20–25.

16. Smith, "Dope With Lime," *North Georgia Review* 6, Nos. 1-4 (Winter 1941), 6.

17. Snelling, review of W. J. Cash's *The Mind of the South*, *North Georgia Review* 5, Nos. 3-5 (Winter 1940–44), 46–48.

18. Snelling, "Ellen Glasgow and Her South," *North Georgia Review* 6, Nos. 1-4 (Winter 1941), 26–27; Snelling, review of Eudora Welty's *A Curtain of Green*, *South Today* 7, No. 1 (Spring 1942), 61.

19. Snelling, review of James Agee's *Let Us Now Praise Famous Men*, *South Today* 7, No. 1 (Spring 1942), 63.

20. Snelling, "Three Native Sons," *North Georgia Review* 5, No. 1 (Spring 1940), 7–12.

21. Snelling, "Southern Fiction and Chronic Suicide," *North Georgia Review* 3, No. 2 (Summer 1938), 27.

22. Snelling, review of Faulkner's *The Wild Palms*, *North Georgia Review* 3, No. 1 (Spring 1939), 24–25.

23. Smith, "Wisdom Crieth in the Streets," *North Georgia Review* (Fall 1937); reprinted in White and Sugg, *From the Mountain*, pp. 40–46.

24. Smith, "Southern Conference?," *North Georgia Review* 5, No. 1 (Spring 1940), 23–26. In general Smith was more sympathetic to the Southern Conference on Human Welfare than the Southern Regional Council, in part because she resented being excluded from its initial meetings and more importantly because she felt that the Southern Regional Council was wrong in avoiding a clear attack on segregation. See her attack on the Southern Regional Council, "Southern Defensive—II," *Common Ground* 4, No. 3 (Spring 1944), 43–45.

25. Smith, "Coming Over Jordan into Democracy," *South Today* 7, No. 1 (Spring 1942), 46–60.

26. Smith and Snelling, "Buying a New World with Old Confederate Bills," *South Today* 7, No. 2 (Winter 1942–43), 7–30.

27. Smith, "Burning Down Georgia's Back Porch," *Common Ground* 2, No. 2 (Winter 1942), 72.

28. Smith, "Dope With Lime," *South Today* 7, No. 1 (Spring 1942), 9.

29. Gregory Nicola, "War—a Holy Supper," *North Georgia Review* 4, Nos. 2-3 (Autumn 1939), 5–11.

30. Smith, "In Defense of Life," *North Georgia Review* 5, No. 2 (Summer 1940), 11–12.

31. Smith and Snelling, "Man Born of Women," *North Georgia Review* 5, No. 2 (Summer 1940), 7–17.

32. See *South Today* 8, No. 1 (Spring-Summer 1941).

33. Smith and Snelling, "Buying a New World," *South Today*, p. 20.

34. Smith, *Killers*, p. 7.

35. *Ibid.*, p. 49.

36. *Ibid.*, p. 47.

37. *Ibid.*, p. 71.
38. *Ibid.*, p. 72.
39. *Ibid.*, p. 79.
40. *Ibid.*, p. 110.
41. *Ibid.*, p. 187.
42. *Ibid.*, p. 112.
43. *Ibid.*, p. 109.
44. Smith, *Strange Fruit*, p. 247.
45. Smith, *Killers*, p. 113.
46. *Ibid.*, pp. 100–101.
47. *Ibid.*, p. 153.
48. For a powerful argument to the contrary see Philip Rieff, *Triumph of the Therapeutic* (New York: Harper and Row, 1966).

9 FROM THEME TO SETTING: WOLFE, AGEE, WARREN

1. Quoted in Virginia Spencer Carr, *The Lonely Hunter* (Garden City: Doubleday, 1975), p. 266.
2. The two standard, full-length biographies of Wolfe are Elizabeth Nowell's *Thomas Wolfe: A Biography* (Garden City: Doubleday, 1960) and Andrew Turnbull's *Thomas Wolfe* (New York: Scribners, 1967). To date Agee has had only one full-length biography (and not a very good one at that), Genevieve Moreau's *The Restless Journey of James Agee* (New York: Morrow, 1977). Valuable biographical information can be found in David Madden (ed.), *Remembering James Agee* (Baton Rouge: Louisiana State University Press, 1974), Dwight Macdonald's "James Agee" in *Against the American Grain* (New York: Random House, 1962), and particularly Robert Fitzgerald's "A Memoir" in *The Collected Short Prose of James Agee* (Boston: Houghton Mifflin, 1968; Ballantine, 1970). Erik Wensberg, who is at work on a critical biography of Agee, has been more than generous with information and insights.
3. Moreau, *The Restless Journey*, p. 51.
4. James Agee, *Letters of James Agee to Father Flye* (New York: George Braziller, 1962; Bantam, 1963).
5. Elizabeth Nowell (ed.), *The Letters of Thomas Wolfe* (New York: Scribners, 1956), p. 591.
6. Allen Tate, *The Fathers,* (New York: G. P. Putnam, 1938; Swallow Press, 1960), pp. 177, 181. In his "The Sorrows of Thomas Wolfe" in Louis Rubin (ed.), *Thomas Wolfe: A Collection of Critical Essays* (Englewood Cliffs, N.J.: Prentice-Hall, 1973), John Peale Bishop compares Wolfe to Hart Crane, and says that in Wolfe's writing: "There is no idea which would serve as a discipline to the event." Bishop was a

friend of the Agrarians. When we combine that with the fact that Tate and Crane were close friends, it suggests that Crane may have provided a model of sorts for George Posey. This would make the Posey-Wolfe connection even more plausible.

7. W. M. Frohock, *The Novel of Violence in America* (Dallas: Southern Methodist University Press, 1957), p. 215. In his 1960 "Foreword" to *Let Us Now Praise Famous Men* (Boston: Houghton Mifflin, 1941), Walker Evans mentions Agee's studied indifference to his mode of dress. Though without much corroborating evidence, Moreau emphasizes Agee's guilt over the betrayal of his father's (and his own) roots.

8. Esther Jack, George Webber's mistress in *The Web and the Rock* and *You Can't Go Home Again*, is Jewish, as was Aline Bernstein, Wolfe's actual mistress. Only after a visit to Nazi Germany did Wolfe come to see the full implications of anti-Semitism.

9. Agee wrote to Father Flye in 1930 that he felt "committed to writing" but that it was difficult "to decide what I want to write about" (*Letters to Father Flye*, p. 41).

10. See Quentin Anderson's *The Imperial Self* (New York: Knopf, 1971; Vintage, 1972). The imperial self is the (American) cultural expression of the narcissistic personality which swings between engulfment of the world and disappearance altogether into it. Theoretical discussions of narcissism can be found in Otto Kernberg's *Borderline Conditions and Pathological Narcissism* (New York: Jason Aronson, 1975) and Heinz Kohut's *The Analysis of the Self* (New York: International Universities Press, 1971). Kohut talks of the narcissistic swing between the "grandiose self" and the "omnipotent object." The narcissistic personality typically exhibits strong oral traits, and his family situation is often marked by a strong mother and a weak or absent father. This is not to suggest a clinical diagnosis of Agee and Wolfe, but only some interesting analogues between cultural patterns and individual characteristics.

11. Representative Wolfe criticism can be found in Alfred Kazin's *On Native Grounds* (New York: Harcourt, Brace, 1942); Richard Kennedy, *The Window of Memory* (Chapel Hill: University of North Carolina Press, 1962); C. Hugh Holman (ed.), *The World of Thomas Wolfe* (New York: Scribners, 1962) and *The Roots of Southern Writing* (Athens: University of Georgia Press, 1972); Leslie Field (ed.), *Thomas Wolfe: Three Decades of Criticism* (New York: New York University Press, 1968); Rubin (ed.), *Thomas Wolfe;* and Richard Gray, *The Literature of Memory* (Baltimore: Johns Hopkins University Press, 1977). In general Southerners have been kinder to Wolfe than have outsiders or his fellow writers, except for Faulkner, who rated Wolfe highest of his contemporaries because Wolfe had attempted the most.

12. Edward Aswell, Wolfe's editor at Harpers after his break with

Perkins at Scribners, voiced this opinion in 1941. See "A Note on Thomas Wolfe" in Thomas Wolfe, *The Hills Beyond* (New York: New American Library, 1968). It has been most recently expressed in Gray's *The Literature of Memory*. There is something to be said for this assessment of Wolfe's writing; but not a great deal.

13. Wright Morris, in his "The Function of Appetite" in Rubin (ed.), *Thomas Wolfe*, writes that Wolfe's "experience, in substance was essentially vicarious. He got it from books" (p. 91). See Kennedy's *Window of Memory* for a less jaundiced analysis but one which has the same import. Except for the influences of that odd couple of contemporary literature, James Joyce and Sinclair Lewis, Wolfe's precursors were primarily in nineteenth-century English and American fiction, De-Quincey and the Romantics.

14. Louis Rubin, "Carson McCullers: The Aesthetic of Pain," *Virginia Quarterly Review* 53, No. 2 (Spring 1977), 262. In *The Literature of Memory* Gray takes the opposite position by locating Wolfe in the "yeoman" tradition of Southern writing.

15. Wolfe, *Letters*, p. 167.

16. Turnbull writes that Aline Bernstein, who was eighteen years older than Wolfe, was "the soft, enfolding type of female he would have liked for a mother, [she was] different from Julia Wolfe somewhat as a pillow differs from a table edge" (p. 107). Turnbull also shows us Wolfe at his most contemptible. In the presence of both women, Wolfe read his mother a letter Mrs. Bernstein had written him accusing Mrs. Wolfe of avarice and pettiness. Mrs. Wolfe then launched into a diatribe accusing Jews of "jumping for nickels." If that were not outrageous enough, Wolfe sided with his mother (pp. 175–77).

17. Wolfe, *Letters*, p. 333.

18. Wolfe, *The Story of a Novel* (New York: Scribners, 1936), pp. 39, 92. It was Wolfe's tragedy as a writer that, though aware of most of the problems in his writing, he was never able to resolve them.

19. The difference between Wolfe and Fitzgerald lies in the fact that Wolfe closely identified with his protagonists, while Fitzgerald provided distance on Gatsby in the figure of Nick Carraway.

20. See Tom Dardis's *Some Time in the Sun* (New York: Scribners, 1976) for not very revealing accounts of Agee and Faulkner in Hollywood. In general, Faulkner seems to have worked mainly on dialogue and narrative, while Agee was much more interested in the visual aspects of film.

21. Agee's film essays and reviews have been collected in *Agee on Film*, vol. 1 (New York: McDowell, Obolensky, 1958). His published film writings begin in the fall of 1941 when he began reviewing for *Time*. The next fall he started with *The Nation*. Quotations having to do with movies are taken from this volume.

22. Both Dardis and Joseph Blotner in *William Faulkner* (New York: Random House, 1974), 2:1184, note that Faulkner worked on *The Southerner* and was more than usually interested in the film and respected the director, Renoir, more than usual. Agee makes no mention of Faulkner's hand in the work, probably because he knew nothing of it.

23. In *Collected Poems of James Agee* (Boston: Houghton Mifflin, 1968; Ballantine, 1970) this bit of satirical verse was printed under the title "Agrarian." Erik Wensberg called my attention to it and supplied the information on Tate's reaction.

24. Allen Tate perhaps matched Agee's self-awareness but never so explicitly wrote of it as did Agee in *Famous Men*.

25. Agee, *Letters to Father Flye*, p. 41.

26. See "Plans for Work: 1937" in *Collected Short Prose*, pp. 145–66. In places this proposal reads like an agenda for the visual arts in America over the next two decades.

27. Agee, *Letters to Father Flye*, p. 50.

28. Joseph Blotner (ed.), *The Selected Letters of William Faulkner* (New York: Random House, 1977), p. 233.

29. T. S. Matthews, review of Genevieve Moreau's *The Restless Journey* in *The New Republic 176*, No. 16. (April 16, 1966), 31.

30. Mia Agee in *Remembering James Agee*, p. 155.

31. Agee, *Letters to Father Flye*, p. 162. This letter was written in January 1949.

32. *Ibid.*, p. 61.

33. Macdonald, *Against the American Grain*, pp. 153–54.

34. Louis Kronenberger in *Remembering James Agee*, p. 111.

35. James Agee, *The Morning Watch* (Boston: Houghton Mifflin, 1951); *A Death in the Family* (New York: McDowell, Obolensky, 1957). Critical literature on Agee includes W. M. Frohock's "James Agee: The Question of Wasted Talent," in *The Novel of Violence in America*, pp. 212–30; Peter Ohlin, *Agee* (New York: Ivan Obolensky, 1966); Kenneth Seib, *James Agee: Promise and Fulfillment* (Pittsburgh: University of Pittsburgh Press, 1968); Alfred Barson, *A Way of Seeing* (Amherst: University of Massachusetts Press, 1972); and Robert Cole's "Childhood: James Agee's *A Death in the Family*" in *Irony in the Mind's Life* (Charlottesville: University of Virginia Press, 1974), pp. 56–106. As if to rectify the early neglect, most discussions of *Famous Men* tend to take Agee at his word and offer a gloss on his own gloss of his effort. Otherwise Agee criticism tends to become very personal, evoking rather than analyzing his writing.

36. William Stott, *Documentary Expression and Thirties America* (New York: Oxford University Press, 1973), pp. 259–314. Stott presents a fascinating discussion of the genesis of *Famous Men* and the relationship of Evans's photographs and Agee's text in the context of

the 1930s, the decade of the documentary. Although Stott provides the materials for a critical discussion, he fails to develop one. All quotations are from *Let Us Now Praise Famous Men* (Boston: Houghton Mifflin, 1960). This second edition included twice as many photographs as the first edition.

37. Agee, *Collected Short Prose*, p. 142.

38. *Ibid.*, p. 143.

39. Agee, *A Death in the Family*, p. 14.

40. Agee, *Collected Short Prose*, p. 150.

41. I must again emphasize that I am not offering a clinical diagnosis of Agee or a psychoanalytic reading of his work as such. I am rather using psychoanalytic theory as a way of talking about the essential themes of Agee's writings.

42. Art critic Leo Steinberg has noted this tendency in the visual arts, including the abstract expressionists. The emphasis there upon "action," he claims, is part of the "American disdain for art conceived as something too carefully plotted, too cosmetic, too French" (*Other Criteria* (New York: Oxford University Press, 1972), p. 62). This trait of American culture is overdetermined: one might cite the puritan tradition, literary nationalism via the transcendentalists, and the rationalization of the world which Max Weber saw most clearly expressed in America. Interestingly, Americans of this tradition read nature and the machine (e.g. the camera for Agee) as teaching the same functionalist lesson.

43. See Walter Benjamin's *Understanding Brecht* (London: New Left Books, 1977) for essays on Brecht's notion of the epic theater. Agee knew of Brecht's work and mentioned it in "Plans for Work: 1937." I am grateful to Erik Wensberg for calling my attention to this specific reference.

44. The placing of the contour map on equal footing with Bach's music echoes a line in an Eisenstein essay "Word and Image" (published in 1938 as "Montage"), where he writes that a report on a victory of the Spanish Republicans was "more moving than a work by Beethoven" (*Film Sense* (London: Faber and Faber, 1968), p. 37).

45. Jacques Derrida, *Of Grammatology*, trans. with an introduction by G. H. Spivak (Baltimore: Johns Hopkins University Press, 1976).

46. Agee took this position one step farther by preferring the visual gesture over even the spoken word as the "purest" mode of communication.

47. See *Famous Men*, pp. 59–69.

48. John Szarkowski, "Introduction," *Walker Evans* (New York: Museum of Modern Art, 1971), pp. 9–20. Steinberg's observations on American artists apply to Evans as well.

49. Erskine Caldwell and Margaret Bourke-White, *You Have Seen Their Faces* (New York: Modern Age Books, 1937). According to

Stott, Agee and Evans held Bourke-White's photography in the deepest contempt to the point of including (with no comment) a breathlessly written—and damning—newspaper article about Bourke-White in *Famous Men* which made her sound like a frivolous opportunist and self-serving careerist. See pp. 450–54.

50. See Roland Barthes, "The Photographic Message" and "The Rhetoric of the Image" in *Image-Music-Text* (New York: Hill and Wang, 1977); and Victor Burgin, *Two Essays on Art Photography and Semiotics* (London: Robert Self, 1976).

51. Susan Sontag, *On Photography* (New York: Farrar, Straus and Giroux, 1978), p. 29. According to Sontag, Diane Arbus's work marks the end-point of this tradition.

52. *Ibid.*, p. 13.

53. *Ibid.*, p. 15. In "The Rhetoric of the Image" Barthes remarks that photographs present "spatial immediacy and temporal anteriority" (p. 44).

54. Walter Benjamin, "The Work of Art in the Age of Mechanical Reproduction," *Illuminations* (New York: Harcourt, Brace, 1968). Sontag also makes this point in *On Photography,* pp. 121, 140. In a sense photography is always a reproduction in somewhat the same way as the performance of a musical composition is.

55. See Barthes's "The Rhetoric of the Image" for a discussion of the various relationships between image and text.

56. The idea of involving the reader (or viewer) in the production of meaning is central to Eisenstein's concept of montage (the production of an image) as superior to mere representation. See "Word and Image." It also underlies much modernist and post-modernist aesthetics.

57. See Gregory Bateson's "Style, Grace and Information in Primitive Art" and "Redundancy and Coding" in *Steps to an Ecology of Mind* (New York: Ballantine, 1972). Bateson's work is much less pretentious than the work of Barthes and the Structuralists.

58. Barthes, "Photographic Message," p. 17.

59. The crucial word here is "falsify." Iconic messages can falsify or express the negative only with great difficulty.

60. Stott, *Documentary Expression*, p. 266. See also Hugh Kenner's *A Homemade World* (London: Boyars, 1977).

61. In his review of *Let Us Now Praise Famous Men* in *Partisan Review 9,* No. 1 (January-February 1942) Paul Goodman made this point emphatically and also claimed that Agee's poetics were "confusion." I agree with the former but not the latter judgment.

62. Robert Coles, *Irony in the Mind's Life,* p. 58. Stott includes an Evans photograph of Ricketts and his children deeply involved in singing what were presumably hymns. It conveys a quite different sense of Ricketts than the one offered by Agee and Evans in the text of *Famous Men.*

63. Eugene Chesnick, "The Plot Against Fiction: *Let Us Now Praise Famous Men,*" *Southern Literary Journal 4,* No. 1 (Fall 1971), 49.

64. Lionel Trilling, review of *Let Us Now Praise Famous Men* in *Kenyon Review 4,* No. 99 (Winter 1942), 99-102. Trilling also saw Agee's difficulty in living up to the "perfect taste" of Evans's photographs.

65. Stott, *Documentary Expression,* pp. 275, 276.

66. *Ibid.,* p. 286. Stott also quotes from other accounts of share-cropper life in the 1930s which stress their determination, hope, and even political possibility (p. 312).

67. *Ibid.,* p. 287.

68. See Hegel's *Phenomenology of Spirit* for the distinction between consciousness and certainty of self, on the one hand, and self-consciousness on the other. Agee's depiction of the tenants' mode of existence is reminiscent of the way Sutpen sees his family's situation after he has become aware of his own domination in *Absalom, Absalom!.*

69. Agee does make this distinction in passing but comes down heavily on the view that his subjects lack aesthetic consciousness.

70. Barson, *A Way of Seeing,* pp. 99–100.

71. Ohlin, *Agee,* p. 65. Ohlin makes the interesting comparison between Agee's effort and "action painting," which stresses enactment over representation. This would be more acceptable had Agee not continually insisted that he sought to render the full humanity of his subjects as well as his own. *Famous Men* was to be a documentary as well as a meta-documentary.

72. *Ibid.,* pp. 57, 66.

73. In early 1951, Agee had several massive heart attacks and was told that, if he wished to survive, he would have to cut down drastically on his smoking and drinking and on his physical activities. He didn't.

74. All quotations are from *All the King's Men* (New York: Harcourt, Brace & Co., 1946). There are two volumes of critical essays on Warren—Maurice Beebe and Leslie Field (eds.), *All the King's Men: A Critical Handbook* (Belmont, Cal.: Wadsworth, 1966); and John L. Langley, Jr. (ed.), *Robert Penn Warren: A Collection of Critical Essays* (New York: New York University Press, 1965). See also L. Hugh Moore, Jr., *Robert Penn Warren and History* (Hague: Mouton, 1970) and Leonard Casper, *Robert Penn Warren: The Dark and Bloody Ground* (Seattle: University of Washington Press, 1960).

75. Roger Sale, "Having It Both Ways," in Beebe and Field, p. 174. Though Sale's concluding judgment that *All the King's Men* is a "dishonest book" is far too extreme and gratuitous, I have followed his main points in developing my analysis.

76. T. D. Young, *Gentleman in a Dustcoat,* (Baton Rouge: Louisiana State University Press, 1976), p. 413. See also David Wyatt's "Robert Penn Warren: The Critic as Artist," *Virginia Quarterly Review* 53, No. 3 (Summer 1977), 475–87.

77. Warren, *Segregation* (New York: Random House, 1956), p. 26. This has become one of the clichés of recent analyses of the Southern mind. As I have tried to show, Cash's thesis seems to me more apposite.

78. Warren's clearest and most concise statement of his *Weltan-schauung* can be found in "Knowledge and the Image of Man" (1955), in Beebe and Field, pp. 55–62.

79. Blotner, *Faulkner*, 1:662.

80. Warren, "William Faulkner," *Three Decades of Faulkner Criticism*, ed. by F. J. Hoffman and Olga Vickery (East Lansing: Michigan State University Press, 1960), pp. 112–13.

81. Blotner, *Faulkner*, 2:1214.

82. Warren began what was to become *All the King's Men* in Italy in 1938 and thus the portrait of Willie Stark could have reflected some of the currents at work in Mussolini's Italy. The work was originally conceived as a verse drama. See Warren, "Louisiana Politics and *All the King's Men*," in Beebe and Field, pp. 23–28. See also T. Harry Williams's massive *Huey Long* (New York: Knopf, 1969) for an always fascinating discussion of Long's life and political career. Huey's brother, Earl, who was to become governor of Louisiana in the 1950s, also generally avoided racial demagoguery and suffered politically for it. His flamboyant personal life did not help matters either.

83. The interaction of past and present was the main characteristic which Cleanth Brooks saw in the Agrarian poets.

84. There was no Jack Burden in the first version of *All the King's Men*.

10 THE NEW SOUTHERN LIBERALISM: KEY, WOODWARD, WARREN

1. See Morton Sosna's *In Search of the Silent South* (New York: Columbia University Press, 1977), chapter 4 ("Southern Liberals and the New Deal"), and Wilma Dykeman and James Stokely, *Seeds of Southern Change* (Chicago: University of Chicago Press, 1962) for discussions of Southern liberals in New Deal Washington.

2. Alexander Heard, *A Two-Party South?* (Chapel Hill: University of North Carolina Press, 1952), p. 17.

3. See Sosna, *In Search*, chapter 5; and Thomas Krueger's *And Promise To Keep* (Nashville: Vanderbilt University Press, 1967).

4. Herman C. Nixon, *Possum Trot* (Norman: University of Oklahoma Press, 1941) and *The Lower Piedmont Country* (New York: Duell, Sloan and Pearce, 1946).

5. Herman C. Nixon, "Politics of the Hills," *Journal of Politics 8*, No. 2 (May 1946), 124.

6. Frank Owsley, *Plain Folk of the Old South* (Baton Rouge: Louisi-

ana State University Press, 1949; Quadrangle Press, 1965). See Fabian Linden, "Economic Democracy in the Slave South: An Appraisal of Some Recent Views," *Journal of Negro History 31*, No. 1 (January 1946), 140–89, for a critique of Owsley's thesis.

7. Owsley, *Plain Folk*, p. 90.

8. *Ibid.*, p. 133.

9. *Ibid.*, p. 134.

10. *Ibid.*, p. 139.

11. Paul Lewinson, *Race, Class and Party: A History of Negro Suffrage and White Politics* (New York: Oxford University Press, 1932).

12. *Ibid.*, p. 190.

13. See, for examples, Francis Cohen, "Are There Distinctive Political Traditions in the South?" *Journal of Politics 2*, No. 1 (February 1940), 3–23; William G. Carleton, "The Conservative South—a Political Myth," *Virginia Quarterly Review 22*, No. 2 (1946), 179–92; Manning Dauer, "Recent Southern Political Thought," *Journal of Politics 10*, No. 2 (May 1948), 327–53; and Herman C. Nixon, "Southern Regionalism Limited," *Virginia Quarterly Review 26*, No. 2 (Spring 1950), 161–70.

14. Gunnar Myrdal, *An American Dilemma*, vol. 1 (New York: Harper & Bros., 1944; McGraw-Hill, 1964), chapters 20–23.

15. Marian D. Irish, "The Southern One-Party System and National Politics," *Journal of Politics 4*, No. 1 (February 1942), 80; Myrdal, *An American Dilemma*, I:444.

16. Myrdal, *An American Dilemma*, I:580.

17. *Ibid.*, I:440.

18. *Ibid.*, I:465.

19. *Ibid.*, I:469.

20. *Ibid.*, I:466. See David Southern, *"An American Dilemma* Revisited: Myrdalism and White Southern Liberalism," *South Atlantic Quarterly 75*, No. 2 (Spring 1976), 182–97. Odum and Vance, for instance, felt Myrdal was excessively optimistic in his predictions.

21. Myrdal, *An American Dilemma*, I:470.

22. *Ibid.*, I:472.

23. *Ibid.*, I:469.

24. *Ibid.*, I:514.

25. *Ibid.*, I:580.

26. V. O. Key (with the assistance of Alexander Heard), *Southern Politics* (New York: Random House, 1949).

27. *Ibid.*, pp. 15–16. See Theodore Lowi's *The End of Liberalism* (New York: W. W. Norton, 1969) for a description and critique of the pluralist, interest-group political ideology. There is a family resemblance among this ideology, the "end of ideology" school of sociology, the "consensus" American historians, and the "countervailing power" analysis of the American economy. All of them exerted prime influence from the end of World War II until the mid-1960s.

28. Key, *Southern Politics*, chapter 14.

29. *Ibid.*, p. 541.

30. *Ibid.*, p. 550.

31. Besides the work of C. Vann Woodward, the most recent challenge to the Lewinson-Myrdal-Key *fait accompli* thesis comes in J. Morgan Kousser's *The Shaping of Southern Politics: Suffrage Restriction and the Establishment of the One-Party South, 1880–1910* (New Haven: Yale University Press, 1974). Kousser also stresses the extent to which disfranchisement was directed against white insurgents as well as against blacks.

32. W. G. Carleton, "Democracy and the Party System," *Virginia Quarterly Review 26*, No. 1 (Winter 1950), 134–38.

33. Cortez A. M. Ewing, review of V. O. Key's *Southern Politics, Journal of Politics 12*, No. 1 (February 1950), 156.

34. C. Vann Woodward, review of W. J. Cash's *The Mind of the South, Journal of Southern History 8*, No. 3 (August 1941), 400–402.

35. C. Vann Woodward, "The Elusive Mind of W. J. Cash," *American Counterpoint* (Boston: Little, Brown, 1971), p. 280. My suggestion of "inevitable" misreading alludes to Harold Bloom's notion of the "anxiety of influence." As I was formulating this aspect of the Cash-Woodward dispute, Bertram Wyatt-Brown was kind enough to let me read an unpublished talk in which he also made use of Bloom to shed light on the two men's intellectual relationship.

36. The essay on Cash is one of the few explicitly polemical pieces which Woodward has published. It might be compared with Richard Hofstadter's *The Progressive Historians*, since both Woodward's essay and the latter's book are attempts to settle accounts with intellectual precursors-rivals.

37. In the following discussion of Woodward I will examine *Tom Watson: Agrarian Rebel* (New York: Macmillan, 1938; Oxford University Press, 1963); *Origins of the New South, 1877–1913* (Baton Rouge: Louisiana State University Press, 1951); *Reunion and Reaction,* 2nd rev. ed. (Garden City: Doubleday Anchor, 1956); *The Strange Career of Jim Crow,* 2nd rev. ed. (New York: Oxford University Press, 1966); and *The Burden of Southern History* (Baton Rouge: Louisiana State University Press, 1960; Vintage, 1961).

Two essays deal with Woodward's career as a whole: David Potter, "C. Vann Woodward," *Pastmasters,* ed. by Marcus Cunliffe and Robin Winks (New York: Harper and Row, 1969), pp. 375–407; and Michael O'Brien, "C. Vann Woodward and the Burden of Southern Liberalism," *American Historical Review 78*, No. 3 (June 1973), 589–604. I am not concerned here with historiographical skirmishes about Woodward's work and his major theses, except as they bear directly on Woodward as one of those involved in the reassessment of the Southern political and cultural tradition.

38. Dykeman and Stokely, *Seeds of Southern Change,* pp. 155–56.

39. See Arthur S. Link and Rembert W. Patrick (eds.), *Writing Southern History: Essays in Historiography in Honor of Fletcher M. Green* (Baton Rouge: Louisiana State University Press, 1965), particularly Paul Gaston's essay "The New South" and Allen J. Going's "The Agrarian Revolt."

40. Daniel M. Robinson, "From Tillman to Long: Some Striking Leaders of the Rural South," *Journal of Southern History 3,* No. 3 (August 1937), 289–310.

41. See Wendell H. Stephenson, *The South Lives in History: Southern Historians and Their Legacy* (Baton Rouge: Louisiana State University Press, 1955) and *Southern History in the Making: Pioneer Historians of the South* (Baton Rouge: Louisiana State University Press, 1964).

42. See Daniel J. Singall, "Ulrich B. Phillips: The Old South as the New," *Journal of American History 68,* No. 4 (March 1977), 871–91. Singall's analysis of Phillips goes far toward demolishing Eugene Genovese's view that Phillips saw the plantation system as pre-modern and pre-capitalist. Singall claims Phillips also saw it as a sort of rural factory to be run along "rational" lines.

43. David Potter, "An Appraisal of Fifteen Years of the *Journal of Southern History,* 1935–49," *Journal of Southern History 16,* No. 1 (February 1956), 25–32.

44. Woodward, *Tom Watson,* p.iv.

45. *Ibid.,* p. 222.

46. *Ibid.,* pp. 348–49.

47. *Ibid.,* pp. 5, 6.

48. *Ibid.,* p. 125.

49. See Charles Crowe, "Tom Watson, Populists and Blacks Reconsidered," *Journal of Negro History 55,* No. 2 (April 1970), 99–116; and Lawrence J. Friedman, "From Politics to Purity: The Crusade of the Powerless," *White Savage* (Englewood Cliffs, N. J.: Prentice-Hall, 1970), chapter 5.

50. Sheldon Hackney, *Populism to Progressivism in Alabama* (Princeton: Princeton University Press, 1969).

51. C. Vann Woodward, "The South in Search of a Philosophy," *Phi Beta Kappa Series,* No. 1, (University of Florida, 1938), pp. 3–20.

52. *Ibid.,* p. 12.

53. Woodward presumably had Allen Tate (if anyone) in mind here.

54. Woodward, "The South in Search . . . ," p. 15. This lack of enthusiasm for Faulkner is particularly ironic since Woodward later criticized Cash for not recognizing the Mississippian's genius. See Woodward, "What Was the Southern Renaissance?" *Virginia Quarterly Review 51,* No. 2 (Spring 1975), 222–39.

55. Woodward, "The South in Search . . . , p. 20.

56. Woodward, *Origins*, pp. 75–76.

57. Woodward, *Reunion and Reaction*, pp. xii–xiii.

58. *Ibid.*, chapter 12.

59. Woodward, "A Southern Brief for Racial Equality," in *American Counterpoint;* and *The Strange Career of Jim Crow*, pp. 44–47, for his discussions of Blair and Cable.

60. See Fredrickson, *Black Image* (New York: Harper and Row, 1971; Harper Torchbooks, 1972), pp. 216–27; and Friedman, *White Savage*, pp. 99–117.

61. Woodward, *American Counterpoint*, pp. 265–66.

62. Woodward, *Reunion and Reaction*, p. v.

63. Woodward, *Origins*, p. 263.

64. *Ibid.*, p. 289.

65. See Kousser, *Shaping of Southern Politics*, for an extension of this point.

66. Richard Kluger, *Simple Justice* (New York: Knopf, 1976), pp. 623–24, 626.

67. See Woodward's "The Strange Career of a Historical Controversy," *American Counterpoint*, pp. 234–60, for his response to his critics and a modification of his argument. The *Jim Crow* thesis might be compared with Stanley Elkins's *Slavery*, for both books state a point in extreme form which proved to be both untenable (as stated) and extremely valuable in sharpening historical treatments of their respective subjects.

68. Woodward, *Strange Career*, p. 63.

69. Woodward, *American Counterpoint*, p. 260.

70. Later, Woodward students such as Willie Lee Rose in her *Rehearsal for Reconstruction* (Indianapolis: Bobbs-Merrill, 1964) and William McFeeley in his *Yankee Stepfather: A Study of General O. O. Howard and the Freedman's Bureau* (New Haven: Yale University Press, 1968) would document this Northern failure to protect black civil, political, or economic rights. See also Woodward's "The Northern Crusade Against Slavery" and "Seeds of Failure in Radical Race Policy" in *American Counterpoint*.

71. Woodward, "The Populist Heritage and the Intellectual," *The Burden of Southern History*, p. 153. Woodward did get in a sly dig at the critics of Populism by characterizing the Populists as pursuing "interest" politics.

72. *Ibid.*, p. 159.

73. Michael O'Brien makes this point very clearly in his essay on Woodward. Woodward avoided the essentialist approach of Cash and instead stressed the Southern *experience* which would presumably leave open a variety of responses. Nevertheless, he did make claims

about the unity of Southern experience every bit as sweeping as Cash's, even if a characteristic of that experience was disunity and conflict. In short, Woodward and Cash don't disagree on the possibility of calling the Southern experience "Southern"; rather their disagreement lies in how that experience is to be characterized.

74. In attacking American innocence and calling for a more nuanced view of the American past, Woodward ironically joined the consensus historians with whom he otherwise had little in common.

75. Woodward's ironic liberalism bears a certain resemblance to the vision Lionel Trilling proposed in *The Liberal Imagination* (New York: Viking Press, 1950) which attempted to preserve the progressive impulse but to wed it to a more sophisticated vision of human nature and society. If Trilling's vision drew upon Freud and James, Woodward's drew upon Niebuhr, Faulkner, and Warren. In the Southern context, Woodward's liberalism had progressive implications; in the national context, Trilling's pointed in a conservative direction. What Mark Shechner writes on Trilling in "Psychoanalysis and Liberalism: The Case of Lionel Trilling," *Salmagundi 41* (Spring 1978), seems to me appropriate to Woodward: ". . . for he [Trilling] must be included among the intellectuals who transformed the prevailing rhetoric of liberalism from one of social progress and justice to one of sensibility and depth, all the while tidying up the depths by purging them of whatever was embarrassing, childish or undignified" (p. 32).

76. John L. Longley (ed.), "Robert Penn Warren," *Robert Penn Warren: A Collection of Critical Essays* (New York: New York University Press, 1965), pp. 18–45. This interview with Warren originally appeared in *Paris Review.* See also Warren, *Who Speaks for the Negro?* (New York: Random House, 1965), pp. 10–13.

77. Longley, "Robert Penn Warren," p. 27.

78. Robert Penn Warren, "The Briar Patch," *I'll Take My Stand* (New York: Harper & Bros., 1930; Harper Torchbooks, 1962), p. 248.

79. Robert Penn Warren, *John Brown: The Making of a Martyr* (New York: Payson and Clarke, 1929), p. 332.

80. Warren, "The Briar Patch," pp. 254–55.

81. *Ibid.,* pp. 260, 262, 264.

82. I am aware of the dangers involved in identifying "RPW" with Warren himself. Still there is enough consistency between the views of RPW and those of Warren to justify this identity.

83. "Jefferson" is a straw man of considerable proportions in *Brother to Dragons,* a caricature of both Jefferson and Enlightenment attitudes.

84. All quotations are from *Brother to Dragons* (New York: Random House, 1953).

85. This was much truer of *Brother to Dragons* than of *All the King's Men* and thus the superiority of the novel to the verse-drama.

86. The comparison with Faulkner's *Light in August* is instructive, for Joe Christmas's search for identity can be understood on all levels, not just the metaphysical.

87. All quotations are from Warren, *Segregation* (New York: Random House, 1956).

88. Paul Goodman, review of Warren's *Segregation, The Society I Live in Is Mine* (New York: Horizon Press, 1962), pp. 113–21.

89. *Ibid.*, p. 114.

Conclusion

1. Friedrich Nietzsche, *The Use and Abuse of History* (Indianapolis: Bobbs-Merrill, 1957), p. 28.

2. Hayden White, *Metahistory* (Baltimore: Johns Hopkins University Press, 1973), p. 348.

3. Nietzsche, *Use and Abuse*, p. 69.

4. Mircea Eliade, *Cosmos and History: The Myth of the Eternal Return* (New York: Pantheon, 1954; Harper Torchbooks, 1959), p. 5.

5. *Ibid.*, p. 150.

6. J. H. Plumb, *The Death of the Post* (Boston: Houghton Mifflin, 1971).

7. White, *Metahistory*, p. 10.

8. See Philip Rieff's *Freud: The Mind of the Moralist* (New York: Viking, 1959), chapter X; and *The Triumph of the Therapeutic* (New York: Harper and Row, 1966).

9. John Dollard, *Caste and Class in a Southern Town* (New Haven: Yale University Press, 1937; Anchor, 1957), p. 171.

10. Benjamin Nelson, *The Idea of Usury: From Tribal Brotherhood to Universal Otherhood*, 2nd ed. enlarged (Chicago: University of Chicago Press, 1969), p. 249.

11. See Lillian Smith's *The Winner Names the Age* (New York: W. W. Norton, 1978) for a collection of essays and speeches in which she expresses the faith in the evolution of humanity to a common consciousness, an idea she took from Teilhard de Chardin.

12. F. Garvin Davenport, *The Myth of Southern History* (Nashville: Vanderbilt University Press, 1970), chapter 5.

Index

Odum and, 40; Tate on, 100–101, 103; in *Go Down Moses,* 131; Cash on, 147–72; "fear of abstraction," 159–60, 231–32, 284; race over class in, 162, 164, 167; liberal analysis of, 171; Smith on, 173–93; up-country differences, 195–96; Wolfe on, 198–204; Agee and, 227–28; Woodward on, in the 1930s, 264–65; Woodward on the New South, 265–70; as "Solid," 266–68; segregation and disfranchisement, 270–71; Woodward on characteristics of, 274–75; Warren on "self-division" of, 284–85

South Carolina, 174, 175
"South in Search of a Philosophy, The" (Woodward), 264–65
South Looks at Its Past, The (Kendrick and Arnett), 162
Southern Conference on Human Welfare, 49, 180, 245
Southern family romance, 8, 9, 77, 85, 107, 166, 196, 287, 290; explained, 26–38; and Agrarians, 52; Faulkner and, 77–85; Percy and, 94; in *The Fathers,* 105–11; incest, time, and, 116; incest and miscegenation in, 126–28; thematized in *Absalom, Absalom!,* 128; in *Go Down Moses,* 130–39; Cash on, 166–67; Smith's analysis, 184–93; and up-country South, 195–96; Warren and, 234, 236; and politics, 244; and Watson, 263
Southern Farmers Tenant Union, 49
Southern Historical Association, 256, 275
Southern liberals, 7, 16, 174, 176, 179, 183, 235, 268, 272, 281; and New Deal, 25; and Agrarians, 74; Quentin Compson as, 112; and Jefferson, 150; on race and sex, 165; regional analyses, 171; Smith on, 180–81; new variety of, 242–86; Myrdal on, 248–49; and interracial dream of, 255; Woodward as, 256; need for heroes, 261
"Southern Mode of Imagination, The" (Tate), 100–101
"Southern One-Party System and

National Politics, The" (Irish), 248
Southern politics, 8, 24–25, 168; Cash on, 162; Southern family romance and, 234; Warren on, 234, 235–36; characteristics of, 242–46; prospects for two parties, 246–56; rediscovery of Populism, 246, 251–53; Lewinson on, 247–48; *fait accompli* thesis, 248; Myrdal on, 248–49; Key on, 250–57; and Populism, 257–66, 268–70; defense of demagogues, 258; Woodward on Watson in, 259–64; "Redeemer" governments, 260, 265; Progressives as racists in, 261–62; and ironic historical consciousness, 290
Southern Politics (Key), 234; analysis of, 249–57; theory of two-party politics, 250, 253–54; rationality in politics, 250, 254–55; pluralist, interest-group politics of, 250–51, 254–55; discussion of Populism and disfranchisement, 252–53, 255–56; critique of, 253–56
Southern Regional Council, 41
Southern Regions (Odum), 42, 43, 44, 45–47, 154, 204
Southern Renaissance, the, 3, 26, 69, 81, 110, 170, 176, 276, 277, 292; explanations of, 3–9; and World War I, 14; and loss of tradition, 15–19; women in the literature of, 36; Tate on, 101–2; and regional self-scrutiny, 146
Southern Review, 57, 72
Southern tradition of the fathers, 7, 8, 9, 14, 52, 53, 56, 65, 76, 77, 85, 130, 140, 287, 290, 292; and World War I, 13, 15, 93; and historical consciousness, 15–19; and the New South Creed, 31–32; death and defeat as central in, 78; as destructive, 82–83; and Will Percy, 85–98; pattern of decline in, 92; Tate on, 101, 110; collapse of, in *The Sound and the Fury,* 118–19; origins in *Absalom, Absalom!,* 120; miscegenation and, 127; in *Go Down Moses,* 130–39; Smith on, 173–93; Agee